First World War
and Army of Occupation
War Diary
France, Belgium and Germany

3 DIVISION
Headquarters, Branches and Services
General Staff
1 November 1918 - 30 June 1919

WO95/1382

The Naval & Military Press Ltd
www.nmarchive.com
Published in association with The National Archives

Published by

The Naval & Military Press Ltd

Unit 10 Ridgewood Industrial Park,

Uckfield, East Sussex,

TN22 5QE England

Tel: +44 (0) 1825 749494

www.naval-military-press.com

www.nmarchive.com

This diary has been reprinted in facsimile from the original. Any imperfections are inevitably reproduced and the quality may fall short of modern type and cartographic standards.

© **Crown Copyright**

Images reproduced by permission of The National Archives, London, England, 2015.

Contents

Document type	Place/Title	Date From	Date To
Heading	3rd Division War Diaries General Staff November 1918		
War Diary	Quievy	01/11/1918	08/11/1918
War Diary	Frasnoy	09/11/1918	17/11/1918
War Diary	Sous-Le-Bois	18/11/1918	19/11/1918
War Diary	Thuin	24/11/1918	25/11/1918
War Diary	Thuin Loverval	25/11/1918	25/11/1918
War Diary	Thuin	26/11/1918	27/11/1918
War Diary	Loverval	27/11/1918	28/11/1918
War Diary	Bioul	28/11/1918	29/11/1918
War Diary	Bioul Emptinne	30/11/1918	30/11/1918
War Diary	Cousorle	21/11/1918	24/11/1918
War Diary	Thuin	24/11/1918	25/11/1918
War Diary	Thuin Loverval	25/11/1918	27/11/1918
War Diary	Loverval	27/11/1918	27/11/1918
War Diary	Loverval Bioul	28/11/1918	29/11/1918
War Diary	Bioul Emptinne	30/11/1918	30/11/1918
War Diary	Frasnoy	17/11/1918	17/11/1918
War Diary	Sous-Le-Bois	18/11/1918	19/11/1918
War Diary	Cousorle	20/11/1918	20/11/1918
War Diary	Quievy	01/11/1918	08/11/1918
War Diary	Frasnoy	09/11/1918	17/11/1918
Operation(al) Order(s)	3rd Division Operation Order No. 280	01/11/1918	01/11/1918
Miscellaneous	March Table To Accompany 3rd Division Operation Order No. 280		
Miscellaneous	A Form Messages And Signals.		
Miscellaneous			
Miscellaneous	Sixth Corps Wire G.450 1st. Nov, Timed 1545 Hrs.		
Miscellaneous	A Form. Messages And Signals.		
Miscellaneous	Messages And Signals		
Miscellaneous	3rd. Div. Wire G.A. 886 Dated 3rd Nov. Timed 1315.		
Miscellaneous	Copy Of VI Corps Wire No. G. 498 Dated 3rd Nov. Timed 6.0 Pm.		
Miscellaneous	3rd Division. Disposition and Movement Report No. 10. Forecast of for Nov. 4th.	03/11/1918	03/11/1918
Miscellaneous	3rd. Div. Wire G.C. 896 Dated 4th Nov. Timed 0930		
Miscellaneous	A Form Messages And Signals.		
Miscellaneous	3rd Division. Disposition and Movement Report No. 11. Forecast of Location for Nov. 5th.	04/11/1918	04/11/1918
Miscellaneous	A Form Messages And Signals.		
Miscellaneous			
Miscellaneous	G.C. 928 Nov. 6th		
Miscellaneous	3rd. Div. G.B. 951 Dated 7th November. Timed 14.00 Hours.		
Miscellaneous	VI Corps Wire No. G.79 of 7th November Timed 0600 Hrs.		
Miscellaneous	3rd Division. Disposition and Movement Report No. 12	07/11/1918	07/11/1918
Miscellaneous	A Form Messages And Signals		
Miscellaneous	VI Corps Wire No. G.123 of 8th Nov. Timed 0715 Hrs.		
Miscellaneous			
Miscellaneous	Messages And Signals.		

Miscellaneous	A Form Messages And Signals		
Miscellaneous	Messages And Signals.		
Miscellaneous			
Miscellaneous	Messages And Signals.		
Miscellaneous	A Form Messages And Signals.		
Miscellaneous	VI Corps Wire No. G.217 Timed 1930 of 9th November		
Operation(al) Order(s)	3rd. Division Operation Order No. 281.	10/11/1918	10/11/1918
Miscellaneous	A Form Messages And Signals.		
Miscellaneous	Messages And Signals		
Miscellaneous	3rd Division. Disposition and Movement Report No. 13	12/11/1918	12/11/1918
Miscellaneous	VI Corps Wire G.322 Dated 12th November, Timed 22.50 Hours.		
Miscellaneous	A Form Messages And Signals.		
Miscellaneous			
Miscellaneous	A Form Messages And Signals.		
Miscellaneous	A Form Messages And Signals		
Miscellaneous			
Miscellaneous	Instructions To Officers In Charge Education 3rd Division	15/11/1918	15/11/1918
Miscellaneous	3rd. Division G. 2002	15/11/1918	15/11/1918
Miscellaneous	Instructions (To Accompany 3rd. Div. G. 2002)		
Miscellaneous	Messages And Signals		
Miscellaneous			
Miscellaneous	A Form Messages And Signals.		
Miscellaneous	Instructions No. 2. To 3rd. Division G.S. 2002	16/11/1918	16/11/1918
Miscellaneous	A Form Messages And Signals.		
Miscellaneous	Messages And Signals		
Miscellaneous	Instructions No.3. To 3rd. Division G. 2002		
Miscellaneous	Instructions No. 4. To 3rd Division G.S. 2002	18/11/1918	18/11/1918
Miscellaneous	3rd. Division G.S.		
Miscellaneous	3rd. Division Operation Order No. 282		
Miscellaneous			
Miscellaneous	A Form Messages And Signals.		
Miscellaneous	3rd. Division Operation Order No. 283		
Miscellaneous	3rd. Division G.S. 2021		
Miscellaneous	3rd. Division G.S. 2023		
Miscellaneous	3rd. Division Operation Order No. 284	24/11/1918	24/11/1918
Miscellaneous	A Form Messages And Signals.		
Miscellaneous	3rd. Division Operation Order No. 285	25/11/1918	25/11/1918
Miscellaneous	3rd Division G.2002/5.	25/11/1918	25/11/1918
Miscellaneous	3rd. Division Operation Order No. 286	27/11/1918	27/11/1918
Operation(al) Order(s)	3rd Division Operation Order No. 287.	27/11/1918	27/11/1918
Miscellaneous	March Table To Accompany 3rd Division Operation Order No. 287		
Miscellaneous	3rd. Division Operation Order No. 288	29/11/1918	29/11/1918
Operation(al) Order(s)	3rd. Division Operation Order No. 281.	10/11/1918	10/11/1918
Miscellaneous	A Form Messages And Signals.		
Miscellaneous	Messages And Signals.		
Miscellaneous	Demobilization and Reconstruction		
Miscellaneous	3rd Division. Disposition and Movement Report No. 13		
Miscellaneous	A Form Messages And Signals.		
Miscellaneous			
Miscellaneous	VI Corps Wire G.322 Dated 12th November, Timed 22.50 Hours.		
Miscellaneous	A Form Messages And Signals.		

Miscellaneous	Messages And Signals.		
Miscellaneous	A Form Messages And Signals.		
Miscellaneous	VI Corps Wire. No.G.123 of 8th Nov. Timed 0715 Hrs.		
Miscellaneous			
Miscellaneous	Messages And Signals.		
Miscellaneous	A Form Messages And Signals.		
Miscellaneous	Messages And Signals.		
Miscellaneous	VI Corps Wire No. G.217 Timed 1950 of 9th November.		
Miscellaneous	A Form Messages And Signals.		
Miscellaneous	3rd. Div. Wire G.C. 896 Dated 4th Nov. Timed 0930		
Miscellaneous	A Form Messages And Signals.		
Miscellaneous	3rd. Division. Disposition and Movement Report No. 11	04/11/1918	04/11/1918
Miscellaneous	A Form Messages And Signals.		
Miscellaneous			
Miscellaneous	G.C. 928 Nov. 6th		
Miscellaneous	3rd Div. G.B. 951 Dated 7th November. Timed 14.00 Hours.		
Miscellaneous	3rd Division. Disposition and Movement Report No. 12	07/11/1918	07/11/1918
Miscellaneous	A Form Messages And Signals.		
Operation(al) Order(s)	3rd Division Operation Order No. 280.	01/11/1918	01/11/1918
Miscellaneous	March Table To Accompany 3rd Division Operation Order No. 280.		
Miscellaneous	A Form Messages And Signals.		
Miscellaneous			
Miscellaneous	Messages And Signals.		
Miscellaneous	A Form Messages And Signals.		
Miscellaneous	3rd. Div. Wire G.A. 886 Dated 3rd Nov. Timed 1315.		
Miscellaneous	3rd Division. Disposition and Movement Report No. 10	03/11/1918	03/11/1918
Miscellaneous	Messages And Signals		
Miscellaneous			
Miscellaneous	Messages And Signals.		
Miscellaneous	Instructions No. 2. To 3rd. Division G.S. 2002	16/11/1918	16/11/1918
Miscellaneous	A Form Messages And Signals.		
Miscellaneous	Instructions No. 3. To 3rd. Division G. 2002	17/11/1918	17/11/1918
Miscellaneous	Instructions No. 4. To 3rd. Division G.S. 2002	18/11/1918	18/11/1918
Miscellaneous	3rd. Division G.S. 2018		
Miscellaneous			
Miscellaneous	Instructions To Officers In Charge Education 3rd. Division.	15/11/1918	15/11/1918
Miscellaneous	3rd. Division G. 2002	15/11/1918	15/11/1918
Miscellaneous			
Miscellaneous	Instructions (To Accompany 3rd. Div. G. 2002)		
Miscellaneous	3rd. Division Operation Order No. 282	19/11/1918	19/11/1918
Miscellaneous			
Miscellaneous	A Form Messages And Signals.		
Miscellaneous	3rd. Division Operation Order No. 283	22/11/1918	22/11/1918
Miscellaneous	3rd. Division G.S. 2021		
Miscellaneous	3rd. Division G.S. 2023		
Miscellaneous	3rd. Division Operation Order No. 284	24/11/1918	24/11/1918
Miscellaneous	Messages And Signals.		
Miscellaneous	3rd. Division Operation Order No. 285	25/11/1918	25/11/1918
Miscellaneous	3rd Division G. 2002/5.	25/11/1918	25/11/1918
Miscellaneous	3rd. Division Operation Order No. 286	27/11/1918	27/11/1918
Operation(al) Order(s)	3rd Division Operation Order No. 287.	27/11/1918	27/11/1918

Type	Description	Start	End
Miscellaneous	March Table To Accompany 3rd Division Operation Order No. 287		
Map	Marche		
Map	Valenciennes		
Map	Namur		
Heading	3rd Division War Diaries General Staff December 1918		
Heading	General Staff 3rd Division 1st-31st December 1918 Volume 38		
War Diary	Emptinne	01/12/1918	05/12/1918
War Diary	Grand Han	06/12/1918	08/12/1918
War Diary	Salmchateau	08/12/1918	14/12/1918
War Diary	Factory Albnuthen	14/12/1918	16/12/1918
War Diary	Euskirchen	17/12/1918	18/12/1918
War Diary	Duren	19/12/1918	31/12/1918
War Diary	Emptinne	01/12/1918	05/12/1918
War Diary	Grand Han	06/12/1918	08/12/1918
War Diary	Salmchateau	08/12/1918	14/12/1918
War Diary	Factory Albnuthen	14/12/1918	16/12/1918
War Diary	Euskirchen	17/12/1918	19/12/1918
War Diary	Duren	19/12/1918	31/12/1918
Miscellaneous	3rd Division Operation Order No. 289.	02/12/1918	02/12/1918
Miscellaneous	Advance To The Rhine.	02/12/1918	02/12/1918
Miscellaneous	Composition of columns from 2nd December (inclusive). Appendix "A"		
Miscellaneous	8th Inf Bde. 9th Inf Bde.	02/12/1918	02/12/1918
Miscellaneous	3rd Division Operation Order No. 290.	03/12/1918	03/12/1918
Miscellaneous	3rd Division G.S. 2042.	03/12/1918	03/12/1918
Miscellaneous	3rd Division Operation Order No. 291.	04/12/1918	04/12/1918
Miscellaneous	3rd Division G.S. 2048	04/12/1918	04/12/1918
Miscellaneous	3rd Division Operation Order No. 292.	00/12/1918	00/12/1918
Miscellaneous	3rd Division Operation Order No. 293.	06/12/1918	06/12/1918
Miscellaneous	3rd Division Operation Order No. 294.	07/12/1918	07/12/1918
Miscellaneous	3rd Division Operation Order No. 295.	08/12/1918	08/12/1918
Miscellaneous	Roads	09/12/1918	09/12/1918
Miscellaneous	3rd Division Operation Order No. 296	10/12/1918	10/12/1918
Miscellaneous	Report On Roads.	10/12/1918	10/12/1918
Miscellaneous	Reference Germany I.M. 1/100,000.	10/12/1918	10/12/1918
Miscellaneous	Training On Arrival at Our Destination In Germany	10/12/1918	10/12/1918
Miscellaneous	Appendix.		
Miscellaneous	Organization		
Miscellaneous	3rd Division Operation Order. No. 297.	11/12/1918	11/12/1918
Miscellaneous	G.O.C., 9th Inf. Bde.	11/12/1918	11/12/1918
Miscellaneous	3rd Division Operation Order No. 289.	02/12/1918	02/12/1918
Miscellaneous	8th Inf Bde. 9th Inf. Bde.	02/12/1918	02/12/1918
Miscellaneous	Composition of columns from 2nd December (inclusive). Appendix "A"		
Miscellaneous	8th Inf Bde. 9th Inf Bde.	02/12/1918	02/12/1918
Miscellaneous	3rd Division Operation Order No. 290.	03/12/1918	03/12/1918
Miscellaneous	3rd Division G.S. 2042.	03/12/1918	03/12/1918
Miscellaneous	3rd Division Operation Order No. 291.	04/12/1918	04/12/1918
Miscellaneous	3rd Division G.S. 2046	04/12/1918	04/12/1918
Miscellaneous	3rd Division Operation Order No. 292.	06/12/1918	06/12/1918
Miscellaneous	3rd Division Operation Order No. 293.	06/12/1918	06/12/1918
Miscellaneous	Instructions For Crossing The German Frontier.	09/12/1918	09/12/1918
Miscellaneous	16 Units Marches from Gunner officer.		
Miscellaneous	3rd Division Operation Order No. 294.	07/12/1918	07/12/1918

Miscellaneous	3rd Division Operation Order No. 295.	08/12/1918	08/12/1918
Miscellaneous	3rd Division. Roads	08/12/1918	08/12/1918
Miscellaneous	3rd Division Operation Order No. 296.	10/12/1918	10/12/1918
Miscellaneous	Report On Roads. Maldringen-Braunnlauf-Krombach-Neundorf Roads.	10/12/1918	10/12/1918
Miscellaneous	Reference Germany I.M. 1/100,000.	10/12/1918	10/12/1918
Miscellaneous	The Division will march on December 12th in accordance with the following march Table.	02/12/1918	02/12/1918
Miscellaneous	C Form. Messages And Signals		
Miscellaneous	G.O.C., 9th Inf. Bde.		
Miscellaneous	3rd Division Operation Order No. 298	12/12/1918	12/12/1918
Miscellaneous	3rd Division. G. S. 2002/8	12/12/1918	12/12/1918
Miscellaneous	G. O.C. 8th Inf. Bde.	12/12/1918	12/12/1918
Miscellaneous	3rd Division Operation Order No. 299.	13/12/1918	13/12/1918
Miscellaneous	3rd Division G. 7650	13/12/1918	13/12/1918
Miscellaneous	A Form Messages And Signals		
Miscellaneous	G. 7634/2.	13/12/1918	13/12/1918
Miscellaneous	3rd Division Operation Order No. 300.	14/12/1918	14/12/1918
Miscellaneous	G. 7653.		
Miscellaneous	8th Inf Bde. 9th Inf. Bde.	14/12/1918	14/12/1918
Miscellaneous	3rd Division Operation Order No. 301	15/12/1918	15/12/1918
Miscellaneous	3rd Division Operation Order No. 302	16/12/1918	16/12/1918
Miscellaneous	3rd Division Operation Order No. 303	17/12/1918	17/12/1918
Miscellaneous	3rd Division Operation Order No. 304	17/12/1918	17/12/1918
Miscellaneous	G 7670	17/12/1918	17/12/1918
Miscellaneous	3rd Division Operation Order No. 305	18/12/1918	18/12/1918
Miscellaneous	Reference 3rd Division Operation Order No. 305	19/12/1918	19/12/1918
Miscellaneous	3rd Division Operation Order No. 306	18/12/1918	18/12/1918
Miscellaneous	G. 7649/2.	18/12/1918	18/12/1918
Miscellaneous	To All Ranks of The "Iron" Third Division.	23/12/1918	23/12/1918
Miscellaneous	8th Inf Bde. 9th Inf. Bde.	26/12/1918	26/12/1918
Miscellaneous	A Form. Messages And Signals.		
Miscellaneous	3rd Division. Disposition and Movement Report No. 4.	31/12/1918	31/12/1918
Miscellaneous	3rd Division Operation Order No. 298	12/12/1918	12/12/1918
Miscellaneous	3rd Division G.S. 2002/8	12/12/1918	12/12/1918
Miscellaneous	G. O.C. 8th Inf. Bde.	12/12/1918	12/12/1918
Miscellaneous	3rd Division Operation Order No. 299	13/12/1918	13/12/1918
Miscellaneous	3rd Division G. 7650	13/12/1918	13/12/1918
Miscellaneous	A Form Messages And Signals		
Miscellaneous	Road Reconnaissance	13/12/1918	13/12/1918
Miscellaneous	3rd Division Operation Order No. 300	14/12/1918	14/12/1918
Miscellaneous	G. 7653.	14/12/1918	14/12/1918
Miscellaneous	8th Inf. Bde	14/12/1918	14/12/1918
Miscellaneous	3rd Division Operation Order No. 301	15/12/1918	15/12/1918
Miscellaneous	3rd Division Operation Order No. 302	16/12/1918	16/12/1918
Miscellaneous	3rd Division Operation Order No. 303	17/12/1918	17/12/1918
Miscellaneous	3rd Division Operation Order No. 304	17/12/1918	17/12/1918
Miscellaneous	G 7670	17/12/1918	17/12/1918
Miscellaneous	3rd Division Operation Order No. 305	18/12/1918	18/12/1918
Miscellaneous	Reference 3rd Division Operation Order No. 305	18/12/1918	18/12/1918
Miscellaneous	3rd Division Operation Order No. 306	18/12/1918	18/12/1918
Miscellaneous	Road Reconnaissance	18/12/1918	18/12/1918
Miscellaneous	8th Inf Bde. 9th Inf. Bde.	26/12/1918	26/12/1918
Miscellaneous	A Form. Messages And Signals		
Miscellaneous	3rd Division. Disposition and Movement Report No. 4	31/12/1918	31/12/1918

Heading	Northern Division (Late 3rd Division) General Staff Jan-Jun 1919		
War Diary	Duren	01/01/1919	31/01/1919
Heading	General Staff Vol 55 3rd Division 1st-28th February Volume 40		
War Diary	Duren	01/02/1919	28/02/1919
Operation(al) Order(s)	3rd Division Operation Order No. 307	19/02/1919	20/02/1919
Miscellaneous	Table of Reliefs.		
Miscellaneous	Guards Division Locations.		
Miscellaneous	Forecast of Moves and Reliefs	22/02/1919	22/02/1919
Miscellaneous	G. 8074/6.	22/02/1919	22/02/1919
Miscellaneous	9th Inf. Brigade. "Q" 3rd Division	22/02/1919	22/02/1919
Miscellaneous	76th Brigade. "Q"	24/02/1919	24/02/1919
Miscellaneous	76th Inf. Bde. "Q"	25/02/1919	25/02/1919
Miscellaneous	Forecast of Moves and Reliefs.	25/02/1919	25/02/1919
Miscellaneous	A Form Messages And Signals		
War Diary	Duren	01/03/1919	01/03/1919
War Diary	Lindenthal (Cologne)	02/03/1919	31/03/1919
Miscellaneous	A Form Messages And Signals		
Miscellaneous	1/9th DLI. Pioneers.	27/03/1919	27/03/1919
War Diary	Lindenthal (Cologne)	07/04/1919	23/04/1919
War Diary	Cologne	01/05/1919	27/05/1919
Heading	War Diary of General Staff, Northern Division (British Army of The Rhine) June 1919		
War Diary	Lindenthal Cologne	01/06/1919	30/06/1919
Miscellaneous	Northern Division No. G. 8874/17. Appendix A	18/06/1919	18/06/1919
Miscellaneous	Northern Division G. 8874/11	30/05/1919	30/05/1919
Miscellaneous	Reference March Table issued with G.8874/6 dated 27th May.	29/05/1919	29/05/1919
Miscellaneous	Reference March Table issued with G.8874/6 dated 27th May.	28/05/1919	28/05/1919
Miscellaneous	1st Northern Inf Bde. 2nd Northern Inf Bde.	27/05/1919	27/05/1919
Miscellaneous	Instructions for the Advance. No. 1	23/05/1919	23/05/1919
Miscellaneous	Distribution of G. 8874.		
Miscellaneous	March Table		
Miscellaneous	Appendix "A" (To accompany Northern Division G. 8874 dated 23rd May.)		
Miscellaneous	Northern Division. G. 8874 Appendix A.	30/05/1919	30/05/1919
Miscellaneous	Appendix "B"	02/06/1919	02/06/1919
Miscellaneous	Instructions for the Advance Appendix "C"	14/06/1919	16/06/1919
Miscellaneous	Instructions for the Advance Appendix "D"	21/06/1919	21/06/1919
Miscellaneous	Instructions for the advance Appendix "E"	23/06/1919	23/06/1919
Miscellaneous	Reference Northern Division G.8874/20 of 25th June. App B	28/06/1919	28/06/1919
Miscellaneous	1st Northern Inf Bde. 2nd Northern Inf Bde.	25/06/1919	25/06/1919
Miscellaneous	March Table		
Miscellaneous	Guards To Be Taken Over From Light Division.		
Miscellaneous	Northern Division	01/06/1919	01/06/1919
Miscellaneous	Northern Division	20/06/1919	20/06/1919

3rd Division
War Diaries
General Staff

November 1918

QUIEVY. Nov. 1st.

	0515	Weather. Fine, but cold.
	0930	VIth Corps wire & Trincers report timed 2510 31/10. An armistice has been signed by Austrian with It. 17. Adv. G.H.Q. report timed 2210 31/10. An armistice has been signed by Austrian with It. 17.
	1310	3rd. Div. O.O. 280. 3rd. Div. will move into Southern half of VIth Corps Area on 3rd November. 76th Inf. Bde Group will move from GARNIERES to QUIEVY. 9th Inf. Bde Group from GARNIERES to NEVILLERS.
	1515.	Situation wire from VIth Corps timed 1345. Adv. G.H.Q. report lefy Corps Third Army and right and centre Corps First Army attacked this morning S. of VALENCIENNES. No details.
		(vide G.O.350 attached)
		(vide report attached)
		(vide VIth Corps R.450 attd.)

Situation report from VIth Corps.
Situation wire from VIth Corps timed 1345 hours.

Nov. 2nd.

	1145	Weather. Dull and cold with slight rain later. 3rd. Division O.O. 868. Ref. O.O. 280. 53th Fld. Coy. R.E. to move to SOLESMES on 3rd. Nov. 56th and 529th Fld Coy. R.E. to move from BOLE LAB to ST.GEORGES river e. of ESCARMAIN on night 3/4th Nov. (vide G.A. 863 attached).
	1830	3rd. Div. Wire G.A. 867. Ref. O.O. 280. 9th Inf. Bde Group less Fld. Co. to move to QUIEVY vis CAMBLEES and BEVILLIES. (vide G.A. 867 attached).
	1530	3rd. Div. Wire G.A. 869. Ref. O.O. 280 and 3rd. Div. wires G.A. 866 and 868. 9th Inf. Bde to move during daylight on 3rd. Nov. 56th Fld. Co. R.E. to move under orders of G.O.C. 9th. Inf. Bde. (vide G.A. 869 attached).

Situation report timed 06:00 hrs and 10.00 hrs. Distributed to Units.
Situation from VIth Corps wire (G.4773) and VIth Corps wire timed 17.30 hrs. (vide attached)

Nov. 3rd.

	0915	Weather. Fine. Dull later.
	1210	Summary of War news. Distributed to Units. 3rd. Division wire G.A. 884. Orders 76th Inf. Bde. Group (less Fld. Coy.R.E. (vide attached) with one M.G.Co. attached to move on Nov. 4th to ESCARMAIN and RUESNES. 8th Inf. Bde Group with one M.G.Co. attached to SOLESMES. M.G.Batts less two companies to QUIEVY. 56th and 529th Fld. Cos. R.E. to vicinity of ESCARMAIN. All concerned informed. (vide G.A. 884 attached)
	1515.	8th and 76th. Inf. Bdes informed of the distances to be maintained on the march.
	1830	20th K.R.R.C. ordered to move to ROMERIES and move not to interfere with the work on roads in forward area. (vide G.A. 886 attached) (vide G.B.890 attached)

QU.F.V. 5/11/18 contd.

                  (vide 3rd. Div. G.B.891 attd)

1930 Move of 20th K.R.R.C. is cancelled.

   Situation report from VIth Corps G.498 and G.510 timed 1800 and 1725 hours. (vide attached).
   Disposition and Movement Report. Distributed to all concerned. (vide Disposition and movement attached).

Nov.4th Weather. Fine.
0930 3rd. Div. wire G.G. 896. Situation from VIth Corps timed 0838. 62nd Div reports. Right Bde. reports 0750 hrs. Blue objective gained on whole Bde. front. In touch with Divn. on right. Guards Divn. report attack appears to have started satisfactorily from Blue Objective. (vide attached)

0936 3rd. Division wire G.C. 897. VIth Corps wires timed 0600 hrs reads. Summary of war news. Italians capture 100,000 prisoners and 2,200 guns. Hostilities on Italian front ceased on account of armistice which has been concluded. (vide G.C. 897 attached).

1235 VIth Corps wires timed 1150. Aeroplane map shows 62nd Divn on Green objective in touch with IVth Corps. Report indicates Guard Divn. also on Green objective.

1545 Situation report from VIth Corps. Armistice signed with Austria to come into effect at 1500 hrs today.

2000 Brigades to be at one hours notice to move after 0600 hours tomorrow.
2010 VIth Corps wires. Location of house allotted to 3rd. Division for H.Q. is R.14.b.4.4.
2130 3rd. Division wire G.A. 907. Attack progressing satisfactorily on whole front. 2nd and 3rd Divns. ordered to close up their leading Brigades on to the line of Rhonelle river. 76th Inf. Bde. Group (less Fld. Coy. R.E.) with attached M.G.Co. to move to ORSINVAL. 8th Inf. Bde Group less Fld. Coy. R.E. with attached M.G.Co to move to RUESNES. 9th Inf. Bde Group less Fld Co. R.E. to move to ESCARMAIN. H.Q. and two M.G Companies M.G. Battn. to move to ESCARMAIN. The Division will be at one hours notice to move after 0600 hours tomorrow. All concerned informed.
                  (vide G.A. 907 attached)
   Disposition and Movement Report. Distributed to all concerned. (vide Disposition and Movement attached.)

Nov.5th Weather. Rain.
11.30 3rd. Div. wire G.B. 917. The Division will NOT move to day. Advance on Corps front today is meeting with little opposition. (vide G.B.917 attached)
14.45 3rd Div. wire G.B.919. 20th K.R.R.C. to move on Nov 6th to RUESNES from SOLESMES. No restriction as to time. (vide G.B.919 attached).
16.30 3rd. Division wire G.B.922. The Division will not move tomorrow Nov 6th. The Guards and 62nd Divisions are continuing the advance of the Corps front. (vide G.B.922

QUIEVY 5/11/18
Contd.
Nov.6th.
             Situation from VIth Corps. Summary of War's news for distribution to troops. (vide attached.
    11.20   Weather. Rain.
             VIth Corps wire reads 62nd Division on line O.1.d.2.3 O.13.c.9.1 with fresh Brigade.
             3rd. Div. G.O. 928.   Summary of war news for distribution to troops.   (vide G.O.928 attd).

Nov.7th.
             Weather. Rain at short intervals.
    0905.   VIth Corps wire timed 0620 hrs reads. Situation. Right Divn. on Brown line consolidating.
             Left Divn. reach ed Brown line on right in touch with right Divn. Enemy counter attack on
             right of 62nd Div. front but repulsed.   Guards Divn report patrols entered BAVAI about 0430
             Civilians state that enemy retired about 0230 hrs to line 2 kilometres E. of BAVAI.
             VIth Corps wires at 0900 62nd Division had taken HARGNIES and the road from HARGNIES to LA
             LONGUEVILLE in O.18.c.   Guards Divn now pushing E. through O.4.b. and d.
    1230
    14.00   3rd. Div. wire B.B. 951.   Forecast of probable move tomorrow. 76th Inf. Bde. to FRASNOY.
             9th Inf. Bde to ROMERIES. 8th Inf. Bde to remain at SOLESMES.   (vide G.B.951 attached)
    2015.   3rd. Div wire G.B. 957. Following moves to take place on Nov. 8th. 76th Inf. Bde. Group less
             Fld. Coy. R.E. with M.G. Coy. attached from ROMERIES to FRASNOY. 9th Inf. Bde Group less Fld.
             Coy. R.E. from QUIEVY to ROMERIES. H.Q. and 2 Coys. M.G. Bn. from QUIEVY to ROMERIES.
             under orders of G.O.C. 9th Inf. Bde.   (vide G.B.957 attd)

             Situation report from VIth Corps and Summary of war news for distribution to troops.
                                                                                    (vide attached).
             Disposition and movement report. Distributed to all concerned.   (vide attached)
Nov 8th.   Weather. Rain at intervals. and cold.
    18.00   3rd. Div. wire G.B. 972. Div. H.Q. will close at QUIEVY at 12.00 hours Nov. 9th and open
             at FRASNOY at same hour. All concerned informed.   (vide G. . 972 attd.)
    19.55   76th Inf. Bde. to provide parties to work under C.R.E. on clearing mud from certain
             roads on Nov. 9th.
    22.00   3rd. Div. wire G.B. 978. Town Major GOMMEGNIES to allot accommodation all in GOMMEGNIES over
             and above that required for Corps d.Q. to 76th Inf. Bde. Group. Bde. Group will also if
             necessary have accommodation in LE CHAVAL-BLANC- LE GRAND SART Area.   (vide G.B.978 attd).
             VI Corps wires G.H.Q. wire timed 19.40. We hold AVESNES HAUTMONT MALPLAQUET CONDE and western
             half of TOURNAI. Prisoners since Nov. 1st estimated at 18,000.
    23.30   Situation report from VI Corps and Summary of War News for distribution to troops. (vide attached).

FRASNOY. Nov.9th Weather. Fine but cold.
12.17 Divnl. H.Q. closed at QUIEVY at 12.00 hours and opened at FRASNOY at same hour. (vide 3rd. Div. wire att
15.40 3rd Div. wire G.A. 985. Warning Order. Following moves to take place on 10th Nov. 76th. Inf. Bde. Group
       to start at 0900 hours. 76th Bde. Group to LONGUEVILLE. 9th Inf. Bde Group to FRASNOY. 8th Inf.
       Bde. Group and M.G. Coy. to ROMERIES and VERTAIN. 529th Fld. C.OY. R.E. to rejoin its Bde. Group.
       56th and 458th Fld. Coys. R.E. to remain in present area. Tent Division 7th Fld. Ambce. to
       RUESNES and move tonight (Nov. 9th) and rejoin its Bde. Group. One M.G.Co. to move with
       each of 76th and 9th Inf. Bde. Groups. H.Q. and 2 Cos. M.G. Bn. to be located in VERTAIN.
       All concerned informed.   (vide 3rd. Div. G.A.985 attd)
17.15 3rd. Div. wire G.A. 988. Orders for tomorrow 10th Nov. VI Corps front runs as follows.
       Q.17.c. Q.11.a. & b. Q.5.cent. K.30.a. & c. Cavalry patrols in CEREFONTAINE and BOUSSOIS
       3rd Div. to move as follows. 76th Inf. Bde. Group with M.G.Co. attached to ENGLEFONTAINE
       529th Fld Co. R.E. in rear of 76th Inf. Bde. Group. 9th Inf. Bde. Group one M.G.Co. to FRASNOY
       area. 8th Bde. Group and attached M.G. Coy. to ROMERIES. H.Q. and remainder M.G.Co. to
       FRASNOY. Tent Div. 7th Fld. Ambce. to LONGUEVILLE. 56th and 458th Fld. Coys. R.E. will not move.
       All concerned informed.   (vide G.A. 988 attd).
18.45 Location of Units. Divnl. H.Q. FRASNOY. 8th Inf. Bde. SOLESMES. 9th Inf. Bde. ROMERIES
       76th Inf. Bde. FRASNOY.   (vide attached).
       Situation report from VIth Corps.
       VI Corps wire G.153. Summary of War News for distribution to troops. (vide attached.)
Nov. 10th Weather. Fine.
13.40 3rd. Div. wire G.A.11. Orders for to morrow 11th Nov. Moves will be carried out as follows.
       76th Inf. Bde. Group frm LA LONGUEVILLE to ASSEVENT. 9th Inf. Bde. Group from FRASNOY to
       LA LONGUEVILLE. 56th Fld. Co. From ORSINVAL to move in rear of 9th Inf. Bde. Group. 8th Bde.
       Group (less 458th Fld.Co.) from ROMERIES to FRASNOY 458th Fld. Co. from GOMMEGNIES
       to MAUBEUGE. H.Q. and Co. M.G. Bn. from GOMMEGNIES to LA LONGUEVILLE. Tent Div. 7th Fld. Ambce.
       from GOMMEGNIES to MAUBEUGE. All concerned informed.   (vide G.A.11 attached).
15.40 3rd. Division wire G.A. 15. Further to G.A.11. 4th Cavalry Bde. will be moving on the
       LA LONGUEVILLE - DOUZIES - MAUBEUGE Road in front of 76th Inf. Bde. Group. to morrow. In addition
       to ASSEVENT, part of BOUSSOIS West of grid line running N. and S. between L.32 and L.53 is at
       disposal of 76th Inf. Bde. for billetting purposes.   (vide G.A. 15 attached.).
18.00 3rd. Division wire G.A. 14. 40th Bde. R.F.A. to move Nov. 11th to MAUBEUGE. (vide G.A. 14 attached.).
20.00 3rd. Div. wire G.B. 19. 4th Cavalry Bde. will detail one troop to report to 3rd. Div. H.Q.
       Place Verte. MAUBEUGE at 16.00 hours Nov. 12th.

FRASNOY.Nov10 20.50 3rd. Division O.O. 281. Report timed 10.00 hours Nov. 10th. Cavalry patrol fired on by M.G. fire
contd.   in M.21.a. OSTERGNIES and COLLERET reported clear of the enemy. Report timed 13.00 hours Nov.10th
                        enemy holding line of rifle pits R.5.b. Sunken Rd. L.35.B. & d. L.29.c. L.28.b. L.22.a. & d.
                        opposite VI and XVII Corps front. Cavalry report timed 15.15 hrs Nov 10th. Report Right Regt.
                        reached line of LA THURE River. Centre Regt. report FORT DE BOUSSOIS (L.27.d.) and TOWER L.29.a.
                        held by enemy. Line held by us on front of Third Army QUIEVELON (incl) E. of BOUSSOIS - E. of
                        ELESMES - and E. of BETTIGNIES. Advanced Guard to be furnished by VI Corps to keep touch with
                        enemy. Leading Inf. Bde. Group 3rd. Div. with Arty. Bde. to push through present front of VI
                        Corps and be in support of 4th Cavalry Bde. G.O.C. 3rd. Div. assumes command of Advanced
                        Guard at 16.00 hours on 11th Nov. 76th Inf. Bde. to be prepared to advance on 12th Nov. in support
                        of Cavalry. Div. H.Q. closes at FRASNOY and opens at MAUBEUGE at 12.00 hours on 11th November.
                        All concerned. informed.   (vide 3rd. Div. O.O. 281 attached)

          22.20   Aerodrome in R.35.c. reserved for 1st Squadron R.A.F. Out of bounds to all troops.
                        Summary of War News for distribution to troops.   (vide G.O. 2 attached)
Nov.11   02.55   Weather. Fine and cold. Imperial Chancellor to ERZBERGER authorises signature of armistice conditions,
                        VI Corps wires. Slight rain in evening.
          07.10   VI Corps wires. but requests negotiations on certain points affecting food supply.
                        3rd. Div. wire G.O. 29. All moves for today cancelled. All Divnl. Units to remain in present
                        area.
          07.50   3rd. Div. G.O. 30. Hostilities cease at 11.00 to day 11th Nov.   (vide G.O. 29 attached).
          09.10   C.R.E. to arrange with Bdes for work on roads.   (vide G.O. 30 attached).
          09.50   VI Corps wires pending further instructions, aeroplanes will not cross the line of the
                        BEAUMONT-MONS Rd. after 11.00 hours to day.
          14.50   Following message pick up by wireless from Germany, sent in English. Heavy English Gun still
                        fire in direction S.W. of BINCHE, please, an immediate cessation of fire.
          25.12   Conference at Divnl. H.Q. at 11.00 hours to-morrow 12th Nov.
                        Situation report from VI Corps. Company of 3rd Canadian Div. entered MONS at 04.30 hours this
                        morning. Belgians entered GHENT.   (vide copy attached).

          Lecture on "Demobilization and Reconstruction"

Army Form C. 2118.

WAR DIARY
or
INTELLIGENCE SUMMARY.
(Erase heading not required.)

Instructions regarding War Diaries and Intelligence Summaries are contained in F. S. Regs., Part II. and the Staff Manual respectively. Title pages will be prepared in manuscript.

Place	Date	Hour	Summary of Events and Information	Remarks and references to Appendices
FRASNOY.	Nov.12th.		Weather. Fine all day.	
		09.45	VI Corps wires G.H.Q. report timed 22.00 hrs. 11th Nov. General Line reached by British Armies at 11.00 hrs to day approx. as follows. MONT BLIART River, 2000 yds E. of EPPE SAUVAGE through BOIS DE MARTINSART B.11.d. O.O. (Etang dr Frasies) (B.8.b.) to COUSOLRE Stn. (inclusive) W. edge of BOIS DE JEUMONT ERQUELYNNES (incl) E. of ERQUELYNNES GIVRY Rd. to GIVRY (incl) S.15 - VILLERS ST GUISLAIN - VILLE SUR HAINE Stn. - JURBISE- FARM DE JIPTEUX (C.16.) - CHIEVRES - GHISLENGHIEN - LESSINES (all incl) - DE ND River to GRAMMONT Western portion inclusive E. of NEDERBRAKEL -	
		13.00	VI Corps wires G.H.Q. report 09.40 hrs situation as follows. Line reached at 11.00 yesterday E. of MONS now reported as follows. GIVRY - BINCHE Rd. in X.18. VILLERS ST GHISLAIN HAVRE DBOURG ST DENIS CASTEAU all inclusive and as previously reported((in above wire)) North of GRAMMONT line runs due north to P.14.c.	
		17.15	VI Corps wires G.H.Q. timed 15.10. French Line at 11.00 yesterday as follows. Southern Bank of MEUSE from WADELINCOURT to REVIN exclusive NEUVE FORGE - CULDESSARTS - FIEZES - BAILEUX - ROBECHIES - RANCHE (all inclusive)	(vide Disposition and Movement Report attached).
			Disposition and Movement report.	
FRASNOY	Nov.13th		Weather. Fine.	
		09.50	3rd. Div. wire G.B. 56. The Companies of M.G. Battns at present attached to 8th and 76th Inf. Bdes to rejoin their Battn. at SARLOTON to day.	(vide G.B.56 attached).
		11.00	VI Corps wires a Conference will be held at Corps H.Q. at 10.00 hrs tomorrow-Nov.14th. G.O.C. and G.S.O.1 of the Division to attend.	
		11.50	M.G. Company attached to 76th Inf. Bde to remain at LONGUEVILLE. M.G. Company attached 8th Inf. Bde to rejoin its Battan as ordered.	
			VI Corps wires timed 22.50 Nov. 12th. Orders and Discipline, with reference to line gained at 11.00 hours on the 11th Nov.	(vide copy attached).

Army Form C. 2118.

WAR DIARY
or
INTELLIGENCE SUMMARY

(Erase heading not required.)

Instructions regarding War Diaries and Intelligence Summaries are contained in F.S. Regs., Part II. and the Staff Manual respectively. Title pages will be prepared in manuscript.

Place	Date	Hour	Summary of Events and Information	Remarks and references to Appendices
Frasnoy.	Nov.14th	18.00	Weather. Fine. 3rd. Div. wire G.C. 69. Following moves to take place to-morrow Nov. 15th. H.Q. and 3 Coys. M.G. Battn. from GOMMEGNIES and SARLOTON to LA LONGUEVILLE. Route Pioneer Battn from RUESNES to GOMMEGNIES and SARLOTON. 76th Inf. Bde. to allot area in LA LONGUEVILLE to M.G. Bn. Weather Fine. (vide G.C. 69 attached).	
	15/11/18	10.30	3rd. Div. wire G.B.77. Following moves to take place Nov. 16th. 8th. Inf. Bde. Group less Fld. Coy. R.E. from ROMERIES to FRASNOY. 9th Bde. Group from FRASNOY to LA LONGUEVILLE. 76th Inf. Bde. Group from LA LONGUEVILLE to NEUF MESNIL and MON PLAISIR. 20th K.R.R.C. from GOMMEGNIES and SARLOTON to NEUF MESNIL. All concerned informed.(vide G.B. 77 attached).	
		22.00	3rd. Div. wire G.B.81. Forecast of moves on 17th November. A. Group to LOUVROIL. B.Group to SOUS LE BOIS. C. Group to NEUF MESNIL and MON PLAISIR. D. Group no move. (vide G.B. 81 attached).	
	16/11/18		Instruction to Officers in charge of Education 3rd. Division. (vide copy attached). Orders and Instruction with reference to the "March to the RHINE". (vide copy attached). Weather. Fine.	
		14.30	3rd. Div. wire G.B. 84. Following moves to take place on Nov. 17th. A Group from NEUF MESNIL MON PLAISIR Area to LOUVROIL. B Group from LA LONGUEVILLE to SOUS LE BOIS. C Group. from FRASNOY to NEUF MESNIL MON PLAISIR Area. Train Coy. to march behind Bde. Group. Divisional Headquarters to move to SOUS LE BOIS. D Group will not move. Addressed all concerned. (Vide G.B. 84 attached).	
		18.45	3rd. Division wire G.B. 89. Divisional Headquarters closes at FRASNOY at 15.00 hours. Nov. 17th and opens at SOUS LE BOIS at same hour. (vide G.B. 89 attached).	
		22.00	3rd. Division wire G.B. 92. Moves ordered in G.B. 84 to take place on Nov. 17th is cancelled. (vide G.B. 92 attached).	
	17/11/18		Instructions No. 2 to 3rd. Division G.2002. with reference to the "March to the RHINE". Weather. Fine but cold.	
		10.30	3rd. Div. wire G.B. 94. Moves ordered in G.B. 84 and 89 dated Nov. 16th will take place on Nov. 18th. Forecast of moves for Nov. 19th. A Group from LOUVROIL to area COLLERET OSTERGNIES CERFONTAINE FERRIERE LA GRANDE. B & C Groups no change. D. Group to area west of the HAUTMONT - LA LONGUEVILLE - BAVAI Road exclusive Divisional Headquarters to COUSOLRE. Addressed all concerned. (vide G.B. 94 attached).	

Army Form C. 2118.

WAR DIARY
or
INTELLIGENCE SUMMARY
(Erase heading not required.)

Instructions regarding War Diaries and Intelligence Summaries are contained in F.S. Regs., Part II. and the Staff Manual respectively. Title pages will be prepared in manuscript.

Place	Date	Hour	Summary of Events and Information	Remarks and references to Appendices
FRASNOY.	17/11/18. contd.	20.00	3rd. Div. wire G.B. 98. Moves forecasted for 19th Nov. will take place on Nov. 20th. No moves for 19th Nov. B. Group will move to OBIES- HARGNIES - VIEUX MESNIL and accommodation for 2 Bdes. R.F.A. in LA LONGUEVILLE. Addressed all concerned. (vide copy attached).	
			Instruction No. 3. With reference to the "march to the RHINE". (vide copy attached).	
SOUS- LE- BOIS.	18/11/18.	16.00	Weather. Dull. Cold with slight snow in morning. Divisional Headquarters opened at SOUS LE BOIS at 15.00 hours. Instructions No. 4. with reference to the "March to the RHINE" (vide copy attached). Nothing else of interest to report.	
	19/11/18.	15.00	Weather. Dull all day. 3rd. Division operation order No. 282 and G.S. 2018. A Group to move on Nov. 20th to COUSORLE - BERSILLIES A'BBAYE - BOUSIGNIES Area. B Group to COLLERET - CERFONTAINE - OSTERGNIES Area. C Group FERRIERE LA GRANDE Area. D. Group. 2 Bdes R.F.A. to LA LONGUEVILLE 1 Bde. R.F.A. and D.A.C. to VIEUX MESNIL and HARGNIES Area. (vide copies attached).	
			Nothing else of interest to report.	
COUSORLE.	20/11/18	14.00 14.20	Weather. Dull and cold. Mist in evening. Divisional Headquarters opened at COUSORLE. 3rd. Division wire G.B. 118. A. B. & C. Groups will not move tomorrow Nov. 21st. D. Group will move to area ROUSIES - REQUIGNIES - MARPENT. No further move to take place, pending improvement of railway and road communications. (vide G.B. 118 attached).	

Army Form C. 2118.

WAR DIARY
or
INTELLIGENCE SUMMARY.
(Erase heading not required.)

Instructions regarding War Diaries and Intelligence Summaries are contained in F. S. Regs., Part II. and the Staff Manual respectively. Title pages will be prepared in manuscript.

Place	Date	Hour	Summary of Events and Information	Remarks and references to Appendices
GOUSORLE.	21st Nov.		Weather. Fine. Nothing of interest.	
"	22nd Nov.	11.50	Weather. Fine. G.A.130 issued mK to all concerned. (Vide G.A. 130 attached).	
"	23rd Nov.	20.00	Frosty. Fine. 3rd Div. O.O.283 issued mK to all concerned. (Vide O.O.283 attached).	
"	24th Nov.	08.00	Weather. Fine. 3rd Div. O.O.284 issued all concerned. (Vide O.O.284 attached).	
		18.10	3rd Div. G.B.149 issued to all concerned. (Vide G.B.149 attached).	
		09.00	3rd Div. H.Q. opened at THUIN.	
THUIN	25th Nov.		Weather. Fair.	
"		03.00	3rd Div. O.O.285 issued to all concerned. (Vide O.O.285 attached).	
LOVERVAL		20.00	3rd Div.G.S.2002/5 issued to all concerned. (Vide G.S.2002/5 attached).	
"		09.00	3rd Div. H.Q. opened at LOVERVAL.	
THUIN.	26th Nov.		Weather. FINE	
"	27th Nov.		Weather. Slight rain.	
LOVERVAL		12.00	3rd Div.O.O.286 issued to all concerned. (Vide O.O.286 attached).	
		20.30	3rd Div.O.O.287 issued to all concerned. (Vide O.O.287 attached).	
LOVERVAL	28th Nov.		Weather. Dull. Nothing of interest.	
BIOUL.		09.00	3rd Div.H.Q. opened at BIOUL.	
"	29th Nov.	15.00	Weather. Slight rain. 3rd Div.O.O. 288 issued to all concerned. (Vide OO 288 attached)	
DAL. NNE.	30th		Weather. Fine.	

for Brig.G. Moon
to Lieut.Colonel
General Staff 3rd Division

Army Form C. 2118.

WAR DIARY
or
INTELLIGENCE SUMMARY.
(Erase heading not required.)

Instructions regarding War Diaries and Intelligence Summaries are contained in F. S. Regs., Part II. and the Staff Manual respectively. Title pages will be prepared in manuscript.

Place	Date	Hour	Summary of Events and Information	Remarks and references to Appendices
COUSOLRE.	21st Nov.		Weather. Fine. Nothing of interest.	
"	22nd Nov.	11.50	Weather. Fine. G.A. 130 issued to all concerned.	
"	23rd Nov.	20.00	Frosty. Fine. 3rd Div. O.O.283 issued to all concerned.	(Vide O.O.283 attached).
"	24th Nov.	08.00	Weather. Fine. 3rd Div. O.O.284 issued to all concerned.	(Vide O.O.284 attached).
		18.10	3rd Div. G.B.149 issued to all concerned.	(Vide G.B.149 attached).
		09.00	3rd Div. H.Q.opened at THUIN.	
THUIN	25th Nov.		Weather. Fair.	
		08.00	3rd Div. O.O.285 issued to all concerned.	(Vide O.O.285 attached).
THUIN		20.00	3rd Div. G.S.2002/5 issued to all concerned.	(Vide G.S.2002/5 attached).
LOVERVAL	26th Nov.	09.00	3rd Div. H.Q.opened at LOVERVAL.	
"			Weather. Fine.	
"			3rd Div.	
"	27th Nov.		Weather. Slight rain.	
			3rd Div.	
LOVERVAL		13.00	3rd Div. O.O.286 issued to all concerned.	(Vide O.O.286 attached).
		20.30	3rd Div. O.O.287 issued to all concerned.	(Vide O.O.287 attached).
LOVERVAL	28th Nov.		Weather. Dull. Nothing of interest.	
BIOUL.		09.00	3rd Div. H.Q.opened at BIOUL.	
"	29th Nov.	15.00	Weather. Slight rain. 3rd Div. O.O.288 issued to all concerned.	
BIOUL.	30th		Weather. Fine.	

for Lieut. Colonel
Command[in]g 3rd Division

Army Form C. 2118.

WAR DIARY
or
INTELLIGENCE SUMMARY.

(Erase heading not required.)

Instructions regarding War Diaries and Intelligence Summaries are contained in F.S. Regs., Part II. and the Staff Manual respectively. Title pages will be prepared in manuscript.

Place	Date	Hour	Summary of Events and Information	Remarks and references to Appendices
FRASNOY.	17/11/18. contd.	20.00	3rd. Div. wire G.B. 98. Moves forecasted for 19th Nov. will take place on Nov. 20th. No moves for 19th Nov. B. Group will move to OBIES-HARGNIES - VIEUX MESNIL and accommodation for 2 Bdes. R.F.A. in LA LONGUEVILLE. Addressed all concerned. (Vide copy attached).	
			Instruction No. 5. with reference to the "march to the RHINE". (vide copy attached).	
SOUS-LE-BOIS.	18/11/18.	16.00	Weather. Dull. Cold with slight snow in morning. Divisional Headquarters opened at SOUS LE BOIS at 15.00 hours. Instructions No. 4. with reference to the "march to the RHINE" (vide copy attached). Nothing else of interest to report.	
	19/11/18		Weather. Dull all day.	
		15.00	3rd. Division operation order No. 282 and G.S. 2018. A Group to move on Nov. 20th to COUSORLE - BERSILLIES A'BBAYE - BOUSIGNIES Area. B Group to COLLERET - CERFONTAINE - OSTERGNIES Area. C Group FERRIERE LA GRANDE Area. D. Group. 2 Bdes R.F.A. to LA LONGUEVILLE 1 Bde. R.F.A. and D.A.C. to VIEUX MESNIL and HARGNIES Area. (vide copies attached).	
			Nothing else of interest to report.	
COUSORLE.	20/11/18	14.00	Weather. Dull and cold. Mist in evening. Divisional Headquarters opened at COUSORLE.	
		14.20	3rd. Division wire G.B. 113. A. B. & C. Groups will not move tomorrow Nov. 21st. D. Group will move to area ROUSIES - RECQUIGNIES - MARPENT. No further moves to take place, pending improvement of railway and road communications. (vide G.B. 118 attached).	

WAR DIARY
or
INTELLIGENCE SUMMARY

(Erase heading not required.)

Army Form C. 2118.

Place	Date	Hour	Summary of Events and Information	Remarks and references to Appendices
QUIEVY.	Nov. 1st	0553	Weather. Fine, but cold.	
			VIth Corps wires 9 prisoners captured in raid on LA FOLIE Farm.	
		0930	Adv. G.H.Q. report timed 2510 31/10. An armistice has been signed by Austria/with Italy.	
		1330	3rd. Div. O.O. 280. 3rd. Div. will move into Southern half of VIth Corps Area on 3rd November. 76th Inf. Bde Group will move from CARNIERES to BEVILLERS. 9th Inf. Bde Group from CATENNIERES to QUIEVY. M.G. Bn. from CARNIERES to QUIEVY. All concerned informed. (3rd. Div. O.O.280 attached).	
		1515	Situation wire from VIth Corps timed 1345. Adv. G.H.Q. report left Corps Third Army and right and centre Corps First Army attacked this morning S. of VALENCIENNES. No details.	(vide G.Q.850 attached)
			Situation report from VIth Corps.	(vide report attached)
			Situation wire from VIth Corps timed 1545 hours.	(vide VIth Corps G.450 attd).
	Nov. 2nd.	1145	Weather. Dull and cold with slight rain later.	
			3rd. Division G.A. 866. Ref. O.O. 280. 56th Fld. Co. R.E. to move to SOLESMES on 3rd. Nov. 56th and 529th Fld Cos. R.E. to move from SOLESMES to ST.GEORGES river E. of ESCARMAIN on night 3/4th Nov.	(vide G.A. 866 attached).
		1230.	3rd. Div. wire G.A. 867. Ref. O.O. 280. 9th Inf. Bde Group less Fld. Co. to move to QUIEVY via CARNIERES and BEVILLERS.	(vide G.A. 867 attached).
		1330.	3rd. Div. wire G.A. 869. Ref. O.O. 280 and 3rd. Div. wires G.A. 866 and 867. 9th Inf. Bde to move during daylight on 3rd. Nov. 56th Fld. Co. R.E. to move under orders of G.O.C. 9th. Inf. Bde.	(vide G.A. 869 attached)
			Situation report timed 0330 hrs and 10.00 hrs. Distributed to Units	(vide attached)
			Situation from VIth Corps (G.479) and VIth Corps wire timed 17.30 hrs.	(vide attached).
	Nov.3rd.	0915	Weather. Fine. Dull later.	
			Summary of War news. Distributed to Units.	(vide attached)
		1210	3rd. Division wire G.A. 884. Orders 76th Inf. Bde. Group (less Fld. Coy.R.E. and Fld. Ambce.) with one M.G.Co. attached to move on Nov. 4th to ESCARMAIN and RUESNES. 8th Inf. Bde Group with one M.G.Co. attached to SOLESMES. M.G.Battn less two companies to QUIEVY. 56th and 529th Fld. Cos. R.E. to vicinity of ESCARMAIN. All concerned informed.	(vide G.A. 884 attached)
		1315.	8th and 76th. Inf. Bdes informed of the distances to be maintained on the march.	(vide G.A. 886 attached)
		1830	20th K.R.R.C. ordered to move to ROMERIES and move not to interfere with the work on roads in forward area.	(vide G.B.890 attached)

WAR DIARY
or
INTELLIGENCE SUMMARY

(Erase heading not required.)

Army Form C. 2118.

Place	Date	Hour	Summary of Events and Information	Remarks and references to Appendices
QUIEVY.	3/11/18. contd.	19.30	Move of 20th K.R.R.C. is cancelled.	(vide 3rd. Div. G.B.891 attd)
	Nov.4th		Weather. Fine.	
		09.30	Situation report from VIth Corps G.498 and G.510 timed 18.00 and 17.25 hours. Disposition and Movement Report. Distributed to all concerned.	(vide attached). (vide Disposition and movement attached).
			3rd. Div. wire G.C. 896. Situation from VIth Corps timed 08.38. 62nd Div reports. Right Bde. reports 07.50 hrs. Blue objective gained on whole Bde. front. In touch with Divn. on right. Guards Divn. report attack appears to have started satisfactorily from Blue Objective.	(vide attached)
		09.36	3rd. Division wire G.C. 897. VIth Corps wires timed 0600 hrs reads. Summary of war news. Italians capture 100,000 prisoners and 2,200 guns. Hostilities on Italian front ceased on account of armistice which has been concluded.	(vide G.C. 897 attached).
		12.35	VIth Corps wires timed 11.50. Aeroplane map shows 62nd Divn on Green objective in touch with IVth Corps. Report indicates Guard Divn. also on Green objective. Armistice signed with Austria to come into effect at 1500 hrs today.	
		13.45	Situation report from VIth Corps.	
		20.00	Brigades to be at one hours notice to move after 0600 hours tomorrow.	
		20.10	VIth Corps wires. Location of house allotted to 3rd. Division for H.Q. is R.14.b.4.4.	
		21.30	3rd. Division wire G.A. 907. Attack progressing satisfactorily on whole front. 2nd and 3rd Divns ordered to close up their leading Brigades on to the line of Rhonelle river. 76th Inf. Bde. Group (less Fld. Coy. R.E.) with attached M.G.Co. to move to ORSINVAL. 8th Inf. Bde Group less Fld. Coy. R.E. with attached M.G.Co to move to RUESNES. 9th Inf. Bde Group less Fld Co. R.E. to move to ESCARMAIN. H.Q. and two M.G Companies M.G. Battn. to move to ESCARMAIN. The Division will be at one hours notice to move after 0600 hours tomorrow. All concerned informed.	(vide G.A.907 attached)
			Disposition and Movement Report. Distributed to all concerned.	(vide Disposition and Movement attached.)
	Nov 5th		Weather. Rain.	
		11.30	3rd. Div. wire. G.B. 917. The Division will NOT move to day. Advance on Corps front today is meeting with little opposition.	(vide G.B.917.attached)
		14.45	3rd Div. wire G.B.919. 20th K.R.R.C. to move on Nov 6th to RUESNES from SOLESMES. No restriction as to time.	(vide G.B.919 attached).
		16.30	3rd. Division wire G.B.922. The Division will not move tomorrow Nov 6th. The Guards and 62nd Divisions are continuing their advance on the Corps front.	(vide G.B.922 attached)

Army Form C. 2118.

85

WAR DIARY
or
INTELLIGENCE SUMMARY
(Erase heading not required.)

Instructions regarding War Diaries and Intelligence Summaries are contained in F. S. Regs., Part II. and the Staff Manual respectively. Title pages will be prepared in manuscript.

Place	Date	Hour	Summary of Events and Information	Remarks and references to Appendices
QUIEVY	5/11/18 Contd. Nov.6th		Situation from VIth Corps. Summary of Wars news for distribution to troops. (vide attached.	
		11.20	Weather. Rain. VIth Corps wire reads 62nd Division on line O.1.d.2.3 O.13.c.9.1 with fresh Brigade. 3rd. Div. G.C. 928. Summary of war news for distribution to troops. (vide G.C.927 attd).	
	Nov.7th.		Weather. Rain at short intervals.	
		0905.	VIth Corps wire timed 0620 hrs reads. Situation. Right Divn. on Brown line consolidating. Left Divn. reached Brown line on right in touch with right Divn. Enemy counter attack on right of 62nd Div. front but repulsed. Guards Divn report patrols entered BAVAI about 0430 Civilians state that enemy retired about 0230 hrs to line 2 kilometres E. of BAVAI.	
		1230	VIth Corps wires at 0900 62nd Division had taken HARGNIES and the road from HARGNIES to LA LONGUEVILLE in O.18.c. Guards Divn now pushing E. through 0.4.b. and d.	
		14.00	3rd. Div. wire G.B. 951. Forecast of probable move tomorrow. 76th Inf. Bde to FRASNOY. 9th Inf. Bde to ROMERIES. 8th Inf. Bde to remain at SOLESMES. (vide G.B.951 attached)	
		2015.	3rd. Div wire G.B.957. Following moves to take place on Nov. 8th. 76th Inf. Bde. Group less Fld. Fld. Coy. R.E. with M.G. Coy. attached from ROMERIES to FRASNOY. 9th Inf. Bde Group less Fld. Coy. R.E. from QUIEVY to ROMERIES. H.Q. and 2 Coys. M.G. Bn. from QUIEVY to ROMERIES under orders of G.O.C. 9th Inf. Bde. (vide G.B.957 attd)	
			Situation report from VIth Corps and Summary of war news for distribution to troops. (vide attached). Disposition and movement report. Distributed to all concerned. (vide attached)	
	Nov 8th		Weather. Rain at intervals. and cold.	
		13.00	3rd. Div. wire G.B. 972. Div. H.Q. will close at QUIEVY at 12.00 hours Nov. 9th and open at FRASNOY at same hour. All concerned informed. (vide G. . 972 attd.)	
		19.55	76th Inf. Bde. to provide parties to work under C.R.E. on clearing mud from certain roads on Nov. 9th.	
		22.00	3rd. Div. wire G.B. 978. Town Major GOMMEGNIES to allot accommodation all in GOMMEGNIES over and above that required for Corps H.Q. to 76th Inf. Bde. Group. Bde. Group will also if necessary have accommodation in LE CHAVAL-BLANC- LE GRAND SART Area. (vide G.B.978 attd).	
		23.30	VI Corps wires G.H.Q. wire timed 19.40. We hold AVESNES HAUTMONT MALPLAQUET CONDE and western half of TOURNAI. Prisoners since Nov. 1st estimated at 18,000. Situation report from VI Corps and Summary of War News for distribution to troops. (vide attached).	

Army Form C. 2118.

WAR DIARY
INTELLIGENCE SUMMARY.
(Erase heading not required.)

Instructions regarding War Diaries and Intelligence Summaries are contained in F.S. Regs., Part II. and the Staff Manual respectively. Title pages will be prepared in manuscript.

Place	Date	Hour	Summary of Events and Information	Remarks and references to Appendices
FRASNOY	Nov.9th	12.17	Weather. Fine but cold. Divnl. H.Q. closed at QUIEVY at 12.00 hours and opened at FRASNOY at same hour.	(vide 3rd. Div. wire attd)
		15.40	3rd Div. wire G.A. 985. Warning Order. Following moves to take place on 10th Nov. Inf. Bde. Groups to start at 0900 hours. 76th Bde. Group to LONGUEVILLE. 9th Inf. Bde. Group from FRASNOY to Bde. Group and M.G. Coy. to ROMERIES and VERTAIN. 529th Fld. C.Oy. R.E. to rejoin its Bde. Group. 56th and 438th Fld. Coys. R.E. to remain in present area. Tent Division 7th Fld. Ambce. to RUESNES and move tonight (Nov. 9th) and rejoin its Bde. Group. one M.G. Co. to move with each of 76th and 9th Inf. Bde. Groups. H.Q. and 2 Cos. M.G. Bn. to be located in VERTAIN. All concerned informed.	(vide 3rd. Div. G.A. 985 attd)
		17.15	3rd. Div. wire G.A. 988. Orders for tomorrow 10th Nov. VI Corps front runs as follows. Q.17.c. Q.11.a. & b. Q.5.cent. K.30.e. & c. Cavalry patrols in CERFONTAINE and BOUSSOIS 3rd. Div. to move as follows. 76th Inf. Bde. Group with M.G.Co. attached to LONGUEVILLE. 529th Fld Co. R.E. in rear of 76th Inf. Bde. Group. 9th Inf. Bde. Group one M.G.Co. to FRASNOY area. 8th Bde. Group and attached M.G. Coy. to ROMERIES. H.Q. and remainder M.G. Co. to FRASNOY. Tent Div. 7th Fld. Ambce. to LONGUEVILLE. 56th and 438th Fld. Coys. R.E. will not move. All concerned informed.	(vide G.A. 988 attd)
		18.45	Location of Units. Divnl. H.Q. FRASNOY. 8th Inf. Bde. FRASNOY. 76th Inf. Bde. FRASNOY. 9th Inf. Bde. SOLESMES. Bde. ROMERIES. Situation report from VIth Corps. VI Corps wire G.153. Summary of War News for distribution to troops.	(vide attached). (vide attached.)
	Nov. 10th		Weather. Fine.	
		13.40	3rd. Div. wire G.A.11. Orders for to morrow 11th Nov. Moves will be carried out as follows. 76th Inf. Bde. Group from LA LONGUEVILLE to ASEVENT. 9th Inf. Bde. Group from FRASNOY to LA LONGUEVILLE. 56th Fld. Co. from ORSINVAL to move in rear of 9th Inf. Bde. Group. 8th Bde. Group (less 438th Fld.Co.) from ROMERIES to FRASNOY 438th Fld. Co. from GOMMEGNIES to MAUBEUGE. H.Q. and Co. M.G. Bn. from GOMMEGNIES to LA LONGUEVILLE. Tent Div. 7th Fld. Ambce. from GOMMEGNIES to MAUBEUGE. All concerned informed.	(vide G.A.11 attached)
		15.40	3rd. Division wire G.A. 15. Further to G.A. 11. 4th Cavalry Bde. will be moving on the LA LONGUEVILLE – DOUZIES – MAUBEUGE Road in front of 76th Inf.Bde. Group. to morrow. In addition to ASEVENT, part of BOUSSOIS West of grid line running N. and S. between L.32 and L.33 is at disposal of 76th Inf. Bde. for billetting purposes.	(vide G.A. 15 attached.).
		16.00	3rd. Division wire G.A. 14. 40th Bde. R.F.A. to move Nov. 11th to MAUBEUGE	(vide G/A Nr attached)
		20.00	3rd. Div. wire G.B. 19. 4th Cavalry Bde. will detail one troop to report to 3rd. Div. H.Q. Place Verte. MAUBEUGE at 16.00 hours Nov. 12th.	

Army Form C.2118.

WAR DIARY
or
INTELLIGENCE SUMMARY.

(Erase heading not required.)

Instructions regarding War Diaries and Intelligence Summaries are contained in F.S. Regs., Part II. and the Staff Manual respectively. Title pages will be prepared in manuscript.

Place	Date	Hour	Summary of Events and Information	Remarks and references to Appendices
FRASNOY contd.	Nov.10	20.30	3rd. Division O.O. 281. Report timed 10.00 hours Nov. 10th. in.M.21.a. OSTERGNIES and COLLERET reported clear of the enemy. Cavalry patrol fired on by M.G. fire enemy holding line of rifle pits R.5.b. Sunken Rd. L.35.b. & d. L.29.c. L.28.b. L.22.a. & d. opposite VI and XVII Corps front. Cavalry report timed 13.00 hours Nov.10th reached line of LA THURE River. Centre Regt. report FORT DE BOUSSOIS (L.27.d.) and TOWER L.29.a. held by enemy. Line held by us on Front of Third Army QUIEVELON (incl) E. of BOUSSOIS - E. of ELESMES - and E. of BETTIGNIES. Advanced Guard to be furnished by VI Corps to keep touch with enemy. Leading Inf. Bde. Group 3rd. Div. with Arty. Bde. to push through present front of VI Corps and be in support of 4th Cavalry Bde. G.O.C. 3rd. Div. assumes command of Advanced Guard at 16.00 hours on 11th Nov. 76th Inf. Bde to be prepared to advance on 12th Nov. in support of Cavalry. Div. H.Q. closes at FRASNOY and opens at MAUBEUGE at 12.00 hours on 11th November. All concerned informed. (vide 3rd. Div. O.O. 281 attached)	
		22.20	Aerodrome in R.35.c. reserved for 1st Squadron R.A.F. Out of bounds to all troops. Summary of War News for distribution to troops. (vide G.C. 2 attached)	
	Nov.11	02.55	Weather. Fine and cold. Slight rain in evening. VI Corps wires. Imperial Chancellor to ERZBERGER authorises signature of armistice conditions, but requests negotiations on certain points effecting food supply.	
		07.10	3rd. Div. wire G.C. 29. All moves for today cancelled. All Divnl. Units to remain in present area. (vide G.C. 29 attached).	
		07.50	3rd. Div. G.C. 30. Hostilities cease at 11.00 to day 11th Nov. (vide G.C. 30 attached).	
		09.10	C.R.E. to arrange with Bdes for work on roads.	
		09.50	VI Corps wires pending further instructions, aeroplanes will not cross the line of the BEAUMONT-MONS Rd. after 11.00 hours to day.	
		14.59	Following message pick up by wireless from Germany, sent in English. Heavy English Gun still fire in direction S.W. of BINCHE, please an immediate cessation of fire.	
		23.12	Conference at Divnl. H.Q. at 11.00 hours to-morrow 12th Nov. Situation report from VI Corps. Company of 3rd Canadian Div. entered MONS at 04.30 hours this morning. Belgians entered GHENT. (vide copy attached).	
			Lecture on "Demobilization and Reconstruction"	

Army Form C. 2118.

WAR DIARY
or
INTELLIGENCE SUMMARY.
(Erase heading not required.)

Instructions regarding War Diaries and Intelligence Summaries are contained in F. S. Regs., Part II. and the Staff Manual respectively. Title pages will be prepared in manuscript.

Place	Date	Hour	Summary of Events and Information	Remarks and references to Appendices
FRASNOY.	Nov.12th.		Weather. Fine all day.	
		09.45	VI Corps wires G.H.Q. report timed 22.00 hrs. 11th Nov. General Line reached by British British Armies at 11.00 hrs to day approx. as follows. MONT BLIART River, 2000 yds E. of EPPE SAUVAGE through BOIS DE MARTINSART B.11.d.0.0. (Etang dr Frasies) (B.8.b.) to COUSOLRE STN. (inclusive) W. edge of BOIS DE JEUMONT ERQUELYNNES (incl) E. of ERQUELYNNES GIVRY Rd. to GIVRY (incl) S.13 - VILLERS ST GUISLAIN - VILLE SUR HAINE Stn. - JURBISE- FARM DE JIPTEUX (C.16.) - CHIEVRES - GHISLENGHIEN - LESSINES (all incl) - DE ND River to GRAMMONT Western portion inclusive E. of NEDERBRAKEL	
		13.00	VI Corps wires G.H.Q. report 09.40 hrs situation as follows. Line reached at 11.00 yesterday E. of MONS now reported as follows. GIVRY - BINCHE Rd. in X.18. VILLERS ST GHISLAIN HAVRE OBOURG ST DENIS CASTEAU all inclusive and as previously reported((in above wire)) North of GRAMMONT line runs due north to P.14.C.	
		17.15	VI Corps wires G.H.Q. timed 13.10. French Line at 11.00 yesterday as follows. Southern Bank of MEUSE from WADELINCOURT to REVIN exclusive NEUVE FORGE - CULDESSARTS - RIEZES - BAILEUX - ROBECHIES - RANCHE (all inclusive)	
			Disposition and Movement report.	(vide Disposition and Movement Report attached).
FRASNOY	Nov.13th.		Weather. Fine.	
		09.50	3rd. Div. wire G.B. 56. The Companies of M.G. Battns at present attached to 8th and 76th Inf. Bdes to rejoin their Battn. at SARLOTON to day.	(vide G.B.56 attached).
		11.00	VI Corps wires a Conference will be held at Corps H.Q. at 10.00 hrs tomorrow Nov.14th. G.O.C. and G.S.O.1 of the Division to attend.	
		11.30	M.G. Company attached to 76th Inf. Bde to remain at LONGUEVILLE. M.G. Company attached 8th Inf. Bde to rejoin its Battan as ordered.	
			VI Corps wires timed 22.50 Nov. 12th. Orders and Discipline, with reference to line gained at 11.00 hours on the 11th Nov.	(vide copy attached).

Army Form C. 2118.

WAR DIARY
or
INTELLIGENCE SUMMARY.
(Erase heading not required.)

Instructions regarding War Diaries and Intelligence Summaries are contained in F. S. Regs., Part II. and the Staff Manual respectively. Title pages will be prepared in manuscript.

Place	Date	Hour	Summary of Events and Information	Remarks and references to Appendices
Frasnoy.Nov.14th			Weather. Fine.	
		18.00	3rd. Div. wire G.C. 89. Following moves to take place to-morrow Nov. 15th. H.Q. and 3 Coys. M.G. Battn. from GOMMEGNIES and SARLOTON to LA LONGUEVILLE. Rest Pioneer Battn from RUESNES to GOMMEGNIES and SARLOTON. 76th Inf. Bde. to allot area in LA LONGUEVILLE to M.G. Bn.	(vide G.C. 89 attached).
			Weather. Fine.	
	15/11/18	10.30	3rd. Div. wire G.B.77. Following moves to take place Nov. 16th. 8th. Inf. Bde. Group less Fld. Coy. R.E. from ROMERIES to FRASNOY. 9th Bde. Group from FRASNOY to LA LONGUEVILLE. 76th Inf. Bde. Group from LA LONGUEVILLE to NEUF MESNIL and MON PLAISIR. 20th K.R.R.C. from GOMMEGNIES and SARLOTON to NEUF MESNIL. All concerned informed.	(vide G.B. 77 attached).
		22.00	3rd. Div. wire G.B.81. Forecast of moves on 17th November. A. Group to LOUVROIL. B.Group to SOUS LE BOIS. C. Group to NEUF MESNIL and MON PLAISIR. D. Group no Move.	(vide G.B. 81 attached).
			Instruction to Officers in charge of Education 3rd. Division.	(vide copy attached).
			Orders and Instruction with reference to the "March to the RHINE".	(vide copy attached).
	16/11/18		Weather. Fine.	
		14.30	3rd. Div. wire G.B. 84. Following moves to take place on Nov. 17th. A Group from NEUF MESNIL MON PLAISER Area to LOUVROIL. B Group from LA LONGUEVILLE to SOUS LE BOIS. C Group. from FRASNOY to NEUF MESNIL MON PLAISIR Area. Train Coy. to march behind Bde. Group. Divisional Headquarters to move to SOUS LE BOIS. D Group will not move. Addressed all concerned.	(Vide G.B. 84 attached).
		18.45	3rd. Division wire G.B. 89. Divisional Headquarters closes at FRASNOY at 15.00 hours. Nov. 17th and opens at SOUS LE BOIS at same hour.	(vide G.B. 89 attached).
		22.00	3rd. Division wire G.B. 92. Moves ordered in G.B. 84 to take place on Nov. 17th is cancelled.	(vide G.B. 92 attached).
	17/11/18.		Weather. Fine but cold.	
		10.30	3rd. Div. wire G.B. 94. Moves ordered in G.B. 84 and 89 dated Nov. 16th will take place on Nov. 18th. Forecast of moves for Nov. 19th. A Group from LOUVROIL to area COLLERET - OSTERGNIES-CERFONTAINE-FERIERE LA GRANDE. B & C Groups no change. D. Group to area west of the HAUTMONT - LA LONGUEVILLE - BAVAI Road exclusive. Divisional Headquarters to COUSOLRE. Addressed all concerned.	(vide G.B. 94 attached.).

(A8op) Wt.W771/M2231 759,000 5/17 Sch. 82 Forms/C2118/14
D. D. & L., London, E.C.

SECRET.

Copy No. 14

3rd DIVISION OPERATION ORDER NO. 280.

1st November 1918.

1. The 3rd Division will move into the Southern half of the VI Corps area on the 3rd November.

   Moves will be carried out on the 3rd November in accordance with the March Table on reverse.

2. The only distances to be maintained on the march will be 300 yards between Battalions and 100 yards between Battalions and their transport.

3. ACKNOWLEDGE.

Lieut. Colonel.
General Staff, 3rd Division.

1st November 1918.

Issued at 13.30.

Copies to
1. G.O.C.
2. 8th Inf. Bde.
3. 9th Inf. Bde.
4. 76th Inf. Bde.
5. C.R.A.
6. C.R.E.
7. A.D.M.S.
8. "Q".
9. 20th K.R.R.C. (Pioneers).
10. 3rd Div. Signals.
11. VI Corps.
12. 62nd Division.
13. War Diary.
14. War Diary.
15. File.
16. File.
17. File.
18. D.A.G.C.
19. 2nd Division.

MARCH TABLE TO ACCOMPANY 3rd DIVISION
OPERATION ORDER NO. 280.

Reference Sheet 57.B. 1/40,000.

Unit.	From	To	Route	Hour of start & Starting Point.	Instructions.
76th Inf. de.Group. (Less Fld. Coy).	CARNIERES.	QUIEVY	BOUSSIERES - BEVILLERS.	Head of Column to pass cross roads C.21.a.5.4. at 16.50 hours.	
M.G.Battn.	CARNIERES.	BEVILLERS	do.		To move in rear of 76th Inf.Bde. Group under orders of G.O.C.76th Inf. Brigade.
9th Inf. de.Group.	CATTENIERES.	QUIEVY	BEAUVOIS - LA GUISETTE Farm J.7.c.	Head of column to pass road junction C.25.c. at 13.50 hours.	

"A" Form
MESSAGES AND SIGNALS.

Army Form C. 2121
(In pads of 100.)

Prefix......Code......m. Office of Origin and Service Instructions	Words	Charge	This message is on a/c of:	Recd. at......m.
	Sent		...............Service.	Date............
●	At............m.			From............
....	To............			
....	By............		(Signature of "Franking Officer")	By............

TO {

Sender's Number.	Day of Month.	In reply to Number.	A A A
G.S. 85	1/11		

Following from Adv. ...... timed 0930 hrs aaa situation report ... Left Corps Third Army and ... and Centre Corps First Army attacked this morning S. of VALENCIENNES ... no details ... Frontal line N. of VALENCIENNES reported 1800 yds N. ... WARGNIES — ... N. of ... NORTH — ... (1001) ... (1001) — NORTH — 1000 yds N. of ... — ...

From ....
Place 3rd Division.
Time ....

The above may be forwarded as now corrected. (Z) ...... G. LOVELY, Capt.

Censor. Signature of Addressor or person authorised to telegraph in his name
* This line should be erased if not required.

Order No. 1625. Wt. W3253/ P 511. 27/2. H. & K., Ltd. (E. 2634).

Following from Army by wireless timed 0135 today (1/11/18) aaa Summary War news for distribution to troops aaa Official reports state TURKEY and AUSTRIA HUNGARY have signed armistice aaa German wireless states national government formed in AUSTRIA repudiating KAISER KARL and describing note to Wilson as betrayal of Germany aaa Demobilisation Committee established aaa FIUME desires union with ITALY aaa ITALIAN Fleet expected aaa Southern Slav states proclaimed at AGRAM claims territory between ISONZO and VARDAR aaa Austrian Fleet at POLA seized by crews for National Councils of German Austria Southern Slavs and Hungary.

Sixth Corps wire G. 450 1st. Nov. timed 1545 hrs.

    Following from Adv. G.H.Q. timed 1225. Situation report. S. of VALENCIENNES our line believed as follows MARESCHES (incl.) - PRESEAU (doubtful) - PRESEAU-MARLY road to railway - along railway S. of VALENCIENNES to SCHELDT. Prisoners over 1000. Above information not yet confirmed. Terms of Armistice with TURKEY include free passage of DARDANELLES and BOSPHORUS and occupation by Allies of forts on them- Demobilisation of Turkish Army except for police forces- Use of Turkish ports and railways - Immediate repatriation of all Allied prisoners of war. Italian embassy in LONDON reported last night that DIAZ had signed Armistice with AUSTRIA. This not yet confirmed and exact situation uncertain. Austrian plenipotentiaries now at Italian G.H.Q. Allied captures now exceed 50,000 prisoners and 300 guns.

3rd. Div. wire G.A. 866 dated 2/11/18.   timed 11.45 hrs.

Reference 3rd. Div O.O. 280 aaa 56th Fld Co. R.E. will move to SOLESMES on morning of 3rd November under orders of C.R.E. aaa 55th and 526th Fld. Cos. R.E. will move from SOLESMES to ST. GEORGES, river east of ESCARMAIN on the night 3rd/4th November under orders of C.R.E. aaa Move not to commence before 21.00 hours on night 3rd/4th Novr. route via ROMERIES aaa Move of 56th Field Co. on morning of 3rd Novr. to be by sections with 300 yards distance between sections aaa Acknowledge aaa Added C.R.E. 9th Inf. Bde. repeated 76th Inf. Bde "Q" A.D.M.S. 62nd Div. VIth Corps.

All concerned informed.

=#=#=#=#=#=#=#=#=#=#=#=#=#=#=#=#=

3rd. Div. wire G.A. 867 dated 2/11/18.   timed 12.30 hrs.

Reference 3rd. Div. O.O. 280 aaa 9th Inf. Bde Group less Fld Co. will start from road junction C.28.c.5.1 at 17.45 hours and will move to QUIEVY via CARNIERES and BEVILLERS aaa Acknowledge aaa Added 9th Inf. Bde repeated 76th Inf. Bde "Q" and VIth Corps Guards Div.

All concerned informed.

=#=#=#=#=#=#=#=#=#=#=#=#=#=#=#=#=

3rd. Div .wire G.A. 869 dated 2/11/18 timed 13.30 hrs.

Reference 3rd. Div. O.O. 280 and G.A. 866 and 867 aaa 9th Inf. Bde Group will move to QUIEVY during daylight on the 3rd November aaa 56th Fld. Coy. R.E. will move under orders of G.O.C. 9th Inf. Bde and will proceed to SOLESMES moving at the head of 9th Inf. Bde Group aaa 9th I.F. Group will move via CARNIERES and BEVILLERS aaa Tail of column to be east of BEVILLERS by 17.00 hrs on 3rd. November aaa Distances to be maintained on the march as follows aaa 300 yds between companies 300 yds between Battalions 100 yds between Battalions and their transport aaa Acknowledge aaa Addressed 9th Inf. Bde C.R.E. repeated 76th Inf. Bde 8th Inf. Bde. "Q" A.D.M.S. Signals C.R.A. Guards Div. VIth Corps.

=#=#=#=#=#=#=#=#=#=#=#=#=#=#=#=#=

VIth Corps wire timed 0350 hours dated 2nd aaa
Following by wireless aaa Summary of war news for distribution
to the troops aaa German wireless reports financial panic
spreading from western Germany aaa VIENNA quiet aaa New
Government formed securing advisor of troops aaa BUDAPEST
Ex-Premier TISZA shot in streets aaa New situation aaa
REUTER states TURKEYS armistice confirmed - includes
free passage of BOSPHORUS occupation of DARDANELLES
ports and immediate repatriation of all Allied prisoners
aaa AMSTERDAM reports panic amongst RHINE population
owing to rumoured replies of German Government consent
to occupation of COLOGNE and COBLENTZ by Allied Troops aaa
VIth Corps wire timed 10.00 hrs dated 2nd Nov. aaa
Following from   . G.H.Q. timed 22.30 hrs aaa Situation
report. Line South of VALENCIENNES as follows MARESCHES
(incl) PRESEAU (excl) PRESEAU - AULNOY Road to cross
roads S.E. of AULNOY Railway S. of MARLY and along
railway to SCHELDT, counter attack with 5 Tanks this
morning forced back our troops to North outskirts of
MARESCHES three enemy Tanks knocked out. Counter attack
N.W. of PRESEAU also forced line back slightly.
Prisoners to day between 2000 and 3000. French hold
west bank of SCHELDT to BECKE AUDENARDE and EECKE
(excl) DENYZE (incl) Americans have advanced line
West of MEUSE 1½ miles on 8 mile front as follows
ANDEVANNE IMECOURT 1000 yds north of
GRANDPRE about 1100 prisoners. British captures
in France since 1st August 1918 to date. Prisoners
175.000, guns 2380, machine guns 17000, Trench Mortars
2750.   French captured 14th July to 20th October 1918
Prisoners 112,500, guns 1575, machine guns 8000
Trench Mortars 570. British captured since commencement of war (approx) 310,000 prisoners, over 3000 guns
22,000 machine guns 3,700 Trench Mortars.

Sixth Corps wire G. 479 Nov. 2nd.

Following from G.H.Q. timed 1000 hrs. South of VALENCIENNES our troops have reached PRESEAU-MARLY Road N. of cross roads (E.30 a). Patrols in MARLY and fighting in centre of VALENCIENNES. Prisoners yesterday over 3,000. American line west of MEUSE reported BASIEMONT WOOD - ANDEVANE - BARRICOURT WOOD - IMECOURT. Prisoners 1,500. FRENCH Line on VOUZIERS front reported 1,500 yards N.E. of FALAISE - N.W. outskirts of BOIS DE VONCQ - SEMUY. Prisoners about 500. ITALIANS are advancing towards river TAGLIAMENTO 700 guns taken. Later. We have taken VALENCIENNES.

Sixth Corps wire timed 17.30 hrs aaa Following from G.H.Q. timed 15.20. Line in VALENCIENNES Sector reported at midday 1000 yds E. of MARESCHES - Fme. DE WULT (1500 yds east of PRESEAU) 1000 yds north of PRESEAU - along PRESEAU - MARLY road - STEELWORKS (excl) MARLY (incl) eastern outskirts of VALENCIENNES. Third Army reports capture of additional 350 prisoners and 2 tanks Captures by Americans yesterday West of MEUSE 5,600 prisoners and 40 guns.

VIth Corps wire timed 0620 hrs dated 3rd Nov aaa Summary of War News for distribution to troops German wireless reports National Government under KALOLYI took over control of HUNGARY during night aaa Government appeals soldiers and workmen return duty having achieved objects aaa HINDENBURG replying numerous messages confidence appeals for national unity aaa matter at stake Germanys honour freedom future aaa Saxony has admitted three Socialists to Ministry as result constitutional change aaa Reuter says British landed GALLIPOLI Mine sweepers clearing Straits aaa General Allenby promoted Knight Grand Cross of the Bath aaa CZECH National Council assumed control of SKODA Works. aaa

VIth Corps wire timed 12.00 hrs aaa Following from G.H.Q. timed 09.20 aaa General situation unchanged aaa Austrians announce that they are evacuating Italy and Serbia aaa Italians report 84,000 prisoners and 1690 guns aaa American line W. of MEUSE reported CLERY LE PETIT – FOSSE– W. edge of BOIS DE BOURGOGNE aaa French line continues OLIZY – N of LACROIX AUX BOIS and BOIS DE VANDY – LES ALLEUX aaa

MESSAGES AND SIGNALS.

Army Form C. 2121.
(In pads of 100.)

TO	8 Suffolk	COH	Honor Div	62 Div
	O Yorks	OM6	Advance	2 Div
	76 Inf Bde	MMGC	Q	11 Corps

Sender's Number.	Day of Month.	In reply to Number.	
M 884	3rd		AAA

Following moves will take place tomorrow 4th November aaa 76th Inf Bde Group less field Coy and Field Ambulance with one MG Coy attached to ESCARMAIN and ROMERIES aaa Route railway crossing D12a SOLESMES cross roads F1609 ROMERIES aaa to pass cross roads D18c44 at 0745 hours aaa 8th Inf Bde Group with one MG Coy attached to SOLESMES aaa Route QUIEVY railway crossing D12a aaa to pass Road junction C24b46

MESSAGES AND SIGNALS.

at	0830	hours	and
MG	Battalion	less	two
Companies	to	QUIEVY	aaa
to	move	on	rear
of	8th	Inf.	Bde
Tromp	aaa	26th	and
029	Field	Coys	will
move	to	vicinity	of
ESCARMAIN	aaa	to	be
clear	of	SOLESMES	by
0800	hours	aaa	to
76th	Inf	Bde	OBE
Bnde	to	acknowledge	aaa
Addressed	1st A	flanks
62 and 2nd Arms Corps

From: 3rd Div

3rd. Div. wire G.A. 886 dated 3rd Nov. timed 1315.

The distances to be maintained on the march tomorrow will be 300 yards between Battalions and 100 yards between Battalions and their transport. Addsd 8th and 76th.Inf. Bdes.

==*=*=*=*=*=*=*=*

3rd. Division wire G.R. 890 dated 3rd Nov. timed 18.30.

20th K.R.R.C. (Pioneers) will move tomorrow Nov 4th to ROMERIES starting from present billets at 11.15 hours aaa Thiss move is not to interfere wiht work on roads in forward area aaa Pioneers to acknowledge aaa Addressed 20th K.R.R.C. (Pioneers) Repeated 6th Inf. Bde C.R.E. "Q" Signals.

==*=*=*=*=*=*=*=*

3rd. Division wire G.B. 891 dated 3rd Nov. timed 17.30 hours.

Move of 20th K.R.R.C. (Pioneers) ordered in G.B. 890 is cancelled. aaa Addressed all recipients of G.B. 890.

Copy of VI Corps wire No. G.498 dated 3rd Nov. Timed 6.0 pm.

G.H.Q.report timed 22.15 (2nd).aaa 60 Prisoners taken and line advanced in local operation by Fourth Army W.of LANDRECIES we hold steelworks S.of MARLY and high ground 2000 yards N.of village thence line continues ST. SAULVE (incl) - due N. to SCHELDT aaa Total prisoners since morning of Nov.1st on this front over 5,000 aaa 4 Tanks captured and a few guns aaa Belgians report progress towards GHENT and EECLOO and enemy retiring aaa No details aaa American captures July 18th 1918 to 1st Nov. incl. Prisoners 44,000 guns 950 M.Gs. 3200, T.Ls. 280 aaa British troops in Italy have taken over 10,000 prisoners and over 100 guns aaa Later aaa Belgian line reported approx. EEKE-BAARLE - MEERENDRE (all incl) - W. of VINDERHAUTE - WAERSCHOOT - EECLOO (both incl).

****

Copy of VI Corps wire No.E.510 dated 3rd Nov. Timed 17.25.

Following from G.H.Q. 14.45 following enemy withdrawal East of VALENCIENNES First Army have reached following general line SAULTAIN (believed incl) West of ESTREUX West of ONNAING maintaining touch with enemy.

****

3rd. Division.

Disposition and Movement Report No. 10.

Forecast of Locations for Nov. 4th.

Unit No.	Unit.	Location of H.Q. Nov. 4th.
1.	3rd. Division H.Q.	QUIEVY.
2.	3rd. Divnl. Arty. H.Q.	"
3.	8th. Inf. Brigade H.Q.	SOLESMES
4.	9th. Inf. Brigade H.Q.	QUIEVY.
5.	76th. Inf. Brigade H.Q.	ESCARMAIN.
6.	C.R.E.	QUIEVY.
7.	529th. Fld. Coy. R.E.	ESCARMAIN.
8.	438th. Fld. Coy. R.E.	SOLESMES.
9.	56th. Fld. Coy. R.E.	ESCARMAIN.
10.	3rd. Bn. M.G. Corps.	QUIEVY.
11.	20th. K.R.R.C. (PIONEERS)	ROMERIES.
12.	62nd. Division.	ESCARMAIN. (Forward Report Centre R. 20b1.6)
13.	Guards Division.	VERTAIN.
14.	2nd. Division.	ST. PYTHON.
15.	42nd. Division.	BEAUVOIS.
16.	24th. Division.	V. 19 d 4.8 ST. AUBERT.

November 3rd. 1918.

Captain for
Major-General,
Commanding 3rd. Division.

3rd. Div. wire G.C. 845 dated 4th Nov. timed 0930.

Situation from VIth Corps timed 0830 aaa 62nd Divn report right Bde reports 0750 hrs aaa BLUE objective gained on whole from Brigade front aaa In touch with New Zealand Division on right and left brigade on left aaa An earlier report states right battalion had taken 50 prisoners aaa Prisoners know nothing about a withdrawal in this sector aaa Unconfirmed report that prisoners captured at LA FOLIE FARM belong to 12th Res Div. which came into line last night from Belgium aaa Guards Div report attack appears to have started satisfactorily from BLUE objective aaa Addressed 8th 9th 76th Inf. Bdes C.R.A. C.R.E. D.M.G.C.

==*=*=*=*=*

3rd. Div. wire G.C. 897 dated 4/11/18 timed 0936.

Sixth Corps wires timed 0600 hrs reads Summary of War news for distribution to troops aaa German wireless aaa New Hungarian Government absolved by King allegiance aaa Will submit to plebiscite questions of Republic or Monarchy aaa Vienna Delegates invited from from War Officers of the new state to co-operate with war ministry in Demobilization aaa Trieste aaa Joint committee of Italians in Slovines formed to keep order aaa Military government STYRIA taken over by German Austrian State aaa Germany aaa KAISER confirms constitutional amendments aaa Memorandum to chancellor from SCHIEDMANN Secty of State advising abdication of KAISER aaa UKRAINE and Austrain German troops attacked POLES capturing LEMBERG on Nov. 1st and PRZEMYSL later aaa Italians offl. 2 more Italian armies entered battle aaa Seventh advancing into western TRENTO aaa First occupied ROVEN and advanced troops near TRIENT aaa Progress continued elsewhere prisoners counted 100,000 aaa Guns 2200 aaa Austrian offl. aaa Our troops have ceased hostilities in the Italian theatre on account of the armistice which has been concluded aaa Notification of the terms of the armistic armies will be given separately. Addressed 8th 9th 76th Inf. Bdes C.R.A. D.M.G.C. A.D.M.S.

==*=*=*=*=*=*=*

"A" Form
MESSAGES AND SIGNALS.

Army Form C. 2121 (In pads of 100.)

Prefix....Code....m.	Words	Charge.	This message is on a/c of:	Recd. at....m.
Office of Origin and Service Instructions	Sent At....m. To By		...Service	Date From By

TO —
8 Bde	~~CRA~~	Q	2 Div	D.M.G.G
9 Bde	~~CRE~~ Pioneer Bn / ADMS	62 Div	APM
76 Bde	~~ADMS~~ Signals	VI Corps	

Sender's Number.	Day of Month.	In reply to Number.	AAA
GA 907	4th		

Attack is making satisfactory progress on whole front aaa Corps has been ordered to continue operations tomorrow 5th Nov to aaa gain BROWN LINE aaa 62nd and Guards Div are to continue attack at 0600 hours aaa will Corps mounted troops with G Company 6th Whippet Tanks Battalion are to be prepared to push through as opportunity offers aaa 2nd and 3rd Div are to close up their leading Brigades on

From ....
Place ....
Time ....

The above may be forwarded as now corrected. (Z) ....
....
Censor. Signature of Addressor or person authorised to telegraph in his name
* This line should be erased if not required.

Order No 1625 Wt. W3253/ P 511 27/2 H. & K., Ltd (E. 2634)

"A" Form
MESSAGES AND SIGNALS.

Army Form C. 2121
(In pads of 100.)

No. of Message...........

Prefix.........Code..........m.	Words	Charge	This message is on a/c of:	Recd. at......m.
Office of Origin and Service Instructions	Sent		............Service.	Date...........
....	At ....m.			From ....
....	To			
....	By	(Signature of "Franking Officer")		By...............

TO {				

Sender's Number.	Day of Month.	In reply to Number.	AAA

The	line	of	the
RHONELLE	river	tomorrow	aaa
76th	Inf	Bde	Group
len	Field	Co RE	with
attached	M G Co	will	move
to	ORSINVAL	aaa	8th
Inf	Bde	Group	len
Field	Co RE	with	attached
M G Co	to	RUESNES	aaa
9th	Inf	Bde	Group
len	Field Co	RE	to
ESCARMAIN	aaa	H Qrs	and
two	Companies	M G	Battalion
to	ESCARMAIN	aaa	Troops
will	move	across	country
as	far	as	possible
aaa	The	Division	will

From			
Place			
Time			

The above may be forwarded as now corrected. (Z)

....
Censor. Signature of Addressor or person authorised to telegraph in his name

* This line should be erased if not required.

Order No 1625 Wt. W3253/ P 511 27/2 H. & K., Ltd (E. 2634)

"A" Form
MESSAGES AND SIGNALS.

Army Form C. 2121 (In pads of 100.)

be	at	one	hour
notice	to	move	after
0600	hours	tomorrow	aaa
~~7th~~	~~bn~~	~~Bde~~	~~Group~~
~~will~~	~~move~~	~~at~~	~~Zero~~
Zero	hour	for	all
moves	will	be	notified
aaa	76th	bn	Bde
Group	will	pass	Cross
roads	W.17.c	at	Zero
plus	10	minutes	aaa
8th	bn	Bde	Group
will	pass	road	junction
E.2.a.0.8	at	Zero
plus	two	hours	aaa
9th	bn	Bde	Group
will	pass	cross	roads

"A" Form
MESSAGES AND SIGNALS.

Army Form C. 2121 (In pads of 100.)

No. of Message............

Prefix........Code........m.	Words	Charge.	This message is on a/c of :	Recd. at......m.
Office of Origin and Service Instructions	Sent At ....m. To By		..................Service. (Signature of "Franking Officer")	Date........ From .... By........

TO {			
Sender's Number.	Day of Month.	In reply to Number.	AAA
D.16.c	4.4	at	Zero
plus	3	hours	30
minutes	aaa	H Qrs	one
2	Companies	M G	Pa
will	follow	in	rear
of	9th	Inf	Bde
Group	aaa	Routes	for
these	moves	will	be
as	follows	aaa	cross
roads	D 16 C 4.4 —		railway
crossing	D.12.a	—	Road
junction	E 2.a 08	—	ROMERIES
—	road junction	W.17.d	—
ESCARMAIN	—	cross roads	Q 36.a
—	cross roads	R 13 C	— cross
Roads	R 22. central		aaa
adv	Div	HQ	will

From ....
Place ....
Time ....

The above may be forwarded as now corrected. (Z) ....
........................Censor. Signature of Addressor or person authorised to telegraph in his name
* This line should be erased if not required.

Order No 1625 Wt. W3253/ P 511 27/2 H. & K., Ltd (E. 2634)

"A" Form
MESSAGES AND SIGNALS.

Army Form C. 2121
(In pads of 100.)

move	to	RUESNES	R 14
3.4.4	at	an	hour
to	be	notified	aaa
acknowledge	aaa	addressed	list
A	plus	VI Corps	2nd
and	62nd	Div	APM

From: 3 DW
Time: 21.30

3rd. DIVISION.

Disposition and Movement Report No. 11.

Forecast of Locations for Nov. 5th.

Unit No.	UNIT.	Location of H.Q. Nov. 5th.	
1.	3rd. Division H.Q.	RUESNES	R.14.b.
2.	3rd. Divnl. Arty. H.Q.	"	"
3.	8th Inf. Brigade. H.Q.	"	
4.	9th. Inf. Brigade H.Q.	ESCARMAIN	
5.	76th. Inf. Brigade H.Q.	ORSINVAL	
6.	C.R.E.	RUESNES.	
7.	529th Fld. Coy. R.E.		X.1.c.0.5
8.	438th Fld. Coy. R.E.	SOLESMES	
9.	56th Fld. Coy. R.E.		X.1.c.0.5
10.	3rd. Bn. M.G. Corps.	ESCARMAIN	
11.	20th K.R.R.C. (Pioneers)	SOLESMES	
12.	62nd Division.	RUESNES	R.20.b.1.6
13.	Guards Division.	VERTAIN	
14.	2nd Division.	RUESNES	
15.	42nd Division	BEAUVOIS	
16.	24th Division.	BERMERAIN	

Captain, for
Major-General,
Commanding 3rd. Division.

November 4th 1918.

"A" Form
MESSAGES AND SIGNALS.

Army Form C. 2121
(In pads of 100.)

This message is on a/c of:

Priority to
Bdes and
D.M.G.C.

Sd. J.M Lumley.
Major.

TO: 8th 9th 76th Bde. CRA. CRE. DMGC. 20 KRRC
ADMS "D" Signals APM

Sender's Number.	Day of Month.	In reply to Number.	AAA
GB 917.	5.		

The Division will NOT move today aaa
Advance on Corps front today is meeting
with little opposition aaa
Addsd. List A.

From
Place
Time 3rd. Div.
11.30

Lumley. Major.

"A" Form
MESSAGES AND SIGNALS.

Army Form C. 2121
(In pads of 100.)

This message is on a/c of:
Priority to
20th K.R.R.C.
sd J. Lumley. Major.

TO: 20th K.R.R.C.   C.R.E. "Q" Signals.
~~VIth Corps~~   ~~62nd Div.~~

Sender's Number: G.B. 919   Day of Month: 5   AAA

The 20th K.R.R.C. (Pioneers) will move tomorrow Nov. 6th from SOLESMES to RUESNES aaa No restriction as to time - route via ESCARMAIN aaa Only that portion of RUESNES within right Divisional Boundary is available for billetting aaa Pioneer Bn. to acknowledge aaa
Addsd. 20th K.R.R.C. Pioneers reptd. ~~C.R.E. "Q" Signals VIth Corps 62nd Div.~~

From: 3rd. Division.
Place:
Time: 14.45

Sd. J. Lumley. Major.

"A" Form
MESSAGES AND SIGNALS.

Army Form C. 2121
(In pads of 100.)

Prefix........Code............m.	Words	Charge.	This message is on a/c of :	Recd. at......m.
Office of Origin and Service Instructions	Sent			Date............
	At ....m.		....................Service.	From ....
	To			
	By		(Signature of "Franking Officer")	By............

TO: 8-9-76th Bdes. C.R.A. C.R.E. D.M.G.C.
A.D.M.S. "Q" Signals.

Sender's Number.	Day of Month.	In reply to Number.	
G.B. 922.	5		AAA

The Division will NOT move tomorrow
Nov 6th aaa The Guards and 62nd Divs.
are continuing the advance on the
Corps front.

From
Place 3rd. Division.

Time 16.30

The above may be forwarded as now corrected.   (Z)

Censor.   Sd J. Lumly. Major.
* This line should be erased if not required.

Order No. 1625. Wt. W3253/   P 511. 27/2. H. & K., Ltd. (E. 2634).

Summary W/T news for distribution to troops Italians official aaa rout of Austrian Army yielded 300,000 prisoners 5,000 guns aaa Albania aaa SCUTARI occupied aaa German W/T aaa Terms Austrian armistice include complete demobilisation aaa Withdrawal units French front aaa Surrender half artillery in field aaa Allies have free movement for troops throughout Austria aaa Occupy strategical points aaa return all allied prisoners aaa Surrender part fleet rest dismantled aaa Germany aaa Political censorship abolished by decree ministry of war aaa Budapeth aaa New Government claims peaceful revolution completed aaa British Official aaa Serbs have occupied Belgrade.

VIth Corps wires timed 2320 hrs dated 4th Nov aaa Line on Third Army front at 19.00 hrs aaa LES GRANDES PATURES (B.2.c.) - LOCQUIGNOL (excl) - E. of ND DE FLAQUETTES (S.18.a.) - LE RON - DE QUESNE - HERBIGNIES - PETIT MARAIS (M.11.c.) all incl - PREUX AU SART (not confirmed) - WARGNIES LE PETIT- WARGNIES GRAND (all incl) ETH (not confirmed) aaa Estimated prisoners captures over 6000 prisoners and 125 guns prisoners taken from 43 Battns of 20 Regts of 11 Divs aaa   Later from G.H.Q. 2005 hrs line now reported East of FESMY - LANDRECIES (incl) - CARREFOUR DUCHENE MURONNE (A.18) LOCQUIGNOL - HERBIGNIES - FRASNOY - WARGNIES (all incl) - SEBOURQUIAUX (incl) -East of ONNAING aaa Prisoners about 10,000 and 200 guns aaa French First Army line runs GRAND VERLI - West of NEUVILLE-LES-DORENGT - West of ROUR aaa Prisoners about 3000 aaa

G.C. #928   Nov. 6th.

Summary of war news for distribution to Troops. Poles established Government CRACOW. German Embassy in Russia withdrawn. German Government recognised CZECH - SLOVAK State. Will welcome CZECH - SLOVAK Ambassador at BERLIN. Bavarian press urges KAISERS abdication. German Wireless. Italian Expedition arrived TRIESTE crews landed to maintain order Commander claims to have been nominated Governor.

3rd. Div. G.B. 951 dated 7th November. timed 14.00 hours.

Forecast of probable moves to morrow Nov 8th aaa 76th Inf. Brigade to FRASNOY aaa 9th Inf. Bde. to ROMERIES aaa 8th Inf. Bde. to remain at SOLESMES aaa 76th Inf. Bde will reconnoitre FRASNOY today if accommodation in that village is insuufficient portion of ORSINVAL not already occupied may be used aaa Acknowledge. aaa Addressed List A. less Pioneers.

=*=*=*=*=*=*=*=

3rd. Division wire G.B. 957 dated 7th November. timed 20.15 hrs.

Following moves will take place tomorrow Nov. 8th aaa 76th Inf. Bde. Group (less Field Coy. R.E.) with attached M.G. Company from ROMERIES to FRASNOY to start at 09.00 hours route BEAUDIGNIES -LE QUESNOY aaa 9th Inf. Bde Group. (less Fld. Co. R.E.) from QUIEVY to ROMERIES to start at 0900 hours route AUTERTRE Fm. -SOLESMES Station aaa H.Q. and 2 Coys M.G. Bn. will move from QUIEVY to ROMERIES under orders of G.O.C. 9th Inf. Bde. who will allot them accommodation in ROMERIES aaa If 76th Inf. Bde find accommodation in FRASNOY insufficient portion of GOMMEGNIES not reserved for Corps H.Q. may be used aaa Following distances to be maintained on the march between Bns. 1000 yards between Bns. and their transport 300 yards aaa Acknowledge aaa Addressed list A plus VIth Corps 2-62nd Divs. AP.M..

=*=*=*=*=*=*=*=

VI Corps wire No.G.79 of 7th November timed 0600 hrs.

Following from G.H.Q. 2225 hrs 6th AAA Situation report AAA British front AAA No material change AAA Prisoners about 700 AAA French line N. to S. runs RUE DES CHATS - East edge of FORET DE NOUVION - one mile E. of BUIRONFOSSE - W. of SORBAIS - FONTAINELES - VERVINS (incl) - GERCY AAA Thence no change AAA Prisoners since Nov.4th 4000 with 60 guns AAA Ends.

=*=*=*=*=*=

Summary of War News for distribution to troops. Reuter. Wilson's Note VERSAILLES discussion sent Germany yesterday AAA FOCH empowered negotiate German plenipotentiaries AAA Allies declare willingness make peace with Germany on terms embodied Wilson's address 4/1 and subsequent addresses with 2 qualifications AAA One. Must reserve freedom in interpretation expression freedom of seas AAA Two. Expression restoration of invaded territories required definition AAA In their view this embodies compensation for damage to civilians and property AAA Hungarians refused passage to German Danube Divisions under MACKENSEN AAA Presumably will be captured. AAA Hungarians have cut off from Germany Rumanian oil supplies AAA Zurich reports great disorder due rising soldiers AAA Bavarians closed frontier against VORARLBERG AAA Hungarian Government delegate has gone to PADUA to negotiate peace terms with DIAZ AAA German wireless AAA German delegation to conclude armistice left Berlin for Austria Nov.6th.

=*=*=*=*=*=

3rd DIVISION.

Disposition and Movement Report No.12.

Unit No.	UNIT.	Location of H.Q. 7th November.	Probable changes within 24 hours.
1.	3rd Divisional H.Q.	QUIEVY.	
2.	3rd Div'l Arty H.Q.	QUIEVY.	
3.	8th Infantry Brigade H.Q.	SOLESMES E.1.c.45.15.	
4.	9th Infantry Brigade H.Q.	QUIEVY.	ROMERIES.
5.	76th Infantry Brigade H.Q.	ROMERIES.	FRASNOY.
6.	C.R.E.	RUESNES R.14.b.4.4.	
7.	529 Field Coy. R.E.	ORSINVAL R.12.a.2.8.	
8.	438 Field Coy. R.E.	BELLEVUE FERME R.15.b.5.8.	
9.	56th Field Coy. R.E.	ORSINVAL R.12.a.1.9.	
10.	3rd Battn M.G.Corps.	QUIEVY.	
11.	20th K.R.R.C.(Pioneers)	RUESNES R.14.c.8.4.	
12.	62nd Division H.Q.	FRASNOY.	OBIES.
13.	Guards Division.	PREUX AU SART.	AMFROIPRET.
14.	2nd Division H.Q.	ST PYTHON.	

[signature]
Captain,
for Major General,
Commanding 3rd Division.

7th November, 1918.

"A" Form
MESSAGES AND SIGNALS.

Army Form
(In pads of 100.)
No. of Message............

Prefix......Code......m	Words	Charge	This message is on a/c of:	Recd. at......m
Office of Origin and Service Instructions	Sent At ......m To...... By......		..................Service. (Signature of "Franking Officer")	Date...... From...... By......

TO { [illegible handwritten text across multiple lines] }

Sender's Number.	Day of Month.	In reply to Number.	AAA
[illegible]	8		

[Body of message - handwritten, largely illegible]

From: [illegible]
Place: [illegible]
Time: 1800

The above may be forwarded as now corrected.   (Z) [signature]
..................Censor.   Signature of Addressor or person authorised to telegraph in his name
* This line should be erased if not required.

Order No. 1625   Wt. W3253/   P 511.   27/2.   H. & K., Ltd. (E. 2634).

"A" Form
MESSAGES AND SIGNALS.

Army Form C. 2121 (In pads of 100.)

TO 76th Inf Bde

Sender's Number: GB 978
Day of Month: 8/11

Reference conversation following wire has been sent by Corps to Town Major GOMMEGNIES aaa 4th Corps are clearing OBIES area by 1100 hrs 9th Nov aaa By this hour 62nd Div will be east of road running through N 15 Central N 10 Cent aaa Town Major GOMMEGNIES will allot all accommodation in GOMMEGNIES over and above that required for Corps HQ to 76th Inf Bde Group and this Group will also be accommodated if necessary in LE CHEVAL BLANC + LE GRAND SART area aaa Ends aaa Please arrange accommodation for Gordons and MG Co direct with Town Major GOMMEGNIES

From: 3rd Div
Time: 2200

VI Corps wire No.G.123 of 8th Nov. timed 0715 hrs.

From G.H.Q. 2220 hrs 7th AAA Line South of CONDE CANAL reported as follows LA CAPELLE - AVESNES Road East of BOULOGNE - AVESNES (excl) - DOURLERS (incl) - LALONGUEVILLE (excl) - BELLIGNIES (incl) - thence unchanged to ONNEZIES - MONTIGNIES - AUDREGNIES (all incl) AAA Otherwise unchanged AAA Prisoners 300 with 8 guns AAA

Summary of War News for distribution to troops AAA German Wireless AAA German delegation for armistice and peace conditions General Von GUNDELL military Delegate HAGUE Conference General Von WINTERFELD formerly attache PARIS Admiral Von HINTZE former Foreign Secretary Admiral MEURERERZBERGER States Secretary Propaganda OBERNDOFF formerly Minister SOFIA AAA Expected to reach the French lines tonight AAA BERLIN AAA Russian Embassoy left in consequence of discovery Bolshevist intrigue AAA There is evident fear of Bolshevism in Germany AAA Reuter AAA Serious mutiny at KIEL yesterday AAA Battleships KAISER and SCHLESWIG hoisted red flag AAA 20 Officers killed AAA Infantry sent to repress mutiny joined revolutionaries AAA Hussars forced back AAA Sailors council controlled situation AAA Sailors refused obedience until peace is signed AAA Later German Wireless AAA Reports negotiations with sailors going well Chief Petty Officers acting for men AAA Ends

TO: VI Corps 2nd [Div] & 62 Div

Sender's Number: X
Day of Month: 9

Div HQrs closed at QUIEVY at 1200 hours opened at KRASNOY same hour

From: 3rd Div
Time: 1211

MESSAGES AND SIGNALS.

Army Form C. 2121
(In pads of 100.)

Prefix............Code...........m	Words / Charge	This message is on a/c of:	Recd. at......m
Office of Origin and Service Instructions	Sent		Date..........
	At ....m.	............Service.	From
	To		
	By	(Signature of "Franking Officer")	By........

TO { 8-9 76 Inf Bdes CRA CRE HQNS
     Q Branch Signals DADMS

Sender's Number: GA 985
Day of Month: 9
In reply to Number:
AAA

Warning order aaa Following moves will take place tomorrow aaa 10th Nov Inf Bde Groups will start at 0900 hrs aaa 76 Inf Bde Group to LONGUEVAL aaa 9 Inf Bde Group to FRASNOY aaa 8 Inf Bde Group and MG Coy to ROMERIES and VERTAIN aaa 529 Field Co RE will rejoin its Bde Group and move under orders of Bde Group Commander aaa 56 and 438 Field Cos will remain in their present locations aaa Sect divn 7 Field Ambulance will move to VERTAIN tonight under orders of ADMS and will rejoin its Bde Group at LONGUEVAL tomorrow starting from ROMERIES at 0900 hrs aaa Divisional HQ will move in rear of the Advanced Inf Bde Groups Head Qrs to MOB will be located at VERTAIN aaa

From: Acknowledge aaa Addd Rep A
Place: 3rd Div
Time: 1540

The above may be forwarded as now corrected. (Z)

Censor. Signature of Addresser or person authorised to telegraph in his name
* This line should be erased if not required.

Order No. 1625. Wt. W2252/ F511. 27/2. H. & K., Ltd. (E. 2634).

MESSAGES AND SIGNALS.

No. of Message...

TO	8 Bde	CRA	DMGC	Guards Div
	9 Bde	CRE	Q	62 Div
	76 Bde	ADMS	Signals	2 Div. APM

Sender's Number: G.A. 988 Day of Month: 9th In reply to Number: VI Corps AAA

Orders for tomorrow 10th November aaa VI Corps front runs as follows Q.17.c Q.11.a and b Q.5 Central K.30 a and c aaa Cavalry patrols in CEREFONTAINE and BOUSSOIS aaa Guards and 62nd Divs have been ordered to consolidate and billet their troops in depth aaa 3rd Division will move as follows tomorrow 10th November aaa 76 Inf Bde Group with attached M.G.Co to LONGUEVILLE aaa Route AMFROIPRET

MESSAGES AND SIGNALS.

BERMERIES BAVAY aaa 529 Field Co will start at 0900 hours and move in rear of 76th Inf Bde Group aaa 9th Inf Bde Group sixth one M.G. Company to FRASNOY area aaa Route BEAUDIGNIES LE QUESNOY aaa 8th Inf Bde Group and attached M.G. Company to ROMERIES aaa H.Q and remaining M.G. Company to FRASNOY area to move under orders of G.O.C 9th Inf Bde aaa

MESSAGES AND SIGNALS.

Tenth Division 7th Field Ambulance will move to LONGUEVILLE leaving RUESNES at 0900 hours aaa 56 and 438 Field Cos will not move aaa 8th 9th and 76th Inf Bde Groups will start at 0900 hours aaa Large distances will be maintained between units on the march and infantry will move off the road at each halt aaa acknowledge

Addressed List A. repeated 62nd Guards 2nd Divs

From: VI Corps & APM
Place: 3 Div
Time: 1715

"A" Form
MESSAGES AND SIGNALS.

Army Form C. 2121
(In pads of 100.)

No. of Message............

Prefix......Code......m	Words	Charge	This message is on a/c of :	Recd. at......m
Office of Origin and Service Instructions	Sent			Date............
....	At......m		....................Service	From............
....	To............			By............
....	By............		(Signature of "Franking Officer")	

TO {
| E.7-76 | Inf Bde | July 6 | |
| G.R.A | | Q | |

Sender's Number	Day of Month	In reply to Number	AAA
GB 982	6		

Copy of G.H.Q. Troops O.B. No ... ... Summary of War News for distribution to Troops ... Reuter ... Austrian ... HIRE ... ... operation ... Officers and Government and commercial station to make ... ... when they will ... off CONSTANTINOPLE G ... ... EIFFEL TOWER message to GERMAN Chancellor August EGZBERGER ... ... SPA ... ... by 1100 hrs Monday ... German Wireless ... Transmitting ... CUXHAVEN HAMBURG WILHELMSHAVEN OLDENBURG HANOVER ...

From			
Place			
Time			

The above may be forwarded as now corrected.   (Z)

....
Censor.   Signature of Addressor or person authorised to telegraph in his name
* This line should be erased if not required.

Order No. 1625 Wt. W3253/ P 511. 27/2. H. & K., Ltd. (E. 2634).

"A" Form
MESSAGES AND SIGNALS.

Army Form
(In pads of)
No. of Message............

Prefix......Code.........m.	Words	Charge	This message is on a/c of :	Recd. at......m.
Office of Origin and Service Instructions	Sent			Date.............
.................●............................	At ....m.		..................Service.	From ....
....	To		....	
....	By		(Signature of "Franking Officer")	By...........

TO {				

Sender's Number. Day of Month. In reply to Number. **A A A**

Order	...	...	working
had	problems	...	...
Reuter	...	telegraphic	
communication	between	between	
AMSTERDAM	and	BERLIN	HAMBURG
LUBECK	BREMEN	and	
between	BREMEN	...	
COPENHAGEN	...	...	

From ....
Place ....
Time 0900

The above may be forwarded as now corrected. (Z)

Censor. Signature of Addressor or person authorised to telegraph in his name

* This line should be erased if not required.

Order No. 1625 Wt. W3253/ P 511. 27/2. H. & K., Ltd. (E. 2634).

MESSAGES AND SIGNALS.

URGENT OPERATIONS PRIORITY to 3 Bdes and D.M.G.C.
PRIORITY to REMAINDER
Sd. W.H.T.

TO: 8th- 9th-76th Bdes. C.R.A. C.R.E. D.M.G.C. A.D.M.S. "Q" Signals. Pioneer Bn. A.P.M. VIth Corps. 62nd Divn 2nd and Guard Divns.

Sender's Number.	Day of Month.	In reply to Number.	AAA
G.A. 11	10		

Orders for tomorrow 11th November aaa Moves will be carried out tomorrow as follows aaa 76th Inf. Bde Group from LA LONGUEVILLE to ASSEVENT via DOUSIES aaa To be clear of LA LONGUEVILLE by 0940 hours aaa 9th Inf. Bde Group from FRASNOY Area to LA LONGUEVILLE via AMFROIPRET BERMERIES and BAVAI aaa To pass road junction H.32.d.7.0 at 0800 hours and to be clear of FRASNOY Area by 1000 hours aaa 56th Fld Coy. from ORSINVAL will move in rear of 9th Inf. Bde Group under orders of G.O.C. 9th Inf. Bde. aaa 8th Inf. Bde. Group (less 438th Fld. Coy.) from ROMERIES to FRASNOY Area via BEAUDIGNIES and LE QUESNOY aaa To enter LE QUESNOY at 1000 hours aaa 438th Fld. Coy. from GOMMEGNIES to MAUBEUGE via AMFROIPRET BERMERIES BAVAI and LA LONGUEVILLE aaa To pass road junction H.32d.7.0 at 0740 hours aaa H.Q. and One Company M.G. Battn. from GOMMEGNIES to LA LONGUEVILLE aaa Route as for 9th Inf. Bde. Group. aaa Tp pass road junction H.32.d.7.0 at 11.30 hours aaa Tent Division 7th Fld.Amb.

Origin and Service Instructions.			This message is on a c of:		Recd. at m.	
		Sent At m. To By	Service. (Signature of "Franking Officer.")	Date From By		

TO				
Sender's Number.	Day of Month.	In reply to Number.		**AAA**

from GOMMEGNIES to MAUBERGE via AMFROIPRET BERMERIES BAVAI and LA LONGUEVILLE aaa To pass road junction H.32.d.7.0 at 1100 hours in rear of 9th Inf. Bde Group aaa Large distances will be maintained on the march and Infantry will move off the road at each halt aaa Acknowledge aaa Addressed List "A" ~~repeat~~ plus A.P.M. repeated VI Corps 62- 2- and Guard Divns.

From 3rd Division.
Place
Time 13.40 hours.

MESSAGES AND SIGNALS.

TO: 76 Bde
       Signals

Sender's Number: GA15

Further to my GA11 of even date you the with Cavalry Bde will be moving in the...

From: 76 Bde

"A" Form
MESSAGES AND SIGNALS.

Army Form C. 2121
(In pads of 100.)

No. of Message............

Prefix........Code........m. | Words | Charge | This message is on a/c of: | Recd. at......m.
Office of Origin and Service Instructions | Sent | | | Date............
.... | At ....m. | | ....Service. | From ....
.... | To .... | | |
.... | By .... | | (Signature of "Franking Officer") | By........

TO { [illegible handwritten entries across multiple cells]

Sender's Number | Day of Month | In reply to Number | AAA

[Handwritten message body, largely illegible:]

...R.F.A... 11th November... MAUBEUGE... area allotted... to them... both on either bank of MAUBEUGE... LA LONGUEVILLE...
...1200... Route Am E to MET BEUGE to LONGUEVILLE...

From ......
Place ......
Time ......

The above may be forwarded as now corrected. (Z) ....
.... Censor. Signature of Addressor or person authorised to telegraph in his name
* This line should be erased if not required.

Order No. 1625 Wt. W3253/ P 511. 27/2. H. & K., Ltd. (E. 2634).

VI Corps Wire No.G.217 timed 1950 of 9th November.

Following from G.H.Q. timed 1520 AAA Advance of all Armies continues AAA Our troops believed to have reached following general line SAINS DU NORD - SARS - POTERIES - ASSEVENT (East of MAUBEUGE) AULNOIS - JEMAPPES W. along MONS - CONDE CANAL to CANAL D'ANTOING PERUWELZ E. of ANTOING - TOURNAI CHEMIN VERT CELLES - BERCHEM AAA French reported across SCHELDT at MELDEN Line of 1st French Army reported N. to S.E. of SAINS - ANOR - HIRSON (both incl).
 LATER. From G.H.Q. 1725 AAA German wireless states that the KAISER has abdicated and the CROWN PRINCE renounces claim to throne AAA First French Army report cavalry reached FRANCO-BELGIUM frontier AAA Ends.

SECRET.

Copy No. 21

3rd. DIVISION OPERATION ORDER NO. 281.

10th November 1918.

Reference Sheets 51 & 52. 1/40,000
NAMUR and VALENCIENNES Sheets 1/100,000

1. (a) The enemy is reported to be retiring on the Third Army front.

   (i) Report timed 10.00 hours on 10th November states Cavalry patrol fired on by M.G. fire from bank of stream in M.21.a. OSTERGNIES and COLLERET reported clear of the enemy.

   (ii) Report timed 13.00 hours 10th November states enemy is holding a line of rifle pits in R.5.b - Sunken Road L.35.b. & d. - L.29.c. - L.28.b. - L.22.c. & a. opposite the VI and XVII Corps fronts.

   (iii) Cavalry report timed 15.15 hours on 10th November, states Right Regiment reached line of LA THURE River. Centre Regiment reports FORT DE BOUSSOIS (L.27.d.) and TOWER in L.29.a. are held by enemy with machine guns. Left Regiment has been withdrawn.

   (b) The line at present held by us on the front of the Third Army is as follows :-

   QUIEVELON (inclusive) - East of BOUSSOIS - East of ELESMES and East of BETTIGNIES.

2. The direction of further advance of the Third Army is as follows :-

   Southern Boundary. FLOURSIES (exclusive) - BEAUMONT (exclusive) MARCHIENNE au PONT Road (exclusive).

   Northern Boundary. BAVAI - BINCHE Road (inclusive)

3. (a) The task of keeping touch with the enemy on the whole front of the Third Army is to be taken over by an Army Advanced Guard to be furnished by the VI Corps.

   (b) The 4th Cavalry Brigade has been placed under the orders of the VI Corps and has been ordered to maintain touch with the enemy on the whole Army front in the direction of and towards the general line THUIN - BINCHE.
   G.O.C. 4th Cavalry Brigade has resumed command of all Corps Cavalry Regiments including the Northumberland Hussars.

   (c) The Infantry of the advanced guard is to advance in the general direction MAUBEUGE - CHARLEROI, in support of the cavalry.

4. As soon as the VI Corps assumes responsibility for the Army Advanced Guard, Corps have been ordered to withdraw any advanced troops East of the AVESNES - MONS Road, except

troops left for billetting purposes.

Corps will however, still be responsible for the defence of the AVESNES - MONS Road within their own areas and have been ordered to thin out the front, and echelon troops back as far as is necessary to facilitate supply.

5. As soon as the 4th Cavalry Brigade is well clear of the line at present held by the Infantry, the leading Infantry Brigade Group of 3rd Division with an Artillery Brigade is to be pushed through the present front of the VI Corps in support of the 4th Cavalry Brigade.

The 3rd Division and 4th Cavalry Brigade will then become the Advanced Guard under the orders of the G.O.C. 3rd Division, who will assume command of the Advanced Guard at 16.00 hours on 11th November.

6. (a) The 76th Infantry Brigade Group with 40th Brigade R.F.A. and an additional Field Co. R.E. attached, will form the vanguard under the orders of G.O.C. 76th Infantry Brigade and will advance along the valley of the SAMBRE in close support of the 4th Cavalry Brigade.

G.O.C. 76th Infantry Brigade will keep in close touch with G.O.C. 4th Cavalry Brigade, who is establishing his H.Q. at BOUSSOIS on 11th November.

(b) The 8th and 9th Infantry Brigade Groups, one M.G. Co. and the remainder of 3rd Divisional Artillery will form the main guard of the Advanced Guard, and will be moved forward as circumstances permit.

(c) The 63rd Brigade R.G.A. (less 6" How. Batteries) will come under the orders of the G.O.C. 3rd Division. This Brigade will consist of two 60-pdr. Batteries.

7. The 62nd and Guards Divisions will be responsible for the protection of the present Main Line of Resistance on the front of the VI Corps, but as the leading Brigade of the 3rd Division passes through the troops on outpost will be withdrawn.

8. Orders for moves on the 11th November have already been issued to all concerned in G.A. 11 and G.A. 14.

9. (i) The 4th Cavalry Brigade is securing on the 11th November with its main bodies the line of the road BEAUMONT - ROUVEROY, with patrols pushed forward in advance to keep contact with the enemy.

(ii) The 76th Infantry Brigade Group will be prepared to advance on the morning of the 12th November in support of the 4th Cavalry Brigade moving along the valley of the SAMBRE on the North Bank.

(iii) The 76th Infantry Brigade will arrange for its own local protection, but will NOT be required to take over the outpost line from the 4th Cavalry Brigade

/as

3.

as that Brigade will find the outpost line each night.

(iv)   C.R.E. 3rd. Division will arrange for the construction of bridges over the SAMBRE so that troops can be passed from the North to the South Bank if required.

(v)   G.O.C. 76th Infantry Brigade will arrange for the protection of these bridges until that duty can be taken over by the main guard of the Advanced Guard.

10.   The 66th Division with Cavalry attached is carrying out the Advanced Guard duties on the Fourth Army front, with H.Q. at road junction South of the first R. in R. de La CROISETTE - 2 miles N.W. of AVESNES.

11.   Divisional Headquarters will close at FRASNOY and open at MAUBEUGE at 12.00 hours on 11th November.

12.   ACKNOWLEDGE.

Lieut-Colonel,
General Staff, 3rd. Division.

Issued at 20.30 hours

Copies to
1. G.O.C.
2. 8th Inf. Brigade.
3. 9th Inf. Brigade.
4. 76th Inf. Brigade.
5. C.R.A.
6. D.M.G.O.
7. C.R.E.
8. 20th K.R.R.C.
9. A.D.M.S.
10. 3rd Division "Q".
11. 3rd Div. Signals.
12. A.P.M.
13. 3rd Div. Train.
14. Guards Division.
15. 2nd Division.
16. 62nd Division.
17. 66th Division.
18. VIth Corps.
19. 4th Cavalry Brigade.
20. War Diary.
21.   "   "
22. File.
23. File.

"A" Form
MESSAGES AND SIGNALS.

Army Form C. 2121
(In pads of 100.)

"A" Form
Army Form C. 2121
(In pads of 100.)

MESSAGES AND SIGNALS.

No. of Message..........

Prefix..............Code..............m.	Words	Charge.	This message is on a/c of:	Recd. at......m.
Office of Origin and Service Instructions	Sent		..........................Service.	Date..............
....	At ....m.			From ....
....	To		....	
....	By		(Signature of "Franking Officer")	By..................

TO

Sender's Number.	Day of Month.	In reply to Number.	AAA

Revolution in MUNICH and Wittelsbach dynasty deposed [illegible] BAVARIA to be Socialist Republic [illegible] [illegible] disturbances reported HANOVER [illegible] ~~[illegible]~~ official telegram from Berlin communiqué [illegible] early [illegible] from shortage [illegible] [illegible] and [illegible] of [illegible]

From [illegible]			
Place			
Time			

The above may be forwarded as now corrected. (Z) [illegible]

.... Censor. Signature of Addressor or person authorised to telegraph in his name

* This line should be erased if not required.

Order No. 1625 Wt. W3253/ P 511. 27/2. H. & K., Ltd. (**E. 2634**).

MESSAGES AND SIGNALS.   Army Form C. 2121.
(In pads of 100.)

Prefix	Code	m.	Words.	Charge.		This message is on a/c of:	Recd. at ... m.
Office of Origin and Service Instructions.			Sent				Date
			At ... m.			Service.	From
			To				
			By			(Signature of "Franking Officer.")	By

TO

Sender's Number.	Day of Month.	In reply to Number.	AAA
GO 29	11		

All moves for to day cancelled till to-morrow will remain in present location Acknowledge

From
Place
Time

The above may be forwarded as now corrected.   (Z)

Censor.   Signature of Addressee or person authorised to telegraph in his name

*This line, except **A A A**, should be erased if not required.

MESSAGES AND SIGNALS.

Army Form C. 2121.
(In pads of 100.)

Prefix	Code	m.	Words.	Charge.	This message is on a/c of:	Recd. at	m.
Office of Origin and Service Instructions.			Sent			Date	
			At m.		Service.	From	
			To				
			By		(Signature of "Franking Officer.")	By	

TO	* Bde	Div y C	CRE	S. Gds
	G RR	MGC	R	
	7 bde	BRA	Signs	

Sender's Number.	Day of Month.	In reply to Number.	AAA
GC 30	11		

Corps wire and
Artillerie will cease at 1100
hrs today 11th Nov and troops
will stay fast on line reached
at that hour which will be
reported by wire to Corps HQ
No fraternising precautions will
be maintained and there is
to be no intercourse of
any description with the enemy
No Germans are to be
allowed to enter our lines any
doing so will be taken prisoner
Cav Bde will carry out its
moves to BOUSSIÈRES

From 2nd Div
Place
Time 0730

Censor. Signature of Addressor or person authorised to telegraph in his name
G. Hovely Capt

*This line, except AAA, should be erased if not required.
Wt. W 3253/P511. 500,000 Pads. 1/18. B. & S. Ltd. (E2389.)

3rd DIVISION.

Disposition and Movement Report No.13.

12th November

Unit No.	UNIT.	Location of H.Q. at 1900 hrs.	Probable changes during 24 hours.
1.	3rd Divisional H.Q.	FRASNOY.	
2.	3rd Divisional Arty H.Q.	FRASNOY.	
3.	**8th Infantry Brigade H.Q.**	VERTAIN.	
4.	2nd The Royal Scots.	ROMERIES.	
5.	1st Royal Scots Fus.	ROMERIES.	
6.	7th K.S.L.I.	ROMERIES.	
7.	8th T.M.Battery.	ROMERIES.	
8.	8th Field Amblce.	ROMERIES.	
9.	No.3 Coy Train.	ROMERIES.	
10.	**9th Infantry Brigade H.Q.**	FRASNOY M.10.b.4.6.	
11.	1st Northumberland Fus.	M.10.c.6.6. FRASNOY.	
12.	4th Royal Fusiliers.	M.10.b.1.4. FRASNOY.	
13.	13th King's L'pool Regt.	N.14.d.4.5.	
14.	9th T.M.Battery.	FRASNOY M.10.b.4.6.	
15.	**76th Infantry Brigade H.Q.**	LA LONGUEVILLE I.36.a.6.6.	
16.	8th K.O.R.L.Regt.	I.36.b.2.2.	
17.	2nd Suffolk Regt.	I.36.a.8.6.	
18.	1st Gordon Hldrs.	I.30.d.6.6.	
19.	76th T.M.Battery.	I.36.d.7.6.	
20.	7th Field Amblce.	I.36.a.7.7.	
21.	No.2 Coy Train.	I.36.a.6.7.	
22.	**C.R.E.**	FRASNOY	
23.	56th Field Coy, R.E.	ORSINVAL.	
24.	438th " " "	GOMMEGNIES M.12.d.3.2.	
25.	529th " " "	LA LONGUEVILLE I.36.a.6.6.	
26.	**3rd M.G.Battalion.**	SARLOTON N.13.d.5.5.	
27.	"A" Company.	GOMMEGNIES.	
28.	"B" "	do.	
29.	"C" "	LA LONGUEVILLE I.36.a.8.6.	
30.	"D" "	VERTAIN.	
31.	20th K.R.R.C.(Pioneers).	RUESNES R.14.c.8.4.	
32.	Guards Division.	MAUBEUGE.	
33.	2nd Division.	VILLERS POL.	
34.	62nd Division.	Q.8.a.central.	

VI Corps wire G.322 dated 12th November, timed 22.50 hours.

(1) Our troops will not advance East of line gained by them, at hour when hostilities ceased aaa Our aeroplanes will keep at a distance of not less than one mile behind this line except for purpose of driving back hostile aeroplanes as indicated in para 3 aaa (2) There is to be no unauthorised intercourse or fraternisation of any description with enemy aaa He will not be permitted to approach our lines and any attempt to do so will be immediately stopped if necessary by fire aaa Any parties of enemy coming over to our lines under a white flag will be made prisoners and fact reported to Corps H.Q. aaa (3) No enemy aircraft will be permitted to cross the line aaa Should any make the attempt to do so they will be attacked by fire from ground and from air. aaa (4) All Commanders are to pay strictest attention to discipline smartness and well-being of their troops so as to ensure that highest state of efficiency shall be maintained throughout British Forces aaa Troops will be given every opportunity for rest, training, recreation and leave aaa (5) Passage of civilians through our lines in either direction will be regulated in accordance with instructions which will be issued separately aaa In the meantime no civilians will be permitted to cross our lines in either direction aaa Ends. aaa

"A" Form.
MESSAGES AND SIGNALS.

Army Form C. 2121.
(In pads of 100.)

Prefix	Code	Words	Charge	This message is on a/c of	Recd. at ... m.
Office of Origin and Service Instructions		Sent At ... m. To By		Service (Signature of "Franking Officer.")	Date From By

TO

Sender's Number	Day of Month	In reply to Number	
67-56	13		A A A

The Companies of ... Bn. at ... attached to 8th ... 76th Inf Bde will report ... Bn. at BARLOT on ... day upon Orders for moves of these Companies are being issued to them direct by Divn C ...

... 8 and 76 Inf Bde upon Divn C

From
Place
Time 0900

The above may be forwarded as now corrected.   (Z)

Censor.   Signature of Addresser or person authorised to telegraph in his name.

* This line, except A A A, should be erased if not required.

Prefix... Code... m.	Words.	Charge.	This message is on a/c of:		Recd. at ...... m.
Office of Origin and Service Instructions.	Sent				Date ....
	At .... m.		.... Service.		From ....
	To				
	By		(Signature of "Franking Officer.")		By ....

TO	76 Bde	3rd Div. G	Words	
	Div. C	Signal	VI Corps	
	Corps C	APM	100 S	

Sender's Number.	Day of Month.	In reply to Number.	AAA
GC 64	14		

Following moves will take place tomorrow Nov 15th by Div H.Q. and 3 Corps arty Bn from GOMMEGNIES and SARLOTON to LA LONGUEVILLE via Route AMFROIPRET – BERMERIES – BAVAI – LA LONGUEVILLE. To be clear of present billets by 1100 hrs. Bns and Pioneer Bn from BUESNES to GOMMEGNIES and SARLOTON via Route LE QUESNOY – Cross Roads M15c Road Junction M11d 4.8 and not to enter GOMMEGNIES and SARLOTON before 1200 hrs. 76 Bde will allot areas in LA LONGUEVILLE to Div HQ Bn and Pioneer will take over billets vacated by Div Bn HQ. Acknowledge

From	3rd Div
Place	
Time	18 00 hrs

The above may be forwarded as now corrected. (Z)

Censor.   Signature of Addressor or person authorised to telegraph in his name.

* This line, except AAA, should be erased if not required.

A Form
MESSAGES AND SIGNALS.
Army Form C. 2121
(In pads of 100.)

No. of Message............

Prefix..........Code.........m.	Words	Charge	This message is on a/c of:	Recd. at......m.
Office of Origin and Service Instructions	Sent			Date............
	At ....m.		..................Service.	From............
	To			
	By		(Signature of "Franking Officer")	By............

TO

| Sender's Number. | Day of Month. | In reply to Number. | AAA |

Following recce will take place on 11th. Nov. 00 and 5th Cav Bde group to field day from ROMERIES to FRASNOY and to plot road junction at 17 C at 0830 hours and route BERVICELLES LE DUESNOY and 9th Cav Bde group from FRASNOY to LA LONGUEVILLE and to pass in Southern MHC CC at 1100 hours. The 2nd & Ameridan BAVAI and 10th field coy RE to form 9th Cav Bde hours via road running through NJ central and move under orders of GOC 9th Cav Bde and JOC 5th Cav Bde group from LA LONGUEVILLE to NEUF MESNIL and MONTPLAISIR and any route and to start at 1100 hrs and remain the from GOGNIES and SARLOTEN to NEUF MESNIL and to pass

From			
Place			
Time			

The above may be forwarded as now corrected. (Z)

....

Censor. Signature of Addressor or person authorised to telegraph in his name
* This line should be erased if not required.

"A" Form

Army Form C. 2121
(In pads of 100.)

MESSAGES AND SIGNALS.

No. of Message...........

Prefix..........Code..........m.	Words	Charge.	*This message is on a/c of:*	Recd. at......m.
Office of Origin and Service Instructions	Sent		.........................*Service.*	Date:............
	At ....m.			From ....
	To			
	By		(Signature of "Franking Officer")	By..............

TO

Sender's Number.	Day of Month.	In reply to Number.	AAA
* GB77	15		

[illegible] 1912 [illegible] at 1200 hours aaa
Route AMFROIPRET BAVAI [illegible] LONGUEVILLE
aaa 7C [illegible] Inf Bde with attd [illegible]
Pioneer Bn aaa Gd [illegible] Bde Group and
Pioneer Bn will NOT march through the
centre of BAVAI but will use the road
running round the south side of the
town in I 25. a and b aaa
Distances to be maintained on march
by all units as follows aaa 50 yards
between Companies 200 yds between
Battns and [illegible] [illegible] 51
and 51A 1 and 40000 aaa
[illegible] aaa [illegible] R [illegible]
CRA 2 and Gd Div and G Coys

From Gd Div
Place
Time 1030

The above may be forwarded as now corrected. (Z) [illegible signature]

....
Censor. Signature of Addressor or person authorised to telegraph in his name

* This line should be erased if not required.

Order No 1625 Wt. W3253/ P 511 27/2 H. & K.. Ltd. (E. 2634)

Prefix......Code.........m.	Words.	Charge.	This message is on a/c of:		Recd. at......m.
Office of Origin and Service Instructions.	Sent			Service.	Date......
	At......m.				From......
	To......		(Signature of "Franking Officer.")		By......
	By......				

TO

Sender's Number.	Day of Month.	In reply to Number.	AAA
GC 21	12		

Forecast of moves on Nov 9/10 A Group to LOUVREAU B Group to SOUS-LE-BOIS C Group to NEUF MESNIL MON PLAISIR D Group to ...... List A

From: 3rd Corps
Place:
Time: 2200

(Z)

INSTRUCTIONS TO OFFICERS in charge EDUCATION
3rd. DIVISION.

(A). SCOPE OF ARMY EDUCATIONAL SCHEME.

1. Provision of practical instruction with a view to training for particular trades and occupations.

2. More general education with a view largely to giving men a wider view of their duties as citizens of the British Empire, and awakening interest in, and providing knowledge in regard to, the peace settlement and social re-construction.

(B). SCHEME OF INSTRUCTION.

The work under para. A.1. will be carried on mainly by means of classes; that of para. A.2. by means of lectures.

The scheme of practical instruction will be run upon the following lines, and upon the principle that each man requiring Education will be able to devote at the minimum six hours per week to Educational Training :-

(i) Elementary Courses.

Group A. Such subjects as Reading, Writing, Dictation, Elementary Arithmetic, Talks on Imperial History and Civics.) For men who have little or no education (probably includes such categories as Agricultural, Dock, and General Labourers, Carters, etc.,).

(No man should leave the Forces without being able to read and write.)

Group B. Such subjects as Composition, Precis Writing, Practical mathematics, Elementary Civics and Economics.) For men requiring a technical course, Engineers, Electricians, carpenters, builders, fitters etc.,)

Group C. Such subjects as Essay writing, Writing of Commercial letters, Mathematics (including Calculation of prices and amounts.) For men requiring a commercial course, (clerks, salesmen, warehousemen, etc.,)

percentage and discounts; the)
metric system), Commercial)
geography, Elementary economics.)

(ii) Additional Subjects for more Advanced Students.

One Language; either French, German, Italian or Spanish.

Any two of the following; Shorthand, Typewriting, Book keeping, Business methods.

Additional Technical Subjects; such as Elementary Mechanics, Theory of Internal Combustion Engines; Motor Mechanics, Electricity and Magnetism, Chemistry, Physics, Building Construction, Elementary Theory of Agriculture, Gardening and allotments.

Where facilities permit, more detailed training for particular trades such as carpentry, telephony, telegraphy, electric lighting and power, and motor driving may be provided.

(iii) Lectures.

Lectures will be arranged by the Divisional Educational Officer. He will be very glad to have the names of any Officers or other ranks willing to lecture on any subject of general interest.

(C). Duties of Officers i/c Education.

(NOTE :- The Education work is regarded as part time Military duty.)

1. To compile a complete list of available instructors in their units, with their qualifications and the subjects they are able to teach. They should be on the look-out for men who, without special teaching experience, are well enough educated to give instruction in such elementary subjects as those in Group "A"; and should bear in mind that the best qualified teachers are likely to be demobilised early, and that they will need others to fall back upon.

A list of instructors should be sent to the Divisional Educational Officer as soon as possible, and on the 20th of each month a return of additions and casualties should be made in order that the list at Headquarters may be kept up-to-date. In the case of Brigaded Infantry, duplicates of these returns should also be sent to the Brigade Educational Officer.

2. They should make a study of the Educational requirements of the men of their units, and be able to give advice as to what sort of instruction they need for their particular trade. A summary of the information so obtained should be forwarded to the Divisional Educational Officer as soon as possible, and on the 20th of each month this information should be brought up to date by a supplementary return.

The returns should be arranged under trade groups, with the number under instruction in each, e.g.

> "Agriculture   14
> Building trades 20
> Commercial   42", and so on.

3. They are responsible for the filling up by Officers of their units of forms required by the Committee on the Resettlement of Officers. (These forms are to be circulated very shortly).

4. Apart from these preliminary steps, they will have the general responsibility of supervising classes in their own units.

5. As soon as circumstances permit, the Education Scheme will be centralised as much as possible, and will be arranged in groups by Brigades, (Divisional Troops being regarded as constituting one group), but in the meantime a start should be made at once with small classes within units in the most elementary subjects.

(D). Books and Apparatus.

1. <u>Text-books etc.</u>, A list of text-books and other material available on indent will be circulated shortly.

2. <u>Library</u>. A small reference library for the use of instructors is in process of formation at Divisional Headquarters.

[signature] Major.
for Lieut-Colonel,
General Staff, 3rd. Division.

November 15th 1918.

SECRET.   3rd. Division G.2002.
****

8th Inf. Bde.   A.D.M.S.
9th Inf. Bde.   3rd. Div. "Q".
76th Inf. Bde.   3rd. Div. Signals.
C.R.A.   A.P.M.
C.R.E.   3rd. M.T. Coy.
20th K.R.R.C.   3rd. Divnl. Train.
Camp Commdt.   Mob. Vet. Sect.
D.A.D.O.S.   D.M.G.O.

----

1. (a)   In accordance with terms of armistice, all occupied
          portions of FRANCE, BELGIUM, and LUXEMBOURG will be
          evacuated by the enemy by the 26th November.
              A further withdrawal to the East of the RHINE will
          take place at a later date.

    (b)   The Allied forces are to commence to advance on the
          17th instant.

    (c)   The advancing British Forces are being organised in
          two Armies, the Second and Fourth, each of four Corps and
          16 Divisions. The Fourth Army consists of the following
          Corps and Divisions :-

          2nd Cavalry Division

          VI Corps - Guards, 2nd, 3rd, 62nd Divisions.

          IV Corps - 5th, 37th, 42nd, and New Zealand Divisions.

          Australian Corps - 1st, 2nd, 4th, and 5th Australian
                                              Divisions.

          IX Corps - 1st, 6th, 32nd, and 66th Divisions.

2. (a)   The IX and VI Corps are to be the two leading Corps of
          the Fourth Army, with the 2nd Cavalry Division covering
          the whole front of the Army.

    (b)   The boundary between the IX and VI Corps and the
          suggested roads for the advance to the First Line are
          shown on Map "B". These roads may be modified by Corps
          at their discretion on receipt of road reconnaissance
          reports, provided Army and Corps boundaries are not
          crossed.

/3.

3.   The VI Corps has been tansferred to the Fourth Army from 12.00 hours, 14th November.

4.   The cavalry will be from 5 to 10 miles ahead of the leading Divisions and will inform Divisions of bad portions of the road, condition of bridges etc.

5.   The 62nd Division, followed a day later by the 3rd Division, will march on the Southern road.
The Guards Division, followed a day later by the 2nd Division, will march on the Northern road.
The Corps Heavy Artillery will follow the 2nd Division a day later on the Northern road.

6.   The VI Corps will have the use of the road through HAUTMONT and the lorry bridge there over the River SAMBRE.

7.   A <u>Corps Depot</u> and a <u>Depot for each Division</u> will be formed near the railway to consist of what we want to come on later. These Depots will be handed over to the IV Corps and will come on with them by train.

8.   (a)   Every Divisional Unit which is not mobile is to be left behind. Stokes Mortar Batteries are to be taken.

(b)   Units must be medically examined and all weaklings left behind.

9.   Batteries will be reduced to 4 gun batteries of two sections each, and will be brought up to establishment.
The 23rd Brigade R.F.A. will rejoin the Artillery of the Division.

10.   Each echelon will march full.

<u>Supplies etc.</u>

11.   All <u>Schools</u> are to be broken up. The pupils are to return to their units, and the establishments handed over to the Army.

12.   Bands will be and <u>Colours</u> may be taken on the march.

13.   Cameras may be taken.

<u>Cameras</u>.

/14.

3.

14. Censorship. The Censorship will be relaxed.

15. Communications.
(a) Telephones will not be used in the early stages of the advance.
It may be possible later to connect up to the German telephone system.

(b) Wireless sets will be allotted to each Infantry Brigade H.Q. and a Directing Station will be maintained at Divisional Headquarters.

(c) Aeroplanes will also be used for communication purposes.
Each Infantry Brigade H.Q. will have a panel station and a Dropping Ground will be established at Divisional Headquarters.

16. Synchronization of watches & issue of orders. A Staff Officer from Divisional Headquarters will call at each Group Headquarters daily to synchronize watches, and to communicate orders, if necessary, and obtain information on any points which Group Commanders may wish to bring to notice.

17. All References in orders will be to the 1/100,000 map.

18. Notes for Staff and Regimental Officers on the rules of March Discipline will be issued shortly by the Fourth Army at the rate of one copy per Officer.

19. The attached instructions will be strictly adhered to.

20. ACKNOWLEDGE.

November 15th 1916.

Lieut-Colonel,
General Staff, 3rd. Division.

INSTRUCTIONS   (To accompany 3rd. Div. G.2002.)

1.   (a)   The Division will march by Groups, composed as follows:-

"A" GROUP.

76th Infantry Brigade.
529th Field Coy. R.E.
No. 7 Field Ambulance (Less Motor Ambulances).
20th K.R.R.C. (Pioneer Battalion).

"B" GROUP.

9th Infantry Brigade.
56th Field Coy. R.E.
No. 142 Field Ambulance (Less Motor Ambulances).
3rd. Bn. M.G. Corps.

Groups on the March.

"C" GROUP.

8th Infantry Brigade.
458th Field Coy. R.E.
No. 8 Field Ambulance (Less Motor Ambulances).

"D" GROUP.

23rd, 40th, 42nd, Bdes. R.F.A.
D.A.C.
Mobile Veterinary Section.

Divn'l Train.   (b)   3rd. Divisional Train will march as a separate unit in rear of "D" GROUP.
Train Companies will be billeted in the areas of the Group to which they are affiliated.

M.T. Co. & motor Ambulances.   (c)   3rd. M.T. Company and Motor Ambulances will move in rear of the Divisional Train.
Motor Ambulances will rejoin their Field Ambulance at the end of the days march.

(d)   No lorry or motor ambulance, (unless specially ordered) will on any account start from its billeting area until 2 hours has elapsed after the tail of the column has passed the area in which such motor lorry or motor ambulance is billeted.

/2

2.

2. Starting Point.

(a) Starting Point and hour of start for each Group will be laid down by Divisional H.Q.

Groups will pass this starting point punctually at the hour laid down.

3. Halts.

The ten minutes' halt, at ten minutes to each clock hour, will be rigidly adhered to once units have reached the main line of march.

If the distance from billets to the main line of march is such that the troops will be required to march for a prolonged period before halting for the first hourly halt, O.C. Units should time their march to the starting point, so as to allow of a short halt before joining the main column, provided that the road is not blocked to other troops thereby; e.g. time for passing starting point 10.30   Time for leaving billets 09.45; the march should be so timed as to allow troops to halt from 10.20 - 10.30 off the main route.

4. Brigade H.Q.

Brigade H.Q. will invariably be located at the H.Q. occupied by the Brigade of the leading Division.

5. Headquarters of Units & Formations.

The Headquarters of all units and formations must be clearly marked.

All units and formations will report their arrival in billets on the completion of a march to the next higher formation, and will send an orderly to the next higher formation with the location of their Headquarters.

6. Billeting Parties.

Billeting parties mounted on bicycles, will be attached to Groups of the 62nd Division. They will meet their units on arrival and show them their billets.

Staff Captains will invariably reach the new billets in sufficient time in advance of their Groups to make any necessary adjustments.

7. Police.

A.P.M. will arrange to post police at any places along the route where columns are liable to take a wrong turning - this is especially necessary when passing through towns or villages.

Stragglers Posts will be detailed to follow Groups during the march.

8. 1st Line Transport, Lewis Guns and Pack Animals.

Lewis gun limbers and ammunition pack animals will march in rear of their companies.

Remainder of the 1st Line transport will march Brigaded in rear of Groups under the Brigade Transport Officers.

9. Transport Personnel.

Brakesmen, cooks with cookers, will march within the breadth of the wheels of the vehicles, and not outside them as is so often the case. All other men marching with the transport will march in formed bodies in rear of the transport of their unit.

10. Parking of guns & vehicles.

No guns or vehicles are on any account to be parked on main roads.

11. Overloading of Wagons.

Wagons must not be overloaded.

Staff Officers have authority to lighten overloaded wagons by dumping the contents by the road side.

12. Supply Columns.

At a certain hour, which will be notified each day, before which the march will have been completed, all roads will be kept clear for the advance of the supply column. No guns or transport must be parked on roads which can in any way interfere with the forward or backward movement of these lorries to and from re-filling points.

All supply lorries will be clear of the roads by a certain hour in the morning which will be laid down by Corps. That is to say, during the day roads will be employed for the marching troops, and during the night will be kept clear for the advance and return of supply lorries.

13. Distances to be maintained on the march.

The following distances will be maintained on the march :-

In rear of an Infantry Company - 10 yards.

In rear of a battery or other unit not specified - 25 yards.

In rear of an Artillery Brigade or Infantry Battalion - 50 yards.

In rear of a Group. - 200 yards.

/14.

4.

14.
Steel Helmets
BoxRespirators

Steel Helmets and Box Respirators will be carried on the march.
Caps will be worn and steel helmets carried on the person.

15.
S.A.A.

60 rounds S.A.A. will be carried on the man.

==*=*=*=*=*=*

MESSAGES AND SIGNALS.

TO: G-O-76th Inf. Bde. C.R.A. C.R.E. A.D.M.S.
D.H.Q.O. 20/K.R.R.C. G Signals A.P.M.
6 Corps G. 2-62nd Divs. 6 Corps Q. 3rd Div Train

Sender's Number: GB. 54
Day of Month: 16th

AAA

Following moves will take place on Nov. 17th AAA
"A" Group from NEUF MESNIL MON PLAISIR area to
LOUVROIL AAA To cross the FRAMERIES - HAUTMONT
railway at 1200 hours AAA "B" Group from
LA LONGUEVILLE to SOUS LE BOIS to start at
1400 hours AAA "C" Group from FRASNOY area to
NEUF MESNIL-MON PLAISIR area AAA Route BAVAI-
LA LONGUEVILLE AAA To enter LA LONGUEVILLE at
1500 hours and tail to be eclear of road
junction just West of P. in PETIT MARAIS by
1830 hours AAA Train companies will march with
Bde Groups AAA Distances as laid down in para
15 of instructions issued with G.2002 AAA Div.
H.Q. will move to SOUS LE BOIS and open at an
hour to be notified AAA "D" group will not move
AAA ACKNOWLEDGE AAA Added list "A" plus A.P.M.
2nd and 62nd Divs. 6th Corps G. and Q. Train

From
Place: 3rd Divn.
Time: 1430 hours.

Sender's Number.	Day of Month.	In reply to Number.	
GB 87	16		AAA

In continuation of GB 84 of this date our Div HQ will close at Flassoy at 1500 hours Nov 17th and open at SOUS-LE-BOIS at the same hour. Addsd for A plus copies 2.6x Div Arty and Train

From: Div
Place:
Time: 1845

MESSAGES AND SIGNALS.

8-9-96	John Arden	1AA CAB	20 KAA	
TO DADC	ADMS Q	Signals	APM	

Sender's Number: GB 92
Day of Month: 16
In reply to Number:
AAA

Moves ordered in GB 84 dated Nov 16th to take place tomorrow Nov 17th are cancelled all Groups will remain in their present locations now due for Nov 17th will probably now take place on Nov 18th acknowledge Addressed list A plus APM.

From: 3 Div
Place:
Time: 2200

3rd. Division G.S. 2002/2.

INSTRUCTIONS No. 2.

To 3rd. Division G.S.2002.

1. During the advance all military precautions against surprise will be taken.
   Roads must be picketed at night.
   Guards will be mounted on all Battalion Headquarters, Brigade Headquarters, and on Divisional Headquarters.
   Guard for Divisional Headquarters will be found from the nearest Brigade Group.

2. All marches will commence at 08.00 hours, unless otherwise stated.

3. Responsibility of Commanding Officers.

   Commanding Officers will take all possible steps to ensure that blocks on the roads, delays in the issue of orders, unnecessary waiting about by parading too early, etc., do not occur. The issue of instructions alone is not sufficient; Staff Officers must ascertain by personal supervision that the instructions issued are carried out.

4. All Formations will report daily while the march continues as soon as all their troops have reached their billets.

5. Any German stragglers or Escaped Prisoners of War of any nationality will at once be sent to Divisional Headquarters.

6. Supply Arrangements.

   Special attention is drawn to "Divisional Supply Arrangements for an Advance" on page 80 and following pages of Fourth Army Standing Orders, which are being issued direct by the Fourth Army to formations. These supply orders are to be most carefully carried out, otherwise there is likely to be a failure in the arrival of supplies.

7. ACKNOWLEDGE.

November 16th 1918.

Lieut-Colonel,
General Staff, 3rd. Division.

MESSAGES AND SIGNALS.

Prefix	Code	Words	Charge	This message is on a/c of:	Recd. at ... m.
Office of Origin and Service Instructions		Sent At ... m. To By		Priority Service. (Signature of "Franking Officer.")	Date From By

TO — G-O-70th Bdes., Cdn.Cav. Cdn.Cav., Cdn. C. GS HQRS., A.D.M.S., AM., CE MLAC., Trdn., VI Corps O A Q, 2 - 88 DIVs.

Sender's Number.	Day of Month.	In reply to Number.	AAA
G.O. 04	17.		

Moves ordered to take place on Nov. 17th in G.O. 04 and G.O. 90 both dated Nov. 16th will now take place on Nov. 18th aaa forecast of moves to take place on Nov. 19th one "A" group from LOUVIGNY to area COLLERET OBOURG(?) — OBOURGAIN — MONCEAU LA GRANDE aaa "B" & "C" Groups no change aaa "E" Group to area West of the HAUMONT — LA LONGVILLE — NAVAL Road exclusive aaa Div. H.Q. to .... aaa acknowledge aaa addressed list A plus A.P.M., Srdn., VI Corps O A Q, 2 - 88 DIVs.

From: Cdn. Division.
Place:
Time: 10-00

The above may be forwarded as now corrected. (Z)

Censor. .... Major

Signature of Addresser or person authorised to telegraph in his name.

* This line, except AAA, should be erased if not required.

MESSAGES AND SIGNALS.

Prefix......Code......m.	Words	Charge	This message is on a/c of:	Recd. at......m.
Office of Origin and Service Instructions	Sent		......Service.	Date......
	At ......m.			From......
	To			
	By	(Signature of "Franking Officer")	By......

TO { G.O. 75th Inf. Bde., G.O. Div.A.C., 20 KHR., AMC., R.E., APM., Signals., Train., M.Sec.

Sender's Number	Day of Month	In reply to Number	AAA
G.O.98	27		

Moves forecasted for 19th Nov. will take place on Nov. 20th and No moves on 19th and Area allotted to "Y" Group for 20th will be OMIES - MAMMIES - VIEUX ARCENT, and accommodation for 2 Bdes H.Q.s in LA BOUVERIE and ARQUENNES and Advanced Adv A plus A.P.M. Train.

From 3rd. Division.
Place
Time 00.00

3rd. Division G.2002/3.

INSTRUCTIONS No. 3.

To 3rd. Division G.2002.

1. Reference para 6 of Instructions which accompanied G.2002 dated November 15th 1918.

As the 62nd Division will now be moving two marches in front of the Division, billeting parties will not be attached to Groups of this Division.

2. Receipts for operation orders will be handed without delay to the D.R's delivering them.

These receipts to be signed (not initialled) by an Officer of the formation or unit to which they are addressed.

3. It may often happen that an area allotted to a Group contains more accommodation than will actually be required. In such cases troops should be billeted as far forward in the area as possible, so as to keep the troops concentrated and so facilitate the following days march.

November 17th 1918.

Lieut-Colonel,
General Staff, 3rd. Division.

3rd. Division G.S.2002/4.

INSTRUCTIONS No. 4.

To 3rd. Division G.S.2002.

1. Reference Fourth Army No. G.S.128 "Notes on March Discipline". Although no compliments will be paid on the march, each Unit will at the end of the days march before entering its billeting area, march past its Commander or Brigade Commander, paying the usual compliments.

2. Reference para 8 of Instructions issued with G.S.2002. Cookers will march immediately in rear of Battalions.

November 18th 1918.

for Lieut-Colonel,
General Staff, 3rd. Division.

3rd. Division G.S.

The following moves will take place on 10th November

"A" GROUP. to COUSOLRE - BERSILLIES L'ABBAYE

"B" GROUP. to CERFONTAINE - OSTERGNIES - COLLERET

"C" GROUP. to FERRIERE LA GRANDE

"D" GROUP. to LA LONGUEVILLE - MARGNIES -
VIEUX MESNIL

Divisional Headquarters will close at SOUS LE BOIS at 0900 hrs
and open at COUSOLRE on arrival.

ACKNOWLEDGE.

Sd. J. H. Lumley Major
for Lieut-Colonel,
General Staff, 3rd. Division.

9/11/18

Distribution :-   A.D.M.S.
C.R.E.
Camp Commandant.
D.A.D.O.S.
A.D.V.S.
3rd. M.T. Coy.
Signals.
File.
War Diary.

W.P.

3rd. Division Operation Order No. 282

1. The Division will march to-morrow 20 Nov. in accordance with the following March Table.

Reference Sheet. 1/100,000

MARCH TABLE.

Unit.	Starting Point.	Hour of start.	Route.	Destination.	Instructions.
"A" GROUP.		0630	COUSOLRE	COUSOLRE HESTRUD L'AGACHE BOUSIGNIES	
"B" GROUP.		082_	MAUBEUGE — Railway Bridge 12m 3.4.1 m — MAUBEUGE COLLERET	COLLERET CERFONTAINE OSTERGNIES	
"C" GROUP.			MAUBEUGE	FEIGNIES LA GOE	
"D" GROUP.			_ _ LA LONGUEVILLE VIEUX MESNIL + BAGNE		

2. Divisional Headquarters will close at SOUS-LE-BOIS at   and open at COUSOLRE on arrival.
3. ACKNOWLEDGE.

Distribution:— G.O.C., "Q"., G.R.A., Div.Train., A.P.M.,
                8th. Inf. Bde.   VI Corps "G".
                9th. Inf. Bde.   VI Corps "Q".
                76th. Inf. Bde.

                                            Lieut-Colonel,
                                    General Staff, 3rd. Division.

Issued at 1500 hours.

TO 8-9-76 Inf Bdes CRA CRE Q
ADMS 3rd Div Train C Coys & D
Signals

Sender's Number: GB 118
Day of Month: 20

A B & C Groups will not move tomorrow Nov 21st aaa D Group will move to area ROUSIES - RECQUIGNIES - MARPENT no restriction as to time or route aaa No further moves will take place pending improvement of Railway and road communications aaa Separate orders are being issued for work on roads aaa Acknowledge aaa Addd 3 Bdes CRA CRE ADMS Q Train C Coys G & D

From: 3rd Div
Time: 1120

"A" Form.
MESSAGES AND SIGNALS.

Army Form C. 2121.
(In pads of 100.)

TO 8th Inf. Bde. C.R.A. "Q" 3rd M.T.Coy.
9th Inf. Bde. C.R.E. Signals. Train.
     Inf. Bde. ADMS A.D.

| Sender's Number. | Day of Month. | In reply to Number. | AAA |

G.s. 180   22nd

Morning Order aaa 3rd Division will be
prepared to resume the advance on 24th
and 25th November aaa 3rd Division will
have its head on line DOUZIE CHARLEROI
Road by evening 23th November aaa Orders
for march on 24th November will be issued
later aaa ACKNOWLEDGE aaa Addressed 3 Bdes
C.R.A. C.R.E. A.D.M.S. "Q" Signals
A.D. 3rd M.T. Coy. Train.

From
Place 3rd Division.
Time

3rd. Division Operation Order No. 283.

1. The Division will march to-morrow 24th Nov in accordance with the following March Table.

Reference Sheet. 1/100,000

MARCH TABLE.

Unit.	Starting Point.	Hour of start.	Route.	Destination.	Instructions.
"A" GROUP.	Road junction 3C 25 20	10.10	Along route HL 05 95 - Bousignies - road junction 3C 25 10 - road junction 3C 25 40 - road junction 3C 25 35 - Leers et Fosteau	THUIN LUBBES	Bde HQ — THUIN
"B" GROUP.	Cross roads 3B 23 03	09.05	— do —	LEERS ET FOSTEAU RAGNIES BIERGES BOIS DE VILLERS	Bde HQ — Château LEERS ET FOSTEAU
"C" GROUP.	Cross roads 3A 33 14 — LEFONTAING	08.35	COLLERET — West bank of LA THURE river Along route HL 05 95 - BOUSIGNES - road junction 3C 25 10	BERSILLIES L'ABBAYE (BOUSIGNES (MONTIGNIES ST CHRISTOPHE	Bde HQ — MONTIGNIES ST CHRISTOPHE
"D" GROUP.	NO		MOVE		RA HQ — Château RECQUIGNIES
Divnl. H.Q.	Road junction 3C 25 20	09.10	Route as for A Group	THUIN	

2. Divisional Headquarters will close at COUSOLRE at 09.00 and open at THUIN on arrival.
3. ACKNOWLEDGE.

Distribution:— G.O.C., "Q", C.R.A., Div. Train, A.P.M.,
8th. Inf. Bde.   VI Corps "G".
9th. Inf. Bde.   VI Corps "Q".
76th. Inf. Bde.   Camp Commdt.
                      3rd. Div. Signals.

23/11/18

Issued at _____ hrs

Lieut-Colonel,
General Staff, 3rd. Division.

3rd. Division G.S. 2021

The following moves will take place on 24th Novr

"A" GROUP. to   THUIN & LOBBES

"B" GROUP. to   LEERS ET FOSTEAU — RAGNIES — BIERCEE
                BOIS DE VILLERS

"C" GROUP. to   BERSILLIES L'ABBAYE — BOUSSIGNIES —
                MONTIGNIES ST CHRISTOPHE

"D" GROUP. to   NO MOVE

Divisional Headquarters will close at COUSOLRE at 0900 and open at THUIN on arrival.

ACKNOWLEDGE.

                                        Lieut-Colonel,
                                    General Staff, 3rd. Division.

22/11/18

Distribution :-   A.D.M.S.
                   C.R.E.
                   ~~Camp Commandant.~~
                   D.A.D.O.S.
                   A.D.V.S.
                   3rd. M.T. Coy.
                   ~~Signals.~~
                   File.
                   War Diary.

3rd. Division G.S. 2023

The following moves will take place on 25th Nov

"A" GROUP. to NALINES - SOMZEE - GOURDINNE - THYLE CHATEAU

"B" GROUP. to BERZEE - COUR-SUR-HEURE - MARBAIX

"C" GROUP. to GOZEE - THUIN

"D" GROUP. to FONTAINE - VALMONT - HANTES - WIHERIES - SOLRE-SUR-SAMBRE - LA BUISSIERE

Divisional Headquarters will close at THUIN at 0900 and open at LOVERVAL on arrival.

ACKNOWLEDGE.

24/11/18

Lieut-Colonel,
General Staff, 3rd. Division.

Distribution :-   A.D.M.S.
C.R.E.
Camp Commandant.
D.A.D.O.S.
A.D.V.S.
3rd. M.T. Coy.
Signals.
File.
War Diary.

3rd. Division Operation Order No. 284.

1. The Division will march to-morrow 25th Novr in accordance with the following March Table.

Reference Sheet. 1/100,000

MARCH TABLE.

Unit.	Starting Point.	Hour of start.	Route.	Destination.	Instructions.
"A" GROUP.	Cross Roads Road junction 2.D.85.09	10.40	GOZEE HAM SUR HEURE COUR SUR HEURE BERZEE THYLE CHATEAU	NALINES SOMZEE GOURDINNE THYLE CHATEAU	Bde HQ – NALINES Route to NALINES Via HAM SUR HEURE and CLAQUEDENT
"B" GROUP.	Cross Roads Road junction 2.D.24.10	10.30	THUIN GOZEE HAM SUR HEURE COUR SUR HEURE	BERZEE COUR SUR HEURE MARBAIX	Bde HQ – BERZEE
"C" GROUP.	Road junction 3.C.55.33	09.25	LEERS ET FOSTEAU THUIN	GOZEE THUIN	Bde HQ – THUIN
	No restrictions as to route or time.			FONTAINE VALMONT HANTES WIHERIES SOLRE SUR SAMBRE LA BUISSIERE	RA HQ – MERBES le CHATEAU
"D" GROUP.	as for A. Group	10.00	GOZEE MARCINELLE		
Divnl. H.Q.				LOVERVAL	

2. Divisional Headquarters will close at THUIN at 09.00 and open at LOVERVAL on arrival.
3. ACKNOWLEDGE.

Distribution:— G.O.C., "Q", C.R.A., Div. Train., A.P.M.,
8th. Inf. Bde. VI Corps "G"
9th. Inf. Bde. VI Corps "Q"
76th. Inf. Bde. Camp Commdt.
3rd. Div. Signals.

24/11/18
Issued at 0700

Lieut-Colonel,
General Staff, 3rd. Division

"A" Form.
MESSAGES AND SIGNALS.

Army Form C. 2121.
(In pads of 100.)

TO: 8 7/6 By Bdes Div Train CRH
6 Corps E.R. Camp Comdt Granades

Sender's Number: GB 149
Day of Month: 20th
AAA

Cancel Limbers orders
abandon rendezvous hour of
start in 3rd Div Operation
Order No 184 and substitute "Cold"
as A Group 1140 hours and
B Group 1130 hours, C Group 1035
hours and Div HQ 1100 hours and
attention necessary on account of
late arrival of rations aaa
acknowledge aaa addsd all
recipients of OO 284 less CRA

From: 3rd Div
Place:
Time: 1510

(Z)

3rd. Division Operation Order No. 285

1. The Division will march to-morrow Nov. 26TH in accordance with the following March Table.

Reference Sheet. 1/100,000

MARCH TABLE.

Unit.	Starting Point.	Hour of start.	Route.	Destination.	Instructions.
"A" GROUP.	Cross Roads 3 G 0075	1000	GERPINNES FROMIÉE - BIESME	METTET PONTAURY BIESME	Groups will march independently. Train Corps in rear of each group
"B" GROUP.	Cross Roads 3 E 9242	1000	SOMZEE TARCIENNE GERPINNES	GOUGNIES VILLERS POTERIE ACOZ GERPINNES	
"C" GROUP.	Road Junction 2 E 2500	1000	HAM SUR HEURE COUR SUR HEURE THY-LE-CHATEAU GOURDINNE	TARCIENNE SOMZEE NALINES } Route to NALINES VIA CLAQUEDENT	
"D" GROUP.	Road Junction 3 D 0983	1000	THUIN - GOZEE HAM SUR HEURE	GOURDINNE THY. LE. CHATEAU BERZEÉ COUR SUR HEURE MARBAIX	

2. Divisional Headquarters will remain at LOVERVAL and open at on arrival.
3. ACKNOWLEDGE.

Distribution:- G.O.C., "Q", C.R.A., Div. Train, A.P.M.,
8th. Inf. Bde.   VI Corps "G".
9th. Inf. Bde.   VI Corps "Q".
76th. Inf. Bde.   Camp Comdt.
                    3rd Div Signals

25/11/18

Issued at 0800

for Lieut-Colonel,
General Staff, 3rd. Division

SECRET.   3rd Division G.2002/5.

8th Inf.Bde.   A.D.M.S.
9th Inf.Bde.   3rd Div."Q".
76th Inf.Bde.   3rd Div.Signals.
C.R.A.   A.P.M.
C.R.E.   3rd Div.Train.
20th K.R.R.C.   Mob.Vet.Section.
Camp Commdt.   D.M.G.C.
D.A.D.O.S.   3rd Div.M.T.Coy.

ADVANCE TO THE RHINE.

1. The Allied Forces are to cross the German frontier in accordance with the terms of the Armistice, to occupy the German territories West of the RHINE, and to establish bridgeheads on the right bank of that river at MAYENCE, COBLENZ and COLOGNE.

2. (a) British troops are to hold the COLOGNE bridgehead. The American Army will be holding the territory on our right and the Belgian Army the territory on our left.

   (b) The British Sector of German territory is to be occupied by the Second Army consisting of four Corps (11 Divisions) and one British Cavalry Division.
   The Second Army will be composed as follows :-

   II Corps   ...   9, 29, N.Z. Divisions.
   VI Corps   ...   Guards, 2, 3, Divisions.
   IX Corps   ...   1, 6, 62 Divisions.
   Cdn.Corps.   ...   1, 2, Cdn.Divisions.
   1st Cavalry Divn.

   (c) The Sector between the German frontier and the line AVESNES - MAUBEUGE - CHARLEROI - BRUSSELS is to be occupied by the Fourth Army consisting of three Corps (14 Divisions) and Cavalry Corps (less one Cavalry Division).

3. The 62nd Division will complete its march as already ordered on 25th November, and on the 26th and 27th November will (less attached troops) sideslip into the IX Corps area, with its head at HAID (inclusive) and tail at DINANT (exclusive) along the Northern route of the IX Corps.

4. The 3rd Division will become the leading Division of the VI Corps on the Southern road. The 3rd Division will therefore continue its march on 26th November, so that its head reaches METTET. The 3rd Division (less Divisional Headquarters) will halt on 27th November.
   Divisional Headquarters will move to METTET on 27th November.

5. The advance of the VI and IX Corps is to be resumed on 28th November.

6. The VI Corps has been ordered to arrange its march as follows :-

   (a) The march will be in two columns within the boundaries already allotted to the VI Corps, as far as the line GRANDMENIL - HARRE. (See Map "B" issued with G.2002 dated 15th November and attached Map "C".)

   (b) After leaving above line the VI Corps is to march with its right column via BELLE HAIE - REGNE - SALMCHATEAU to VIELSALM, passing through IX Corps area during this part of the march, and its left column via WERBOMONT - BASSE BODEUX to TROIS PONTS.

(c) The leading troops of the VI Corps are to reach the line VIELSALM - TROIS PONTS by evening 4th December, unless the weather and state of the roads render this impossible without inflicting undue hardship and discomfort on the troops.

(d) All orders for the further march eastwards from VIELSALM and TROIS PONTS are to be issued to the VI Corps by Second Army, but the VI Corps is to be ready to resume the advance on 5th December.

7. The IX Corps is to continue its march as far as LAROCHE which place its leading troops are to reach by evening 4th December.
On reaching LAROCHE, the IX Corps is to halt until the whole of the VI Corps has crossed the German frontier.

8. (a) The Cavalry attached to the Second Army (1st Cavalry Division) is to cross the German frontier on 1st December, and is to take over the whole of the new front of the Second Army.
The 2nd Cavalry Division is not now required to cross the German frontier on 1st December.

(b) The 2nd Cavalry Division has been ordered, during the 1st December to close to its right, so that by the evening of that day it may be South and clear of the LAROCHE - SALMCHATEAU - VIELSALM - POTEAU Road.

(c) The 2nd Cavalry Division is to occupy billets in the area bounded on the North by the above road (leaving clear all billets required by the VI Corps), on the east by the German frontier, and on the South by the Fourth Army Southern Boundary.

9. (a) The following troops at present attached to the 62nd Division will be transferred to the 3rd Division from midnight 25th/26th November when these units will come under the orders of the G.O.C.76th Infantry Brigade.

    2 Troops Australian Horse   ) Location will
    1 Coy. 4th Cyclist Battalion) be notified.

(b) 132 A.T.Company, R.E. will be transferred to the 3rd Division from midnight 27th/28th November and will remain as permanent maintenance gang at the bridges over the MEUSE under the orders of the C.R.E.
When the 3rd Division has crossed the MEUSE this unit will be transferred to the VI Corps Heavy Artillery.

(c) C.C.Cable Section and one Section 174th Tunnelling Company will be transferred from 62nd to 3rd Division from midnight 27th/28th November.

10. The 3rd Division will be re-grouped as follows :-

"A" Group.

Commander -

Brig.Genl.F.E.METCALFE,
C.M.G., D.S.O.

{ 2 Troops Australian Horse.
{ 1 Coy.4th Cyclist Battalion.
{ 76th Inf.Bde.
{ 1 Brigade, R.F.A. *
{ 529th Field Coy. R.E.
{ 20th K.R.R.C.(Pioneer Battalion).
{ 7th Field Ambulance.
{ No.2 Coy. Divisional Train.
{ One Section,174th Tunnelling Coy.

/ "B" Group.

* To be selected by C.R.A.

"B" Group.	(9th Inf.Bde.
	(56th Field Company, R.E.
Commander -	(3rd Battalion, Machine Gun Corps.
	(142 Field Ambulance.
Brig.Genl.H.C.POTTER,	(No.4 Coy. Divisional Train.
C.M.G., D.S.O.	

"C" Group.	(8th Inf.Bde.
	(438th Field Coy. R.E.
Commander -	(8th Field Ambulance.
	(No.3 Coy. Divisional Train.
Brig.Gen. B.D.FISHER, D.S.O.	
Brig.Genl.C.YATMAN, C.M.G., D.S.O. (Temporarily Commanding)	

"D" Group.	(23rd Brigade R.F.A.	)Less Brigade
	(40th Brigade R.F.A.	)attached "A"
	(42nd Brigade R.F.A.	) Group.
Commander -	(D.A.C.	
	(No.XI Mobile Vet. Section.	
Brig.Genl.J.S.OLLIVANT, C.M.G., D.S.O., R.A.	(No.1 Coy. Divisional Train.	

Divisional H.Q.Group.	(Divisional H.Q.Transport.
	(H.Q.Section, Div.Signal Coy.
	(C.C. Cable Section.

11. ACKNOWLEDGE.

[signature]

Lieut.Colonel.
General Staff, 3rd Division.

25th November 1918.

* Maps issued to units starred.

3rd. Division Operation Order No. 28.

1. The Division will march to-morrow 28th in accordance with the following March Table.

Reference Sheet. 1/100,000

MARCH TABLE.

Unit.	Starting Point.	Hour of start.	Route.	Destination.	Instructions.
"A" GROUP	Cross Roads 3 I 35.75	1000	BIOUL	ANNEVOIE ROUILLON	Train Companies will march in rear of their groups
"B" GROUP	Railway Level Crossing 2 H 00.20	0935	BIOUL River Junction 2 J 6702 WARNANT	WARNANT ANHEE	
			BIESME SERY PONTAURY	ST GERARD	
			BIESME - SERY METTET-Cross Roads 3 I 35 75	BIOUL	
"C" GROUP	Cross Roads 3 G 20.65	1000	HANZINNE HANZINELLE ORET STATION Cross Roads 3 H 95 67	GRAUX FURNAUX DENEE	
	Sp. to be fixed by C.R.A. not to enter SOMZEE before 10.45		SOMZEE GERPINNES BIESME	BIESME METTET SERY PONTBURY	
"D" GROUP	Horse- Cross Roads ½ mile NE of first L in LOVERVAL	1000	VILLERS POTERIE BOUVIGNES BIESME METTET		Long halt for feeding will be made immediately after clearing METTET

2. Divisional Headquarters will close at LOVERVAL at 0900 and open at BIOUL on arrival.
3. ACKNOWLEDGE.

Distribution:- G.O.C., "Q", C.R.A., Div. Train., A.P.M.,
8th. Inf. Bde.   VI Corps "G".
9th. Inf. Bde.   VI Corps "Q".
76th. Inf. Bde.   Camp Commdt.
                  3rd. Div. Signals.

Lieut-Colonel,
General Staff, 3rd. Division.

27/11/18

Issued at 1200 hrs

WN

SECRET.

Copy No. 19

3rd DIVISION OPERATION ORDER NO. 287.

27th November 1918.

Reference NAMUR and MARCHE Sheets
1/100,000.

1. The Division will march in accordance with the attached March Table on the 29th November.

   The order of march will be as follows :-

   (i)   "A" Group.)   Less 1st Line Transport.
         "B" Group.)   (Only vehicles laid down in G.7359
         "C" Group.)   will accompany units).

   (ii)   "A" Group.)
          "B" Group.)   1st Line Transport.
          "C" Group.)

   (iii)   "A" Group.   Train Company.
           "B" Group.   do.
           "C" Group.   do.

   (iv)   "D" Group.

2. For the march on the 29th November the 1st Line Transport of Groups will be under the orders of the O.C. Divisional Train who will issue orders direct to Brigade Transport Officers as regards Starting Points and hour of start. Order of march will be in accordance with para 1.

3. As soon as the 1st Line Transport of Groups has crossed the bridge at YVOIR the whole of the Train (Less 1 Company with D.A.) will close up with its head on the bridge and will cross the MEUSE in rear of the 1st Line Transport, in order of groups.

4. (a) Each Infantry Brigade will leave an infantry party of 2 Officers and 50 other ranks in YVOIR to report to the O.C. Divisional Train - rendezvous for these parties - east end of YVOIR Bridge.
   As soon as these parties are no longer required O.C. Divisional Train will order them to proceed on their march and rejoin their units.

/(b)

(2)

    (b)   Each Group will hand over all spare horses to the O.C. of their affiliated Train Company before commencing the march on the 29th November.

5.   On all marches in future the greatcoat will be carried on the man.

6.   The C.R.A. will detail 12 pairs of horses (with drivers and harness) to report at Divisional H.Q. BIOUL on the afternoon of November 28th, these will be handed over to the O.C. Divisional Train for rations and accommodation and will be used by him on hill East of the YVOIR on November 29th.

7.   A Staff Officer will be on the hill just east of YVOIR with orders to dump excess baggage on overloaded wagons.

8.   Divisional Headquarters will remain at BIOUL on Nov. 29th.

9.   ACKNOWLEDGE.

                          Major
                        for Lieut. Colonel,
                General Staff, 3rd Division.

Issued at 20.30 hours.

Copies to :-

1.	G.O.C.	11.	A.P.M.
2.	8th Inf.Bde.	12.	3rd Div.M.T.Coy.
3.	9th Inf.Bde.	13.	VI Corps "G".
4.	76th Inf.Bde.	14.	VI Corps "Q".
5.	C.R.A.	15.	Guards Division.
6.	C.R.E.	16.	D.A.D.O.S.
7.	"Q".	17.	D.A.D.V.S.
8.	A.D.M.S.	18.	Camp Commdt.
9.	3rd Div.Signals.	19.	War Diary.
10.	3rd Div.Train.	20.	War Diary.
		21 - 24	File.

MARCH TABLE TO ACCOMPANY 3rd DIVISION OPERATION ORDER NO. 287.

Unit.	Starting Point.	Hour of start.	Route.	Destination.	Instructions
"A" Group. (Less 1st Line Transport).	Bridge 3.K.50.85.	09.00	EVREHAILLES.	DORINNE.	
"B" Group. (Less 1st Line Transport).	Road Junction 2.J.67.02.	09.15	Cross Roads 2.K.21.18. Western Bank of MEUSE to Bridge at 3.K.50.85. EVREHAILLES.	} Areas will be notified by "Q".	
"C" Group. (Less 1st Line Transport).	Cross Roads 3.J.03.91.	09.00	BIOUL. Cross Roads 2.K.21.18. Western Bank of MEUSE to Bridge at 3.K.50.85. EVREHAILLES.	BIOUL	
"D" Group.	Cross Roads 3.I.33.75.	11.15	BIOUL Road Junction 2.J.67.02.	ANNEVOIE ROUILLON. WARNANT ACHEE	Road ROUILLON — Bridge at 3.K.50.85 is not to be used.

3rd. Division Operation Order No. 288

Reference Sheet. 1/100,000

1. The Division will march tomorrow Nov. 30th in accordance with the following March Table.

MARCH TABLE.

Unit.	Starting Point.	Hour of start.	Route.	Destination.	Instructions.
"A" GROUP.	To be clear of present area by 0930 hours		Any	ACHET or CINEY NOIRIVILLE PESSOUX	3rd Div "Q" will notify whether ACHET or CINEY is allotted
"B" GROUP.	SPONTIN	0900	Any	NATOYE BRAIBANT SOVET	1st Line Transport and Train Companies will march in rear of their Group
"C" GROUP.	EVREHAILLES	0900	Any	SPONTIN DORINNE	
"D" GROUP.	Bridge at YVOIR	1130	Any	PURNODE EVREHAILLES YVOIR GODINNE	
Divl HQ Motor transport and Signal Section	2 J 66 02	0800	ANNEVOIE ROUILLON Bridge at YVOIR	CHATEAU DE FONTAIN at 0900 and open at sous EMPTINNE on arrival.	

2. Divisional Headquarters will close at BIOUL at 0900 and open at sous EMPTINNE on arrival.
3. ACKNOWLEDGE.

Distribution:- G.O.C., "Q", C.R.A., Div. Train., A.P.M.,
8th. Inf. Bde.   VI Corps "G",
9th. Inf. Bde.   VI Corps "Q".
76th. Inf. Bde.   Camp Cdt
                  3rd Div. Signals

29/11/18

Issued at 14h30

[signature] Lieut-Colonel,
General Staff, 3rd. Division.

SECRET.

Copy No. 20

3rd. DIVISION OPERATION ORDER NO. 281.

10th November 1918.

Reference Sheets 51 & 52. 1/40,000
NAMUR and VALENCIENNES Sheets 1/100,000

1. (a) The enemy is reported to be retiring on the Third Army front.

   (i) Report timed 10.00 hours on 10th November states Cavalry patrol fired on by M.G. fire from bank of stream in M.21.a. OSTERGNIES and COLLERET reported clear of the enemy.

   (ii) Report timed 13.00 hours 10th November states enemy is holding a line of rifle pits in R.5.b. - Sunken Road L.35.b. & d. - L.29.c. - L.28.b. - L.22.c. & a. opposite the VI and XVII Corps fronts.

   (iii) Cavalry report timed 15.15 hours on 10th November, states Right Regiment reached line of LA THURE River. Centre Regiment reports FORT DE BOUSSOIS (L.27.d.) and TOWER in L.29.a. are held by enemy with machine guns. Left Regiment has been withdrawn.

   (b) The line at present held by us on the front of the Third Army is as follows :-

   QUIEVELON (inclusive) - East of BOUSSOIS - East of ELESMES and East of BETTIGNIES.

2. The direction of further advance of the Third Army is as follows :-

   Southern Boundary. FLOURSIES (exclusive) - BEAUMONT (exclusive) MARCHIENNE au PONT Road (exclusive).

   Northern Boundary. BAVAI - BINCHE Road (inclusive)

3. (a) The task of keeping touch with the enemy on the whole front of the Third Army is to be taken over by an Army Advanced Guard to be furnished by the VI Corps.

   (b) The 4th Cavalry Brigade has been placed under the orders of the VI Corps and has been ordered to maintain touch with the enemy on the whole Army front in the direction of and towards the general line THUIN - BINCHE.
   G.O.C. 4th Cavalry Brigade has resumed command of all Corps Cavalry Regiments including the Northumberland Hussars.

   (c) The Infantry of the advanced guard is to advance in the general direction MAUBEUGE - CHARLEROI, in support of the cavalry.

4. As soon as the VI Corps assumes responsibility for the Army Advanced Guard, Corps have been ordered to withdraw any advanced troops East of the AVESNES - MONS Road, except

troops left for billetting purposes.

Corps will however, still be responsible for the defence of the AVESNES - MONS Road within their own areas and have been ordered to thin out the front, and echelon troops back as far as is necessary to facilitate supply.

5. As soon as the 4th Cavalry Brigade is well clear of the line at present held by the Infantry, the leading Infantry Brigade Group of 3rd Division with an Artillery Brigade is to be pushed through the present front of the VI Corps in support of the 4th Cavalry Brigade.

The 3rd Division and 4th Cavalry Brigade will then become the Advanced Guard under the orders of the G.O.C. 3rd Division, who will assume command of the Advanced Guard at 16.00 hours on 11th November.

6. (a) The 76th Infantry Brigade Group with 40th Brigade R.F.A. and an additional Field Co. R.E. attached, will form the vanguard under the orders of G.O.C. 76th Infantry Brigade and will advance along the valley of the SAMBRE in close support of the 4th Cavalry Brigade.

G.O.C. 76th Infantry Brigade will keep in close touch with G.O.C. 4th Cavalry Brigade, who is establishing his H.Q. at BOUSSOIS on 11th November.

(b) The 8th and 9th Infantry Brigade Groups, one M.G. Co. and the remainder of 3rd Divisional Artillery will form the main guard of the Advanced Guard, and will be moved forward as circumstances permit.

(c) The 63rd Brigade R.G.A. (less 6" How. Batteries) will come under the orders of the G.O.C. 3rd Division. This Brigade will consist of two 60-pdr. Batteries.

7. The 62nd and Guards Divisions will be responsible for the protection of the present Main Line of Resistance on the front of the VI Corps, but as the leading Brigade of the 3rd Division passes through the troops on outpost will be withdrawn.

8. Orders for moves on the 11th November have already been issued to all concerned in G.A. 11 and G.A. 14.

9. (i) The 4th Cavalry Brigade is securing on the 11th November with its main bodies the line of the road BEAUMONT - ROUVEROY, with patrols pushed forward in advance to keep contact with the enemy.

(ii) The 76th Infantry Brigade Group will be prepared to advance on the morning of the 12th November in support of the 4th Cavalry Brigade moving along the valley of the SAMBRE on the North Bank.

(iii) The 76th Infantry Brigade will arrange for its own local protection, but will NOT be required to take over the outpost line from the 4th Cavalry Brigade

/as

as that Brigade will find the outpost line each night.

- (iv) C.R.E. 3rd. Division will arrange for the construction of bridges over the SAMBRE so that troops can be passed from the North to the South Bank if required.

- (v) G.O.C. 76th Infantry Brigade will arrange for the protection of these bridges until that duty can be taken over by the main guard of the Advanced Guard.

10. The 66th Division with Cavalry attached is carrying out the Advanced Guard duties on the Fourth Army front, with H.Q. at road junction South of the first R. in R. de La CROISETTE - 2 miles N.W. of AVESNES.

11. Divisional Headquarters will close at FRASNOY and open at MAUBEUGE at 12.00 hours on 11th November.

12. ACKNOWLEDGE.

Lieut-Colonel,
General Staff, 3rd. Division.

Issued at 20.30 hours

Copies to
1. G.O.C.
2. 8th Inf. Brigade.
3. 9th Inf. Brigade.
4. 76th Inf. Brigade.
5. C.R.A.
6. D.M.G.C.
7. C.R.E.
8. 20th K.R.R.C.
9. A.D.M.S.
10. 3rd Division "Q".
11. 3rd Div. Signals.
12. A.P.M.
13. 3rd Div. Train.
14. Guards Division.
15. 2nd Division.
16. 62nd Division.
17. 66th Division.
18. VIth Corps.
19. 4th Cavalry Brigade.
20. War Diary.
21. "   "
22. File.
23. File.

"A" Form
MESSAGES AND SIGNALS.

Army Form C. 2121
(In pads of 100.)

No. of Message............

Prefix............Code............m. | Words | Charge. | This message is on a/c of : | Recd. at......m.
Office of Origin and Service Instructions | Sent | | ....Service. | Date............
.... | At ....m. | | | From ....
.... | To | | .... |
C49 | By .... | (Signature of "Franking Officer") | By ....

TO { Div Artk.

| Sender's Number. | Day of Month. | In reply to Number. | AAA |
| GC2. | 10 | | |

VI Corps. wire timed 0230 hrs reads Summary of war news for distribution to troops aaa German wireless aaa German Emperor has abdicated Crown Prince renounces throne aaa Majority Socialist EBERT to be Chancellor when abdication complete and constituent assembly to be elected to decide future government and boundary of Germany aaa Revolution has broken out in BERLIN and Council of workers and soldiers in charge of city under leadership of social democrats aaa order maintained and few casualties aaa New Government alleged to have support of Officer delegates from Guards Battn aaa Similar movement reported from other parts of Germany aaa Reuters

From
Place
Time

The above may be forwarded as now corrected. (Z)

....
Censor. Signature of Addressor or person authorised to telegraph in his name
* This line should be erased if not required.

Order No. 1625 Wt. W3253/ P 511 27/2 H. & K., Ltd. (E. 2634).

"A" Form
MESSAGES AND SIGNALS.

Army Form C. 2121
(In pads of 100.)

No. of Message............

Prefix.........Code..........m.	Words	Charge.	This message is on a/c of :	Recd. at......m.
Office of Origin and Service Instructions	Sent		...................Service.	Date............
	At ....m.			From ....
(50)	To			
	By		(Signature of "Franking Officer")	By........

TO {

Sender's Number.   Day of Month.   In reply to Number.   **A A A**

Revolution in MUNICH Wittelsbach dynasty deposed BAVARIA to be Socialist republic Serious disturbance reported HANOVER Serious disturbance reported official telegram from Berlin announces early alleviation food shortage owing to peace and raising of blockade

From ....
Place ....
Time ....

The above may be forwarded as now corrected.   (Z) ....

Censor.   Signature of Addressor or person authorised to telegraph in his name
* This line should be erased if not required.

Order No. 1625   Wt. W3253/   P 511.   27/2.   H. & K., Ltd. (**E. 2634**).

MESSAGES AND SIGNALS. Army Form C. 2121.
(In pads of 100.)

Prefix	Code	Words	Charge			
Office of Origin and Service Instructions.		Sent At ... m. To ... By ...	This message is on a/c of: (5) (Signature of "Franking Officer.")	Recd. at ... m. Date ... From ... By ...

TO:
8 Bde	CRA	Div C	y Cl
9 Bde	CRE	20th M.G.	
76 Bde	Adms	Signs	

Sender's Number	Day of Month	In reply to Number	AAA
GC 29	11		

All moves for today cancelled all Divisional will remain in present location aaa acknowledge

From: 3rd Div
Place:
Time: 0910

(Z) for G Lively
Signature of Addressor or person authorised to telegraph in his name

*This line, except AAA, should be erased if not required.
Wt. W 3253/P511. 500,000 Pads. 1/18. B. & S. Ltd. (E2389.)

MESSAGES AND SIGNALS.

Army Form C. 2121.
(In pads of 100.)

TO	8 Bde	Divy C	CRE	Signals
	9 Bde	KKC	Q	
	7 Bde	BRA	Adms	

Sender's Number.	Day of Month.	In reply to Number.	AAA
GC 30	11		

Corps wire aaa Hostilities will cease at 1100 hrs today 11th Nov aaa troops will stand fast on line reached at that hour which will be reported by wire to Corps HQ aaa Defensive precautions will be maintained aaa There is to be no intercourse of any description with the enemy aaa No Germans are to be allowed to enter our lines any doing so will be taken prisoners aaa Bde will carry out its moves to BOUSSOIS

From 2nd OW
Place
Time 0756

G Kingsley Capt

DEMOBILIZATION AND RECONSTRUCTION.

A Lecture delivered at G.H.Q., on 12-10-1918.
by
MAJOR D. BORDEN-TURNER.

The object of this lecture is the communication of the principles upon which the Government has decided to carry out demobilization.

Lest the announcement of this subject should cause some alarm, I hasten to assure you that this lecture is not to be taken as any indication that the end is in sight. As a matter of fact, the Government decided long ago that it was not going to be caught napping by peace as it was found unprepared for war. It is no less than two years since the plans for Demobilization were put in hand, and these have been worked at ever since - six months ago the pamphlet which I have in my hand, and which forms the basis of what I say, was issued by the War Office as a guide to lecturers on the subject - for the authorities desired and do desire to take the soldier into their confidence in regard to these plans; feeling sure that if the troops are informed of these plans and made acquainted with the reasons for taking certain measures, they will give their willing co-operation and make every effort of their own free will to ensure the smooth and rapid working of the system to be followed.

It may as well be stated, at the very beginning, in order to remove some grave fears that are widely entertained, that the men who stayed at home, either of choice or necessity, either in military service or engaged in war production, are not going to be given priority in the matter of resettlement, simply because they are on the spot. The man in France will have an equal chance with the man at home in getting settled comfortably and happily into civil life.

In general, the principle on which the Government has decided to carry out Demobilization is "Demobilization by individuals in accordance with Trade requirements, and not by units in accordance with Military requirements," in other words, it is not primarily the convenience of the War Office that will be consulted, but the economic future of the individual soldier.

After former wars, men were disbanded according to military convenience with little regard to what was going to happen to them, with, in very many cases, the most distressing consequences. They were thrown on to the Labour Market without any consideration as to the ability of the Labour Market to absorb them. The nation is determined that, after this war, not only will the discharged soldier be given a fair chance, but he will be given every chance of satisfactory resettlement.

/Mr.

Mr. Roberts, the Minister of Labour, speaking in France the other day, said that he would rather keep men in the Army in France for an extended period than have them go home only to create a large army of unemployed.

I have said that the plan of demobilization is not designed to meet the convenience of the War Office. I do not wish to imply that the War Office is opposed to it - far from it. The War Office is well aware that, if, after conducting this war to a glorious conclusion, it succeeds in restoring to the country the men it has taken, in a happy and contented spirit, fit to reap individually the fruits of a victorious peace, it will add a golden spray to its laurel wreath and will build itself a monument more lasting than brass.

The release, then, of men from the army will be governed largely by the ability of industry to absorb them. And here a very pertinent question arises. "Will industry be able to absorb us all ?. And will the process be very slow ?" We know something about the slowness of leave allotments. Is there any hope of industry reviving quickly, or must we envisage the prospect of inflicting ourselves for an indefinite period on the long-suffering French. I shall refer in a moment to certain considerations which will delay demobilization. I have, however, the authority of the Minister of Labour for saying that there is evry prospect of a speedy and marked boom in industry which will continue for a number of years. The Labour Minister has been advised in this respect by a committee of expert economists, who have made a careful study of the main industries of the country, and have come to the conclusion, that there will be such a rise in the volume of trade soon after the cessation of hostilities, that not only will there be work for all the men in the country and the men in the armies, but that it will be possible to absorb also those of the women of the country, who have entered the field of industry under the abnormal conditions of the war, and who desire to continue in it.

It must not be supposed however, that we are all going home within ten days or a month; even if there were a Channel tunnel, and we could run trains through without stopping night and day, it would take months before the men and especially the material accumlated out here during these years could be taken home.

Demobilization will necessarily be a slow process and there are four considerations which will militate against any great rapidity in the operation :-

1. The transformation of factories, etc., from war to peace conditions. This will inevitably take time, but I do not want you to imagine that plans for this are being left till

/the

3. (54)

the necessity actually arises. It is all being arranged and thought out now, and I have excellent authority for saying that the process in most cases is not going to be nearly so slow as many people fear - but of course it is not going to be accomplished over the week end.

2. The removal from France to England of an immense quantity of material which has been borrowed from the industry of the country, and which will have to go back before the normal life of the country is resumed. There are many locomotives and hundreds of miles of railway truck which will have to be taken back before the necessary transport services of the country are restored.

3. There is a great scarcity of raw material. We have made havoc of the world's stocks of all kinds of raw material, and these raw materials must be secured before industry can get into full swing. The Government is engaged on the problem of seeking out all available sources of supply and in securing control of them, but this is undoubtedly one of the most serious problems which has to be met.

4. The lack of transport. This will be acute at first, but will improve as the months pass. It is transport for goods that will be the difficulty; there will be enough transport to take us home as fast as the country is ready to receive us.

Subject to these considerations the process of demobilization will be carried through as quickly as possible. It is all to the interest of the Government to have no delay for it will be costing the Government money to keep us in France, and the country will be losing our productive effort.

The Government too is quite alive to the fact that the Germans have a very much easier task than we have to get their troops demobilized: in fact they may very likely all be in their own country when that moment arrives, and we are not anxious in the very least to let the Germans have any sort of start in restoring the normal industrial life.

In what order shall we go? This is the question that interests us all. This I can tell you for certain, that you will not/go in the order of the numbers inscribed in your A.B.64, so that those who are registered Group 1, 2, 3, 4, 5 may at once cease to cherish the belief that they are for home by the first or second boat. We shall go, as we can be spared, and as we are required, and no one can at the present moment forecast with/any accuracy what these requirements are going to be.

/The

The first men to be released from their Units, and the release will probably take effect as soon as peace is in sight and before general demobilization actually commences will be :-

1. Those who are required in their military or civil capacity for the actual work of demobilization. It is quite clear that a machine must be created and that men will be required to run it.

2. Regular soldiers with more than two years unexpired colour service to form the nucleus of a new regular army. Part of this new army will be required to take as soon as possible the places of the units serving in India and other places who must themselves be released. It has not been decided what the size of the new army will be, but it will certainly not be smaller than the "contemptible little army" of 1914. Nor have the conditions of service been laid down, but it is quite certain they will be considerably more attractive than those which obtained in the old army. The army has come into its own during this war and the status of the soldier will be a very different thing in future, not only as regards pay, but as regards position in the social scale. Every household in the land knows now what the soldier is - his calling has gained the respect and honour to which it was always entitled but which he did not always receive.

I can think of no more attractive career for a man whose future is not clearly laid out for him, than service in the new regular army.

3. Those known as "pivotal" men - that is, the key men in the various trades and industries - the men without whom the rest of the workers cannot be employed.

These three classes being disposed of, there remains the question of the way in which priority will be applied to the rest of us.

There will be two categories of priority :-

(a) of Industries.

(b) of Individuals.

(a) No priority list of Industries has been made yet, nor is it possible to make one at present. Even when such a list is drawn up it will not remained fixed but will change according to the industrial situation. The trade that is

/at

the head of the list one day may be sixth or seventh a few days later. As a matter of fact the whole of the industry hangs together and all trades must go forward at the same time.

(b) Priority will be accorded to individuals for these three reasons :-

    (1) For long service. 10% of those who go from France will be chosen on account of long service and for no other reason.

    (2) For assured employment. Immediately hostilities have ceased, or possibly before, every man in the Army will be required to fill up a form showing, amongst other things, whether he has a promise of re-employment and from whom, or where he would like to be employed.

In the former case the statements will be verified; in the latter case every endeavour will be made to secure employment, and, as soon as employment is guaranteed to any man, a release slip will be made out in his favour and forwarded to his Officer Commanding. This will secure him priority.

    (3) Priority will also be given to married men other things being equal.

When the actual work of Demobilizing the B.E.F. commences, the Minister of Labour, who has been charged by the Government with the carrying out of the arrangements, will have before him two returns on which he will base his demands.

    (1) A return showing the total numbers of men in the B.E.F. according (a) to their industrial groups, and (b) according to the districts of Great Britain and Ireland to which they wish to go.

    (2) A return from the employment exchanges throughout the country showing the estimated demand for labour in each district in different trades.

We will suppose that at the outset the maximum rate of dispersal from France will be 15,000 men per diem, and that of this total, the Liverpool district can absorb 12%, i.e. 1,250 men each day.

G.H.Q. will therefore receive from the War Office a daily allotment of 1,250 men for this district, and at the same time a priority list of industrial groups as determined by the Ministry of Labour.

We will suppose that the first three groups are those

/of

of Butchers, Bakers and Candlestick Makers in that order.

Vacancies for dispersal in the Liverpool district are sub-allotted down the chain of formations from G.H.Q. downwards to units, until the O.C. 1st Rutlands receives an allotment of 20 men, and at the same time is told the priority list - Butchers, Bakers and Candlestick Makers.

He turns up his roll of men going to the Liverpool district and is guided by four considerations in choosing the men from the list to make that day's draft.

1. He chooses first 10%.i.e. the two men with the longest service irrespective of their trades or anything else.

2. He next chooses every man for whom he has a release slip, again irrespective of their trades. Let us suppose there are 13 of these. Five vacancies are left.

3. He then calls for the Butchers as Butcher stands first on Priority list. Three butchers are found and are put down for the draft.

    He proceeds to call for the Bakers. There happen to be none.
    He then looks up the Candlestick Makers and finds there are four.
    He has only two places and so

4. He selects the married men; there are three of those and he chooses the two with the longest military service.

Simultaneously with the return home of individuals in this way, there will go on the process of returning units. Generally speaking, a unit will not leave the country until it has been reduced to what is called cadre strength, i.e., that strength which is necessary for the care of its arms, equipment and stores. Most units of the regular army, however, will go home early, and will take with them all men with two years unexpired colour service to run, whether they are "old regulars" or men who have enlisted on regular attestations out here.

Let me now trace the history of the man from the time he leaves his unit in France. He will proceed by rail or motor lorry or march route through a series of camps on the direct line towards the port of embarkation, where he will be put into a draft proceeding direct to the dispersal station in Great Britain nearest to his own home. There he will hand in his arms and equipment and he will receive

    (1) A Railway warrant to his destination.

    (2) The War Gratuity.

(3) An allowance for civilian clothes.

(4) A certificate entitling him to draw pay and allowances including separation allowance for 28 days, in other words, 28 days leave.

(5) An Unemployment Donation Policy valid for a year.

During his four weeks leave he will be expected to get himslef re-settled in civil life. If he has an appointment waiting for him so much the better, but if not he will have the assistance of the local employment exchange. In case of any difficulty either in getting back to his old employment or in finding a new job, he can appeal to the Local Advisory Committee of his district. These committees made up of an equal number of employers and work-people have been set up all over the country by the Ministry of Labour and make it their business to see that the discharged soldier is satisfactorily re-settled. They have already dealt with large numbers of discharged men and experience has shown that not only can employers be relied upon to keep loyally the promises of re-employment given to their men but that these committees are willing to take an infinity of trouble in finding suitable situations for the discharged soldier. In one case no less than 43 positions were found for one man. The soldier therefore can be sure that on his release from the army, if he is in need of advice or assistance he may go, not to an Official body hampered by regulations, but to a tribunal of his fellow citizens who are prepared to give not only sympathy but active and generous help

And now gentlemen I have told you what the country is prepared to do for you. May I say a word or two about what you can do for the country.

1. In the first place, it is one thing for the Government to get us back to work in civil life, it will be another and entirely different thing to insure that we shall all be able to pick up our work again. Many of us are going to find it extraordinary difficult to do so – we have so completely lost touch with the old life that it will seem exceedingly hard and possibly very irksome to resume it. Few out here are doing the same sort of work they were doing at home and whatever their work was, they have lost the knack of it to a greater or lesser degree. The army has taught us many things but has not necessarily made us any better at our own job. This is a loss not to ourselves only but to the whole nation. More than ever after the war the country will need efficient men. There is going to be a great economic struggle after this war with our

/present.

present enemies, and an industrial race - a friendly one no doubt, but a contest all the same, with our allies, and the firing of the last gun will be the signal for the start. We should be getting ready to get off the mark. Every hour of study devoted towards his future career that a man can put in before he goes home is going to help him, and not only him, but the whole country.

2. In the second place; we have as an army a great reputation to sustain. You remember the message sent by Lord Kitchener to the troops who first came to France. The expectation of that message has been more than abundantly fulfilled. The patience and good temper, the kindly courtesy and cheerful self-sacrifice of the men in France have been beyond all praise. It is a great record and one which must not be spoiled. Some of us are going to be kept here till near the end, some of us to the very end, either because we are too useful, or useless, or through sheer bad luck, and we are going to sit and watch the others going home. It is going to be hard. With the removal of the tremendous discipline of battle self-discipline is going to be more difficult, but it is our duty so to carry ourselves that when we all do finally leave the country, our hospitable allies will have absolutely nothing to regret but our departure, so to comport ourselves that not one stain shall fall on that bright shield of honour which our men have carried so gallantry these four long years.

3. In the third place; the government has carried out in the last three years several great measures of reform. They are contemplating other measures designed to secure a better country in the future for us all; but all those measures will be unavailing unless the spirit of the nation keeps pace with its legislation. Were a social system perfect in every detail to come down to us from above it would be entirely futile unless it were quickened by the breath of life. It is to the men from France that the country is looking for the incoming of that spirit the spirit of good sense and good humour and courage and discipline and broadmindedness which has so marvellously chracterized the Army in France. Consider what a wonderful enlargement of mind has come to us during these four years. We have been taken up from our small circles, swept out of our narrow grooves and brought out to live in this country amongst people foreign in language, customs, and ideas. We have learned to appreciate the many great qualities of our allies but we have not learned to love our own country any the less. We have for the first time in our history come into an intimate contact with the men of the dominions, we have seen them and lived with them and

/we

we have fought with these magnificent men from Australia, Canada, Newfoundland, South Africa, New Zealand, and we have felt proud to belong to the same empire and the same race. We have realized for the first time what the British Empire means.

More than that we have come to know our own people as never before - men from every walk and class of life have been ground together in the mill of battle, stirred together in this great melting pot of war, from every corner of our islands from John O'Groats to Lands' End from Killarney to the Norfolk Broads, English, Scotch, Welsh, Irish, we have all got to know one another. Add to that enlargement of mind the sense of the value of discipline and of the imperious necessity of leadership which we have learned by the bitterest of all experience in the hardest of all schools. If we can but gather this all up together into one great spiritual dynamic, we shall send back to our country after the war a body of men capable of an intelligent and high minded participation in the affairs of the country such as no nation has ever dreamed of possessing.

At no time in our history has there ever been vouchsafed to the men of the nation such an opportunity as will come to each one of us to take a determining part in the working out of the destiny of our race. Whether we will it or no, that power will rest with us - whether we realise it or not - we shall go back with a tremendous influence to wield for evil or for good. "We are beginning", says a recent writer, "to wonder whether we cannot introduce into our civil ways of life some of the influences which have clothed the men on the field of battle with imperishable spiritual splendour." The country is looking anxiously eagerly, expectantly, for us to supply that spiritual momentum which is the country's greatest need. We are a great citizen army, so long as we live we shall be proud of the fact that we served as soldiers in this great war. Should we be any the less proud of the fact that we are citizens of an empire which, when this war is over, will be more than ever incontestably the greatest empire that the world has seen. The day will come when most of us will have to take off these uniforms we wear. Are we simply going to discard them, and with them, all that this khaki has brought us, all that this khaki has taught us, or are we going to carry back with us into the life of the country some of that imperishable spiritual splendour and show to the world a new thing in a citizenship that will be enlightened and heroic and inspired.

==*=*=*=*=*=*=*=

3rd DIVISION.

Disposition and Movement Report No.13.

12th November

Unit No.	UNIT.	Location of H.Q. at 1900 hrs.	Probable changes during 24 hours.
1.	3rd Divisional H.Q.	FRASNOY.	
2.	3rd Divisional Arty H.Q.	FRASNOY.	
3.	8th Infantry Brigade H.Q.	VERTAIN.	
4.	2nd The Royal Scots.	ROMERIES.	
5.	1st Royal Scots Fus.	ROMERIES.	
6.	7th K.S.L.I.	ROMERIES.	
7.	8th T.M.Battery.	ROMERIES.	
8.	8th Field Amblce.	ROMERIES.	
9.	No.3 Coy Train.	ROMERIES.	
10.	9th Infantry Brigade H.Q.	FRASNOY M.10.b.4.6.	
11.	1st Northumberland Fus.	M.10.d.6.6.	FRASNOY.
12.	4th Royal Fusiliers.	M.10.b.1.4.	FRASNOY.
13.	13th King's L'pool Regt.	N.14.d.4.5.	
14.	9th T.M.Battery.	FRASNOY M.10.b.4.6.	
15.	76th Infantry Brigade H.Q.	LA LONGUEVILLE I.36.a.6.6.	
16.	8th K.O.R.L.Regt.	I.36.b.2.2.	
17.	2nd Suffolk Regt.	I.36.a.8.6.	
18.	1st Gordon Hldrs.	I.30.d.6.6.	
19.	76th T.M.Battery.	I.36.d.7.6.	
20.	7th Field Amblce.	I.36.a.7.7.	
21.	No.2 Coy Train.	I.36.a.6.7.	
22.	C.R.E.	FRASNOY	
23.	56th Field Coy, R.E.	ORSINVAL.	
24.	438th " " "	GOMMEGNIES M.12.d.3.2.	
25.	529th " " "	LA LONGUEVILLE I.36.a.6.6.	
26.	3rd M.G.Battalion.	SARLOTON N.13.d.5.5.	
27.	"A" Company.	GOMMEGNIES.	
28.	"B" "	do.	
29.	"C" "	LA LONGUEVILLE I.36.a.8.6.	
30.	"D" "	VERTAIN.	
31.	20th K.R.R.C.(Pioneers).	RUESNES R.14.c.8.4.	
32.	Guards Division.	MAUBEUGE.	
33.	2nd Division.	VILLERS POL.	
34.	62nd Division.	Q.8.a.central.	

"A" Form.
MESSAGES AND SIGNALS.

Army Form C. 2121.
(In pads of 100.)

Prefix... Code... m. | Words | Charge | This message is on a/c of: | Recd. at ... m.
Office of Origin and Service Instructions. | Sent | | | Date
| At ... m. | (59) | Service | From
| To | | |
| By | (Signature of "Franking Officer.") | By

TO: 8th & 76 Inf Bde ... Army C

| Sender's Number | Day of Month | In reply to Number | AAA |
| G.66 | 13 | | |

The Companies of Machine
Gun Bn. at present
attached to 8th and
76th Inf Bdes will rejoin
this Bn at SARLOT 21d
today. Orders for moves
of these Companies
are being issued to
them direct by Army C.
Addressed 8 and 76 Inf Bde
rptd Army C

From: Inf Bn
Place:
Time: 0950

(Z) L. .... Capt

Prefix	Code	m.	Words	Charge	This message is on a/c of:		Recd. at	m.
Office of Origin and Service Instructions			Sent				Date	
			At	m.	Service		From	
(61)			To				By	
			By		(Signature of "Franking Officer.")			

TO	76 Bde	3rd Div Q	Comds
	D.A.G.C	Signal	VI Corps
	201 RRC	APM	GSI

Sender's Number	Day of Month	In reply to Number	AAA
GC 69	14		

Following moves will take place tomorrow Nov 15th aaa Hqs and 3 Corps MG Bn from GOMMEGNIES and SARLOTON to LA LONGUEVILLE aaa Route AMFROIPRET – BERMERIES – BAVAI – LA LONGUEVILLE aaa To be clear of present billets by 1200 hrs aaa Pioneer Bn from RUESNES to GOMMEGNIES and SARLOTON aaa Route LE QUESNOY – Cross Roads M15c Road junction M11d 4.8 aaa Not to enter GOMMEGNIES and SARLOTON before 1200 hrs aaa 76 Bde will allot an area in LA LONGUEVILLE to MG Bn aaa Pioneers will take over billets vacated by MG Bn aaa Acknowledge

From	3rd Div		
Place			
Time	18 50 hrs		

The above may be forwarded as now corrected. (Z)

Censor. Signature of Addressor or person authorised to telegraph in his name.

* This line, except AAA, should be erased if not required.
Wt. W 3253/P511. 500,000 Pads. 1/18. B. & S. Ltd. (E2389.)

I Corps wire G.322 dated 12th November, timed 22.50 hours.

(1) Our troops will not advance East of line gained by them at hour when hostilities ceased aaa Our aeroplanes will keep at a distance of not less than one mile behind this line except for purpose of driving back hostile aeroplanes as indicated in para 3 aaa (2) There is to be no unauthorised intercourse or fraternisation of any description with enemy aaa He will not be permitted to approach our lines and any attempt to do so will be immediately stopped if necessary by fire aaa Any parties of enemy coming over to our lines under a white flag will be made prisoners and fact reported to Corps H.Q. aaa (3) No enemy aircraft will be permitted to cross the line aaa Should any make the attempt to do so they will be attacked by fire from ground and from air. aaa (4) All Commanders are to pay strictest attention to discipline smartness and well-being of their troops so as to ensure that highest state of efficiency shall be maintained throughout British Forces aaa Troops will be given every opportunity for rest, training, recreation and leave aaa (5) Passage of civilians through our lines in either direction will be regulated in accordance with instructions which will be issued separately aaa In the meantime no civilians will be permitted to cross our lines in either direction aaa Ends. aaa

"A" Form
MESSAGES AND SIGNALS.

Order [illegible] taken over by workers and soldiers committees and Reuter and Telegraphic communication closed between AMSTERDAM and BERLIN HAMBURG LUBECK BREMEN and between BERLIN and COPENHAGEN and [illegible]

From 3rd Div
Time 0900

MESSAGES AND SIGNALS.

MESSAGES AND SIGNALS.

(43)

From GOMMEGNIES to FRASNOY area via BEAUDIGNIES and LE QUESNOT aaa to eighth LE QUESNOT at 1800 ... +38 ... Co from GOMMEGNIES to MAUBEUGE via AMFROIPRET BERMERIES BAVAI and LA LONGUEVILLE ... to pass road junction H32d.7.0 at 0740 hours ... HQ with one Co MG from GOMMEGNIES to LA LONGUEVILLE ... Route as for 9th ... group ... to pass road junction H32d.7.0 at 1130 hours ... Division 7th Field Amb ...

MESSAGES AND SIGNALS.

From Gommegnies to Maubeuge via Amfroipret Bermeries Bavai and La Longueville are to pass road junction H 32. d. 7. 0 at 1100 hours in rear of 9th Inf. Bde Group AAA Three distances will be maintained on the march and Infantry will move off the road at each halt AAA Acknowledge AAA Added list A plus APM repld XI Corps 62nd 2nd and Guards Divs

From: [signature]
Place: [illegible]
Time: 1040

MESSAGES AND SIGNALS.

Prefix......Code......m.	Words	Charge	This message is on a/c of:	Recd. at......m.
Office of Origin and Service Instructions	Sent			Date......
	At ......m.		......Service.	From *......
(45)	To			
	By		(Signature of "Franking Officer")	By ......

TO 76 Bde
Signals

Sender's Number.	Day of Month.	In reply to Number.	AAA
GA 15	10		

Further to my GA 11 of even date the 4th Cavalry Bde will be moving on the LA LONGUEVILLE – DOUZIES – VIAUDEUGE Road in front of the 76 Bde tomorrow AAA the Cavalry Bde will be clear of cross roads J 31 c0 5 by 0745 hrs AAA in addition to ASSEVENT that part of BOUSOIS which is West of the grid line running N and S between L32 and L33 is also placed at disposal of 76 Bde for billeting purposes

From
Place   BW BW
Time   1540

The above may be forwarded as now corrected. (Z) Lt W Ellison Capt

"A" Form
MESSAGES AND SIGNALS.

Army Form C. 2121
(In pads of 100.)

Prefix....Code....m.	Words	Charge.	This message is on a/c of:	Recd. at....m.
Office of Origin and Service Instructions	Sent At....m. To By		....................Service. (Signature of "Franking Officer")	Date.... From.... By....

TO: CRA / G Bde / 76 Bde — Dvly C / CP / Asst C — Signals / VI Corps / Guard Div. — 8th CRE / KRRC

Sender's Number.	Day of Month.	In reply to Number.	AAA
GH 14	10		

76 Bde RJA will move tomorrow 11th November to MAUBEUGE an area allotted to this Bde on either side of MAUBEUGE LA LONGUEVILLE road in square Q1 a and b and Q2 a and b aaa 76 Bde will move in rear of HQ and one company only Battalion and will not pass road junction 432 d 7.0 before 1200 hours aaa Route AMFROIPRET BERMERIES BAVAI LA LONGUEVILLE aaa large distance will be maintained between units on the march aaa acknowledge aaa Addressed 6RA repeated G 76 Bde Dvly C CP Asst C Signal VI Corps Guard Div

From: ......
Place: ......
Time: 1600

The above may be forwarded as now corrected. (Z) W H T

Censor. Signature of Addressor or person authorised to telegraph in his name
* This line should be erased if not required.

Order No. 1625 Wt. W3253/ P 511. 27/2. H. & K., Ltd. (E. 2634).

VI Corps wire No. G.123 of 8th Nov. timed 0715 hrs.

From G.H.Q. 2220 hrs 7th AAA Line South of CONDE CANAL reported as follows LA CAPELLE - AVESNES Road East of BOULOGNE - AVESNES (excl) - DOURLERS (incl) - LALONGUEVILLE (excl) - BELLIGNIES (incl) - thence unchanged to ONNEZIES - MONTIGNIES - AUDREGNIES (all incl) AAA Otherwise unchanged AAA Prisoners 300 with 8 guns AAA

Summary of War News for distribution to troops AAA German Wireless AAA German delegation for armistice and peace conditions General Von GUNDELL Military Delegate HAGUE Conference General Von WINTERFELD formerly attache PARIS Admiral Von HINTZE former Foreign Secretary Admiral MEURER ERZBERGER States Secretary Propaganda OBERNDOFF formerly Minister SOFIA AAA Expected to reach the French lines tonight AAA BERLIN AAA Russian Embassey left in consequence of discovery Bolshevist intrigue AAA There is evident fear of Bolshevism in Germany AAA Reuter AAA Serious mutiny at KIEL yesterday AAA Battleships KAISER and SCHLESWIG hoisted red flag AAA 20 Officers killed AAA Infantry sent to repress mutiny joined revolutionaries AAA Hussars forced back AAA Sailors council controlled situation AAA Sailors refused obedience until peace is signed AAA Later German Wireless AAA Reports negotiations with sailors going well Chief Petty Officers acting for men AAA   Ends

TO: VI Corps 2nd Gds & 62 Div

Sender's Number: X
Day of Month: 9

Div HQrs closed at QUIEVY at 1200 hours opened at FRASNOY same hour

From: 3rd Div
Time: 1217

(Sd) G. Lively

MESSAGES AND SIGNALS.

Army Form C. 2121
(In pads of 100.)

TO: 8-9-16 Inf Bdes CRA CRE ADMS
Q Pioneer Bn Signals DHQC

Sender's Number: GA 985
Day of Month: 9
AAA

Warning order aaa Following moves will take place tomorrow aaa 10th Nov Inf Bde Groups will start at 0900 hrs aaa 76 Inf Bde Group to LONGUEVILLE aaa 9 Inf Bde Group to FRASNOY aaa 8 Inf Bde Group and MG Coy to ROMERIES and VERTAIN aaa 529 Field Co RE will rejoin its Bde Group and move under orders of Bde Group Commander aaa 56 and 438 Field Cos will remain in their present locations aaa Sent divn. 7 Field Ambulance will move to RUESNES tonight under orders of ADMS and will rejoin its Bde Group at LONGUEVILLE tomorrow starting from RUESNES at 0900hrs aaa One MG Coy will move with each of the 76 and 9 Inf Bde Groups HQ and two Cos MG Bn will be located in VERTAIN aaa

From: Acknowledge aaa Added hy A
Place: 3rd Div
Time: 1540

GA 947

MESSAGES AND SIGNALS.

Army Form C. 2121
(In pads of 100.)

No. of Message............

Prefix......Code......m.	Words	Charge.	This message is on a/c of:	Recd. at......
Office of Origin and Service Instructions		Sent		Date............
C30		At		From........
		To		
		By	(Signature of "Franking Officer")	By........

TO: [illegible addressees]

Sender's Number | Day of Month | In reply to Number | AAA

Orders for tomorrow 10th
November are as Corps will
move as follows Q at
Q H Q moved to Q at
Central KD... C
and Cavalry patrols to
BELLEFONTAINE and BOUSSOIS
[illegible]
[illegible]
the Corps [illegible]
[illegible]
10th November Inf
Bde group with attached
M.G.C. to LONGUEVILLE
[illegible]

From..........
Place..........
Time..........

The above may be forwarded as now corrected. (Z)
....
Censor. Signature of Addressor or person authorised to telegraph in his name
* This line should be erased if not required.
Order No. 1625. Wt. W2253/ P 511. 27/2. H. & K., Ltd. (E. 2634).

MESSAGES AND SIGNALS.   Army Form C. 2121 (In pads of 100.)

Prefix....Code....m.	Words	Charge.	This message is on a/c of:	Recd. at....m.
Office of Origin and Service Instructions		Sent		
		At........m.	..............Service.	Date........
		To........		From........
		By........	(Signature of "Franking Officer")	By........

TO { (37) }

Sender's Number.   Day of Month.   In reply to Number.   **AAA**

BERMERIES BAVAI ...
... will start
at 0900 ...
move ...
7th Inf Bde ...
9th Inf Bde ...
with ... MG Company
to FRASNOY
Route BEAUDIGNIES ...
QUESNOY ... 8th Inf Bde
... and ...
MG Company
ROMERIES ...
Company to FRASNOY area
to move ...
... 9th Inf ...

From
Place
Time

The above may be forwarded as now corrected. (Z)

Censor.   Signature of Addressor or person authorised to telegraph in his name

* This line should be erased if not required.

Order No. 1625. Wt. W3253/   P 511. 27/2. H. & K., Ltd. (E. 2634).

MESSAGES AND SIGNALS. No. of Message..........

Prefix.........Code.........m.	Words	Charge.	This message is on a/c of:	Recd. at......m.
Office of Origin and Service Instructions	Sent		.........................Service.	Date............
	At ....m.			From ....
	To			
	By		(Signature of "Franking Officer")	By............

TO (38)

Sender's Number.	Day of Month.	In reply to Number.	AAA

1st Division 7th Field Ambulance will move to LUNGUEVILLE leaving RUESNES at 0900 hours and 56 and 438 Field Cos will not move and 8th 9th and 76th Inf Bdes [illegible] will also start at 0900 hours and long distances will be maintained between units in the march and infantry will move off the road at each halt [illegible] acknowledge [illegible] [illegible] A repeated 63rd Guards 2nd Div VI Corps & APM

From 3rd Div

Place

Time 17.5

The above may be forwarded as now corrected. (Z) Sd WH [illegible]

Censor. Signature of Addressor or person authorised to telegraph in his name

* This line should be erased if not required.

Order No. 1625. Wt. W3252/ P 511. 27/2. H. & K., Ltd. (E. 2634).

(39)

<u>VI Corps Wire No.G.217 timed 1930 of 9th November.</u>

Following from G.H.Q. timed 1520 AAA Advance of all Armies continues AAA Our troops believed to have reached following general line SAINS DU NORD - SARS - POTERIES - ASSEVENT (East of MAUBEUGE) AULNOIS - JEMAPPES W. along MONS - CONDE CANAL to CANAL D'ANTOING PERUWELZ E. of ANTOING - TOURNAI CHEMIN VERT CELLES - BERCHEM AAA French reported across SCHELDT at HELDEN Line of 1st French Army reported N. to S.E. of SAINS - ANOR - HIRSON (both incl).
    LATER. From G.H.Q. 1725 AAA German wireless states that the KAISER has abdicated and the CROWN PRINCE renounces claim to throne AAA First French Army report cavalry reached FRANCO-BELGIUM frontier AAA Ends.

"A" Form
MESSAGES AND SIGNALS.

Army Form C. 2121
(In pads of 100.)

Prefix	Code	Words	Charge	This message is on a/c of:	Rec'd at....m.
Office of Origin and Service Instructions		Sent			Date
		At....m.		Service	From
		To		(40)	
		By		(Signature of "Franking Officer")	By

TO: E-9-76 Inf Bdes — Duty C — CRE
CRA — Q

Sender's Number	Day of Month	In reply to Number	AAA
GB 982	9		

6 Corps wire G 153 timed 0630 hrs reads aaa summary of war news for distribution to troops aaa Reuter aaa Disturbances KIEL were due to opposition of Officers new Government and rumoured intention to make naval attack England aaa Men thereupon arrested Officers aaa Allied fleet will anchor off CONSTANTINOPLE 9th inst aaa EIFFEL TOWER message to GERMAN CHANCHELLOR signed ERZBERGER aaa announces despatch armistice conditions to SPA and requests answer by 1100 hrs Monday aaa German wireless aaa Spread revolutionary movement CUXHAVEN HAMBURG WILHELMSHAVEN OLDENBERG HANOVER aaa

From
Place
Time

The above may be forwarded as now corrected. (Z)

Censor. Signature of Addressor or person authorised to telegraph in his name
* This line should be erased if not required.

Order No. 1625 Wt. W3253/ P 511. 27/2. H. & K., Ltd. (E. 2634).

3rd. Div. wire G.C. 896 dated 4th Nov. timed 0930.

    Situation from VIth Corps timed 0830 aaa 62nd Divn report right Bde reports 0750 hrs aaa BLUE objective gained on whole from Brigade front aaa In touch with New Zealand Division on right and left brigade on left aaa An earlier report states right battalion had taken 50 prisoners aaa Prisoners know nothing about a withdrawal in this sector aaa Unconfirmed report that prisoners captured at LA FOLIE FARM belong to 12th Res Div. which came into line last night from Belgian aaa Guards Div report attack appears to have started satisfactorily from BLUE objective aaa Addressed 8yh 9th 76th Inf. Bdes C.R.A. C.R.E. D.M.G.C.

==*=*=*=*=*=*

3rd. Div. wire G.C. 897 dated 4/11/18 timed 0936.

    Sixth Corps wires timed 0600 hrs reads Summary of War news for distribution to troops aaa German wireless aaa New Hungarian Government absolved by King allegeance aaa Will submit to plebiscite questions of Republic or Monarchy aaa Vienna Delegates invited from from War Officers of the new state to co-operate with war ministry in Demobilization aaa Trieste aaa Joint committee of Italians in Slovines formed to keep order aaa Military government STYRIA taken over by German Austrian State aaa Germany aaa KAISER confirms constitutional amendments aaa Memorandum to chancellor from SCHIEDMANN Secty of State advising abdication of KAISER aaa UKRAINE and Austrain German troops attacked POLES capturing LEMBERG on Nov. 1st and PRZEMYSL later aaa Italians offl. 2 more Italian armies entered battle aaa Seventh advancing into western TRENTO aaa First occupied ROVEN and advanced troops near TRIENT aaa Progress continued elsewhere prisoners counted 100,000 aaa Guns 2200 aaa Austrian offl. aaa Our troops have ceased hostilities in the Italian theatre on account of the armistice which has been concluded aaa Notification of the terms of the armistic armies will be given separately. Addressed 8th 9th 76th Inf. Bdes C.R.A. D.M.G.C. A.D.M.S.

==*=*=*=*=*=*=*

"A" Form
MESSAGES AND SIGNALS.

Army Form C. 2121
(In pads of 100.)

No. of Message............

Prefix......Code......m.	Words	Charge	*This message is on a/c of:*	Recd. at......m.
Office of Origin and Service Instructions	Sent		......Service.	Date............
....	At......m.			From............
....	To			
	By		(Signature of "Franking Officer")	By............

TO {

Sender's Number.	Day of Month.	In reply to Number.	A A A

From
Place
Time

The above may be forwarded as now corrected (Z)

....
Censor.   Signature of Addressor or person authorised to telegraph in his name
* This line should be erased if not required.

Order No 1625   Wt. W3253/   P 511   27/2   H. & K., Ltd. (**E. 2634**)

"A" Form
MESSAGES AND SIGNALS.

Army Form C. 2121
(In pads of 100.)

No. of Message............

Prefix......Code......In	Words	Charge	This message is on a/c of:	Recd. at......m
Office of Origin and Service Instructions	Sent		..................Service.	Date............
	At ......m			From............
	To			
	By		(Signature of "Franking Officer")	By............

TO {

Sender's Number.	Day of Month.	In reply to Number.	A A A

The	line	of	the
RHONELLE	river	tomorrow	aaa
76th	Inf	Bde	Group
less	Field	Co RE	with
attached	MG Co	will	move
to	ORSINVAL	aaa	8th
Inf	Bde	Group	less
Field	Co RE	with	attached
MG Co	to	ROESNES	aaa
9th	Inf	Bde	Group
less	Field Co	RE	to
ESCARMAIN	aaa	HQrs	and
the	Companies	MG	Battalion
to	ESCARMAIN	aaa	Troops
will	move	every	country
as	far	as	Poirville
aaa	the	Division	will

From
Place
Time

The above may be forwarded as now corrected   (Z)

....
Censor.   Signature of Addressor or person authorised to telegraph in his name
* This line should be erased if not required.

Order No 1625   Wt. W3253/   P 511   27/2   H. & K., Ltd (E. 2634)

“A” Form
Army Form C. 2121
(In pads of 100.)

MESSAGES AND SIGNALS.

No. of Message............

Prefix.............Code.............m. Office of Origin and Service Instructions	Words / Charge.	This message is on a/c of:	
(18)	Sent At ....m. To .... By	........................Service. .... (Signature of “Franking Officer”)	Recd. at......m. Date.............. From.......... By..............

TO

Sender's Number.	Day of Month.	In reply to Number.	AAA
*			

be	set	[illegible]	[illegible]
[illegible]	15	[illegible]	[illegible]
[illegible]	[illegible]	[illegible]	[illegible]
~~76th~~	~~Inf~~	~~Bde~~	~~[illegible]~~
~~[illegible]~~	~~[illegible]~~	~~[illegible]~~	~~[illegible]~~
Zero	hour	for	[illegible]
[illegible]	will	be	[illegible]
[illegible]	76th	Inf	Bde
[illegible]	[illegible]	have	cross
roads	W.17.c	2.6	Zero
plus	10	[illegible]	[illegible]
8th	Inf	Bde	[illegible]
will	have	[illegible]	junction
E.2.a.0.8.		at	zero
plus	two	hours	and
9th	Inf	Bde	[illegible]
will	have	[illegible]	[illegible]

From
Place
Time

The above may be forwarded as now corrected. (Z) ....

.... *Censor.* Signature of Addressor or person authorised to telegraph in his name

* This line should be erased if not required.

Order No 1625 Wt. W3253/ P 511 27/2 H. & K., Ltd (E. 2634)

"A" Form
MESSAGES AND SIGNALS.

Army Form C. 2121
(In pads of 100.)

No. of Message............

Prefix.........Code..........m.	Words	Charge	This message is on a/c of :	Recd. at......m.
Office of Origin and Service Instructions	Sent		..................Service.	Date............
(19)	At ....m.			From............
	To			
	By		(Signature of "Franking Officer")	By............

TO {

Sender's Number. | Day of Month. | In reply to Number. | **AAA**

D.16.c	4.4	at	Zero
plus	3	hours	30
minutes	aaa	H.Q.	one
2	Companies	M.G.	Bn
will	follow		rear
of	7th	left	Bde
Group	aaa	Route	for
these	moves	will	be
as	follows	aaa	Cross
road	D.16.c.4.4	—	Railway
crossing	D.12.2	—	Road
Junction	E.2.a.08	—	ROMERIES
—	Road Junction	W.17.d	—
ESCARMAIN	—	cross roads Q.36.a	
—	cross roads R.13.c	—	Cross
Roads	R.22.central		aaa
adv	Div	H.Q.	will

From
Place
Time

The above may be forwarded as now corrected. (Z)

....
Censor. Signature of Addressor or person authorised to telegraph in his name
* This line should be erased if not required.

Order No 1625   Wt. W3253/   P 511 27/2 H. & K., Ltd (E. 2634)

"A" Form
MESSAGES AND SIGNALS.

Army Form C. 2121 (In pads of 100.)

Prefix....Code....m	Words	Charge	This message is on a/c of:	Recd. at....m
Office of Origin and Service Instructions	Sent At ....m		....Service	Date....
(20)	To			From ....
	By		(Signature of "Franking Officer")	By....

TO				

Sender's Number	Day of Month	In reply to Number	AAA
	5	ROESNES	R 14
6.4.a			
	be		
A			
			APM

From 3 DW
Place
Time 21.30

The above may be forwarded as now corrected. (Z)

Censor. Signature of Addressor or person authorised to telegraph in his name
* This line should be erased if not required.

Order No 1625 Wt. W3253/ P 511 27/2 H. & K., Ltd. (E. 2634)

3rd. DIVISION.

Disposition and Movement Report No. 11.

Forecast of Locations for Nov. 5th.

Unit No.	UNIT.	Location of H.Q. Nov. 5th.	
1.	3rd. Division H.Q.	RUESNES	R.14.b.
2.	3rd. Divnl. Arty. H.Q.	"	"
3.	8th Inf. Brigade, H.Q.	"	
4.	9th. Inf. Brigade H.Q.	ESCARMAIN	
5.	76th. Inf. Brigade H.Q.	ORSINVAL	
6.	C.R.E.	RUESNES.	
7.	529th Fld. Coy. R.E.		X. 1.c.0.5
8.	438th Fld. Coy. R.E.	SOLESMES	
9.	56th Fld. Coy. R.E.		X. 1.c.0.5
10.	3rd. Bn. M.G. Corps.	ESCARMAIN	
11.	20th K.R.R.C. (Pioneers)	SOLESMES	
12.	62nd Division.	RUESNES	R.20.b.1.6
13.	Guards Division.	VERTAIN	
14.	2nd Division.	RUESNES	
15.	42nd Division	BEAUVOIS	
16.	24th Division.	BERMERAIN.	

Captain, for
Major-General,
Commanding 3rd. Division.

November 4th 1918.

"A" Form
MESSAGES AND SIGNALS.

Army Form C. 2121 (In pads of 100.)

This message is on a/c of:
Priority to Bdes and D.M.G.C.
Sd. J.M Lumley.
Major.

TO 8th 9th 76th Bde. CRA. CRE. DMGC. 20 KRRC ADMS "Q" Signals APM.

Sender's Number: GB 917.
Day of Month: 5.

AAA

The Division will NOT move today aaa
Advance on Corps front today is meeting
with little opposition aaa
Addsd. List A.

From / Place: 3rd. Div.
Time: 11.30

(Z) Sd. J.M. Lumley. Major.

"A" Form
MESSAGES AND SIGNALS.

Army Form C. 2121
(In pads of 100.)

This message is on a/c of:
Priority to
20th K.R.R.C.
sd J. Lumley. Major.

TO: 20th K.R.R.C.   C.R.E.   "Q" Signals.
    VIth Corps   62nd Div.

Sender's Number.	Day of Month.	In reply to Number.	AAA
G.B. 919	5		

The 20th K.R.R.C. (Pioneers) will move
tomorrow Nov. 6th from SOLESMES to
RUESNES aaa No restriction as to time -
route via ESCARMAIN aaa Only that portion
of RUESNES within right Divisional
Boundary is available for billetting aaa
Pioneer Bn. to acknowledge aaa
Addsd. 20th K.R.R.C. Pioneers reptd.
C.R.E. "Q" Signals VIth Corps 62nd Div.

From: 3rd. Division.
Place:
Time: 14.45

Sd. J. Lumley. Major.

"A" Form
MESSAGES AND SIGNALS.

Army Form C. 2121
(In pads of 100.)

TO: 8-9-76th Bdes. C.R.A. C.R.E. D.M.G.C.
A.D.M.S. "Q" Signals.

Sender's Number: G.B. 922.
Day of Month: 5
AAA

The Division will NOT move tomorrow Nov 6th aaa The Guards and 62nd Divs. are continuing the advance on the Corps front.

From Place: 3rd. Division.
Time: 16.30

Sd. J. Lumly. Major.

Order No. 1625. Wt. W3253/ P 511. 27/2. H. & K., Ltd. (E. 2634).

Summary W/T news for distribution to troops Italians official
aaa rout of Austrian Army yielded 300,000 prisoners 5,000
guns aaa Albania aaa SCUTARI occupied aaa German W/T aaa
Terms Austrian armistice include complete demobilisation aaa
Withdrawal units French front aaa Surrender half artillery
in field aaa Allies have free movement for troops throughout
Austria aaa Occupy stratigical points aaa return all allied
prisoners aaa Surrender part fleet rest dismantled aaa
Germany aaa Political censorship abolished by decree
ministry of war aaa Budapeth aaa New Government claims
peaceful revolution completed aaa British Official
aaa Serbs have occupied Belgrade.

VIth Corps wires timed 2320 hrs dated 4th Nov aaa
Line on Third Army front at 19.00 hrs aaa LES GRANDES PATURES
(B.2.c.) - LOCQUIGNOL (excl) - E. of ND DE FLAQUETTES
(S.18.a.) - LE RON - DE QUESNE - HERBIGNIES - PETIT MARAIS
(M.11.c.) all incl - PREUX AU SART (not confirmed) -
WARGNIES LE PETIT- WARGNIES GRAND (all incl) ETH (not confirmed)
aaa Estimated captures over 6000 prisoners and
125 guns prisoners taken from 43 Battns of 20 Regts of 11
Divs aaa   Later from G.H.Q. 2005 hrs line now reported
East of FESMY - LANDRECIES (incl) - CARREFOUR DUCHENE
MURONNE (A.18) LOCQUIGNOL - HERBIGNIES - FRASNOY - WARGNIES
(all incl) - SEBOURQUIAUX (incl) -East of ONNAING aaa
Prisoners about 10,000 and 200 guns aaa French First
Army line runs GRAND VERLI - West of NEUVILLE-LES-
DORENGT - West of ROUR aaa Prisoners about 3000 aaa

G.C. 928   Nov. 6th.   (26)

Summary of war news for distribution to Troops. Poles established Government CRACOW. German Embassy in Russia withdrawn. German Government recognised CZECH - SLOVAK State. Will welcome CZECH - SLOVAK Ambassador at BERLIN. Bavarian press urges KAISERS abdication. German Wireless. Italian Expedition arrived TRIESTE crews landed to maintain order Commander claims to have been nominated Governor.

3rd. Div. G.B. 951 dated 7th November. timed 14.00 hours.

Forecast of probable moves tomorrow Nov 8th aaa 76th Inf. Brigade to FRASNOY aaa 9th Inf. Bde. to ROMERIES aaa 8th Inf. Bde. to remain at SOLESMES aaa 76th Inf. Bde will reconnoitre FRASNOY today if accommodation in that village is insufficient portion of ORSINVAL not already occupied may be used aaa Acknowledge. aaa Addressed List A. less Pioneers.

==*=*=*=*=*

3rd. Division wire G.B. 957 dated 7th November. timed 20.15 hrs.

Following moves will take place tomorrow Nov. 8th aaa 76th Inf. Bde. Group (less Field Coy. R.E.) with attached M.G. Company from ROMERIES to FRASNOY to start at 09.00 hours route BEAUDIGNIES -LE QUESNOY aaa 9th Inf. Bde Group. (less Fld. Co. R.E.) from QUIEVY to ROMERIES to start at 0900 hours route AUTERTRE Fm. -SOLESMES Station aaa H.Q. and 2 Coys M.G. Bn. will move from QUIEVY to ROMERIES under orders of G.O.C. 9th Inf. Bde. who will allot them accommodation in ROMERIES aaa if 76th Inf. Bde find accommodation in FRASNOY insufficient portion of GOMMEGNIES not reserved for Corps H.Q. may be used aaa Following distances to be maintained on the march between Bns. 1000 yards between Bns. and their transport 300 yards aaa Acknowledge aaa Addressed list A plus VIth Corps 2-62nd Divs. AP.M..

=*=*=*=*=*=*=*=

VI Corps wire No.G.79 of 7th November timed 0600 hrs.

Following from G.H.Q. 2225 hrs 6th AAA Situation report AAA British front AAA No material change AAA Prisoners about 700 AAA French line N. to S. runs RUE DES CHATS - East edge of FORET DE NOUVION - one mile E. of BUIRONFOSSE - W. of SORBAIS - FONTAINELES - VERVINS (incl) - GERCY AAA Thence - no change AAA Prisoners since Nov.4th 4000 with 60 guns AAA Ends.

=*=*=*=*=*=

Summary of War News for distribution to troops. Reuter. Wilson's Note VERSAILLES discussion sent Germany yesterday AAA FOCH empowered negotiate German plenipotentiaries AAA Allies declare willingness make peace with Germany on terms embodied Wilson's address 4/1 and subsequent addresses with 2 qualifications AAA One. Must reserve freedom in interpretation expression freedom of seas AAA Two. Expression restoration of invaded territories required definition AAA In their view this embodies compensation for damage to civilians and property AAA Hungarians refused passage to German Danube Divisions under MACKENSEN AAA Presumably will be captured. AAA Hungarians have cut off from Germany Rumanian oil supplies AAA Zurich reports great disorder due rising soldiers AAA Bavarians closed frontier against VORARLBERG AAA Hungarian Government delegate has gone to PADUA to negotiate peace terms with DIAZ AAA German wireless AAA German delegation to conclude armistice left Berlin for Austria Nov.6th.

=*=*=*=*=*=

3rd DIVISION.

Disposition and Movement Report No.12.

Unit No.	UNIT.	Location of H.Q. 7th November.	Probable changes within 24 hours.
1.	3rd Divisional H.Q.	QUIEVY.	
2.	3rd Div'l Arty H.Q.	QUIEVY.	
3.	8th Infantry Brigade H.Q.	SOLESMES E.1.c.45.15.	
4.	9th Infantry Brigade H.Q.	QUIEVY.	ROMERIES.
5.	76th Infantry Brigade H.Q.	ROMERIES.	FRASNOY.
6.	C.R.E.	RUESNES R.14.b.4.4.	
7.	529 Field Coy. R.E.	ORSINVAL R.12.a.2.8.	
8.	438 Field Coy. R.E.	BELLEVUE FERME R.15.b.5.8.	
9.	56th Field Coy, R.E.	ORSINVAL R.12.a.1.9.	
10.	3rd Battn M.G. Corps.	QUIEVY.	
11.	20th K.R.R.C. (Pioneers)	RUESNES R.14.c.8.4.	
12.	62nd Division H.Q.	FRASNOY.	OBIES.
13.	Guards Division.	PREUX AU SART.	AMFROIPRET.
14.	2nd Division H.Q.	ST PYTHON.	

Captain,
for Major General,
Commanding 3rd Division.

7th November, 1918.

"A" Form
MESSAGES AND SIGNALS.

Sent At (20) m.

TO:
8-9-76	Bdes	CRA	CRE	DADGS
22 KRRC	Coms	Q	Signal	
2-62	Div	VI Corps		

Sender's Number: GB 972
Day of Month: 8
AAA

Div HQ will close at QUIEVY at 12.00 hours Nov 9th and open at BRUNOY at the same hour. Add address list A plus VI Corps 2-62 Div.

From: 3rd Div
Place:
Time: 1800

J Kinley Major

"A" Form
MESSAGES AND SIGNALS.

Army Form C. 2121 (In pads of 100.)

Prefix......Code......m.	Words	Charge.	This message is on a/c of:	Recd. at......m.
Office of Origin and Service Instructions	Sent At (31) m. To...... By......		..................Service. (Signature of "Franking Officer")	Date...... From...... By......

TO — 76th Inf Bde

Sender's Number.	Day of Month.	In reply to Number.	AAA
GB 978	8/11		

Reference conversation following wire has been sent by Corps to Divs quote GOMMEGNIES now being cleared of British by 1160 hrs 9 Nov AAA By this hour 62 Div will be east of road running through N15 cent N16 cent AAA GHQ require GOMMEGNIES will clear all accommodation in GOMMEGNIES over and above that required for Corps HQ to 76th Inf Bde Group and this

From
Place
Time

The above may be forwarded as now corrected. (Z)
....
Censor. Signature of Addressor or person authorised to telegraph in his name
* This line should be erased if not required.

Order No. 1625. Wt. W3253/ P 511. 27/2. H. & K., Ltd. (E. 2634).

"A" Form
MESSAGES AND SIGNALS.

Prefix....Code....m.	Words	Charge.	This message is on a/c of:	Recd. at......m.
Office of Origin and Service Instructions	Sent At (32) m. To By		....................Service. (Signature of "Franking Officer")	Date............ From............ By............

TO {

Sender's Number.	Day of Month.	In reply to Number.	AAA

Group will also be accommodated if necessary in LE CHEVAL BLANC - LE GRAND SART. Also ____ _____ ___ Please arrange accommodation for Gordons and MG Co direct with Town Major GOMMEGNIES

From 3rd Div
Place
Time 2200

SECRET.

Copy No. 13

3rd DIVISION OPERATION ORDER NO. 280.

1st November 1918.

1. The 3rd Division will move into the Southern half of the VI Corps area on the 3rd November.

   Moves will be carried out on the 3rd November in accordance with the March Table on reverse.

2. The only distances to be maintained on the march will be 300 yards between Battalions and 100 yards between Battalions and their transport.

3. ACKNOWLEDGE.

Lieut. Colonel.
General Staff, 3rd Division.

1st November 1918.

Issued at 13.30.

Copies to
1. G.O.C.
2. 8th Inf. Bde.
3. 9th Inf. Bde.
4. 76th Inf. Bde.
5. C.R.A.
6. C.R.E.
7. A.D.M.S.
8. "Q".
9. 20th K.R.R.C. (Pioneers).
10. 3rd Div. Signals.
11. VI Corps.
12. 62nd Division.
13. War Diary.
14. War Diary.
15. File.
16. File.
17. File.
18. D.A.G.C.
19. 2nd Division.

MARCH TABLE TO ACCOMPANY 3rd DIVISION
OPERATION ORDER NO. 280.

Reference Sheet 57.B. 1/40,000.

Unit.	From	To	Route	Hour of start & Starting Point.	Instructions.
76th Inf. Bde.Group. (Less Fld. Coy).	CARNIERES.	QUIEVY	BOUSSIERES - BEVILLERS.	Head of Column to pass cross roads C.21.a.5.4 at 16.50 hours.	
M.G.Battn.	CARNIERES	BEVILLERS	do.		To move in rear of 76th Inf.Bde. Group under orders of G.O.C.76th Inf. Brigade.
9th Inf. do.Group.	CATTENIERES.	QUIEVY	BEAUVOIS - LA GUISETTE Farm J.7.c.	Head of column to pass road junction C.25.c. at 16.50 hours.	

"A" Form
MESSAGES AND SIGNALS.

Army Form C. 21[?]
(In pads of 100.)

No. of Message..........

Prefix......Code......m.	Words	Charge	This message is on a/c of :	Recd., at......m.
Office of Origin and Service Instructions	Sent			Date............
	At.........m.		............Service.	From........
D.R.L.S.	To..........		(2)	
	By..........		(Signature of "Franking Officer")	By............

TO: B-g 76 Bde / BRA / Div C / BRA / WMB / CR / 2nd ANZAC

Sender's Number.	Day of Month.	In reply to Number.	AAA
G.A. 85	1/11		

Following from Adv. G.H.Q. timed 0930 hrs aaa Situation report aaa Left Corps Third Army and Right and Centre Corps First Army attacked this morning S. of VALENCIENNES aaa No details aaa French line N. of MESGNIN reported 1500 yds N. of HOUDIGNIES - S. of N. of MORGNE - DE LELVE DOUTER (incl) KERSPRINGHEM (excl) HUFFRUCHES - 1000 yds E. of STRAGBERT - POIGNIES

From Place: 3rd. Division.

Time: ....

The above may be forwarded as now corrected. (Z) ...A. S. Lovely, Capt.

Censor. Signature of Addressor or person authorised to telegraph in his name

* This line should be erased if not required.

Order No. 1625. Wt. W3253/ P 511. 27/2. H. & K., Ltd. (E. 2634).

(3)

Following from Army by wireless timed 0135 today (1/11/18) aaa
Summary War news for distribution to troops aaa Official
reports state TURKEY and AUSTRIA HUNGARY have signed
armistice aaa German wireless states national government
formed in AUSTRIA repudiating KAISER KARL and describing
note to Wilson as betrayal of Germany aaa Demobilisation
Committee established aaa FIUME desires union with ITALY
aaa ITALIAN Fleet expected aaa Southern Slav states
proclaimed at AGRAM claims territory between ISONZO and
VARDAR aaa Austrian Fleet at POLA seized by crews for
National Councils of German Austria Southern Slavs and
Hungary.

(4)

<u>Sixth Corps wire G. 450 1st. Nov. timed 1545 hrs.</u>

  Following from Adv. G.H.Q. timed 1225. Situation report. S. of VALENCIENNES our line believed as follows MARESCHES (incl.) - PRESEAU (doubtful) - PRESEAU-MARLY road to railway - along railway S. of VALENCIENNES to SCHELDT. Prisoners over 1000. Above information not yet confirmed. Terms of Armistice with TURKEY include free passage of DARDANELLES and BOSPHORUS and occupation by Allies of forts on them-Demobilisation of Turkish Army except for police forces- Use of Turkish ports and railways - Immediate repatriation of all Allied prisoners of war. Italian embassy in LONDON reported last night that DIAZ had signed Armistice with AUSTRIA. This not yet confirmed and exact situation uncertain. Austrian plenipotentiaries now at Italian G.H.Q. Allied captures now exceed 50,000 prisoners and 300 guns.

(5)

3rd. Div. wire G.A. 866 dated 2/11/18.   timed 11.45 hrs.

Reference 3rd. Div O.O. 280 aaa 56th Fld Co. R.E. will move to SOLESMES on morning of 3rd November under orders of C.R.E. aaa 56th and 520th Fld. Cos. R.E. will move from SOLESMES to ST. GEORGES river east of ESCARMAIN on the night 3rd/4th November under orders of C.R.E. aaa Move not to commence before 21.00 hours on night 3rd/4th Novr. route via ROMERIES aaa Move of 56th Field Co. on morning of 3rd Novr. to be by sections with 300 yards distance between sections aaa Acknowledge aaa Addsd C.R.E. 9th Inf. Bdes repeated 76th Inf. Bde "Q" A.D.M.S. 62nd Div. VIth Corps.
All concerned informed.

==*=*=*=*=*=*=*=*=*=*=*=*=*=*

3rd. Div. wire G.A. 867 dated 2/11/18.   timed 12.30 hrs.

Reference 3rd. Div. O.O. 280 aaa 9th Inf. Bde Group less Fld Co. will start from road junction C.25.c.5.1 at 17.45 hours and will move to QUIEVY via CARNIERES and BEVILLERS aaa Acknowledge aaa Addsd 9th Inf. Bde repeated 76th Inf. Bde "Q" and VIth Corps Guards Div.
All concerned informed.

==*=*=*=*=*=*=*=*=*=*=*=*=*=*

3rd. Div.wire G.A. 869 dated 2/11/18 timed 13.30 hrs.

Reference 3rd. Div. O.O. 280 and G.A. 866 and 867 aaa 9th Inf. Bde Group will move to QUIEVY during daylight on the 3rd November aaa 56th Fld. Coy. R.E. will move under orders of G.O.C. 9th Inf. Bde and will proceed to SOLESMES moving at the head of 9th Inf. Bde Group aaa 9th Inf. Group will move via CARNIERES and BEVILLERS aaa Tail of column to be east of BEVILLERS by 17.00 hrs on 3rd. November aaa Distances to be maintained on the march as follows aaa 300 yds between companies 300 yds between Battalions 100 yds between Battalions and their transport aaa Acknowledge aaa Addressed 9th Inf. Bde C.R.E. repeated 76th Inf. Bde. 8th Inf. Bde. "Q" A.D.M.S. Signals C.R.A. Guards Div. VIth Corps.

==*=*=*=*=*=*=*=*=*=*=*=*=*=*

(6)

VIth Corps wire timed 0350 hours dated 2nd aaa
Following by wireless aaa Summary of war news for distribution
to the troops aaa German wireless reports financial panic
spreading from western Germany aaa VIENNA quiet aaa New
Government formed securing advisor of troops aaa BUDAPEST
Ex-Premier TISZA shot in streets aaa New situation aaa
REUTER states TURKEYS armistice confirmed - includes
free passage of BOSPHORUS occupation of DARDANELLES
ports and immediate repatriation of all Allied prisoners
aaa AMSTERDAM reports panic amongst RHINE population
owing to rumoured replies of German Government consent
to occupation of COLOGNE and COBLENTZ by Allied Troops aaa
VIth Corps wire timed 10.00 hrs dated 2nd Nov. aaa
Following from G.H.Q. timed 22.30 hrs aaa Situation
report. Line South of VALENCIENNES as follows MARESCHES
(incl) PRESEAU (excl) PRESEAU - AULNOY Road to cross
roads S.E. of AULNOY Railway S. of MARLY and along
railway to SCHELDT, counter attack with 5 Tanks this
morning forced back our troops to North outskirts of
MARESCHES three enemy Tanks knocked out. Counter attack
N.W. of PRESEAU also forced line back slightly.
Prisoners to day between 2000 and 3000. French hold
west bank of SCHELDT to BECKE AUDENARDE and EECKE
(excl) DENYZE (incl) Americans have advanced line
West of MEUSE 1½ miles on 8 mile front as follows
ANDEVANNE IMECOURT 1000 yds north of
GRANDPRE about 1100 prisoners. British captures
in France since 1st August 1918 to date. Prisoners
175.000, guns 2380, machine guns 17000, Trench Mortars
2750. French captured 14th July to 20th October 1918
Prisoners 112,500, guns 1575, machine guns 8000
Trench Mortars 570. British captured since commencement of war (approx) 310,000 prisoners, over 3000 guns
22,000 machine guns 3,700 Trench Mortars.

(7)

Sixth Corps wire G. 479 Nov. 2nd.
    Following from G.H.Q. timed 1000 hrs. South of VALENCIENNES our troops have reached PRESEAU-MARLY Road N. of cross roads (E.30 a). Patrols in MARLY and fighting in centre of VALENCIENNES. Prisoners yesterday over 3,000. American line west of MEUSE reported BABIEMONT WOOD - ANDEVANE - BARRICOURT WOOD - IMECOURT. Prisoners 1,500. FRENCH Line on VOUZIERS front reported 1,500 yards N.E. of FALAISE - N.W. outskirts of BOIS DE VONCQ - SEMUY. Prisoners about 500. ITALIANS are advancing towards river TAGLIAMENTO 700 guns taken. Later. We have taken VALENCIENNES.

Sixth Corps wire timed 17.30 hrs aaa Following from G.H.Q. timed 15.20. Line in VALENCIENNES Sector reported at midday 1000 yds E. of MARESCHES - Fme. DE WULT (1500 yds east of PRESEAU) 1000 yds north of PRESEAU - along PRESEAU - MARLY road - STEELWORKS (excl) MARLY (incl) eastern outskirts of VALENCIENNES. Third Army reports capture of additional 350 prisoners and 2 tanks Captures by Americans yesterday West of MEUSE 3,600 prisoners and 40 guns.

VIth Corps wire timed 0620 hrs dated 3rd Nov aaa Summary of War News for distribution to troops German wireless reports National Government under KAROLYI took over control of HUNGARY during night aaa Government appeals soldiers and workmen return duty having achieved objects aaa HINDENBURG replying numerous messages confidence appeals for national unity aaa matter at stake Germanys honour freedom future aaa Saxony has admitted three Socialists to Ministry as result constitutional change aaa Reuter says British landed GALLIPOLI Mine sweepers clearing Straits aaa General Allenby promoted Knight Grand Cross of the Bath aaa CZECH National Council assumed control of SKODA Works. aaa

VIth Corps wire timed 12.00 hrs aaa Following from G.H.Q. timed 09.20 aaa General situation unchanged aaa Austrains announce that they are evacuating Italy and Serbia aaa Italians report 84,000 prisoners and 1600 guns aaa American line W. of MEUSE reported CLERY LE PETIT - FOSSE- W. edge of BOIS DE BOURGOGNE aaa French line continues OLIZY - N of LACROIX AUX BOIS and BOIS DE VANDY - LES ALLEUX aaa

MESSAGES AND SIGNALS.

Prefix... Code... m.	Words. Charge.	This message is on a/c of:	Recd. at ... m.	
Office of Origin and Service Instructions.	Sent		Date...	
	At... m.	Service.	From	
(9)	To...		By	
	By...	(Signature of "Franking Officer.")		

TO	8 Inf Bde	CRA	Corps Bn	62 Div
	9 Inf Bde	CRE	AMMUS	2 Div
	76 Inf Bde	DMSC	&	VI Corps

Sender's Number.	Day of Month.	In reply to Number.	AAA
GA 884	3rd		

Following moves will take place tomorrow 4th November aaa 76th Inf Bde Group (less Field Coy and Field Ambulance) with one M G Coy attached to ESCARMAIN and ROMERIES aaa Route Railway crossing D12a SOLESMES cross roads E16.09 ROMERIES aaa To pass cross roads D16c44 at 0745 hours aaa 8th Inf Bde Group with one M G Coy attached to SOLESMES aaa Route QUIEVY Railway crossing D12a aaa To pass Road junction C24b4.6

From
Place
Time

The above may be forwarded as now corrected. (Z)

Censor. Signature of Addressor or person authorised to telegraph in his name.

*This line, except AAA, should be erased if not required.

MESSAGES AND SIGNALS.

A Form. Army Form C. 2121. (In pads of 100.)

Sender's Number.	Day of Month.	In reply to Number.	A A A

at 0830 hours aaa M G Battalion less two Companies to QUIEVY aaa To move in rear of 8th Inf Bde Group aaa 56th and 529 Field Coys will move to vicinity of ESCARMAIN aaa To be clear of SOLESMES by 0800 hours aaa 8th 76th Inf Bdes CRE DIV bc to acknowledge aaa Addressed List A repeated 62 and 2nd Divs VI Corps

From 3rd Div

Place

Time 1210

(11)

3rd. Div. wire G.A. 886 dated 3rd Nov. timed 1315.

The distances to be maintained on the march tomorrow will be 300 yards between Battalions and 100 yards between Battalions and their transport. Addsd.8th and 76th.Inf. Bdes.

==*=*=*=*=*

(11)

3rd. Division wire G.B. 890 dated 3rd Nov. timed 18.30.

20th K.R.R.C. (Pioneers) will move tomorrow Nov 4th to ROMERIES starting from present billets at 11.15 hours aaa This move is not to interfere with work on roads in forward area aaa Pioneers to acknowledge aaa Addressed 20th K.R.R.C. (Pioneers) repeated 76th Inf. Bde C.R.E. "Q" Signals.

==*=*=*=*=*

3rd. Division wire G.B. 891 dated 3rd NOv. timed 19.30 hours.

Move of 20th K.R.R.C. (Pioneers) ordered in G.B. 890 is cancelled. aaa Addressed all recipients of G.B. 890.

==*=*=*=*=*=*=*=*=*

Copy of VI Corps wire No. G.498 dated 3rd Nov. Timed 6.0 pm.

G.H.Q. report timed 22.15 (2nd). aaa 60 Prisoners taken and line advanced in local operation by Fourth Army W. of LANDRECIES we hold steelworks S. of MARLY and high ground 2000 yards N. of village thence line continues ST. SAULVE (incl) - due N. to SCHELDT aaa Total prisoners since morning of Nov. 1st on this front over 5,000 aaa 4 Tanks captured and a few guns aaa Belgians report progress towards GHENT and EECLOO and enemy retiring aaa No details aaa American captures July 18th 1918 to 1st Nov. incl. Prisoners 44,000 guns 950 M.Gs. 3200, T.Ls. 280 aaa British troops in Italy have taken over 10,000 prisoners and over 100 guns aaa Later aaa Belgian line reported approx. EEKE-BAARLE - MEERENDRE (all incl) - W. of VINDERHAUTE - WAERSCHOOT - EECLOO (both incl).

****

Copy of VI Corps wire No. G.510 dated 3rd Nov. Timed 17.25.

Following from G.H.Q. 14.45 following enemy withdrawal East of VALENCIENNES First Army have reached following general line SAULTAIN (believed incl) West of ESTREUX West of ONNAING maintaining touch with enemy.

****

3rd. Division.

Disposition and Movement Report No. 10.

Forecast of Locations for Nov. 4th.

Unit No.	Unit.	Location of H.Q. Nov. 4th.
1.	3rd. Division H.Q.	QUIEVY.
2.	3rd. Divnl. Arty. H.Q.	"
3.	8th. Inf. Brigade H.Q.	SOLESMES
4.	9th. Inf. Brigade H.Q.	QUIEVY.
5.	76th. Inf. Brigade H.Q.	ESCARMAIN.
6.	C.R.E.	QUIEVY.
7.	529th. Fld. Coy. R.E.	ESCARMAIN.
8.	438th. Fld. Coy. R.E.	SOLESMES.
9.	56th. Fld. Coy. R.E.	ESCARMAIN.
10.	3rd. Bn. M.G. Corps.	QUIEVY.
11.	20th. K.R.R.C. (PIONEERS)	ROMERIES.
12.	62nd. Division.	ESCARMAIN. (Forward Report Centre R. 20b1.6)
13.	Guards Division.	VERTAIN.
14.	2nd. Division.	ST. PYTHON.
15.	42nd. Division.	BEAUVOIS.
16.	24th. Division.	V. 19 d 4.8 ST. AUBERT.

November 3rd. 1918.

Captain for Major-General,
Commanding 3rd. Division.

MESSAGES AND SIGNALS.

Prefix......Code......m. Office of Origin and Service Instructions	Words / Charge Sent At......m. To......... By.........	This message is on a/c of: PRIORITY Service. (Signature of "Franking Officer")	Recd. at......m. Date............ From............ Major. By............

TO: 8-9-76th Inf. Bdes.   G.R.A.   C.R.E.   A.D.M.S.
    D.H.Q.   20/K.R.R.C.   Q Signals   A.P.M.
    6 Corps G. 2-62nd Divs. 6 Corps Q. 3rd Div Train

Sender's Number.	Day of Month.	In reply to Number.	AAA
Gb. 84	16th		

Following moves will take place on Nov.17th AAA "A" Group from NEUF MESNIL MON PLAISIR area to LOUVROIL AAA To cross the FRAMERIES - HAUTMONT railway at 1200 hours AAA "B" Group from LA LONGUEVILLE to SOUS LE BOIS to start at 1400 hours AAA "C" Group from FRASNOY area to NEUF MESNIL MON PLAISIR area AAA Route BAVAI LA LONGUEVILLE AAA To enter LA LONGUEVILLE at 1500 hours and tail to be clear of road junction just West of P. in PETIT MARAIS by their 1230 hours AAA Train companies will march with Bde Groups AAA Distances as laid down in para 15 of instructions issued with G.2002 AAA Div. H.Q. will move to SOUS LE BOIS and open at an hour to be notified AAA "D" Group will not move AAA ACKNOWLEDGE AAA Added list "A" plus A.P.M. 2nd and 62nd Divs. 6th Corps G. and Q. Train

From Place: 3rd Divn.
Time: 1430 hours.

The above may be forwarded as now corrected. (Z) .... Major GS
Censor. Signature of Addressor or person authorised to telegraph in his name
* This line should be erased if not required.

TO 8-9-76 Inf Bde RA RE Duke Coms
Q Signals 2/KRRC VI Corps G&Q
12-62 Div Div Train

Sender's Number: GB89
Day of Month: 16
AAA

In continuation of GB84 of this date aaa Div HQ will close at Briastony at 1500 hours Nov 17th and open at SOUS-LE-BOIS at the same hour aaa Addsd List A plus Corps 2-62 Div Arm and Train.

From: Div
Time: 18.45

MESSAGES AND SIGNALS.

8-9-16	to Bdes	CRA CRE	2 KRR
DMGC	ADMS Q	Signals	APM

Sender's Number: GB 92
Day of Month: 16
AAA

Moves ordered in GB 84 dated Nov 16th to take place tomorrow Nov 17th are cancelled aaa All Groups will remain in their present locations aaa The moves ordered for Nov 17th will probably now take place on Nov 18th aaa Acknowledge Addressed list A plus APM.

From: 3 Div
Place:
Time: 2200

3rd. Division G.S. 2002/2.

INSTRUCTIONS No. 2.

To 3rd. Division G.S.2002.

1. During the advance all military precautions against surprise will be taken.
   Roads must be picketed at night.
   Guards will be mounted on all Battalion Headquarters, Brigade Headquarters, and on Divisional Headquarters.
   Guard for Divisional Headquarters will be found from the nearest Brigade Group.

2. All marches will commence at 08.00 hours, unless otherwise stated.

3. **Responsibility of Commanding Officers.**

   Commanding Officers will take all possible steps to ensure that blocks on the roads, delays in the issue of orders, unnecessary waiting about by parading too early, etc., do not occur. The issue of instructions alone is not sufficient; Staff Officers must ascertain by personal supervision that the instructions issued are carried out.

4. All Formations will report daily while the march continues as soon as all their troops have reached their billets.

5. Any German stragglers or Escaped Prisoners of War of any nationality will at once be sent to Divisional Headquarters.

6. **Supply Arrangements.**

   Special attention is drawn to "Divisional Supply Arrangements for an Advance" on page 80 and following pages of Fourth Army Standing Orders, which are being issued direct by the Fourth Army to formations. These supply orders are to be most carefully carried out, otherwise there is likely to be a failure in the arrival of supplies.

7. ACKNOWLEDGE.

November 16th 1918.

Lieut-Colonel,
General Staff, 3rd. Division.

"A" Form.
MESSAGES AND SIGNALS.

Army Form C. 2121.

TO S=Q=76th Bdes., C.R.A., C.R.E., D.A.D.O.S., 20 SBAC., A.P.M., A.D.M.S., Q., Signals., Train., VI Corps C.E.O. 2 - 62 Divs.

Sender's Number.	Day of Month.	In reply to Number.	
G.B. 94	17.		AAA

Moves ordered to take place on Nov. 17th in G.B. 84 and G.B. 89 both dated Nov. 16th will now take place on Nov. 18th aaa Forecast of moves to take place on Nov. 19th aaa "A" Group from LOUVROIL to area COLLERET OSTERGNIES - CERFONTAINE - FERRIERE LA GRANDE aaa "B" & "C" Groups no change aaa "D" Group to area West of the HAUTMONT - LA LONGUEVILLE - BAVAI Road exclusive aaa Div. H.Q. to COUSOLRE aaa Acknowledge aaa

Addressed list A plus A.P.M., Train., VI Corps, G & Q., 2 - 62 Divs.

From 3rd. Division.
Time 10.50

"A" Form
MESSAGES AND SIGNALS.

Army Form C. 2121
(In pads of 100.)

No. of Message............

Prefix........Code........m.	Words	Charge.	This message is on a/c of :	Recd. at......m.
Office of Origin and Service Instructions	Sent			Date..........
....	At ....m.		(b) ....Service.	From ....
....	To			
	By		(Signature of "Franking Officer")	By ....

TO— 0-0-7th Diss Coy.Sg. G.H.Q.g.R.O.C.Sg.
~~No R.D.~~, ADSSg 7g APDg Signalsg Traing
~~F~~

Sender's Number.	Day of Month.	In reply to Number.	A A A
R.O. 78	7		

Moves forecasted for 19th Nov. will take
place on Nov. 20th and no moves on 19th and
Area allotted to "B" Group for 20th will
be OMLES – RAWERES – VIEUX RENEL and
accommodation for 2 Bdes Def.Aa in
LA LONGUEVILLE. ~~All ~~ ACKNOWLEDGE. Cen
Addressed List A plus A.P.Mg Traing
~~Signs~~ Censors.

From BGRGS 3lvasion.
Place
Time 19.00

The above may be forwarded as now corrected. (Z)
....
Censor. Signature of Addressor or person authorised to telegraph in his name
* This line should be erased if not required.

3rd. Division G.2002/3.

INSTRUCTIONS No. 3.

To 3rd. Division G.2002.

1. Reference para 6 of Instructions which accompanied G.2002 dated November 15th 1918.

As the 62nd Division will now be moving two marches in front of the Division, billeting parties will not be attached to Groups of this Division.

2. Receipts for operation orders will be handed without delay to the D.R's delivering them.

These receipts to be signed (not initialled) by an Officer of the formation or unit to which they are addressed.

3. It may often happen that an area allotted to a Group contains more accommodation than will actually be required. In such cases troops should be billeted as far forward in the area as possible, so as to keep the troops concentrated and so facilitate the following days march.

November 17th 1918.

Lieut-Colonel,
General Staff, 3rd. Division.

3rd. Division G.S.2002/4.

INSTRUCTIONS No. 4.

To 3rd. Division G.S.2002.

1. Reference Fourth Army No. G.S.128 "Notes on March Discipline". Although no compliments will be paid on the march, each Unit will at the end of the days march before entering its billeting area, march past its Commander or Brigade Commander, paying the usual compliments.

2. Reference para 8 of Instructions issued with G.S.2002. Cookers will march immediately in rear of Battalions.

November 18th 1918.

Lieut-Colonel,
General Staff, 3rd. Division.

(79)

3rd. Division G.S. 2018

The following moves will take place on 20th November

"A" GROUP. to area COUSOLRE – BIERSILLIES L'ABBAYE

"B" GROUP. to CERFONTAINE – OSTERGNIES – COLLERET area

"C" GROUP. to FERRIERE LA GRANDE

"D" GROUP. to area LA LONGUEVILLE – HARGNIES – VIEUX MESNIL

Divisional Headquarters will close at SOUS LE BOIS at 0900hrs and open at COUSOLRE on arrival.

ACKNOWLEDGE.

Sd J.M Lumley Major
for Lieut-Colonel,
General Staff, 3rd. Division.

19/11/18

Distribution :-   A.D.M.S.
C.R.E.
Camp Commandant.
D.A.D.O.S.
A.D.V.S.
3rd. M.T. Coy.
Signals.
File.
War Diary.

TO	8 Bde	RA	Pioneer Bn	Sigs 3rd Div
	9 "	CRE	Trains	4th? 2 Div
	76 "			C Corps

Sender's Number.	Day of Month.	In reply to Number.	AAA
CB 77	15		

Following moves will take place on 16" Nov aaa 8th Inf Bde group less field Co from ROMERIES to FARNOY aaa by pass road junction W 9 c at 0830 hours aaa route BEAUDIGNIES LE QUESNOY aaa 9th Inf Bde group from FARNOY to LA LONGUEVILLE aaa by pass road junction M 11 c a at 1000 hours aaa route AMFAUPRET BAVAI aaa. 76 field Co RE to join 9th Inf Bde group via road running through M 9 central and move under orders of CRE 9th Inf Bde aaa 76th Inf Bde group from LA LONGUEVILLE to NEUF MESNIL and MONPLAISIR aaa any route aaa to start at 1100 hours aaa horses batt from COMMEGNIES and HARGOTON to NEUF MESNIL aaa by pass cross roads M 12 d at 1100 hours aaa.

Prefix......Code........ m.	Words.	Charge.		No. of Message.	
Office of Origin and Service Instructions.			This message is on a/c of:	Recd. at ...... m.	
	Sent			Date	
(b3)	At	m.	...............Service.	From	
	To			By	
	By		(Signature of "Franking Officer.")		

TO	2		
Sender's Number.	Day of Month.	In reply to Number.	AAA

Route AMFROMRET DAVAY LA GONGUEVILLE road 7th Inf Bde will allot Colots to Pioneer Battn and 9th Inf Bde Group and Pioneer Battn will NOT march through the centre of DAVAY but will use the roads running round the south side of the town in Sa & and to and Distances to be maintained on march by all units as follows nave 50 yards between companies 200 yards between battalions and full reference to charts 51 and 51 A sover up too and Acknowledge and addresses list A plus HPm 2-6a Divs 6Corps

From	3rd Div
Place	
Time	1030

The above may be forwarded as now corrected. (Z)

Censor. Signature of Addresser or person authorised to telegraph in his name.

Prefix	Code	m.	Words.	Charge.	This message is on a/c of:	Recd. at	m.
Office of Origin and Service Instructions.			Sent		Phone Service.	Date	
WB (64)			At	m.	to Bgze	From	
			To		Col Tunley	Major	
			By		(Signature of "Franking Officer.")	By	

TO 8-9-76 Inf Bdes CRA CRE
    Div E DADMS Adm'n f

Sender's Number.	Day of Month.	In reply to Number.	AAA
*GB 81	15		

Forecast of moves on Nov 17th aaa A Group to LOUVROIL aaa B Group to SOUS-LE-BOIS aaa C Group to NEUF MESNIL and MON PLAISIR aaa D Group no move aaa added list A

From Ld &w
Place
Time 2200

The above may be forwarded as now corrected. (Z) Sd /s/ Tunley
Censor. Signature of Addresser or person authorised to telegraph in his name.

* This line, except AAA, should be erased if not required.

percentage and discounts; the)
metric system), Commercial)
geography, Elementary economics.)

(ii) Additional Subjects for more Advanced Students.

One Language; either French, German, Italian or Spanish.

Any two of the following; Shorthand, Typewriting, Book keeping, Business methods.

Additional Technical Subjects; such as Elementary Mechanics, Theory of Internal Combustion Engines; Motor Mechanics, Electricity and Magnetism, Chemistry, Physics, Building Construction, Elementary Theory of Agriculture, Gardening and allotments.

Where facilities permit, more detailed training for particular trades such as carpentry, telephony, telegraphy, electric lighting and power, and motor driving may be provided.

(iii) Lectures.

Lectures will be arranged by the Divisional Educational Officer. He will be very glad to have the names of any Officers or other ranks willing to lecture on any subject of general interest.

(C). Duties of Officers i/c Education.

(NOTE :- The Education work is regarded as part time Military duty.)

1. To compile a complete list of available instructors in their units, with their qualifications and the subjects they are able to teach. They should be on the look-out for men who, without special teaching experience, are well enough educated to give instruction in such elementary subjects as those in Group "A"; and should bear in mind that the best qualified teachers are likely to be demobilised early, and that they will need others to fall back upon.
   A list of instructors should be sent to the Divisional Educational Officer as soon as possible, and on the 20th of each month a return of additions and casualties should be made in order that the list at Headquarters may be kept up-to-date. In the case of Brigaded Infantry, duplicates of these returns should also be sent to the Brigade Educational Officer.

INSTRUCTIONS TO OFFICERS in charge EDUCATION
3rd. DIVISION.

(A). SCOPE OF ARMY EDUCATIONAL SCHEME.

1. Provision of practical instruction with a view to training for particular trades and occupations.

2. More general education with a view largely to giving men a wider view of their duties as citizens of the British Empire, and awakening interest in, and providing knowledge in regard to, the peace settlement and social re-construction.

(B). SCHEME OF INSTRUCTION.

The work under para. A.1. will be carried on mainly by means of classes; that of para. A.2, by means of lectures.

The scheme of practical instruction will be run upon the following lines, and upon the principle that each man requiring Education will be able to devote at the minimum six hours per week to Educational Training :-

(i) Elementary Courses.

Group A. Such subjects as Reading, Writing, Dictation, Elementary Arithmetic, Talks on Imperial History and Civics.) For men who have little or no education (probably includes such categories as Agricultural, Dock, and General Labourers, Carters, etc.,).

(No man should leave the Forces without being able to read and write.)

Group B. Such subjects as Composition, Precis Writing, Practical mathematics, Elementary Civics and Economics.) For men requiring a technical course, Engineers, Electricians, carpenters, builders, Fitters etc.,)

Group C. Such subjects as Essay writing, Writing of Commercial letters, Mathematics (including Calculation of prices and amounts,) For men requiring a commercial course, (clerks, salesmen, warehousemen, etc.,)

2. They should make a study of the Educational requirements of the men of their units, and be able to give advice as to what sort of instruction they need for their particular trade. A summary of the information so obtained should be forwarded to the Divisional Educational Officer as soon as possible, and on the 20th of each month this information should be brought up to date by a supplementary return.

The returns should be arranged under trade groups, with the number under instruction in each, e.g.

"Agriculture   14
Building trades 20
Commercial   42", and so on.

3. They are responsible for the filling up by Officers of their units of forms required by the Committee on the Resettlement of Officers. (These forms are to be circulated very shortly).

4. Apart from these preliminary steps, they will have the general responsibility of supervising classes in their own units.

5. As soon as circumstances permit, the Education Scheme will be centralised as much as possible, and will be arranged in groups by Brigades, (Divisional Troops being regarded as constituting one group), but in the meantime a start should be made at once with small classes within units in the most elementary subjects.

(D). Books and Apparatus.

1. Text-books etc., A list of text-books and other material available on indent will be circulated shortly.

2. Library. A small reference library for the use of instructors is in process of formation at Divisional Headquarters.

November 15th 1918.

Major.
for Lieut-Colonel,
General Staff, 3rd. Division.

SECRET. (67)   3rd. Division G.2002.
****

- 8th Inf. Bde.   A.D.M.S.
- 9th Inf. Bde.   3rd. Div. "Q".
- 76th Inf. Bde.   3rd. Div. Signals.
- C.R.A.   A.P.M.
- C.R.E.   3rd. M.T. Coy.
- 20th K.R.R.C.   3rd Divnl. Train.
- Camp Comndt.   Mob. Vet. Sect.
- D.A.D.O.S.   D.M.G.C.

---

1. (a) In accordance with terms of armistice, all occupied portions of FRANCE, BELGIUM, and LUXEMBOURG will be evacuated by the enemy by the 26th November.
    A further withdrawal to the East of the RHINE will take place at a later date.

   (b) The Allied forces are to commence to advance on the 17th instant.

   (c) The advancing British Forces are being organised in two Armies, the Second and Fourth, each of four Corps and 16 Divisions. The Fourth Army consists of the following Corps and Divisions :-

   2nd Cavalry Division

   VI Corps - Guards/ 2nd, 3rd, 62nd Divisions.

   IV Corps - 5th, 37th, 42nd, and New Zealand Divisions.

   Australian Corps - 1st, 2nd, 4th, and 5th Australian Divisions.

   IX Corps - 1st, 6th, 32nd, and 66th Divisions.

2. (a) The IX and VI Corps are to be the two leading Corps of the Fourth Army, with the 2nd Cavalry Division covering the whole front of the Army.

   (b) The boundary between the IX and VI Corps and the suggested roads for the advance to the First Line are shown on Map "B". These roads may be modified by Corps at their discretion on receipt of road reconnaissance reports, provided Army and Corps boundaries are not crossed.

2.

(67A)

3. The VI Corps has been tansforred to the Fourth Army from 12.00 hours, 14th November.

4. The Cavalry will be from 5 to 10 miles ahead of the leading Divisions and will inform Divisions of bad portions of the road, condition of bridges etc.

5. The 62nd Division, followed a day later by the 3rd Division, will march on the Southern road.
The Guards Division, followed a day later by the 2nd Division, will march on the Northern road.
The Corps Heavy Artillery will follow the 2nd Division a day later on the Northern road.

6. The VI Corps will have the use of the road through HAUTMONT and the lorry bridge there over the River SAMBRE.

7. A Corps Depot and a Depot for each Division will be formed near the railway to consist of what we want to come on later. These Depots will be handed over to the IV Corps and will come on with them by train.

8. (a) Every Divisional Unit which is not mobile is to be left behind. Stokes' Mortar Batteries are to be taken.

(b) Units must be medically examined and all weaklings left behind.

9. Batteries will be reduced to 4 gun batteries of two sections each, and will be brought up to establishment.
The 23rd Brigade R.F.A. will rejoin the Artillery of the Division.

10. Each echelon will march full.

Supplies etc.

11. All Schools are to be broken up. The pupils are to return to their units, and the establishments handed over to the Army.

12. Bands will be and Colours may be taken on the march.

13. Cameras may be taken.

Cameras.

/14.

3. (68)

14. <u>Censorship</u>.	The Censorship will be relaxed.
15. <u>Communications</u>.	(a) Telephones will not be used in the early stages of the advance. It may be possible later to connect up to the German telephone system. (b) Wireless sets will be allotted to each Infantry Brigade H.Q. and a Directing Station will be maintained at Divisional Headquarters. (c) Aeroplanes will also be used for communication purposes. Each Infantry Brigade H.Q. will have a panel station and a Dropping Ground will be established at Divisional Headquarters.
16. <u>Synchronization of watches & issue of orders</u>.	A Staff Officer from Divisional Headquarters will call at each Group Headquarters daily to synchronize watches, and to communicate orders, if necessary, and obtain information on any points which Group Commanders may wish to bring to notice.
17.	<u>All References</u> in orders will be to the 1/100,000 map.
18.	Notes for Staff and Regimental Officers on the rules of <u>March Discipline</u> will be issued shortly by the Fourth Army at the rate of one copy per Officer.
19.	The attached instructions will be strictly adhered to.
20.	ACKNOWLEDGE.

Lieut-Colonel,
General Staff, 3rd. Division.

November 15th 1918.

2.

2. Starting Point. (a) Starting Point and hour of start for each Group will be laid down by Divisional H.Q.
Groups will pass this starting point punctually at the hour laid down.

3. Halts.
The ten minutes' halt, at ten minutes to each clock hour, will be rigidly adhered to once units have reached the main line of march.
If the distance from billets to the main line of march is such that the troops will be required to march for a prolonged period before halting for the first hourly halt, O.C. Units should time their march to the starting point, so as to allow of a short halt before joining the main column, provided that the road is not blocked to other troops thereby; e.g. time for passing starting point 10.30   Time for leaving billets 09.45; the march should be so timed as to allow troops to halt from 10.20 - 10.30 off the main route.

4. Brigade H.Q.
Brigade H.Q. will invariably be located at the H.Q. occupied by the Brigade of the leading Division.

5. Headquarters of Units & Formations.
The Headquarters of all units and formations must be clearly marked.
All units and formations will report their arrival in billets on the completion of a march to the next higher formation, and will send an orderly to the next higher formation with the location of their Headquarters.

6. Billeting Parties.
Billeting parties mounted on bicycles, will be attached to Groups of the 62nd Division. They will meet their units on arrival and shew them their billets.
Staff Captains will invariably reach the new billets in sufficient time in advance of their Groups to make any necessary adjustments.

7. Police.
A.P.M. will arrange to post police at any places along the route where columns are liable to take a wrong turning - this is especially necessary when passing through towns or villages.
Stragglers Posts will be detailed to follow Groups during the march.

/8.

INSTRUCTIONS   (To accompany 3rd. Div. G.2002.)

1. (a) The Division will march by Groups, composed as follows:-

"A" GROUP.

76th Infantry Brigade.
529th Field Coy. R.E.
No. 7 Field Ambulance (Less Motor Ambulances).
20th K.R.R.C. (Pioneer Battalion).

"B" GROUP.

9th Infantry Brigade.
56th Field Coy. R.E.
No. 142 Field Ambulance (Less Motor Ambulances).
3rd. Bn. M.G. Corps.

Groups on the March.

"C" GROUP.

8th Infantry Brigade.
438th Field Coy. R.E.
No. 8 Field Ambulance (Less Motor Ambulances).

"D" GROUP.

23rd, 40th, 42nd, Bdes. R.F.A.
D.A.C.
Mobile Veterinary Section.

Divn'l Train. (b) 3rd. Divisional Train will march as a separate unit in rear of "D" GROUP.
   Train Companies will be billeted in the areas of the Group to which they are affiliated.

M.T. Co. & motor Ambulances. (c) 3rd. M.T. Company and Motor Ambulances will move in rear of the Divisional Train.
   Motor Ambulances will rejoin their Field Ambulance at the end of the days march.

(d) No lorry or motor ambulance, (unless specially ordered) will on any account start from its billeting area until 2 hours has elapsed after the tail of the column has passed the area in which such motor lorry or motor ambulance is billeted.

/2

3.

8.
1st Line Transport, Lewis Guns and Pack Animals.

Lewis gun limbers and ammunition pack animals will march in rear of their companies.

Remainder of the 1st Line transport will march Brigaded in rear of Groups under the Brigade Transport Officers.

9.
Transport Personnel.

Brakesmen, cooks with cookers, will march within the breadth of the wheels of the vehicles, and not outside them as is so often the case. All other men marching with the transport will march in formed bodies in rear of the transport of their unit.

10.
Parking of guns & vehicles.

No guns or vehicles are on any account to be parked on main roads.

11.
Overloading of Wagons.

Wagons must not be overloaded.

Staff Officers have authority to lighten overloaded wagons by dumping the contents by the road side.

12.
Supply Columns.

At a certain hour, which will be notified each day, before which the march will have been completed, all roads will be kept clear for the advance of the supply column. No guns or transport must be parked on roads which can in any way interfere with the forward or backward movement of these lorries to and from re-filling points.

All supply lorries will be clear of the roads by a certain hour in the morning which will be laid down by Corps. That is to say, during the day roads will be employed for the marching troops, and during the night will be kept clear for the advance and return of supply lorries.

13.
Distances to be maintained on the march.

The following distances will be maintained on the march :-

    In rear of an Infantry Company — 10 yards.

    In rear of a battery or other unit not specified — 25 yards.

    In rear of an Artillery Brigade or Infantry Battalion — 50 yards.

    In rear of a Group. — 200 yards.

/14.

(70A)

14.
Steel Helmets
Box Respirators

Steel Helmets and Box Respirators will be carried on the march.
Caps will be worn and steel helmets carried on the the person.

15.
S.A.A.

60 rounds S.A.A. will be carried on the man.

3rd. Division Operation Order No. 282

1. The Division will march tomorrow 25th Nov, in accordance with the following March Table.

Reference 1/100,000

MARCH TABLE.

Unit.	Starting Point.	Hour of start.	Route.	Destination.	Instructions.
"A" GROUP.	Rest Crossing 4½ mile NW of F. in FERRIERE LA GDE (NAMUR Sheet)	0830	COLLERET	COUSOLRE BERSILLIES L'ABBAYE BOUSIGNIES	Train to move in rear of C Group also vehicles of Pioneer Bn Brampton Horses
"B" GROUP.	Cross roads 600 yds NE of Fleur S in SOUS LE BOIS	0830	MAUBEUGE – Railway Bridge 1200yds S of M in MAUBEUGE – COLLERET	COLLERET CERFONTAINE OSTERGNIES	Train to move in rear of C Group
"C" GROUP.	Cross roads 600 yds NE of Fleur S in SOUS LE BOIS	0925	MAUBEUGE	FERRIERE LA GDE	Do
"D" GROUP.	2 Bde R.F.A. to LA LONGUEVILLE 1 Bde R.F.A. & Div ammn column entire of CRA		6 VIEUX MESNIL + HARGNIES		

2. Divnl. H.Q. will close at SOUS LE BOIS at 0900 and open at COUSOLRE on arrival.
3. ACKNOWLEDGE.

Distribution { G.O.C. 3 Bde R.F.A., Div train Div Sup Col. CRA A.P.M. } VI Corps (G) VI Corps (Q)

14th November 1918.
Transport 1500 hrs.

F. Furneaux Major,
for Lieut-Colonel,
General Staff, 3rd. Division.

SIGNALS.

TO: 8-9-76 Inf Bdes CRA CRE Q ADMS 3rd Div Train 6 Corps G & Q Signals

Sender's Number: GB 118
Day of Month: 20

AAA

A B & C Groups will not move tomorrow Nov 21st aaa D Group will move to area ROUSIES - RECQUIGNIES - MARPENT no restriction as to time or route aaa No further moves will take place pending improvement of railway and road communications aaa Separate orders are being issued for work on roads aaa Acknowledge aaa Addd 3 Bdes CRA CRE ADMS Q Train 6 Corps G & Q

From: 3rd Divn
Time: 1420

"A" Form.
MESSAGES AND SIGNALS.

Army Form C. 2121.
(In pads of 100.)

TO 8th Inf. Bde.   C.R.A.   "Q"   3rd M.T.Coy.
    9th Inf. Bde.   C.R.E.   Signals.   Train.
    76th Inf. Bde. ADMS.   A.P.M.

Sender's Number.	Day of Month.	In reply to Number.	
G.A. 130	22nd		AAA

Warning Order aaa 3rd Division will be prepared to resume the advance on 24th and 25th November aaa 3rd Division will have its head on line SOMZEE CHARLEROI Road by evening 25th November aaa Orders for March on 24th November will be issued later aaa ACKNOWLEDGE aaa Addressed 3 Bdes C.R.A. C.R.E. A.D.M.S. "Q" Signals A.P.M. 3rd M.T. Coy. Train.

From: 3rd. Division.

Secret

3rd. Division Operation Order No. 223

1. The Division will march tomorrow 24th Nov in accordance with the following March Table.

Reference Sheet. 1/100,000

MARCH TABLE.

Unit.	Starting Point.	Hour of start.	Route.	Destination.	Instructions.
"A" GROUP.	Road junction 3C 25.20	10-10	Cross roads HC 05.75 – BOUSIGNES – cross junction 3C 35.20 – cross junction 3C 35.40 – west junction 3C 55.33 – LEERS ET FOSTEAU	THUIN LOBBES	Rd HQ – THUIN
"B" GROUP. (88)	Cross roads 3 B 23.03	09 05	– do –	LEER ET FOSTEAU RAGNIES BIERCEE BOIS DE VILLIERS	Bn HQ – Château LEERS ET FOSTEAU
"C" GROUP.	Cross roads 3A 33.14 in CERFONTAINE	08 35	COLLERET – West bank of LA THURE River – cross roads HC 05.75 – BOUSIGNES – cross junction 3C 35.20	BERSILLIES L'ABBAYE BOUSIGNES MONTIGNIES ST CHRISTOPHE	Bde HQ – MONTIGNIES ST CHRISTOPHE
"D" GROUP.	NO		MOVE		
Divnl. H.Q.	Road junction 3C 25.20	09 10	Route as for A Group	THUIN	Rd HQ – Château REC RUIGNIES

2. Divisional Headquarters will close at COUSOLRE at 0900 and open at THUIN on arrival.
3. ACKNOWLEDGE.

Distribution:— G.O.C., "Q", C.R.A., Div. Train., A.P.M.,
8th. Inf. Bde.   VI Corps "G".
9th. Inf. Bde.   VI Corps "Q".
76th. Inf. Bde.   Camp Commdt.
                  3rd. Div. Signals.

Lieut-Colonel,
General Staff, 3rd. Division.

23/11/18
Issued at 20.50 hrs.

(84)

3rd. Division G.S. 2021

The following moves will take place on 24th Nov.

"A" GROUP. to   THUIN & LOBBES

"B" GROUP. to   LEERS ET FOSTEAU – RAGNIES – BIERCEE
                BOIS DE VILLERS

"C" GROUP. to   BERSILLIES L'ABBAYE – BOUSSIGNIES –
                MONTIGNIES ST CHRISTOPHE

"D" GROUP. to   No Move

Divisional Headquarters will close at COUSOLRE at 0900 and open at THUIN on arrival.

ACKNOWLEDGE.

M Traill
Lieut-Colonel,
General Staff, 3rd. Division.

22/11/18

Distribution :-   A.D.M.S.
                  C.R.E.
                  ~~Camp Commandant.~~
                  D.A.D.O.S.
                  A.D.V.S.
                  3rd. M.T. Coy.
                  ~~Signals.~~
                  File.
                  War Diary.

(85)   3rd. Division G.S. 2023.

The following moves will take place on 25th Nov
==*=*=*=*=*

"A" GROUP. to   NALINES - SOMZEE - GOURDINNE - THYLE CHATEAU.

"B" GROUP. to   BERZEE - COUR SUR HEURE - MARBAIX.

"C" GROUP. to   GOZEE - THUIN.

"D" GROUP. to   FONTAINE - VALMONT - HANTES - WIHERIES SOLRE SUR SAMBRE - LA BUISSIERE.

Divisional Headquarters will close at THUIN at 09.00 and open at LOVERVAL on arrival.

ACKNOWLEDGE.

for Lieut-Colonel,
General Staff, 3rd. Division.

24/11/18.

Distribution :-   A.D.M.S.
C.R.E.
Camp Commandant.
D.A.D.O.S.
A.D.V.S.
3rd. M.T. Coy.
Signals.
File.
War Diary.

3rd. Division Operation Order No. 284

1. The Division will march to-morrow 25th Nov. in accordance with the following March table.

Reference Sheet. 1/100,000

MARCH TABLE.

Unit.	Starting Point.	Hour of start.	Route.	Destination.	Instructions.
"A" GROUP.	Cross Roads 2D 85.09	10.40	GOZEE / HAM SUR HEURE / COUR SUR HEURE / BERZEE / THYLE CHATEAU	NALINES / SOMZEE / GOURDINNE / THYLE CHATEAU	Bde H.Q. - NALINES. Route to NALINES via HAM SUR HEURE and CLAQUEDENT
"B" GROUP.	Cross Roads 2D 24.10	10.30	THUIN / GOZEE / HAM SUR HEURE / COUR SUR HEURE	BERZEE / COUR SUR HEURE / MARBAIX	Bde H.Q. BERZEE
"C" GROUP.	Road Junction 3C 55.33	09.25	LEERS ET FOSTEAU / THUIN	GOZEE / THUIN	Bde H.Q. THUIN
"D" GROUP.	No instructions as to route on time			FONTAINE VALMONT / HANTES WIHERIES / SOLRE SUR SAMBRE / LA BUISSIERE	R.A.H.Q. MERBES-le-CHATEAU
DIVL. H.Q.	As for A Group	10.00	GOZEE / MARCINELLE	LOVERVAL	

2. Divisional Headquarters will close at THUIN at 09.00 and open at LOVERVAL on arrival.
3. ACKNOWLEDGE.

Distribution:- G.O.C.; "Q"; O.R.A.; Div. Train.; A.P.M.;
8th. Inf. Bde.   VI Corps "G"
9th. Inf. Bde.   VI Corps "Q"
76th. Inf. Bde.   Camp Comdt
                       Indois. Sig.

24/11/18
Issued at 0800 hrs

[signature]
Lieut-Colonel,
General Staff, 3rd. Division.

MESSAGES AND SIGNALS.

Army Form C. 2121.

Prefix... Code... m.	Words.	Charge.	This message is on a/c of:	Recd. at... m. Date... From By
Office of Origin and Service Instructions. W/	Sent At... m. To (87) By		...Service. (Signature of "Franking Officer.")	

TO	8-9-16 Inf Bde cav Brig ADMS
	G.Cops BHQ camp Cdt Signals

Sender's Number.	Day of Month.	In reply to Number.	AAA
G B 146	24		

Camel lines given in column headed in 2nd Div Operation order No 284 and substitute aaa A Group 1140 hours aaa B Group 1130 hours C Group 1025 hours aaa Div HQ 1100 hours aaa Alteration necessary on account of late arrival of rations aaa Acknowledge aaa Addd all recpt of OO 284 less Cdt

From: Ind Div
Place:
Time: 1810

3rd. Division Operation Order No. 285

1. The Division will march to-morrow Nov 26th in accordance with the following March Table.

Reference Sheet. 1/100,000

MARCH TABLE.

Unit.	Starting Point.	Hour of start.	Route.	Destination.	Instructions.
"A" GROUP.	Cross Roads 2E.23.00	10.00	GERPINNES FROMIÉE - BIESME	METTET PONTAURY BIESME	Groups will march independently from Coys.
"B" GROUP.	Cross Roads 3E.92.42	10.00	SOMZEE TARCIENNE GERPINNES	GOUGNIES VILLERS POTERIE ACOZ GERPINNES	in rear of each Group.
"C" GROUP.	Road Junction 3G.00.75	10.00	HAM-SUR-HEURE COUR-SUR-HEURE THY LE CHATEAU GOURDINNE	TARCIENNE Route to SOMZEE (Malines NALINES) via CLAQUEDENT	
"D" GROUP.	Road Junction 3D.09.83	10.00	THUIN - GOZEE HAM SUR HEURE	GOURDINNE THY-LE CHATEAU BERZEE COUR SUR HEURE MARBAIX	

2. Divisional Headquarters will close at LOVERVAL and open at _____ on arrival.
3. ACKNOWLEDGE.

Distribution:- G.O.C., "Q", C.R.A., Div. Train.; A.P.M.;
8th. Inf. Bde.   VI Corps "G"
9th. Inf. Bde.   VI Corps "Q"
76th. Inf. Bde.   Army Cav.
                     3rd Div Signals

25/11/18

Issued at 0800.

f. _____
Lieut-Colonel,
General Staff, 3rd. Division.

SECRET. 3rd Division G.2002/5.

8th Inf.Bde.	A.D.M.S.
9th Inf.Bde.	3rd Div."Q".
76th Inf.Bde.	3rd Div.Signals.
C.R.A.	A.P.M.
C.R.E.	3rd Div.Train.
20th K.R.R.C.	Mob.Vet.Section.
Camp Commdt.	D.A.G.C.
D.A.D.O.S.	3rd Div.M.T.Coy.

ADVANCE TO THE RHINE.

1. The Allied Forces are to cross the German frontier in accordance with the terms of the Armistice, to occupy the German territories West of the RHINE, and to establish bridgeheads on the right bank of that river at MAYENCE, COBLENZ and COLOGNE.

2. (a) British troops are to hold the COLOGNE bridgehead. The American Army will be holding the territory on our right and the Belgian Army the territory on our left.

   (b) The British Sector of German territory is to be occupied by the Second Army consisting of four Corps (11 Divisions) and one British Cavalry Division.
   The Second Army will be composed as follows :-

II Corps	9, 29, N.Z. Divisions.
VI Corps	Guards, 2,3, Divisions.
IX Corps	1, 6, 62 Divisions.
Cdn.Corps.	1, 2, Cdn.Divisions.
1st Cavalry Divn.	

   (c) The Sector between the German frontier and the line AVESNES - MAUBEUGE - CHARLEROI - BRUSSELS is to be occupied by the Fourth Army consisting of three Corps (14 Divisions) and Cavalry Corps (less one Cavalry Division).

3. The 62nd Division will complete its march as already ordered on 25th November, and on the 26th and 27th November will (less attached troops) sideslip into the IX Corps area, with its head at HAID (inclusive) and tail at DINANT (exclusive) along the Northern route of the IX Corps.

4. The 3rd Division will become the leading Division of the VI Corps on the Southern road. The 3rd Division will therefore continue its march on 26th November, so that its head reaches METTET. The 3rd Division (less Divisional Headquarters) will halt on 27th November.
   Divisional Headquarters will move to METTET on 27th November.

5. The advance of the VI and IX Corps is to be resumed on 28th November.

6. The VI Corps has been ordered to arrange its march as follows :-

   (a) The march will be in two columns within the boundaries already allotted to the VI Corps, as far as the line GRANDMENIL - HARRE. (See Map "B" issued with G.2002 dated 15th November and attached Map "C".)

   (b) After leaving above line the VI Corps is to march with its right column via BELLE HAIE - REGNE - SALMCHATEAU to VIELSALM, passing through IX Corps area during this part of the march, and its left column via WERBOMONT - BASSE BODEUX to TROIS PONTS.

/(c)

(89A)

(c) The leading troops of the VI Corps are to reach the line VIELSALM - TROIS PONTS by evening 4th December, unless the weather and state of the roads render this impossible without inflicting undue hardship and discomfort on the troops.

(d) All orders for the further march eastwards from VIELSALM and TROIS PONTS are to be issued to the VI Corps by Second Army, but the VI Corps is to be ready to resume the advance on 5th December.

7. The IX Corps is to continue its march as far as LAROCHE which place its leading troops are to reach by evening 4th December.

On reaching LAROCHE, the IX Corps is to halt until the whole of the VI Corps has crossed the German frontier.

8. (a) The Cavalry attached to the Second Army (1st Cavalry Division) is to cross the German frontier on 1st December, and is to take over the whole of the new front of the Second Army.

The 2nd Cavalry Division is not now required to cross the German frontier on 1st December.

(b) The 2nd Cavalry Division has been ordered, during the 1st December to close to its right, so that by the evening of that day it may be South and clear of the LAROCHE - SALMCHATEAU - VIELSALM - POTEAU Road.

(c) The 2nd Cavalry Division is to occupy billets in the area bounded on the North by the above road (leaving clear all billets required by the VI Corps), on the east by the German frontier, and on the South by the Fourth Army Southern Boundary.

9. (a) The following troops at present attached to the 62nd Division will be transferred to the 3rd Division from midnight 25th/26th November when these units will come under the orders of the G.O.C.76th Infantry Brigade.

  2 Troops Australian Horse) Location will
  1 Coy. 4th Cyclist Battalion) be notified.

(b) 132 A.T.Company, R.E. will be transferred to the 3rd Division from midnight 27th/28th November and will remain as permanent/gang at the bridges over the MEUSE under the orders of the C.R.E.

When the 3rd Division has crossed the MEUSE this unit will be transferred to the VI Corps Heavy Artillery.

(c) C.C.Cable Section and one Section 174th Tunnelling Company will be transferred from 62nd to 3rd Division from midnight 27th/28th November.

10. The 3rd Division will be re-grouped as follows :-

"A" Group.   (2 Troops Australian Horse.
       (1 Coy. 4th Cyclist Battalion.
Commander - (76th Inf.Bde.
       (1 Brigade, R.F.A. *
Brig.Genl.F.E.METCALFE,(529th Field Coy. R.E.
 C.M.G., D.S.O. (20th K.R.R.C.(Pioneer Battalion).
       (7th Field Ambulance.
       (No.2 Coy. Divisional Train.
       (One Section,174th Tunnelling Coy.

/ "B" Group.

* To be selected by C.R.A.

(90)

"B" Group.　　　　　　　(9th Inf.Bde.
　　　　　　　　　　　　(56th Field Company, R.E.
Commander -　　　　　　(3rd Battalion, Machine Gun Corps.
　　　　　　　　　　　　(142 Field Ambulance.
Brig.Genl.H.C.POTTER,　(No.4 Coy. Divisional Train.
　　　C.M.G., D.S.O.　　(

"C" Group.　　　　　　　(8th Inf.Bde.
　　　　　　　　　　　　(458th Field Coy. R.E.
Commander -　　　　　　(8th Field Ambulance.
　　　　　　　　　　　　(No.3 Coy. Divisional Train.
Brig.Gen. B.D.FISHER,
　　　　　D.S.O.

Brig.Genl.C.YATMAN,
　　　C.M.G.,D.S.O.
(Temporarily Commanding)

"D" Group.　　　　　　　(23rd Brigade R.F.A.) Less Brigade
　　　　　　　　　　　　(40th Brigade R.F.A.) attached "A"
　　　　　　　　　　　　(42nd Brigade R.F.A.) Group.
Commander -　　　　　　(D.A.C.
　　　　　　　　　　　　(No.XI Mobile Vet. Section.
Brig.Genl.J.S.OLLIVANT,(No.1 Coy. Divisional Train.
　　C.M.G.,D.S.O.,R.A.

Divisional H.Q.Group.　(Divisional H.Q.Transport.
　　　　　　　　　　　　(H.Q.Section, Div.Signal Coy.
　　　　　　　　　　　　(C.C. Cable Section.

11.　　ACKNOWLEDGE.

　　　　　　　　　　　　　　　　　　　　Lieut.Colonel,
　　　　　　　　　　　　　　　　General Staff, 3rd Division.

25th November 1918.

* Maps issued to units starred.

3rd. Division Operation Order No. 286

1. The Division will march tomorrow 28th Nov in accordance with the following March Table.

Reference Sheet. 1/100,000

MARCH TABLE.

Unit.	Starting Point.	Hour of start.	Route.	Destination.	Instructions.
"A" GROUP	Cross Road 3 I 35 75	10 00	BIOUL	ANNEVOIE ROUILLON	
			BIOUL Road Junction 2 J 67 02 WARNANT	WARNANT ANHEE	Train Companies will march in rear of their groups
"B" GROUP	Railway level crossing 2 H 00 20	09 35	BIESME SERY PONTAURY	ST GERARD	
			BIESME — SERY METTET — Cross Road 3 I 35.75	BIOUL	
"C" GROUP	Cross Roads 3 G 20 65	10 00	HANZINNE HANZINELLE ORET STATION Cross Roads 3 H 95.67	GRAUX FURNAUX DENEE	
"D" GROUP	S.P. to be fixed by CRA not to enter SOMZEE before 10 45		SOMZEE GERPINNES BIESMES	BIESMES METTET SERY PONTAURY	
	Div H.Q. Horse Transport/Signal of first L in LOVERVAL Cross roads ½ mile N.E	10 00	VILLERS POTERIE COUGNIES BIESMES METTET		Long halt by feeding will be made immediately after clearing METTET

2. Divisional Headquarters will close at LOVERVAL at 0900 and open at BIOUL on arrival.
3. ACKNOWLEDGE.

Distribution:- G.O.C., "Q", C.R.A., Div. Train, A.P.M.,
8th. Inf. Bde.
9th. Inf. Bde. VI Corps "G".
76th. Inf. Bde. VI Corps "Q".
Camp Comdt
Signals

27/11/18.

Issued at 1200 hours

_____
for _____ Major
for Lieut-Colonel,
General Staff, 3rd. Division.

SECRET.
Copy No. 20

3rd DIVISION OPERATION ORDER NO. 287.

27th November 1918.

Reference NAMUR and MARCHE Sheets
1/100,000.

1. The Division will march in accordance with the attached March Table on the 29th November.

    The order of march will be as follows :-

    (i) "A" Group.) Less 1st Line Transport.
        "B" Group.) (Only vehicles laid down in G.7359
        "C" Group.)   will accompany units).

    (ii) "A" Group.)
         "B" Group.) 1st Line Transport.
         "C" Group.)

    (iii) "A" Group. Train Company.
          "B" Group.   do.
          "C" Group.   do.

    (iv) "D" Group.

2. For the march on the 29th November the 1st Line Transport of Groups will be under the orders of the O.C. Divisional Train who will issue orders direct to Brigade Transport Officers as regards Starting Points and hour of start.
    Order of march will be in accordance with para 1.

3. As soon as the 1st Line Transport of Groups has crossed the bridge at YVOIR the whole of the Train (Less 1 Company with D.A.) will close up with its head on the bridge and will cross the MEUSE in rear of the 1st Line Transport, in order of groups.

4. (a) Each Infantry Brigade will leave an infantry party of 2 Officers and 50 other ranks in YVOIR to report to the O.C. Divisional Train - rendezvous for these parties - east end of YVOIR Bridge.
    As soon as these parties are no longer required O.C. Divisional Train will order them to proceed on their march and rejoin their units.

/(b)

(2)

(b) Each Group will hand over all spare horses to the O.C. of their affiliated Train Company before commencing the march on the 29th November.

5. On all marches in future the greatcoat will be carried on the man.

6. The C.R.A. will detail 12 pairs of horses (with drivers and harness) to report at Divisional H.Q. BIOUL on the afternoon of November 28th, these will be handed over to the O.C. Divisional Train for rations and accommodation and will be used by him on hill East of the YVOIR on November 29th.

7. A Staff Officer will be on the hill just east of YVOIR with orders to dump excess baggage on overloaded wagons.

8. Divisional Headquarters will remain at BIOUL on Nov. 29th.

9. ACKNOWLEDGE.

Lieut.Colonel,
General Staff, 3rd Division.

Issued at 20.30 hours.

Copies to :-

1. G.O.C.
2. 8th Inf.Bde.
3. 9th Inf.Bde.
4. 76th Inf.Bde.
5. C.R.A.
6. C.R.E.
7. "Q".
8. A.D.M.S.
9. 3rd Div.Signals.
10. 3rd Div.Train.
11. A.P.M.
12. 3rd Div.M.T.Coy.
13. VI Corps "G".
14. VI Corps "Q".
15. Guards Division.
16. D.A.D.O.S.
17. D.A.D.V.S.
18. Camp Commdt.
19. War Diary.
20. War Diary.
21 - 24 File.

MARCH TABLE TO ACCOMPANY 3rd DIVISION OPERATION ORDER NO. 287.

Unit.	Starting Point.	Hour of start.	Route.	Destination.	Instructions.
"A" Group. (Less 1st Line Transport).	Bridge 3.K.50.85.	09.00	EVREHAILLES.	DORINNE.	
"B" Group. (Less 1st Line Transport).	Road Junction 2.J.67.02.	09.15	Cross Roads 2.K.21.18. Western Bank of LEUSE to Bridge at 3.K.50.85. EVREHAILLES.	} Areas will be notified by "Q".	
"C" Group. (Less 1st Line Transport).	Cross Roads 3.J.03.91.	09.00	BIOUL. Cross Roads 2.K.21.18. Western Bank of MEUSE to Bridge at 3.K.50.85. EVREHAILLES.	BIOUL	
"D" Group.	Cross Roads 3.J.33.75.	11.15	BIOUL. Road Junction 2.J.67.02.	ANNEVOIE ROUILLON. WARNANT ATHEE	Road ROUILLON— Bridge at 3.K.50.85 is not to be used.

BELGIUM 1:100.000

MARCHE

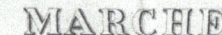

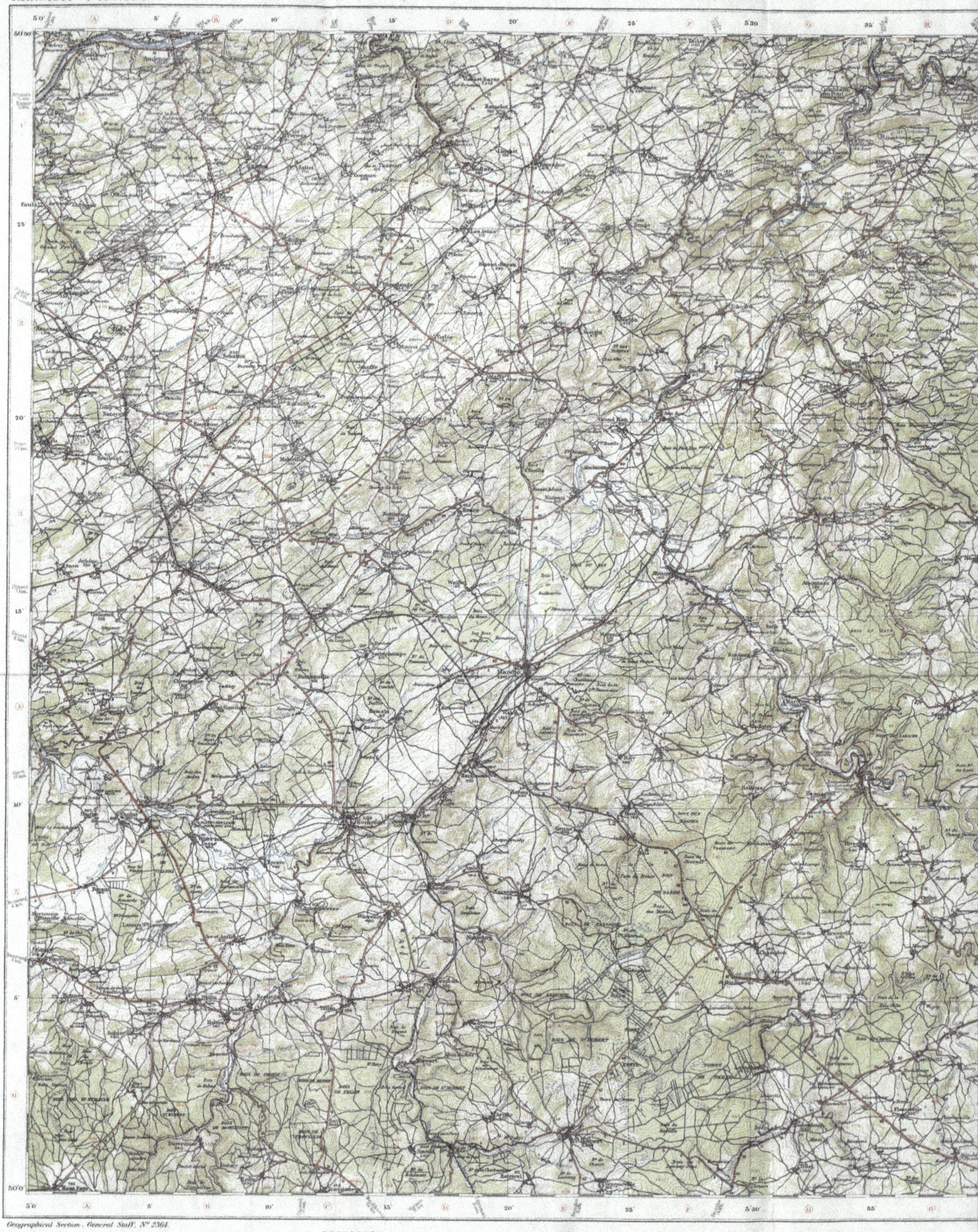

Geographical Section, General Staff, Nº 2364.

REFERENCE

Townships	Thuin
Hamlets	Larroir
Canal or waterway	Lock, Ferry, Ford, Dam or Weir
Chateau, Farm	Chau Fe
Church or Chapel, Tower	
Fort	
Frontier line	
Heights in metres (10 metres 32·8 feet)	
Lighthouse	L.H.
Orchard	

Scale $\frac{1}{100000}$ or 1 Inch to 1·58 Miles

Mile 1 0 1 2 3 4 5 6 7 8 9 10 Miles

Kilometre 1 0 1 2 3 4 5 6 7 8 9 10 11 12 13 14 15 Kilometres

1 Centimetre to 1 Kilometre

Contour interval 10 metres every 100 accentuated. Woods shown in green.

MARCHE

FOR OFFICIAL USE ONLY.

9.

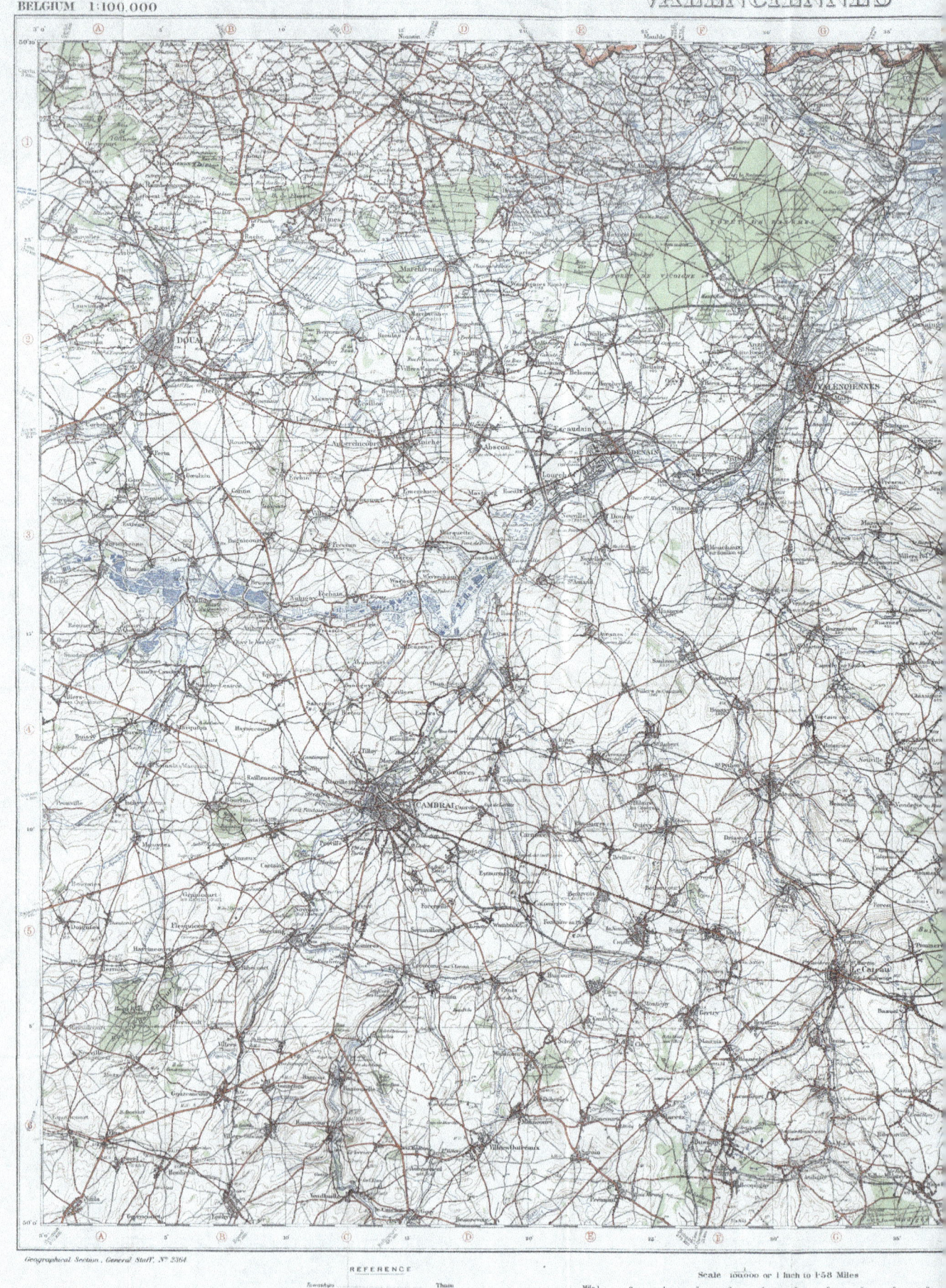

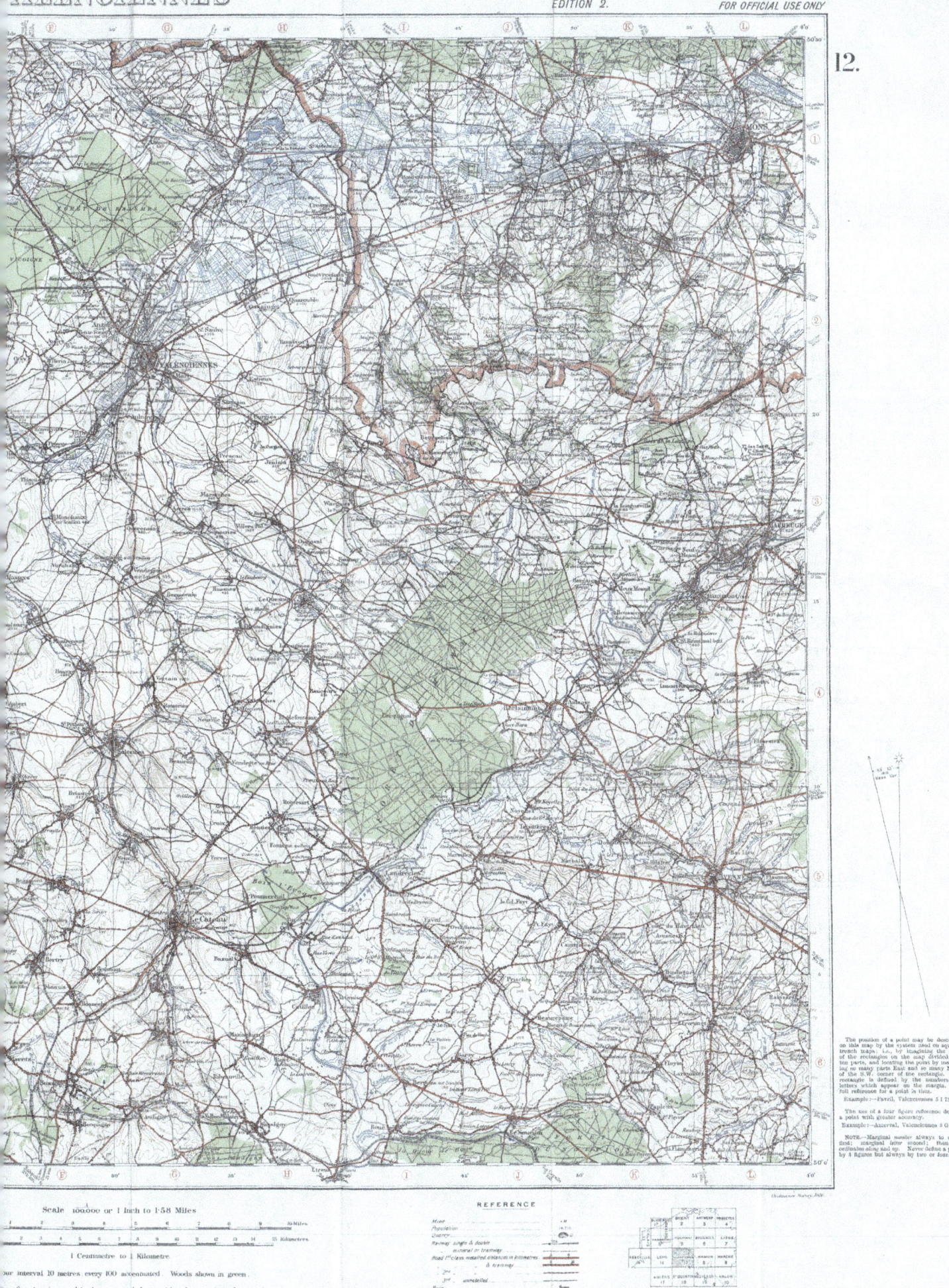

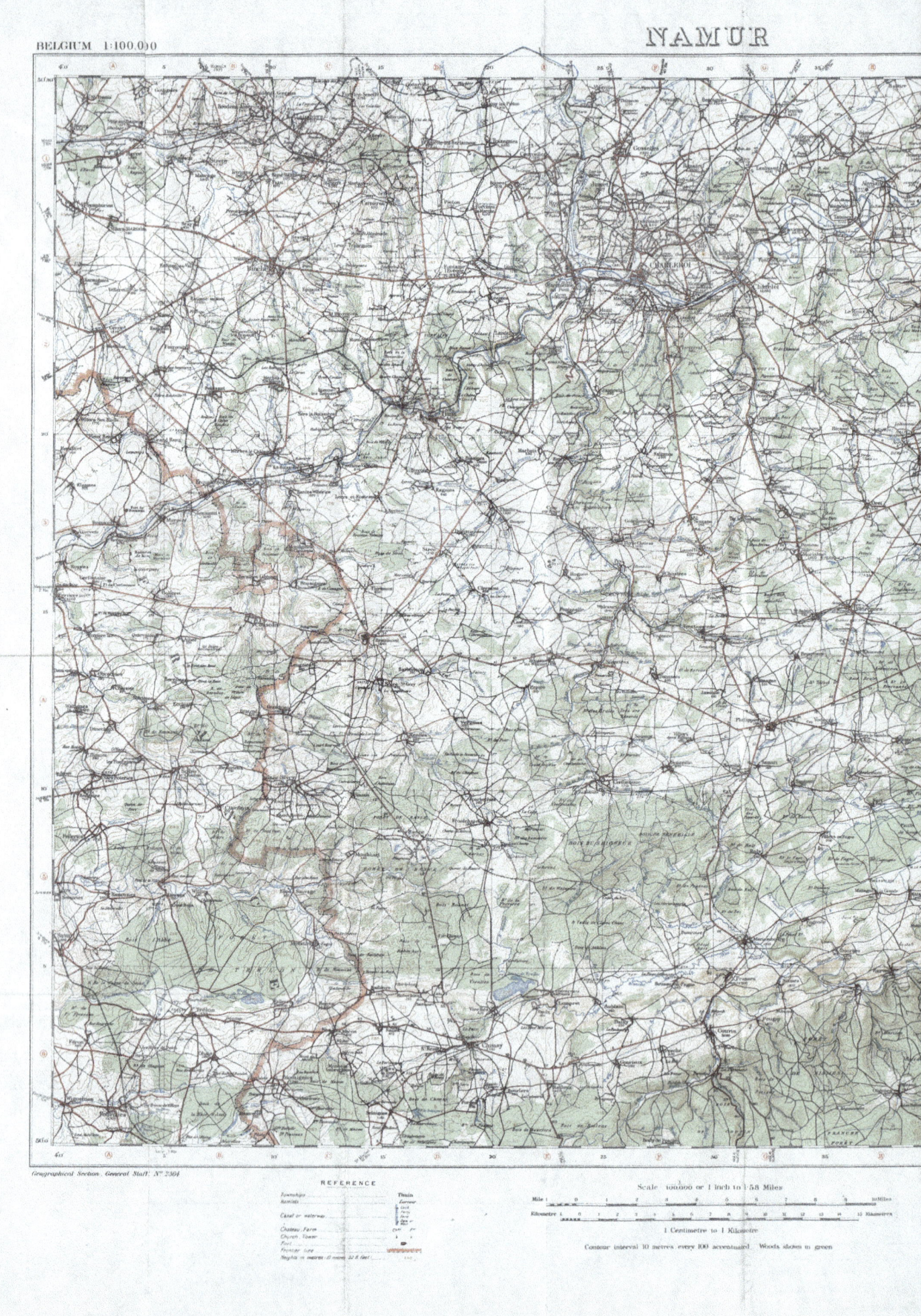

3rd Division

War Diaries

General Staff

December 1918

CONFIDENTIAL

GENERAL STAFF
3rd DIVISION
WAR DIARY
1st – 31st DECEMBER 1915
VOLUME 38

Army Form C. 2118.

WAR DIARY
INTELLIGENCE SUMMARY.

(Erase heading not required.)

Instructions regarding War Diaries and Intelligence Summaries are contained in F. S. Regs., Part II and the Staff Manual respectively. Title pages will be prepared in manuscript.

Place	Date	Hour	Summary of Events and Information	Remarks and references to Appendices
EMPTINNE.	1st Dec.		Weather. Fine. Nothing of interest.	
"	2nd Dec.	20.00 - -	Weather. Dull. 3rd Division Operation Order No.289 issued to all concerned. 3rd Division G.S.2002/6 issued to all concerned. (Vide copy attached). (Vide G.S.2002/6 attached) 3rd Division G.S.2002/7 issued to all concerned. (Vide G.S.2002/7 attached).	
"	3rd Dec.	20.00 -	Weather. Wet. 3rd Division Operation Order No.290 issued to all concerned. (Vide O.O.290 attached). Report on Roads issued to all concerned. (Vide G.S.2042 attached).	
"	4th Dec.	20.00 -	Weather. Wet. 3rd Division Operation Order No.291 issued to all concerned. (Vide O.O.291 attached) Report on Roads issued to all concerned. (Vide G.S.2046 attached).	
"	5th Dec.	09.00.	Weather. Fine but overcast. 3rd Division H.Q.closed at EMPTINNE and opened at GRAND HAN.	
GRAND HAN	6th Dec.	07.00. 20.30.	Weather. Fine. 3rd Division Operation Order No.292 issued to all concerned. (Vide O.O.292 attached). 3rd Division Operation Order No.293 issued to all concerned. (Vide O.O.293 attached).	

Army Form C. 2118.

WAR DIARY
or
INTELLIGENCE SUMMARY.
(Erase heading not required.)

Instructions regarding War Diaries and Intelligence Summaries are contained in F. S. Regs., Part II. and the Staff Manual respectively. Title pages will be prepared in manuscript.

Place	Date	Hour	Summary of Events and Information	Remarks and references to Appendices
GRAND HAN.	7th Dec.	18.00.	Weather. Fine. 3rd Division Operation Order No.294 issued to all concerned. (Vide O.O.294 attached).	
"	8th Dec.	09.00. 19.30.	Weather. Fine. 3rd Division H.Q. closed at GRAND HAN and opened at SALMCHATEAU. 3rd Division Operation Order No. 295 issued to all concerned. (Vide O.O.295 attached).	
"	9th Dec.		Weather. Fine. Report on roads issued to all concerned. (Vide G.2062 attached).	
"	10th Dec.	07.00.	Weather. Dull. Slight rain. 3rd Division Operation Order No.296 issued to all concerned. (Vide O.O.296 attached). 3rd Division G.7629 issued to all concerned. (Vide G.7629 attached). 3rd Division G.7634 issued to all concerned. (Vide G.7634 attached). Training on arrival at our destination in Germany issued to all concerned. (Vide copy attached).	
SALMCHATEAU.	11th Dec.	07.00.	Weather. Wet. 3rd Division Operation Order No.297 issued to all concerned. (Vide G.C.297 attached). During the morning the Corps Commander and Divisional Commander inspected the 76th Inf. Bde. and 20th K.R.R.C.(Pioneers) and 9th Infantry Brigade as they crossed the frontier into Germany.	
"		—	G.O.Cs. letter of congratulation to 9th Inf. Bde. and 76th Inf. Bde.Group.(Vide G.7643 and 7642 attached).	

Army Form C. 2118.

WAR DIARY
or
INTELLIGENCE SUMMARY.

(Erase heading not required.)

Instructions regarding War Diaries and Intelligence Summaries are contained in F. S. Regs., Part II. and the Staff Manual respectively. Title pages will be prepared in manuscript.

Place	Date	Hour	Summary of Events and Information	Remarks and references to Appendices
SALMCHATEAU	12th Dec.	07.00	Weather. Wet.	
			3rd Division Operation Order No.298 issued to all concerned.	(Vide O.O.298 attached).
			3rd Division G.S.2002/8 issued to all concerned.	(Vide G.S.2002/8 attached).
			During the morning the Divisional Commander inspected the M.G.Battalion and 8th Inf.Bde. as they passed the frontier into Germany.	
			G.O.Cs.letter of congratulation to 8th Inf.Bde. and M.G.Battalion.	(Vide G.7646 and 7647 attd).
"	13th Dec.	07.00	Weather. Wet all day.	
			3rd Division Operation Order No.299 issued to all concerned.	(Vide O.O.299 attached).
			G.O.Cs.letter of congratulation to R.A.M.C., R.E. on fine marching when crossing the frontier into Germany.	(Vide G.7650 attached).
			3rd Division G.O. 201 issued to all concerned.	(Vide G.O. 201 attached).
			Report on road reconnaissance issued to all concerned.	(Vide H.7634/2 attached).
"	14th Dec.	06.30	Weather. Dull.	
			3rd Division Operation Order No.300 issued to all concerned.	(Vide O.O.300 attached).
		09.00	3rd Division H.Q.closed at SALMCHATEAU and opened at the Factory, ALBNUTHEN.	
			During the morning the Divisional Commander inspected the Divisional Artillery, 35th Bde. R.G.A. and 132 A.T.Company as they crossed the frontier this morning.	(Vide G.7653 attached).
			3rd Division G.S.2002/9 issued to all concerned.	(Vide G.S.2002/9 attached).
FACTORY ALBNUTHEN	15th Dec.		Weather. Cold and dull.	
			3rd Division Operation Order No.301 issued to all concerned.	(Vide O.O.301 attached).
"	16th Dec.	06.30	Weather. Rain during morning, fine later.	
			3rd Division Operation Order No.302 issued to all concerned.	(Vide O.O.302 attached).
		09.00	3rd Division H.Q.closed at the Factory, ALBNUTHEN and opened at EUSKIRCHEN.	

Army Form C. 2118.

WAR DIARY
or
INTELLIGENCE SUMMARY.
(Erase heading not required.)

Instructions regarding War Diaries and Intelligence Summaries are contained in F. S. Regs., Part II. and the Staff Manual respectively. Title pages will be prepared in manuscript.

Place	Date	Hour	Summary of Events and Information	Remarks and references to Appendices
EUSKIRCHEN	17th Dec.	06.30. 10.30.	Weather. Slight rain. 3rd Division Operation Order No.303 issued to all concerned. 3rd Division Operation Order No.304 issued to all concerned. Report on roads issued to all concerned.	(Vide O.O.303 attached) (Vide O.O.304 attached) (Vide G.7670 attached)
"	18th Dec.	06.50. 14.00	Weather. Dull. 3rd Division Operation Order No.305 issued to all concerned. Addition to O.O.305 issued to all concerned. 3rd Division Operation Order No.306 issued to all concerned. Road Reconnaissance Report issued to all concerned.	(Vide O.O.305 attached). (Vide copy attached). (Vide O.O.306 attached). (Vide G.7649/2 attached).
"	19th Dec.	09.00.	Weather. Cold. and windy. 3rd Division H.Q. closed at EUSKIRCHEN and opened at DUREN.	
DUREN	20th Dec.		Weather. Slight rain. Nothing of interest.	
"	21st Dec.		Weather. Fine. Nothing of interest.	
"	22nd Dec.		Weather. Fine. Nothing to report.	

Army Form C. 2118.

WAR DIARY
INTELLIGENCE SUMMARY.
(Erase heading not required.)

Instructions regarding War Diaries and Intelligence Summaries are contained in F.S. Regs., Part II. and the Staff Manual respectively. Title pages will be prepared in manuscript.

Place	Date	Hour	Summary of Events and Information	Remarks and references to Appendices
DUREN.	23rd Dec.		Weather. Wet. G.O.Cs. letter to all ranks of the 3rd (Iron) Division issued to all concerned. (Vide G.7716 attached).	
"	24th Dec.		Weather. Fine. Nothing to report.	
"	25th Dec.		Weather. Snow during morning. Fine later. Nothing of interest.	
"	26th Dec.		Weather. Rain with bright intervals. 3rd Div. G.7738 re move of portion of 8th and 9th Brigades. (Vide G.7738 attached). 3rd Div. G.A.288 re above issued to 8th and 9th Brigades. (Vide G.A.288 attached).	
"	27th Dec.		Weather. Wet. Nothing of interest.	
"	28th Dec.		Weather. Wet. Nothing to report.	
"	29th Dec.		Weather. Fine. Nothing to report.	
"	30th Dec.		Weather. Fine. Nothing of interest.	
"	31st Dec.		Weather. Fine. Nothing to report.	

F. Hume Maj.
for Lieut-Colonel
General Staff 3rd Division.

Army Form C. 2118.

WAR DIARY
INTELLIGENCE SUMMARY.
(Erase heading not required.)

Instructions regarding War Diaries and Intelligence Summaries are contained in F. S. Regs., Part II. and the Staff Manual respectively. Title pages will be prepared in manuscript.

Place	Date	Hour	Summary of Events and Information	Remarks and references to Appendices
EMPTINNE.	1st Dec.		Weather. Fine. Nothing of interest.	
"	2nd Dec.	20.00. — —	Weather. Dull. 3rd Division Operation Order No.289 issued to all concerned. 3rd Division G.S.2002/6 issued to all concerned. 3rd Division G.S.2002/7 issued to all concerned.	(Vide copy attached). (Vide G.S.2002/6 attached). (Vide G.S.2002/7 attached).
"	3rd Dec.	20.00. —	Weather. Wet. 3rd Division Operation Order No.290 issued to all concerned. Report on Roads issued to all concerned.	(Vide O.O.290 attached). (Vide G.S.2042 attached).
"	4th Dec.	20.00. —	Weather. Wet. 3rd Division Operation Order No.291 issued to all concerned. Report on Roads issued to all concerned.	(Vide O.O.291 attached). (Vide G.S.2046 attached).
"	5th Dec.	09.00.	Weather. Fine but overcast. 3rd Division H.Q. closed at EMPTINNE and opened at GRAND HAN.	
GRAND HAN	6th Dec.	07.00. 20.30.	Weather. Fine. 3rd Division Operation Order No. 292 issued to all concerned. 3rd Division Operation Order No.293 issued to all concerned.	(Vide O.O.292 attached). (Vide O.O.293 attached).

Army Form C. 2118.

WAR DIARY
or
INTELLIGENCE SUMMARY.
(Erase heading not required.)

Instructions regarding War Diaries and Intelligence Summaries are contained in F. S. Regs, Part II. and the Staff Manual respectively. Title pages will be prepared in manuscript.

Place	Date	Hour	Summary of Events and Information	Remarks and references to Appendices
GRAND HAN.	7th Dec.	18.00.	Weather. Fine. 3rd Division Operation Order No.294 issued to all concerned.	(Vide O.O.294 attached).
"	8th Dec.	09.00. 19.30.	Weather. Fine. 3rd Division H.Q.closed at GRAND HAN and opened at SALMCHATEAU. 3rd Division Operation Order No. 295 issued to all concerned.	(Vide O.O.295 attached).
SALMCHATEAU.	9th Dec.		Weather. Fine. Report on roads issued to all concerned.	(Vide G.2062 attached).
"	10th Dec.	07.00.	Weather. Dull. Slight rain. 3rd Division Operation Order No.296 issued to all concerned. 3rd Division G.7629 issued to all concerned. 3rd Division G.7634 issued to all concerned. Training on arrival at our destination in Germany issued to all concerned.	(Vide O.O.296 attached). (Vide G.7629 attached). (Vide G.7634 attached). (Vide copy attached).
"	11th Dec.	07.00. —	Weather. Wet. 3rd Division Operation Order No.297 issued to all concerned. During the morning the Corps Commander and Divisional Commander inspected the 76th Inf.Bde. and 20th K.R.R.C.(Pioneers) and 9th Infantry Brigade as they crossed the frontier into Germany. G.O.Cs.letter of congratulation to 9th Inf. Bde. and 76th Inf.Bde.Group.	(Vide G.C.297 attached). (Vide G.7643 and 7642 attached).

Army Form C. 2118.

WAR DIARY
or
INTELLIGENCE SUMMARY.
(Erase heading not required.)

Instructions regarding War Diaries and Intelligence Summaries are contained in F. S. Regs., Part II. and the Staff Manual respectively. Title pages will be prepared in manuscript.

Place	Date	Hour	Summary of Events and Information	Remarks and references to Appendices
SALMCHATEAU.	12th Dec.	07.00	Weather. Wet. 3rd Division Operation Order No.298 issued to all concerned. 3rd Division G.S.2002/8 issued to all concerned. During the morning the Divisional Commander inspected the M.G.Battalion and 8th Inf.Bde. as they passed the frontier into Germany. G.O.Cs.letter of congratulation to 8th Inf.Bde. and M.G.Battalion.	(Vide O.O.298 attached). (Vide G.S.2002/8 attached). (Vide G.7646 and 7647 attd).
"	13th Dec.	07.00	Weather. Wet all day. 3rd Division Operation Order No.299 issued to all concerned. G.O.Cs.letter of congratulation to R.A.M.C., R.E. on fine marching when crossing the frontier into Germany. 3rd Division G.C. 201 issued to all concerned. Report on road reconnaissance issued to all concerned.	(Vide O.O.299 attached). (Vide G.7650 attached). (Vide G.C. 201 attached). (Vide H.7634/2 attached).
"	14th Dec.	06.30 09.00	Weather. Dull. 3rd Division Operation Order No.300 issued to all concerned. 3rd.Division H.Q.closed at SALMCHATEAU and opened at the Factory, ALBNUTHEN. During the morning the Divisional Commander inspected the Divisional Artillery, 35th Bde. R.G.A. and 132 A.T.Company as they crossed the frontier this morning. 3rd Division G.S.2002/9 issued to all concerned. G.O.Cs.letter of congratulations to Div.Arty., 35th Bde.RGA., 132 A.T.Coy. and Div.Train on fine marching when crossing the frontier.	(Vide O.O.300 attached). (Vide G.7655 attached). (Vide G.S.2002/9 attached). (Vide G.7653 attd).
FACTORY ALBNUTHEN	15th Dec.		Weather. Cold and dull. 3rd Division Operation Order No.301 issued to all concerned.	(Vide O.O.301 attached).
"	16th Dec.	06.30 09.00	Weather. Rain during morning, fine later. 3rd Division Operation Order No.302 issued to all concerned. 3rd Division H.Q.closed at the Factory, ALBNUTHEN and opened at EUSKIRCHEN.	(Vide O.O.302 attached).

Army Form C. 2118.

WAR DIARY
or
INTELLIGENCE SUMMARY.

(Erase heading not required.)

Instructions regarding War Diaries and Intelligence Summaries are contained in F.S. Regs., Part II. and the Staff Manual respectively. Title pages will be prepared in manuscript.

Place	Date	Hour	Summary of Events and Information	Remarks and references to Appendices
EUSKIRCHEN	17th Dec.	06.30 10.30	Weather. Slight rain. 3rd Division Operation Order No.303 issued to all concerned. (Vide O.O.303 attached) 3rd Division Operation Order No.304 issued to all concerned. (Vide O.O.304 attached) Report on roads issued to all concerned. (Vide G.7670 attached)	
"	18th Dec.	06.30 — 14.00	Weather. Dull. 3rd Division Operation Order No.305 issued to all concerned. (Vide O.O.305 attached). Addition to O.O.305 issued to all concerned. (Vide copy attached). 3rd Division Operation Order No.306 issued to all concerned. (Vide O.O.306 attached). Road Reconnaissance Report issued to all concerned. (Vide G.7649/2 attached).	
"	19th Dec.	09.00	Weather. Cold, and windy. 3rd Division H.Q. closed at EUSKIRCHEN and opened at DUREN.	
DUREN	20th Dec.		Weather. Slight rain. Nothing of interest.	
"	21st Dec.		Weather. Fine. Nothing of interest.	
"	22nd Dec.		Weather. Fine. Nothing to report.	

Army Form C. 2118.

WAR DIARY
INTELLIGENCE SUMMARY.
(Erase heading not required.)

Instructions regarding War Diaries and Intelligence Summaries are contained in F. S. Regs., Part II. and the Staff Manual respectively. Title pages will be prepared in manuscript.

Place	Date	Hour	Summary of Events and Information	Remarks and references to Appendices
DUREN.	23rd Dec.		Weather. Wet. G.O.Cs. letter to all ranks of the 3rd (Iron) Division issued to all concerned. (Vide G.7716 attached).	
"	24th Dec.		Weather. Fine. Nothing to report.	
"	25th Dec.		Weather. Snow during morning. Fine later. Nothing of interest.	
"	26th Dec.		Weather. Rain with bright intervals. 3rd Div. G.7738 re move of portion of 8th and 9th Brigades. (Vide G.7738 attached). 3rd Div. G.A.288 re above issued to 8th and 9th Brigades. (Vide G.A.288 attached).	
"	27th Dec.		Weather. Wet. Nothing of interest.	
"	28th Dec.		Weather. Wet. Nothing to report.	
"	29th Dec.		Weather. Fine. Nothing to report.	
"	30th Dec.		Weather. Fine. Nothing of interest.	
"	31st Dec.		Weather. Fine. Nothing to report.	

f. Emmers Hoon
for Lieut Colonel
General Staff 3rd Division

3rd DIVISION OPERATION ORDER NO. 289.

1. The Division will march on December 4th in accordance with the following March Table.
Reference Sheet 1/100,000.

MARCH TABLE

Unit.	Starting Point.	Route.	Destination.	Instructions.
"A" Group.	To be clear of present area by 09.30.	Any	BAILLONVILLE. HEURE. NETTINNE. SINSIN.	
"B" Group.	Head of column not to pass east of present area before 08.30, tail to be clear of it by 09.30.	Any	MOHIVILLE. PESSOUX. ACHET. CINEY.	
"C" Group.	Head of column not to pass east of present area before 08.30 hours, tail to be clear of it by 09.30.	Any	NATOYE. BRAIBANT.	
"D" Group.	Not to leave PURNODE before 09.30 and to be clear of that village by 11.30.	Any	SOVET. SPONTIN. DORINNE. DURNAL. PURNODE. AVAGNE.	
35th Bde. R.G.A.	Not to enter PURNODE before 11.30.	Any		

2. Divisional Headquarters will remain at CHATEAU DE FONTAIN on December 4th.
3. ACKNOWLEDGE.

Distributions:— G.O.C., "Q". C.R.A. Div.Train.
8th Inf.Bde. VI Corps "G".
9th Inf.Bde. VI Corps "Q".
76th Inf.Bde. 35th Bde.R.G.A.

2/12/18. for Lemley
Issued at 20.00. Major
for Lieut.Colonel.
General Staff, 3rd Division.

SECRET. 3rd Div. G.S.2002/6.

```
* 8th Inf.Bde.        A.D.M.S.         35th Bde. R.G.A. *
* 9th Inf.Bde.      * 3rd Div."Q".
* 76th Inf.Bde.       3rd Div.Sigs.
* C.R.A.              A.P.M.
* C.R.E.              3rd Div.M.T.Coy.
  20th K.R.R.C.       3rd Div.Train.
  Camp Commdt.        Mob.Vet.Section.
  D.A.D.O.S.          D.M.G.O.
```

ADVANCE TO THE RHINE.

1. The distribution of the Second Army in German territory is shewn on Rhine Valley No.1 Map issued to all concerned.

2. The advance to the occupation of the Bridgehead is to be carried out by

   Canadian Corps   )
   1 Cavalry Brigade   ) on the right.

   II Corps.   )
   1st Cavalry Divn.   ) on the left.
   (less 1 Cavalry   )
       Brigade)   )

3. The Canadian and II Corps will be followed by the VI Corps.

4. The composition of the Columns of the VI Corps is shewn in Appendix "A".
   G.Os.C.Divisions will assume responsibility for their Columns from 23.59 hours 1st December.

5. The main road allotted for the advance of each column and the dividing line between columns for billeting purposes are shewn on the attached Maps "D" and "E".

6. When the frontier has been crossed, although the comfort of the troops is the first consideration, military precautions against surprise must be taken.

7. Any enemy encountered on the march are to be taken prisoners.

8. ACKNOWLEDGE.

                                              Lieut.Colonel.
                                        General Staff, 3rd Division.

2nd December 1918.

* Maps "D" and "E" attached.

APPENDIX "A".

Composition of columns from 2nd December (inclusive).

RIGHT COLUMN.   Maj.Genl. C.J. DEVERELL, C.B.
                                      3rd Division.

    3rd Division.
    35th Mobile Brigade, R.G.A.
    "CC" Cable Section.
    132nd Army Troops Coy. R.E.
    70th Sanitary Section.
    H.Q. and 2½ Sections 21st A.A. Horse Coy.

CENTRE COLUMN.   Maj.Genl. T.G. MATHESON, C.B.
                                      Guards Division.

    Guards Division.
    63rd Mobile Brigade R.G.A.
    No.5 Group Sharpshooters (Lovats Scouts).
    "C" Cable Section.
    280th Army Troops Coy. R.E.
    38th Sanitary Section.
    One Section 13th A.A. Horse Coy.
    One Section 15th A.A. Horse Coy.
    Half Section 21st A.A. Horse Coy.

LEFT COLUMN.   Maj.Genl. C.E. PEREIRA, C.B., C.M.G.
                                      2nd Division).

    2nd Division.
    92nd Mobile Brigade R.G.A.
    "M" A.A. Battery.
    No.7 AA. Searchlight Section.
    H.Q. and 2 Sections 15th A.A. Horse Coy.
    33rd Sanitary Section,

                                                                    P.T.O.

CORPS HEADQUARTERS GROUP.

VI Corps Headquarters.
Headquarters VI Corps Heavy Artillery.
6th Cyclist Battalion.
'F' Corps Signal Coy.
Nos.13,20 .93 Motor Airline Sections.
"A" Cable Section.
One Light Motor Wireless Section.
174th Tunnelling Coy. R.E.
Half 30th M.A.C.
H.Q.and 2 Sections 13th AA.Horse Coy.
No.6 Vet.Evac.Station.

12th Squadron R.A.F.

SECRET. 3rd Div.G.S.2002/7.

8th Inf.Bde.	VI Corps "G".
9th Inf.Bde.	VI Corps "Q".
76th Inf.Bde.	3rd Div."Q".
C.R.A.	A.D.M.S.
C.R.E.	Camp Commdt.
3rd Div.Train.	D.A.D.O.S.
A.P.M.	D.A.D.V.S.
D.M.G.C.	3rd Div.Signals.
20th K.R.R.C.	

Reference N.W.Europe. Sheet 5. 1/250,000.

Forecast of moves to take place after 4th December at dates to be notified later.

	Approximate position of head of Column.
1st Day.	SOY
2nd Day.	MANHAY
3rd Day.	SART
4th Day.	BEHO
5th Day.	ST. VITH.
6th Day.	ANDLER.

2nd November 1918.

for Lieut.Colonel.
General Staff, 3rd Division.

3rd Division Operation Order No.290.

1. The Division will march on 5th December in accordance with the following March Table.

Reference Sheet 1/100,000.

MARCH TABLE

Unit.	Starting Point.	Hour of Start.	Route.	Destination.	Instructions.
"A" Group.	Cross Roads 3.E.20.50.	10.00.	NOISEUX – FRONVILLE – HOTTON.	SOY – NY – HOTTON. NONVILLE.	Units proceeding to SOY march via NY but all transport of their units will move by route given.
"B" Group.	Road Junction 3.C.63.32.	10.00	BAILLONVILLE.	FRONVILLE – DEULIN GD.ENEILLE –NOISEUX BAILLONVILLE.	
Div.H.Q. Transport & Sig.Section.	Road Junction 3.B.55.82.	07.00.	Cross Roads 3.C.17.60. MAFFE – Road Junction 2.E.50.15.	GRAND HAN.	
"C" Group.	Head of Column not to pass Cross Roads 3.C.15.41 before 10.30 hours. Tail of column to be clear of NATOYE – LEIGNON Railway by 09.00 hours.		Cross Roads. 3.C.15.41	MARESSEE. HEURE. NETTINNE. SINSIN.	Train Companies will march in rear of their groups.
"D" Group.	Railway Crossing 3.A.89.72.	09.30	Any	PESSOUX. – SOY. MOHIVILLE –AGIET.	
35 Bde.RGA. with 132 A.T. Coy.R.E.	Not to leave present area before 10 hours.		SPONTIN. BRABANT.	CINEY.	

2. Divisional Headquarters will close at EMPTINNE at 09.00 hours and open at GRAND HAN on arrival.
3. ACKNOWLEDGE.

Distribution :- G.O.C. C.R.A. Div.Train. A.P.M.
8th Inf.Bde. "Q". VI Corps "G". Camp Commdt.
9th Inf.Bde. VI Corps "Q". 3rd Div.Sigs.
76th Inf.Bde. 35th Bde.R.G.A.

for Lieut.Colonel.
General Staff, 3rd Division.

3/12/18.
Issued at 20.00 hours.

3rd Division G.S.2042.

8th Inf.Bde.
9th Inf.Bde.
76th Inf.Bde.
C.R.A.
35th Bde. R.G.A.
3rd Div.Train.

The main road between HOTTON and SOY is good.

Between HOTTON and SOY there is a steep gradient from HOTTON to the second kilometre stone and again from the Fourth kilometre stone into SOY. The road between the second and fourth kilometre stones is level.

In moving transport over this road Group Commanders should make arrangements for spare horses and parties of men to assist heavily laden wagons up these two gradients in case of necessity.

Troops can march via NY which is 1¾ miles shorter than by the main road via HOTTON but it is not advisable to take the transport via NY as there is a steep gradient of a mile in length between NY and SOY and the road is not good for transport.

Sd. W.H.Traill.Lieut.Colonel.
General Staff, 3rd Division.

3/12/18

3rd Division.

Copy to 1st Division for information.

3rd Division Operation Order No.291.

1. The Division will march on 6th DEC. in accordance with the following March Table.
2. Train Coys. will march in rear of their groups.

Reference Sheet 1/100,000.

MARCH TABLE.

Unit.	Starting Point.	Hour of start.	Route.	Area	Instruction.
"A" Group.	Cross Roads 3.G.30.47.	10.00	EREZEE. GRANDMENIL.	ODEIGNE. MALEMPRE. VAUX CHAVANNE. GRANDMENIL.	
"B" Group.	Cross Roads, 3.F.17.44.	10.00	HOTTON SOY.	EREZEE. NORMONT. FANZEL.	
"C" Group.	Cross Roads 3.D.77.61.	09.30	NOISEUX. FRONVILLE.	SOY. NY. HOTTON.	Units moving to SOY can march via NY all transport of these units will move by main road via HOTTON.
"D" Group.	Road Junction, 3.C.63.32.	09.30	HEURE.	MONVILLE. FRONVILLE. NOISEUX.	
35th Bde. RGA. 132 AT.Coy.RE.	Cross Roads 3.B.30.53.	09.30	PESSOUX. HEURE.	BAILLONVILLE.	

3. Divisional Headquarters will remain at GRAND HAN.
4. ACKNOWLEDGE.

f. Lindsay Major.
for Lieut. Colonel.
General Staff, 3rd Division.

Distribution:- G.O.C., "Q", G.R.A. Div.Train. A.P.M. VI Corps "G"
9th Inf.Bde. VI.Corps "Q" 2nd Division. 35/Gen R30.
76th Inf.Bde. Guards Div. 6th Division.
AT.Coy.RE. 3rd.Division. VI Corps H.A.

4/12/18.
Issued at 20.00.

3rd Division.
G.S.2046.

8th Inf.Bde.
9th Inf.Bde.
76th Inf.Bde.
C.R.A.
3rd Div.Train.
35th Bde.R.G.A.

    The road between EREZEE and GRANDMENIL is very muddy and there is a long steep gradient leading from the river AISNE up to the village of EREZEE and a short steep gradient between the 11th and 12th kilometre stones East of EREZEE.

    There is also a long steep gradient between the 15th [13/15] and 17th kilometre stones West of GRANDMENIL.

    The usual precautions should be taken to assist heavily laden wagons up these gradients if necessary.

                                          Lieut.Colonel.
                                  General Staff, 3rd Division.

4th December 1918.

Copy to 1st Division for information.

3rd Division Operation Order No.292.

1. The Division will march on December 7th in accordance with the following March Table.
Reference Sheet 1/100,000.

MARCH TABLE

Unit.	Starting Point.	Hour of Start.	Route.	Destination.	Instruction.
"A" Group.	Road Junction 3.I.37.42.	10.00	Any	ELHAIN. REGNE. MALEMPRE. ODEIGNE. VAUX CHAVANNE.	
"B" Group.			Any	GRANDMENIL. HORMONT. FANZEL.	Not to leave present area, before 08.50. Tail to be clear of present area by 10.00.
Div. H.Q. Transport & Sig. Sec.	GRAND HAN.	10.00	HOTTON EREZEE.	CLERHEID.	
"C" Group.			ANY	EREZEE.	Not to leave present area before 09.15, tail to be clear of it by 10.00.
"D" Group.	MONVILLE.	09.30	ANY	SOY. OPPAGNE. Nr. HOTTON MONVILLE. FRONVILLE.	
35th Bde. RGA. 132. A.T.Coy. RE.				DEULIN. MOISEUX. BAILLONVILLE.	

2. Divisional H.Q. will remain at GRAND HAN.
3. ACKNOWLEDGE.

Distribution:—
G.O.C.	"Q"	C.R.A.	Div. Train.	A.P.M.
8th Inf. Bde.		VI Corps "G"	VI Corps "Q"
9th Inf. Bde.		Camp Commdt.	3rd Div. Sigs.
76th Inf. Bde.		35th Bde. RGA.	Guards Div. 6th Div.
1st Division.		G.R.E.	A.D.M.S.
3rd Div. M.T. Coy.		VI Corps H.A.	A.D.V.S.
		File.	D.A.D.O.S. War Diary.

6/12/18.
Issued at 27.00.

[signature] Major
for Lieut. Colonel.
General Staff, 3rd Division.

1. The Division will march on 8th December in accordance with the following March Table.

Reference Sheet 1/100,000.

MARCH TABLE.

Unit.	Starting Point.	Hour of Start.	ROUTE	DESTINATION.	INSTRUCTIONS.
"A" Group.	Tail to be clear of Road Junction 3.K.09.14.by 11.30.		Any.	BOUVIGNY. COURTIL. GRAND SART. PETIT SART. JOUBIEVAL.	
"B" Group.	Head not to leave present area before 08.15. Tail to be clear of Road junction 3.I.37.42 by 10.30.		Any.	VERLEUMONT. HEBRONVAL. OTTRE. REGNÉ. FRAITURE. ODEIGNE. MALEMPRE.	
Div.H.Q. Transport & Sig.Sec.	CLERHEID.	08.30.	GRANDMENIL. REGNÉ.	SALME CHATEAU.	
"C" Group.	Not to pass Cross Roads 3.H.57.56 before 09.45.		Any	VAUX CHAVANNE. GRAND MENIL. LA BOSSE. LA BATTY.	
"D" Group. 35th Bde. RGA. 132 AT.Coy.RE			NO MOVE.		

2. Divisional Headquarters will close at GRAND HAN at 09.00 and open at SALME CHATEAU on arrival.
3. ACKNOWLEDGE.

Distribution :- G.O.C.   "Q"   CRA   Div.Train.
               8th Inf.Bde.   A.P.M.   VI Corps "G".
               9th Inf.Bde.   VI Corps "Q".   Camp Comdt.
               76th Inf.Bde. 3rd Div.Sigs.   35th Bde.R.G.A.
               Guards Div.   6th Division.   1st Division.
               VI Corps H.A. C.R.E.   A.D.M.S.
               D.A.D.O.S.   3rd Div.M.T.Coy.File.   War Diary.

5/12/18.
Issued at 20.30.

[signature]
for Lieut.Colonel,
General Staff, 3rd Div.

3rd Division Operation Order No.294.

1. The Division will march on the 9th December in accordance with the following March Table.

Reference Sheet 1/100,000.

MARCH TABLE.

Unit.	Starting Point.	Hour of Start.	ROUTE.	DESTINATION.	INSTRUCTIONS.
"A" Group.	Tail of column to be clear of present area by 11.30		Any.	BEHO. OURTHE. WATERMAL. GOUVY. HALCONREUX.	
"B" Group.	Not to pass Cross Roads 3.K.18.18 before 09.30. Tail to be clear of that point by 12.00.		SALM-CHATEAU.	COURTIL. BOVIGNY. ROGERY. BECH.	
"C" Group.	Road Junction 3.I.37.45.	09.30	REGNE.	GRAND SART. JOUBIEVAL. OTTRE. BIHAIN. REGNE. HEBRONVAL. VERLEUMONT.	
"D" Group.	Cross Roads, 3.G.28.48.	09.00	EREZEE. GRANDMENIL.	VAUX CHAVANNE. LALEMPRE. ODEIGNE. LA FOSSE. LE BATTY. GRANDMENIL.	
35th Bde. R.G.A.	Road Junction, 3.E.70.70.	09.00.	FISENNE. SOUS LE BOIS.	FANZEL. MORMONT.	Route from MONVILLE to SOY for marching detachments of Seige Batteries and 132 A.T. Coy. is via NY.
132 A.T. Coy R.E.				EREZEE.	

2. Divisional Headquarters will remain at SALM-CHATEAU.
3. ACKNOWLEDGE.

Distribution :-

G.O.C.	"Q"	C.R.A.	Div.Train.
8th Inf.Bde.	A.P.M.		VI Corps "G".
9th Inf.Bde.	VI Corps "Q".		Camp Commdt.
76th Inf.Bde.	3rd Div.Signals.		35th Bde.RGA.
Guards Div.	6th Division.		1st Division.
VI Corps H.A.	C.R.E.		A.D.M.S.
D.A.D.O.S.	3rd Div.M.T.Coy.		File. War Diary.

7/12/18.
Issued at 18.00.

[signature] Megr.
Lieut.Colonel.
General Staff, 3rd Division.

3rd Division Operation Order No. 295.

1. 3rd Division Operation Order No. 294 is cancelled.
2. The Division will march on December 9th in accordance with the following March Table.
Reference Sheet 1/100,000.

MARCH TABLE.

Unit.	Starting Point.	Hour of Start.	Route.	Destination.	Instructions.
"A" Group.	Tail to be clear of Road junction in SALM CHATEAU by 11.30.		Any.	BEHO – ROGERY CIEREUX – HONVELEZ BOVIGNY – COURTIL PROUVE DROUX	
"B" Group.	Tail to be clear of Cross Roads 3.J.40.05 by 10.30. Not to enter JOUBIEVAL before 10.30.		Any	COMTE – SART JOUBIEVAL – OTTRE- VERLEUMONT – HERRONVAL – REGNE.	
"C" Group.	Not to pass Cross Roads 3.I.85.00 before 10.00 and to be clear of VAUX-CHAVANNE and GRANDMENIL by 10.30.		Any	FRAITURE. MALEMPRE. ODEIGNE – LA FOSSE LA BAILLY – MANHAY. GRANDMENIL. VAUX – CHAVANNE EREZEE – FISENNE.	
"D" Group.	Cross Roads, 3.G.28.48.	09.00	EREZEE.		
55th Bde. RGA. 132 AT.Coy. RE.	Road Junction, 3.E.70.70.	09.00	FISENNE. SOUS LE BOIS.	FANZEL. MORMONT.	Route from MONVILLE to SOY for marching detachments of Siege Batteries and 132 A.T.Coy. is via NY.

3. Divisional Headquarters will remain at SALMCHATEAU.
4. ACKNOWLEDGE.

Distribution :–
G.O.C.   "Q".   C.R.A.   A.P.M.
8th Inf.Bde.   VI Corps "Q".   VI Corps "G"   3rd 10 is from
9th Inf.Bde.   Camp Commdt.   3rd Div.Signal.
76th Inf.Bde. 35th Bde.RGA. Guards Division.
6th Division. 1st Division. VI Corps H.A.
C.R.E.   A.D.M.S.   D.A.D.O.S.
3rd Div.MT.Coy.File.   War Diary.

W M Froll
Lieut.Colonel.
General Staff, 3rd Division.

8/12/18.
Issued at 19.30 hours.

3rd Division.

ROADS.

1. SALMCHATEAU – LONGCHAMPS – BEHO Road generally solid and fit for single lorry traffic in bad weather. It is very muddy and near the 8th kilometre stone there are some bad ruts.

2. BEHO – MALDINGEN – ST.VITH similar to 1 and very muddy. Sharp pull about ½ kilometre into ST.VITH. Some other sharp rises but none should affect wagons with ordinary loads.

3. Cross Roads ½ m north of GRUFFLINGEN to OUDLER and BURG REULAND reported good but muddy by C.R.E. Corps Troops.

4. MALDINGEN – BRAUNLAUF – KRONBACH – ST.VITH a rather soft road. Canadians have taken all forms of horse transport over this road, but it is now rather cut up and it is doubtful if it will take more than cookers and limbers.

5. ALDRINGEN – ESPELER – THOMMEN. The ALDRINGEN end appears suitable for horse transport, the THOMMEN end is poor and may only take limbers and cookers.

6. NEUNDORF due South to main road. Near the main road is only gravelled and only fit for cookers and limbers, further north it improves.

7. The turn to SALMEN off the main road appears sound for horse transport. It was not fully inspected.

8. BOVIGNY – COURTIL – HALCONREUX good for horse transport. Passable to Lorries (one way).

9. HALCONREUX – GOUVY – BEHO. Single lorry was very muddy.

I will endeavour to make a more detailed examination on 4.5.6.7. on horseback early, as it was risky to take a car along them owing to danger of being bogged.

Arrangements have been made for the inhabitants to clear the mud from the main roads under the local authorities.

8/12/18.

Sd. G.P.Walsh. Lieut.Col.RE.
C.R.E. 3rd Division.

-S-

For information.

9th December 1918.

Lieut.Colonel.
General Staff, 3rd Division.

3rd Division Operation Order No.296.

1. The Division will march on December 11th in accordance with the following March Table.
Reference Sheet 1/100,000.

MARCH TABLE.

Unit.	Starting Point.	Hour of Start.	Route.	Destination.	Instructions.
"A" Group.	Road Junction 400 yards North of B in BEHO. (Paper Map 1/100,000.)	10.00	MALDINGEN	NEIDINGEN. NEUNDORF. KROMBACH. WEISTEN. BRAUNLAUF. THOMMEN. GRUFFLINGEN. MALDINGEN.	
"B" Group.	Road Junction, S.K.95.00.	10.45	BEHO	BEHO. ALDRINGEN. ESPELER. DEYFELDT. BECH.	
"C" Group.	Cross Roads, 3.J.41.05.	10.30	REGNE.	CONTE. GRAND SART. PETIT SART. JOUBIEVAL. OTTRE. PROVE DROUX.	
"D" Group.			Any	BIHAIN. REGNE. HEBRONVAL. FRAITURE. MALEMPRE. SDEIGNE. VAUX CHAVANNE.	Head not to leave present area before 09.00. Tail to be clear of Cross Roads 3.I.12.52 by 11.30.
35 Bde.RGA. 132 A.T.Coy. R.E.			Road Junction 3.I.00.50	GRANDMENIL. HANHAY.	Not to pass Road Junction 3.I.00.50 before 12.00.

2. Divisional H.Q. will remain at SALMCHATEAU.
3. ACKNOWLEDGE.

Distribution:- G.O.C.   "Q"   G.S.O.A.   3rd Div.Train.
8th Inf.Bde.   A.P.M.   VI Corps "Q".
9th Inf.Bde.   VI Corps "G"   Camp Commdt.
76th Inf.Bde.   3rd Div.Sigs.   35th Bde.RGA.
1st Division.   Guards Div.   6th Division.
VI Corps H.A.   C.R.E.   A.D.M.S.
D.A.D.O.S.   3rd Div.M.T.Coy.   File.
    War Diary.

10/12/18.
Issued at 07.00.

/s/ Lieut.Colonel.
General Staff, 3rd Division.

8th Inf.Bde.
9th Inf.Bde.
76th Inf.Bde.
C.R.A.
35th Bde.RGA.
"Q".

G.7629.

REPORT ON ROADS.

MALDRINGEN - BRAUNLAUF - KROMBACH - NEUNDORF Roads.

1. From MALDRINGEN to BRAUNLAUF. Road is about 22 feet wide and was originally metal in the centre about 15 feet - the metal has now been broken and road is no better than a cross country track and is not fit for Infantry transport.

2. The road from the main BEHO - ST.VITH road half way between MALDRINGEN and Cross Roads at GRUFFLINGEN is the same as No.1 at the BRAUNLAUF end.

3. From BRAUNLAUF - KROMBACH same as No.1.
Not fit for horse transport.

4. From KROMBACH to NEUNDERF road is in a better condition in places but on hills is very bad.

5. From NEUNDERF towards ST.VITH road appears to be fairly good for 600 - 700 yards astride village, if this village was used for billeting troops they would have to proceed via ST.VITH.

All roads would be very heavy indeed for infantry marching.

Road ALDRINGEN - ESPELER - THOMMEN.

From cross roads N.of ALDRINGEN Road is in bad condition.
Width - 10 feet metal, 3 feet berm.
Thickness of metal 3" - 5".
Metal Shale Rock.
From ALDRINGEN through ESPELER to cross roads S.of THOMMEN Road good 12 feet metal. 3 feet berm.
From cross roads S.of ESPELER to THOMMEN - fair.
The above road will take Horse Transport.

Road ESPELER - OUDLER.

Road fair for first 100 yards, after this point road is in good condition.
Width 10 feet metal 3 feet berm.
Civilians working on clearing roads in OUDLER.

All roads in above report have no grades which are impassable for horse transport.

Sd.J.N.LUMLEY, Major.
for Lieut. Colonel.
10th December 1918.   General Staff, 3rd Division.

Copy to 1st Division for information.

G.7634.

8th Inf.Bde.
9th Inf.Bde.
76th Inf.Bde.
C.R.A.
35th Bde.RGA.
"Q".

Reference Germany I.M. 1/100,000.

1. Reference report on roads forwarded under G.7629 dated 9th December.

Personal reconnaissance shews that this report is unduly pessimistic in the following respects :-

Para 2. of G.7629.

The road mentioned in this para. though not good is passable for horse transport at the BRAUNLAUF end.

Para.5.of G.7629.

The route to NEUNDORF is not via ST.VITH.
The road from NEUBRUCK to NEUNDORF is the road to be used (see C.R.E's report attached).

2. Road from THOMMEN to cross roads ½ mile N.W. of first G in GRUFFLINGEN is passable for horse transport.

3. Units billeted in WEISTEN, KROMBACH and NEUNDORF must not use the NEUNDORF - ST.VITH road as this leads through the Guards Division area.

From NEUNDORF transport must gain the main road via ~~NEUNDORF~~ NEUBRUCK. Troops can possibly use a track (not shewn) running along the north side of the Railway (shewn on paper map 1/100,000) This should be reconnoitred.

4. In NEUNDORF there are cases of foot and mouth disease - no animals should be accommodated in this village.

10th December 1918.
         Sd. W.H.TRAILL. Lieut:Colonel.
         General Staff, 3rd Division.

Copy to 1st Division for information.

TRAINING ON ARRIVAL AT OUR DESTINATION IN GERMANY.

1. The objects to be attained are :-

   (a) Security in an enemy's country.
   (b) To keep all ranks fit, smart, well disciplined, comfortable and contented.
   (c) The education of individuals as a matter of supreme national importance to take their places in Civil life.

2. The methods by which the above can be secured are :-

   (i) Ordinary daily training for all ranks to consist of - drill - physical exercises - musketry - ceremonial - outpost duties.
   This training should not exceed two hours daily with the exception of one day per week after 1st January 1919 when all dismounted units will carry out one route march weekly.
   The exact programme to be carried out each day will be worked out in advance - all training will be carried out smartly and with the strictest attention to discipline.
   The work must be made interesting and all delays in getting to work etc. absolutely forbidden.

   (ii) Recreational Training. Every endeavour is to be made to keep all ranks fit by a well organized system of games both outdoor and indoor. Outdoor games will be arranged so as not to be confined only to Battalion teams, but platoon, company and similar unit matches must be arranged.
   The afternoons should be kept entirely free for these games, and all men encouraged to take part in them.
   It is intended to hold Divisional Football Tournaments - Association for 1st, 2nd 3rd elevens of units Also Rugby Tournament.
   A Comittee has been formed and its proposals are awaited by the G.O.C.
   The Divisional Cinema will be available for performing in the different groups - entertainment troupes are now being formed. All units will ensure the provision of indoor games and a good supply of British papers to enable men to pass the long winter evenings comfortably.
   Rooms must be set apart for this purpose in all units, and kept clean, warm and comfortable.
   The bands of all Regular Battalions have been asked for, and are expected shortly from England.

/The

(2)

The G.O.C. wishes to impress on all Commanders that this recreational training is to commence immediately on arrival at our destination, and its immediate organization must be taken in hand.

(iii)(a) <u>Educational Training</u>. This Education must be recognised as part of a daily programme, and it is with this object in view that ordinary military training has been confined to the bare essentials to keep men fit, smart and disciplined.

For this educational training there can be no compulsion but there must be every opportunity.

To relegate almost the whole of the work of education to a man's leisure time, would be to foster the idea that education is a mere side issue instead of a matter of supreme national importance.

Thus the ordinary daily military training of men who desire to engage seriously in this educational training may be restricted to the minimum weekly to keep all fit and efficient. At the same time it is no part of the scheme that men who desire only to spend their time in leisure should be given unrestricted opportunity for this purpose, but other work and training must be found for them to keep them from leading an idle life.

The successful execution of this scheme requires constant supervision and watchfulness by all commanders, and considerable discretion must be used, and is required.

(b) For this education scheme instructors are required, and for the efficient performance of their duties they will be required to devote considerable time not only to the actual teaching but also to the preparation and subsequent correction of the work done.

It is therefore to be made clear at once that this work will not be entirely extra work coming out of their spare time. Their work is to be recognised as of national consequence. It is recognised that Commanders of sub-units etc. cannot be entirely relieved of their responsibilities — Captains of Companies for instance must continue to command their companies — but all Commanding Officers will do all in their power to ensure that all instructors are relieved of all ordinary routine duties and given every reasonable opportunity of devoting time other than their spare time to their instructional duties.

It is not possible to lay down definite rules how this is to be done but Unit Commanders will be able to do much to ensure the principles herein laid down being carried out in the proper spirit.

/(c)

(c) Rooms will have to be provided for educational purposes in each unit. Classes cannot be conducted to any advantage in odd corners of cold and noisy billets.

The capacity to provide adequate accommodation conditions the whole educational scheme. It is useless to set apart one room for one or two hours in the day as that would mean the teaching of one subject only to, say 50 men, whereas the demand is for the teaching of at least nine large groups to over 5,000 men.

(d) An annexure to this memorandum shows the numbers so far as known at present who have expressed a desire to learn or instruct, and their particular subjects, and also describes the organization and general scheme to be followed.

(iv) The Divisional Commander wishes to make it quite clear that whilst this memorandum contains his orders as to general lines to be followed in all forms of training on arrival at our destination, they cannot be considered detailed orders. He directs that these orders be followed and adhered as a general basis for the more detailed orders by all subordinate commanders. He feels that much can and will be done by all commanders to maintain the very high character of the Division, and to fit all for their duties in their military and civil lives hereafter.

10th December 1918.

Lieut.Colonel.
General Staff, 3rd Division.

APPENDIX.

An analysis of the returns to date showing by groups numbers of instructors available, and applicants for instruction within the Division :-

GROUP.	NO. OF INSTRUCTORS.	APPLICANTS FOR INSTRUCTION IN SUBJECTS IN GROUP.
A.	46	907
B.	35	707
C.	9	181
D.	6	72
E.	15	78
F.	11	725
G.	34	789
H.	11	563
I.	3	73
J.	2	24
K.	31	478
L.	18	1414

TOTAL NUMBER OF INSTRUCTORS - 200.

ORGANIZATION.

The returns show that in some subjects the larger units at all events are able to supply their own instructors but this is not always the case. Consequently the educational unit for certain subjects will have to be a formation whose resources in instructors can be pooled.

(ii) The Infantry Brigade satisfies these requirements as a rule. A similar group can be made of the Artillery Brigades and the Divisional Ammunition Column. On the supposition that Field Ambulances, Field Companies R.E. will be attached to their respective Infantry Brigades, this will only leave Divisional Headquarter Troops, Pioneers Machine Gun Battalion and the Divisional Train A.S.C. outside the Group system, and if their locations are sufficiently close together these will be formed into a fifth group.

There is already an officer responsible for education within the Brigade on Headquarters of each Infantry Brigade; to make the system symmetrical there will be an officer (not necessarily an additional officer, but one of those already appointed) to co-ordinate the education within each of these two other groups. It would be the duty of the education officer for each group to arrange the syllabus required by students, and the supply of instructors, hours at their disposal, and accommodation available. The Divisional Education Officer will indicate the priority of importance of the subjects demanded and any external resources in the way of instructors that it might be possible to put at the disposal of the group officer. It would also be for the group officer to decide which subjects could be taught adequately within each unit and for which he would have to make centralized provision in his group.

(iii) There are certain specialised subjects for which a thoroughly expert instructor is essential, which the returns show could not be properly taught on this system; for example Economics, questions of Reconstruction and Peace Settlement, Engineering Subjects, Art and Design. There are only two or three really qualified teachers of these subjects in the Division. In these subjects the best plan would appear to be to arrange courses to be taken by these specialists either at Divisional Headquarters if sufficiently central or in each Brigade in which a demand for these subjects exists.

SCHEME.

1. The chief emphasis in the scheme should be put upon subjects of general education. Ref. War Office Army Education Circular No.2 :- "A proper course of vocational training demands a longer time than Education Officers are likely to have at their disposal, so far as the course of events after cessation of hostilities can reasonably be foreseen. While no estimate can be formed of the probable duration of an armistice the most informed opinion on the actual demobilisation period indicates that it will not last very long, certainly not long enough to make it worth while to draw up technical training courses"

/To

"To avoid misunderstanding, it maybe said at once that every
"effort is being made to provide facilities for trade and
"technical education in the present circumstances, abroad as
"well as at home, and to secure such larger facilities as may
"be obtainable on the cessation of hostilities. But except in
"special cases Education Officers must aim at effecting, in
"preparation for the return to civil life, a training of the mind
"which will make it more receptive of specialised training, rather
"than the specialised training itself. They should contemplate
"returning a more intelligent man to his trade, not a technically
"higher-grade man".

This type of education includes such subjects as Elementary
English, Arithmetic and Elementary Mathematics, Citizenship,
Elementary English History, Geography, English Language and
Literature, English History (political, social and industrial)
and European History.

2. The aim in such technical training as is provided (e.g.
engineering subjects) should be to give practice to those who
have got elementary knowledge already and who simply wish to
refurbish, and not to teach beginners. The practical side of this
instruction could best be given in R.E.workshops (possibly also
in pioneer workshops) under the direction of the C.R.E. Especially
with regard to training for practical mechanics, for which there
is a large demand, the warning is necessary that with the great
supply already existing of fairly expert and experienced labour
there are not likely to be many openings for beginners; but a
limited amount of instruction can be provided by the Mechanical
Transport Company or under Corps arrangements. Courses in France
are being arranged by G.H.Q. in technical subjects, with allotments
down to Divisions.

3. It is suggested in the G.H.Q. education scheme that Handyman
Trades in Group "K" such as shoemaking, tailoring, haircutting,
cookery, should be taught and practised in connection with the
shops and cook-houses of units, but it seems doubtful if this
would prove a satisfactory system, whether sufficient materials
would be available, and whether more than a very few men could
be dealt with efficiently. This will be left to Education Officers
and C.Os. in units to decide whether this is a practicable system
for small numbers.

Simple Carpentry on the other hand, probably could be taught
with advantage through the R.E.workshops and pioneer workshops
of units.

4. With a view (i) to strengthening the general education and (ii) to providing guidance and information on questions of peace settlement and national reconstruction, courses of lectures will be delivered at Divisional Headquarters if sufficiently central, or in the different groups, under the direction of the Divisional Education Officer. These courses would embrace such subjects as British and European History, English Literature, Economics, Economic History, Geography and Civics (or Public Administration).

5. It will probably be possible also to arrange for occasional lectures on miscellaneous subjects of general interest, e.g. Music Art, Places of interest in the neighbourhood. It may be possible to obtain lantern slides to illustrate lectures of this nature.

6. Inasmuch as some of these who have volunteered as teachers have had no experience in teaching, it will be necessary to provide a class for teachers or at any rate occasional conferences of instructors to discuss their difficulties.

7. It is intended to establish at Division H.Q. if possible in the same building as the Education Office a reading room where the reference library would be kept and also, if obtainable, copies of the best reviews and of such periodicals as the "Cornhill" and "Blackwood". This room could also be used for lecture, debates, instructor's classes and reading circles.

8. A subsidiary function of the Education Department is to provide information and advice with regard to resettlement and training not only in the forces but on demobilisation at home. The department is regularly supplied by G.H.Q. with current news relating to these matters.

****

3rd Division Operation Order. No.297.

1. The Division will march on December 12th in accordance with the following March Table.

Reference Sheet 1/100,000.

MARCH TABLE.

Unit.	Starting Point.	Hour of Start.	Route.	Destination.	Instructions.
"A" Group.	Railway Crossing 400 yards South of S in ST.VITH. (Paper Map 1/100,000).	10.00.	ATZERATH	KREWINKEL. HASENVENN. HANDERFELD. WECKERATH. ANDLER. SCHONBERG. MACKENBACH. SETZ	
"B" Group.	Not to enter new area before 08.50 to be clear of present area by 10.30.		Any.	MELDINGEN. NEUNDORF. KROMBACH. WEISTEN. BRAUMLAUF. THOMM. GRUEFLINGEN.	
"C" Group.	Road Junction, 3.K.95.00.	10.00	BEHO	HALDINGEN. BEHO. ALDRINGEN. ESPELER. DEYFELD.	
"D" Group.	Road Junction, 3.J.88.12.	10.00	Cross Roads SALMCHATEAU.	COURTIL. BOUVIGNY. ROGERY. CIERREUX.	
35th Bde R.G.A. 152 M.T.Coy. R.E.	Road Junction 3.I.35.57.	10.00	REGNE.	PROVE DROUX. GOUTE. GRAND SART. PETIT SART. JOUDIEVAL.	

2. The move of Divisional Headquarters will be notified later.
3. ACKNOWLEDGE.

Distribution :-
G.O.C.   "Q".   G.R.A.
8th Inf.Bde. VI Corps "G".
9th Inf.Bde. Camp Commdt.
26th Inf.Bde. 35th Bde.R.G.A.
1st Division. VI Corps H.A.
A.D.M.S.   D.A.D.O.S.
File.   War Diary.

A.P.M.
VI Corps "Q".
3rd Div.Sigs.
Guards Div.
C.R.E.
3rd Div.M.T.Coy.
Section Train.
64 Div

11/12/18.
Issued at
0730

f. [signature]
for Lieut.Colonel.
General Staff, 3rd Division.

G.O.C., 9th Inf.Bde.

Please convey to all ranks of your Brigade my congratulations on their fine marching and smart soldierlike appearance, when crossing the frontier this morning. The care and hard work required to bring about the result attained is much appreciated.
All ranks may well be proud.

            Sd. C.J.Deverell.Major General.
            Commanding, 3rd Division.

11th Dec.1918.

         G.7642.

G.O.C., 76th Inf.Bde.

Please convey to all ranks of all units of your group my congratulations on their fine appearance and marching this morning when crossing the frontier. The care and hard work required to bring about the result attained, is much appreciated.
All ranks may well be proud.

            Sd. C.J.Deverell.Maj.General.
            Commanding, 3rd Division.

11th December 1918.

3rd DIVISION OPERATION ORDER NO. 289.

1. The Division will march on December 4th in accordance with the following March Table.

Reference Sheet 1/100,000.

M A R C H   T A B L E

Unit.	Starting Point.	Route.	Destination.	Instructions.
"A" Group.	To be clear of present area by 09.30.	Any	BAILLONVILLE. HEURE. NETTINNE. SINSIN.	
"B" Group.	Head of column not to pass east of present area before 08.30, tail to be clear of it by 09.30.	Any	MOHIVILLE PESSOUX ACHET CINEY.	
"C" Group.	Head of column not to pass east of present area before 08.30 hours, tail to be clear of it by 09.30.	Any	NATOYE BRAIBANT	
"D" Group.	Not to leave PURNODE before 09.30 and to be clear of the village by 11.30.	Any	SOVET SPONTIN DORINNE DURNAL	
35th Bde. R.G.A.	Not to enter PURNODE before 11.30.	Any	PURNODE AWAGNE	

2. Divisional Headquarters will remain at CHATEAU DE FONTAIN on December 4th.
3. ACKNOWLEDGE.

Distributions:- G.O.C.,   C.R.A.   Div. Train.
               8th Inf. Bde.   "Q".   VI Corps "G".
               9th Inf. Bde.   VI Corps "Q".
               76th Inf. Bde.   35th Bde. R.G.A.

Acknowledgment Signals.

f. Hundley Major
for Lieut.Colonel.
General Staff, 3rd Division.

2/12/18.
Issued at 20.00

SECRET.   3rd Div. G.S.2002/6.

```
* 8th Inf.Bde.      A.D.M.S.       35th Bde. R.G.A. *
* 9th Inf.Bde.    * 3rd Div."Q".
* 76th Inf.Bde.    3rd Div.Sigs.
* C.R.A.           A.P.M.
* C.R.E.           3rd Div.M.T.Coy.
  20th K.R.R.C.    3rd Div.Train.
  Camp Commdt.     Mob.Vet.Section.
  D.A.D.O.S.       D.M.G.C.
```

ADVANCE TO THE RHINE.

1. The distribution of the Second Army in German territory is shewn on .... Rhine Valley No.1 Map issued to all concerned.

2. The advance to the occupation of the Bridgehead is to be carried out by

   Canadian Corps   )
   1 Cavalry Brigade   ) on the right.

   II Corps.   )
   1st Cavalry Divn.   ) on the left.
   (less 1 Cavalry   )
      Brigade)   )

3. The Canadian and II Corps will be followed by the VI Corps.

4. The composition of the Columns of the VI Corps is shewn in Appendix "A".
   G.Os.C.Divisions will assume responsibility for their Columns from 23.59 hours 1st December.

5. The main road allotted for the advance of each column and the dividing line between columns for billeting purposes are shewn on the attached Maps "D" and "E".

6. When the Frontier has been crossed, although the comfort of the troops is the first consideration, military precautions against surprise must be taken.

7. Any enemy encountered on the march are to be taken prisoners.

8. ACKNOWLEDGE.

[signature]

Lieut.Colonel.
General Staff, 3rd Division.

2nd December 1918.

* Maps "D" and "E" attached.

APPENDIX "A".

Composition of columns from 2nd December (inclusive).

RIGHT COLUMN. Maj.Genl.C.J.DEVERELL. C.B.
3rd Division.

3rd Division.
35th Mobile Brigade, R.G.A.
"CC" Cable Section.
132nd Army Troops Coy. R.E.
70th Sanitary Section.
H.Q. and 2½ Sections 21st A.A.Horse Coy.

CENTRE COLUMN. Maj.Genl. T.G.MATHESON, C.B.
Guards Division.

Guards Division.
63rd Mobile Brigade R.G.A.
No.5 Group Sharpshooters (Lovats Scouts).
"O" Cable Section.
280th Army Troops Coy. R.E.
38th Sanitary Section.
One Section 13th A.A.Horse Coy.
One Section 15th A.A.Horse Coy.
Half Section 21st A.A.Horse Coy.

LEFT COLUMN. Maj.Genl, C.E.PEREIRA,C.B., C.M.G.
2nd Division).

2nd Division.
92nd Mobile Brigade R.G.A.
"M" A.A.Battery.
No.7 AA.Searchlight Section.
H.Q. and 2 Sections 15th A.A.Horse Coy.
33rd Sanitary Section,

P.T.O.

CORPS HEADQUARTERS GROUP.

VI Corps Headquarters.
Headquarters VI Corps Heavy Artillery.
6th Cyclist Battalion.
'F' Corps Signal Coy.
Nos.13, 20 .93 Motor Airline Sections.
"A" Cable Section.
One Light Motor Wireless Section.
174th Tunnelling Coy. R.E.
Half 30th M.A.C.
H.Q. and 2 Sections 13th AA.Horse Coy.
No.6 Vet.Evac.Station.

12th Squadron R.A.F.

SECRET.   3rd Div.G.S.2002/7.

8th Inf.Bde.	VI Corps "G".
9th Inf.Bde.	VI Corps "Q".
76th Inf.Bde.	3rd Div."Q".
C.R.A.	A.D.M.S.
C.R.E.	Camp Commdt.
3rd Div.Train.	D.A.D.O.S.
A.P.M.	D.A.D.V.S.
D.M.G.O.	3rd Div.Signals.
20th K.R.R.C.	

Reference N.W.Europe. Sheet 5. 1/250,000.

Forecast of moves to take place after 4th December at dates to be notified later.

                               Approximate position of
                               head of Column.

1st Day.	SOY
2nd Day.	MANHAY
3rd Day.	SART
4th Day.	BEHO
5th Day.	ST. VITH.
6th Day.	ANDLER.

2nd November 1918.

for Lieut.Colonel.
General Staff, 3rd Division.

1. The Division will march on 5th December in accordance with the following March Table.

Reference Sheet 1/100,000.

MARCH TABLE

Unit.	Starting Point.	Hour of Start.	Route.	Destination.	Instructions.
"A" Group.	Cross Roads 3.E.20.50.	10.00.	NOISEUX - FRONVILLE - HOTTON.	SOY - N. HOTTON. NOSIVILLE.	Units proceeding to SOY march via MY but all transport of their units will move by route given.
"B" Group.	Road Junction 3.J.65.32.	10.00	BAILLONVILLE.	FRONVILLE - DEULIN GD.ENEILLE -NOISEUX BAILLONVILLE.	
Div.H.Q. Transport & Sig.Section.	Road Junction 3.B.55.82.	07.00.	Cross Roads 3.C.17.40. NAFFE - Road Junction 2.E.50.15.	GRAND HAN.	
"C" Group.	Head of Column not to pass Cross Roads 3.C.15.41 before 10.50 hours. Tail of column to be clear of NATOYE - LEIGNON Railway by 09.00 hours.		Cross Roads. 3.C.15.41.	MARESSE. HEURE. NETTINNE. SINSIN.	Train Companies will march in rear of their groups.
"D" Group. 35 Bde.RGA. with 132 A.T. Coy.R.E.	Railway Crossing 3.A.89.72.	09.30.	SPONTIN - BRAIBANT.	PESSOUX. - SGY. MOHIVILLE -AGHET. CINEY.	

2. Divisional Headquarters will close at EMPTINNE at 09.00 hours and open at GRAND HAN on arrival, before 10 hours.
3. ACKNOWLEDGE.

Distribution :- G.O.C. "Q". C.R.A. Div.Train. A.P.M.
8th Inf.Bde. VI Corps "G". Camp Commdt.
9th Inf.Bde. VI Corps "Q". 3rd Div.Sigs.
76th Inf.Bde. 35th Bde.R.G.A. *[signature]*

5/12/18. *[signature]*
Issued at 20.00 hours.

for Lieut.Colonel,
General Staff, 3rd Division.

3rd Division G.S.2042.

8th Inf.Bde.
9th Inf.Bde.
76th Inf.Bde.
C.R.A.
35th Bde.RGA.
3rd Div.Train.

The main road between HOTTON and SOY is good.

Between HOTTON and SOY there is a steep gradient from HOTTON to the second kilometre stone and again from the Fourth kilometre stone into SOY. The road between the second and fourth kilometre stones is level.

In moving transport over this road Group Commanders should make arrangements for spare horses and parties of men to assist heavily laden wagons up these two gradients in case of necessity.

Troops can march via NY which is 1½ miles shorter tan by the main road via HOTTON but it is not advisable for to take the transport via NY as there is a steep gradient of a mile in length between NY and SOY and the road is not good for transport.

                        Sd. W.H.Traill. Lt.Col.
                       General Staff, 3rd Division.

3/12/18.

Copy to 1st Division for information.

3rd Division Operation Order No. 291.

1. The Division will march on 5th DEC. in accordance with the following March Table.
2. Train C'ys will march in rear of their groups.

Reference Sheet 1/100,000.

MARCH TABLE.

Unit.	Starting Point.	Hour of start.	Route.	Area	Instruction.
"A" Group.	Cross Roads 3.G.30.47.	10.00	EREZEE. GRANDMENIL.	ODEIGNE. MALEMPRE. VAUX CHAVANNE. GRANDMENIL.	
"B" Group.	Cross Roads, 3.F.17.44.	10.00	HOTTON SOY.	EREZEE. MORMONT. FANZEL.	
"C" Group.	Cross Roads 3.D.77.61.	09.30	NOISEUX. FRONVILLE.	SOY. NY. HOTTON.	Units moving to SOY can march via NY all transport of these units will move by main road via HOTTON.
"D" Group.	Road Junction, 3.C.63.32.	09.30	HEURE.	MONVILLE. FRONVILLE. NOISEUX.	
35th Bde. RGA. 132 AT.Coy.RE.	Cross Roads, 3.E.30.53.	09.30	PESSOUX. HEURE.	BAILLONVILLE.	

3. Divisional Headquarters will remain at GRAND HAN.
4. ACKNOWLEDGE.

Distribution:- G.O.C., "Q", G.R.A. Div.Train. A.P.M. VI Corps "G".
8th Inf.Bde. VI Corps "Q". 2nd Division.
9th Inf.Bde. Guards Div. 6th Division.
76th Inf.Bde. 1st.Division. VI Corps H.A.

f. hunter. Major.
for Lieut. Colonel.
General Staff, 3rd Division.

4/12/18.
Issued at 20.00.

Road Re

3rd Division.
G.S.2048.

8th Inf.Bde.
9th Inf.Bde.
76th Inf.Bde.
C.R.A.
3rd Div.Train.
35th Bde.R.G.A.

The road between EREZEE and GRANDMENIL is very muddy and there is a long steep gradient leading from the river AISNE up to the village of EREZEE and a short steep gradient between the 11th and 12th kilometre stones East of EREZEE.

There is also a long steep gradient between the 15th [13/15] and 17th kilometre stones West of GRANDMENIL.

The usual precautions should be taken to assist heavily laden wagons up these gradients if necessary.

H.W.Fraill
Lieut.Colonel,
General Staff, 3rd Division.

4th December 1918.

Copy to 1st Division for information.

3rd Division Operation Order No. 292.

1. The Division will march on December 7th in accordance with the following March Table.
Reference Sheet 1/100,000.

MARCH TABLE

Unit.	Starting Point.	Hour of Start.	Route.	Destination.	Instruction.
"A"Group.	Road Junction 3.I.37.42.	10.00	Any	BIHAIN. REGNE. MALEMPRE. ODEIGNE.	
"B"Group.			Any	VAUX CHAVANNE. GRANDMENIL. HORMONT. FANZEL.	Not to leave present areas before 08.50. Tail to be clear of present area by 10.00.
Div. H.Q. Transport & Sig.Sec.	GRAND HAN.	10.00	HOTTON EREZEE.	CLERHEID.	
"C"Group.			Any	EREZEE. SOY. OPPAGNE.	Not to leave present area before 09.15, tail to be clear of it by 10.00.
"D"Group.	MONVILLE.	09.30	ANY	N. HOTTON. MONVILLE. FRONVILLE.	
35th Bde RGA. 152 A.T.Coy. RE.				DEULIN. NOISEUX. BAILLONVILLE.	Not to enter BAILLONVILLE before 10.00.

2. Divisional H.Q. will remain at GRAND HAN.
3. ACKNOWLEDGE.

Distribution:-
G.O.C.   "Q"   G.R.A.   Div.Train.   A.P.M.
8th Inf.Bde.   VI Corps   VI Corps   "Q"
9th Inf.Bde.   Camp Commdt.   3rd Div.Sigs.
76th Inf.Bde.   35th Bde.RGA.   Guards Div.   6th Div.
1st Division.   VI Corps H.A.   A.D.M.S.
3rd Div.M.T.Coy. File.   G.R.E.   D.A.D.O.S.   War Diary.

6/12/18.   for Lindsay, Major
Issued at 77.00.   for Lieut.Colonel.
                                                       General Staff, 3rd Division.

1. The Division will march on 5th December in accordance with the following March Table.

Reference Sheet 1/100,000.

MARCH TABLE.

Unit.	Starting Point.	Hour of Start.	ROUTE	DESTINATION.	INSTRUCTIONS.
"A" Group.	Tail to be clear of Road Junction 3.K.09.14. by 11.30.		Any.	BOUVIGNY. COURTIL. GRAND SART. PETIT SART. JOUBIEVAL.	
"B" Group.	Head not to leave present area before 08.15. Tail to be clear of Road Junction 3.I.37.42 by 10.30.		Any.	VERLEUMONT. HEBRONVAL. OTTRE. REGNÉ. FRAITURE. ODEIGNE. MALEMPRE.	
Div.H.Q. Transport & Sig.Sec.	CLEPHEID.	08.30.	GRANDMENIL. REGNE.	SALME CHATEAU.	
"C" Group.	Not to pass Cross Roads 3.H.57.56 before 09.45.		Any	VAUX CHAVANNE. GRAND MENIL. LA BOSSE. LA BATTY.	
"D" Group.			NO MOVE.		
35th Bde. RGA. 132 AT.Coy.RE.					

2. Divisional Headquarters will close at GRAND HAN at 09.00 and open at SALME CHATEAU on arrival.
3. ACKNOWLEDGE.

Distribution :- G.O.C.   "Q".   C.R.A.   Div.Train.
               8th Inf.Bde.   A.P.M.   VI Corps "G".
               9th Inf.Bde.   VI Corps "Q".   Camp Comndt.
               76th Inf.Bde. 3rd Div.Sigs.   35th Bde.R.G.A.
               Guards Div.   6th Division.   1st Division.
               VI Corps H.A. C.R.E.   A.D.M.S.
               D.A.D.O.S.   3rd Div.M.T.Coy.File.   War Diary.

f. Lewis Cary Major
for Lieut.Colonel.
for General Staff, 3rd Div.

5/12/18.
Issued at 20.30.

8th Inf.Bde.	3rd Div.Train.	20th K.R.R.C.
9th Inf.Bde.	35th Bde.RGA.	D.M.G.C.
76th Inf.Bde.	VI Corps.	G.7625.
C.R.A.	A.P.M.	
C.R.E.	Camp Commdt.	
A.D.M.S.	"Q"	
	3rd Div.Sigs.	

INSTRUCTIONS FOR CROSSING THE GERMAN FRONTIER.

1. The leading unit will cross the frontier at 10.15 hours on the 11th.
   The Divisional Commander will march at the head of the Division followed by the G.O.C., 76th Inf.Bde. and Divisional and Brigade Staffs.

2. The Corps Commander will take the salute at the frontier.
   Bayonets will be fixed and colours will be carried uncased and flying. Bands will play the Regimental Marches of Units.

3. Divisional Band will play the Machine Gun Battalion and Artillery Units across the frontier – accommodation for them being arranged accordingly.

4. A similar procedure will be adopted on the 12th and 13th until the whole Division has crossed.

5. An Order of Battle is being prepared and copies will be distributed to all Units for Record.

6. G.O.C., Infantry Brigades, C.R.E. and O.C., 3rd Divisional Train will attend to the saluting of transport units which is at present below the standard of smartness required.
   The saluting of all Brigades R.F.A. is very good. D.A.C. still require improvement.
   Flags of Allied Nations are not to be carried by troops or placed on vehicles.

7. It is hoped that photographs of all units crossing the frontier will be taken.

8. The crossing of the frontier will be considered as an inspection by the Corps Commander. Every effort will be made to present a very smart soldierlike appearance.
   The marching of the whole Division has been of a very high standard throughout the advance and has been much appreciated.
   All that remains to be done is a general smartening up of equipment and vehicles to an inspection standard for an historic and unique occasion.

   Lieut.Colonel.
   General Staff, 3rd Division.

9th December 1918.

16 mile marches
from Games Officer

3rd Division Operation Order No.294.

1. The Division will march on the 9th December in accordance with the following March Table.

Reference Sheet 1/100,000.

MARCH TABLE.

Unit.	Starting Point.	Hour of Start.	ROUTE.	DESTINATION.	INSTRUCTIONS.
"A" Group.	Tail of column to be clear of present area by 11.30.		Any.	BEHO. OURTHE. WATTERMAL. GOUVY. HALCONREUX.	
"B" Group.	Not to pass Cross Roads 3.K.18.18 before 09.30. Tail to be clear of that point by 12.00.		SALM-CHATEAU.	COURTIL. BOVIGNY. ROGERY. BECH.	
"C" Group.	Road Junction 3.I.57.43.	09.30.	REGNE.	GRAND SART. JOUBIEVAL. OTTRE. BIHAIN. REGNE. HEBRONVAL. VERLEUMONT.	
"D" Group.	Cross Roads, 3.G.28.48.	09.00.	EREZEE. GRANDMENIL.	VAUX CHAVANNE. MALEMPRE. ODEIGNE. LA FOSSE. LE BATTY. GRANDMENIL.	
35th Bde. R.G.A.	Road Junction, 3.E.70.70.	09.00.	FISENNE. SOUS LE BOIS.	FANZEL. MORMONT.	Route from MONVILLE to SOY for marching detachments of Seige Batteries and 132 A.T. Coy. is via NY.
132 A.T.Coy R.E.				EREZEE.	

2. Divisional Headquarters will remain at SALM-CHATEAU.
3. ACKNOWLEDGE.

Distribution :-
G.O.C.   "Q"   C.R.A.   Div.Train.
8th Inf.Bde.   A.P.M.   VI Corps "G".   VI Corps "Q".
9th Inf.Bde.   VI Corps "Q". Camp Commdt.
76th Inf.Bde.   3rd Div.Signals. 35th Bde.RGA.
Guards Div.   6th Division. 1st Division.
VI Corps H.A.   C.R.E.   A.D.M.S.
D.A.D.O.S.   3rd Div.M.T.Coy. File. War Diary.

7/12/18.
Issued at 18.00.

Lieut.Colonel.
General Staff, 3rd Division.

1. 3rd Division Operation Order No.294 is cancelled.
2. The Division will march on December 9th in accordance with the following March Table.
Reference Sheet 1/100,000.

MARCH TABLE.

Unit.	Starting Point.	Hour of Start.	Route.	Destination.	Instructions.
"A" Group.	Tail to be clear of Road junction in SALM CHATEAU by 11.30.		Any.	BEHO – ROGERY CIEREUX – HONVELEZ BOVIGNY – COURTIL. PROUVE DROUX	
"B" Group.	Tail to be clear of Cross Roads 3.J.40.05 by 10.30. Not to enter JOUBIEVAL before 10.30.		Any	COMTE – SART. JOUBIEVAL – OTTRE- VERLEUMONT – HERPONVAL – REGNE. FRAITURE.	
"C" Group.	Not to pass Cross Roads 3.I.85.00 before 10.00 and to be clear of VAUX-CHAVANNE and GRANDMENIL by 10.30.		Any	MALEMPRE. ODEIGNE – LA FOSSE LA BAILLY – MANHAY. GRANDMENIL.	
"D" Group.	Cross Roads, 3.G.28.48.	09.00	EREZEE.	VAUX –CHAVANNE EREZEE – FISENNE.	
55th Bde. RGA., 132 A.T.Coy. RE.	Road Junction, 3.E.70.70.	09.00	FISENNE. SOUS LE BOIS.	FANZEL. MORMONT.	Route from MONVILLE to SOY for marching detachments of Siege Batteries and 132 A.T.Coy. is via NY.

3. Divisional Headquarters will remain at SALMCHATEAU.
4. ACKNOWLEDGE.

Distribution :-
G.O.C.   "Q".   C.R.A.   A.P.M.
8th Inf.Bde.   VI Corps "G".   VI Corps "Q".
9th Inf.Bde.   Camp Commdt.   3rd Div.Signal.
76th Inf.Bde.   35th Bde.RGA.   Guards Division.
6th Division.   1st Division.   VI Corps H.A.
C.R.E.   A.D.M.S.   D.A.D.O.S.
3rd Div.MT.Coy.File.   War Diary.

8/12/18.
Issued at 19.30 hours.

W.M.Freeland
Ira. 10th Train. Lieut.Colonel.
General Staff, 3rd Division.

S.S.100/G/12.

3rd Division.

R O A D S.

1.   MALMEDY - LIGNEUVILLE - RECHT Road generally solid and fit for single lorry traffic in bad weather. It is very muddy and near the 8th kilometre stone there are some bad ruts.

2.   RECHT - HALENFELD - ST.VITH similar to 1 and very muddy. Sharp pull about ½ kilometre into ST.VITH. Some other sharp rises but none should affect wagons with ordinary loads.

3.   Cross Roads ½ m north of LIGNEUVILLE to OUDLER and BORN REULAND reported good but muddy by C.R.E. Corps Troops.

4.   HALENFELD - MEDERLAND - RESHBACH - ST.VITH a rather soft road. Canadians have taken all forms of horse transport over this road, but it is now rather cut up and it is doubtful if it will take more than cookers and limbers.

5.   ALDRINGEN - ESPELER - THOMMEN. The ALDRINGEN end appears suitable for horse transport, the THOMMEN end is poor and may only take limbers and cookers.

6.   WEISSBORN due South to main road. Near the main road is only gravelled and only fit for cookers and limbers, further north it improves.

7.   The turn to SHAKEN off the main road appears sound for horse transport. It was not fully inspected.

8.   LOVAGNE - COURTIL - HANDOMONT Good for horse transport. Passable to lorries (one way).

9.   MALMEDY - BEUVY - RECHT. Single lorry was very muddy.

I will endeavour to make a more detailed examination on 4.5.6.7. or horseback early, as it was risky to take a car along them owing to danger of being bogged.

Arrangements have been made for the inhabitants to clear the mud from the main roads under the local authorities.

Sd. C.P.Walsh. Lieut.Col. RE.
C.R.E. 3rd Division.

5/12/18.

8th Inf.Bde.
9th Inf.Bde.
76th Inf.Bde.
25th Bde.R.F.A.

For information.

Lieut.Colonel,
General Staff, 3rd Division.

December 1918.

3rd Division Operation Order No.296.

1. The Division will march on December 11th in accordance with the following March Table. Reference Sheet 1/100,000.

MARCH TABLE.

Unit.	Starting Point.	Hour of Start.	Route.	Destination.	Instructions.
"A" Group.	Road Junction 400 yards North of B in BEHO. (Paper map 1/100,000)	10.00	MALDINGEN	NEIDINGEN. NEUNDORF. KROMBACH. WEISTEN. BRAUNLAUF. THOMEN. GRUFFLINGEN. MALDINGEN.	
"B" Group.	Road Junction, 5.K.95.00.	10.45	BEHO	BEHO. ALDRINGEN. ESPELER. DEYFELDT. BECH.	
"C" Group.	Cross Roads, 3.J.41.05.	10.30	REGNE.	COMTE. GRAND SART. PETIT SART. JOUBIEVAL. OTTRE. PROVE DROUX.	
"D" Group.	Head not to leave present area before 09.00. Tail to be clear of Cross Roads 3.I.12.52 by 11.30.		Any	BIHAIN. REGNE. HEBRONVAL. FRAITURE. MALEMPRE. SDEIGNE.	
35 Bde.RGA. 132 AT.Coy. R.J.	Not to pass Road Junction 3.I.00.50 before 12.00.		Road Junction 3.I.00.50.	VAUX CHAVANNE. GRANDMENIL. HANHAY.	

2. Divisional H.Q. will remain at SALMCHATEAU.

3. ACKNOWLEDGE.

Distribution:—
G.O.C.   G.R.A.   3rd Div.Train.
8th Inf.Bde.   A.P.M.   VI Corps "Q".
9th Inf.Bde.   VI Corps"G"   Camp Commdt.
76th Inf.Bde.   3rd Div.Sigs.   35th Bde.RGA.
1st Division.   Guards Div.   6th Division.
VI Corps H.A.   C.R.E.   A.D.M.S.
                 D.A.D.O.S.   3rd Div.M.T.Coy. File.
                                 War Diary.

10/12/18.
Issued at 07.00.

/s/ [signature]
/s/ Lieut. Colonel.
General Staff, 3rd Division.

8th Inf.Bde.
9th Inf.Bde.
76th Inf.Bde.
G.R.A.
35th Bde.RGA.
"Q".

G.7629.

REPORT ON ROADS.

MALDRINGEN - BRAUNLAUF - KROMBACH - NEUNDORF Roads.

1. From MALDRINGEN to BRAUNLAUF. Road is about 22 feet wide and was originally metal in the centre about 15 feet – the metal has now been broken and road is no better than a cross country track and is not fit for Infantry transport.

2. The road from the main BEHO - ST.VITH road half way between MALDRINGEN and Cross Roads at GRUFFLINGEN is the same as No.1 at the BRAUNLAUF end.

3. From BRAUNLAUF - KROMBACH same as No.1.
Not fit for horse transport.

4. From KROMBACH to NEUNDERF road is in a better condition in places but on hills is very bad.

5. From NEUNDERF towards ST.VITH road appears to be fairly good for 600 - 700 yards astride village, if this village was used for billeting troops they would have to proceed via ST.VITH.

All roads would be very heavy indeed for infantry marching.

Road ALDRINGEN - ESPELER - THOMMEN.

From cross roads N.of ALDRINGEN Road is in bad condition.
Width - 10 feet metal , 3 feet berm.
Thickness of metal 3" - 5".
Metal Shale Rock.
From ALDRINGEN through ESPELER to cross roads S.of THOMMEN Road good 12 feet metal. 3 feet berm.
From cross roads S.of ESPELER to THOMMEN - fair.
The above road will take Horse Transport.

Road ESPELER - OUDLER.

Road fair for first 100 yards, after this point road is in good condition.
Width 10 feet metal 3 feet berm.
Civilians working on clearing roads in OUDLER.

All roads in above report have no grades which are impassable for horse transport.

Sd.J.N.LUMLEY. Major.
for Lieut.-Colonel.
10th December 1918.   General Staff, 3rd Division.

Copy to 1st Division for information.

G.7634.

8th Inf.Bde.
9th Inf.Bde.
76th Inf.Bde.
C.R.A.
55th Bde.RGA.
"Q".

Reference Germany I.M. 1/100,000.

1.   Reference report on roads forwarded under G.7629 dated 9th December.

Personal reconnaissance shews that this report is unduly pessimistic in the following respects :-

Para 2. of G.7629.

The road mentioned in this para. though not good is passable for horse transport at the BRAUNLEUF end.

Para.5.of G.7629.

The route to NEUNDORF is not via ST.VITH.
The road from NEUBRUCK to NEUNDORF is the road to be used (see C.R.E's report attached).

2.   Road from THOMMEN to cross roads ½ mile N.W. of first G in GRUFFLINGEN is passable for horse transport.

3.   Units billeted in WEISTEN, KROMBACH and NEUNDORF must not use the NEUNDORF - ST.VITH road as this leads through the Guards Division area.

From NEUNDORF transport must gain the main road via NEUBRUCK. Troops can possibly use a track (not shewn) running along the north side of the Railway (shewn on paper map 1/100,000) This should be reconnoitred.

4.   In NEUNDORF there are cases of foot and mouth disease - no animals should be accommodated in this village.

Sd. W.H.TRAILL. Lieut.Colonel.
10th December 1918.   General Staff, 3rd Division.

Copy to 1st Division for information.

1. The Division will march on December 12th in accordance with the following March Table.

Reference Sheet 1/100,000.

MARCH TABLE.

Unit.	Starting Point.	Hour of Start.	Route.	Destination.	Instructions.
"A" Group.	Railway Crossing 400 yards South of S in ST.VITH.(Paper Map 1/100,000).	10.00.	ATZERATH	KREWINKEL. HASEN- VENN. MANDERFELD. WECKERATH. ANDLER. SCHONBERG. MACKENBACH. SETZ. NEIDINGEN.	
"B" Group.			Any.	NEUNDORF. KROMBACH. WEISTER. BRAUNLAUF. THOMMEN. GRUFFLINGEN.	Not to enter new area before 08.30 to be clear of present area by 10.30.
"C" Group.	Road Junction, 3.K.95.00.	10.00	BEHO	MALDINGEN. BEHO. ALDRINGEN. ESPELER. DEIFELD.	
"D" Group.	Road Junction, 3.J.88.12.	10.00	Cross Roads SALMCHATEAU.	COURTIL. BOUVIGNI. ROGERY. CIERREUX. PROVE DROUX. CONTE.	
55th Bde RGA. 132 m.T.Coy. RE.	Road Junction, 3.I.35.37.	10.00	REGNE.	GRAND SART. PETIT SART. JOUBIEVAL.	

2. The move of Divisional Headquarters will be notified later.
3. ACKNOWLEDGE.

Distribution :- G.O.C. "Q". C.R.A. A.P.M.
8th Inf.Bde. VI Corps "G". VI Corps "Q".
9th Inf.Bde. Camp Commdt. 3rd Div.Sigs.
76th Inf.Bde. 35th Bde.R.G.A. Guards Div.
1st Division. VI Corps H.A. C.R.E.
A.D.M.S. D.A.D.O.S. 3rd Div. M.T.Coy.
File. War Diary. 3rd Div. Train.

11/12/18.
Issued at 0700

f. [signature]
Major
for Lieut.Colonel
f. [signature]
for Lieut.Colonel
General Staff, 3rd Division.

6th Divn.

"C" FORM.
MESSAGES AND SIGNALS.

Army Form C. 2123.
(In books of 100.)
No. of Message..............

Prefix......Code......Words......	Received.	Sent, or sent out.	Office Stamp.
£ s. d.	From......	At............m.	
Charges to Collect	By......	To..............	
Service Instructions		By..............	

Handed in at................Office............m. Received......./.....m.

TO .... 8th Bn

*Sender's Number.	Day of Month.	In reply to Number.	AAA°
M957	7		

Following moves will take place tomorrow nov 5th
an 9th Inf Bde Group (less Fld Coy
RE) with attached MG Coy from ROMERIES to
PRESNOY to start at 0900 hrs route BEAUDIGNIES
– LE QUESNOY aaa 7th Inf
Bde Group (LESS Field
Coy RE) from QUIEVY
to ROMERIES to start
at 0900 hrs route
BUTERTRE PN – SOLESMES aaa from
aaa HQ and 2
Companies MG Battn will
move from QUIEVY to

FROM
PLACE & TIME

"C" FORM.
MESSAGES AND SIGNALS.

Army Form C. 2123.
(In books of 100.)

No. of Message..................

Prefix........Code.....Words..........
£ s. d.
Charges to Collect
Service Instructions

Received.
From................
By..................

Sent, or sent out.
At..................m.
To..................
By..................

Office Stamp.

Handed in at.....................................Office..........m. Received..........m.

TO (2)

* Sender's Number.	Day of Month.	In reply to Number.	AAA
ROMERIES under orders of			
GOC	9th	Infantry	Bde
who	will	allot	them
accommodation in ROMERIES aaa			
If	9th	Inf	Bde
find	accommodation in FRASNOY		
insufficient portion of			TOURMIGNIES
not reserved for			Corps
HQ	may	be	used
aaa Following distances will			
be maintained on the			
march between Bns			1000
yards between Bn			and
their transport 300			yards
aaa acknowledge aaa addsd			
List A M530 plus			6
Corps 2		62	Divs

FROM
PLACE & TIME

9pm 3rd DIV
2015

G.7643.

G.O.C., 9th Inf.Bde.

Please convey to all ranks of your Brigade my congratulation on their fine marching and smart soldierlike appearance, when crossing the frontier this morning. The care and hard work required to bring about the result attained is much appreciated.

All ranks may well be proud.

11th Dec.1918.

Sd. C.J.Deverell.Major General.
Commanding, 3rd Division.

G.7642.

G.O.C., 76th Inf.Bde.

Please convey to all ranks of all units of your group my congratulations on their fine appearance and marching this morning when crossing the frontier. The care and hard work require to bring about the result attained, is much appreciated.

All ranks may well be proud.

11th December,1918.

Sd. C.J.Deverell.Maj.General.
Commanding, 3rd Division.

3rd DIVISION OPERATION ORDER NO. 298.

1. The Division will march on December 13th in accordance with the following March Table.

Reference Sheet 1/100,000.

MARCH TABLE.

Unit.	Starting Point.	Hour of start.	Route.	Destination.	Instructions.
"A" Group.	To be clear of present area by 12.00.		Any.	BAASEN - BERK KRONENBURG - FRAUENKRON HALLSCHLAG - SCHEID LOSHEIM - ALBUTHEN.	
"B" Group.	Railway Crossing 400 yards south of S in ST.VITH (Paper map 1/100,000.)	10.00	ATZERATH.	KREWINKEL - HASENVENN MANDERFELD - ANDLER WECKERATH - SCHONBERG MACKENBACH - SETZ.	
"C" Group.	Not to enter new area before 08.30. To be clear of present area by 10.30.		Any.	NEIDINGEN - WEUNDORF KROMBACH - WEISTEN BRAUNLAUF - THOMMEN GRUFFLINGEN.	
"D" Group.	Head of column not to leave present area before 09.30 to be clear of present area except ROGERY by 11.30.		Any.	LALDINGEN - BEHO ALDRINGEN - ESPELER DAYFELD - ROGERY.	
				BOUVIGNY.	
35th Bde. RGA. 132 A.T.Coy. R.E.	Cross Roads, 3.K.28.21.	10.30	Gen. Roads SALMCHATEAU.	COURTIL.	

2. Divisional Headquarters will remain at SALMCHATEAU.
3. ACKNOWLEDGE.

Distribution :-
G.O.C.,   "Q"
8th Inf.Bde.   Div.Train.   G.R.A.
9th Inf.Bde.   VI Corps "G"   A.P.M.
76th Inf.Bde.   Camp Commdt.   VI Corps "Q"
35th Bde.RGA.   Guards Div.   3rd Div.Sigs.
1st Division.   VI Corps H.A.C.R.E. 6th Division.
A.D.M.S.   D.A.D.O.S.   3rd Div.M.T.Coy.
D.A.D.V.S.   File.   War Diary.

12/12/18.
Issued at 07.00

f. Munby Major
f. Lieut.Colonel.
General Staff, 3rd Division.

3rd Division.
G.S.2002/8.

8th Inf. Bde.   A.D.M.S.
9th Inf. Bde.   3rd Div. "Q".
76th Inf. Bde.   3rd Div. Signals.
C.R.A.   A.P.M.
C.R.E.   3rd M.T.Coy.
20th K.R.R.C.   3rd Div'l Train.
Camp Comndt.   XI Mobile Vet. Secn.
D.A.D.O.S.   D.M.G.C.
35th Bde R.G.A.

Reference para.1 of G.S.2002/2 dated 16th November.

1.   During the march through Germany, roads need not be picketed at night, but guards must be mounted over ammunition, also on groups of billets, gun parks, horse lines, and at all Headquarters.
    Inlying picquets must be detailed in every unit, and be ready to turn out at very short notice.

12th December, 1918.

Lieut.Colonel,
General Staff, 3rd Division.

G.7646.

G.O.C.8th Inf.Bde.

    Will you please accept yourself and convey to all ranks of your fine Brigade by congratulations on their good marching and smart soldierlike appearance when crossing the frontier this morning. I am well aware of, and appreciate highly, the care and hard work required to bring about the results attained. All ranks may well be proud.

12th Dec.1918.

                                    Sd.C.J.Deverell.Major General.
                                      Commanding, 3rd Division.

G.7647.

O.C.3rd M.G.Bn.

    Please accept your self and convey to all ranks of your fine Battalion my congratulations on their fine marching and smart soldierlike appearance when crossing the frontier this morning. I am well aware of, and appreciate, the care and hard work which has been required to produce the results attained.
    All ranks may well be proud.

12th Dec.1918.

                                      Sd.C.J.Deverell.Major General.
                                      Commanding, 3rd Division.

3rd Division Operation Order No.299.

1. The Division will march on December 14th in accordance with the following March Table.
Reference Sheet 1/100,000.

M A R C H   T A B L E.

Unit.	Starting Point.	Hour of Start.	Route.	Destination.	Instructions.
"A" Group.	Road Junction 1000 yards N.W. of S. in STADTKYLL. (Paper Map 1/100,000).	11.00	DAHLEM.	BLANKENHEIM. BLANKENHEIMERDORF. SCHMIDTHEIM.	
"B" Group.	Not to enter new area before 09.00. To be clear of present area by 12.00.		Any	DAASEM. KRONENBURG. HALLSCHLAG. SCHEID. LOSHEIM.	
Div.H.Q. Transport & Sig.Section.	SALMCHATEAU.	09.00.	GIERREUX. ROGERY-BEHO. Road Junction 800 yards N.W. of V.G in GRUFFLINGEN. ST.VITH.	HEUEM HEUEM (Staging Area).	1st
"C" Group.	Railway Crossing 400 yards South of S in ST.VITH. (Paper Map 1/100,000).	10.00.	ATZERATH.	KREWINKEL. HASENVENN. HANDERFELD. ANDLER-NECKERATH. SCHONBERG. ATZERATH.	
"D" Group.	Not to enter new area before 08.30. To be clear of present area by 10.45.		Any	NEIDINGEN. NEUNDORF - KROMBACH. BRAUNLAUF. THOMMEN - GRUFFLINGEN.	
33 Bde.RE. 132 A.Coy. RE.	Road Junction 1 mile East of Y in BOUVIGNY.	09.30.	BEHO	MALDINGEN. ALDRINGEN.	

2. Divisional H.Q. will close at SALMCHATEAU at 09.00 and open at Factory ½ mile S.E. of Cross Roads at point 572 in square 4.I. Sheet I.A. Germany 1/100,000 and 1¾ miles S.S.E. of LOSHEIM on arrival.

3. Acknowledge.
Distribution:- G.O.C.   "Q". G.S.O.   Div. Train.
                8th Inf.Bde. A.P.M.   VI Corps "G".
                9th Inf.Bde. VI Corps "Q".   Camp Commdt.
                76th Inf.Bde. 3rd Div.Sigs.   35th Bde.RGA.
                Guards Div.   6th Division.   1st Division.
                VI Corps H.A. C.R.E.   A.D.M.S. D.A.D.V.S.
                Dam.D.O.S.   3rd Div.M.T.Coy. File. War Diary.

Issued at 03.30.
13/12/18.

A. *[signature]* Major.
for Lieut-Colonel.
General Staff, 3rd Division.

3rd Division.
G.7650.

A.D.M.S.

Will you please convey to all ranks of the 3 Field Ambulances of this Division my congratulations on their fine marching and smart soldierlike appearance when crossing the Frontier. I appreciate the care and hard work required to bring about the results attained. All ranks may well be proud.

13th Dec. 1918.

(Sgd.) C.J.DEVERELL, Major-General,
Commanding, 3rd Division.

C.R.E.

Will you please convey to all ranks of the three Field Companies of this Division my congratulations on their fine marching and smart and soldierlike appearance when crossing the Frontier. I appreciate the care and hard work of all ranks required to bring about the results attained. All ranks may well be proud.

13/12/18.

(Sgd.) C.J.DEVERELL, Major-General,
Commanding, 3rd Division.

"A" Form
MESSAGES AND SIGNALS.

Army Form C. 2121
(In pads of 100.)

No. of Message..........

Prefix....Code.....m.	Words	Charge.	This message is on a/c of:	Recd. at....m.
Office of Origin and Service Instructions	Sent		..............Service.	Date..........
....	At ....m.		....	From ......
....	To		....	
....	By		(Signature of "Franking Officer")	By..........

TO—

Sender's Number.	Day of Month.	In reply to Number.	AAA
SC201	13/2		

From
Place
Time

The above may be forwarded as now corrected. (Z)

....
Censor. Signature of Addressor or person authorised to telegraph in his name
* This line should be erased if not required.

Order No. 1625. Wt. W8252/ P 511. 27/2. H. & K., Ltd. (E. 2634).

G.7634/3.

8th Inf.Bde.
9th Inf.Bde.
76th Inf.Bde.
C.R.A.
38th Bde.,R.A.

ROAD RECONNAISSANCE.

1. SCHONBERG – AMEL – MANDERFELD. This road is similar to that between ST.VITH and SCHONBERG. There is about 12" to 18" of metalling but the sides are very muddy. Lorries can pass anywhere going slow.
   For 3 kilometres N.from AMEL there is a heavy winding pull up the first kilometre having a very soft surface though the soling seems very soft underneath. Civilians are clearing this hill and replacing the surface as far as possible.

2. MANDERFELD – PT.572 – HALLSCHLAG similar to (1). About 1000 yards steady pull up N.E. of HALLSCHLAG.

3. MANDERFELD – KRUWINKEL to LOSHEIM – PRUM Road reported by staff officers suitable for all horse transport to KRUWINKEL. Beyond KRUWINKEL only partly examined and found passable for all horse transport. But so heavy that only transport of troops using KRUWINKEL village should use it, and cookers etc. of troops using the ammunition factory.

4. PT.572 (A.A) to Munition Factory near WELDTIUGELST/ Road similar to (1) in sound condition but muddy. A railway runs along side the road.

5. PT.572 – ALMUTHEM good road for all horse transport to entrance of village, then very soft and muddy.

6. HALLSCHLAG – KRONENBURG – STADTKYLL – Similar to (1) sound muddy but most of centre scraped. Several rises and falls but none serious.

7. From road (6) above to BERK narrow road. Hard, suitable for all horse transport. Branch to FRAUENKRON stated by Burgomeister to be equally good.

8. Road past 2nd N. in KRONENBURG – BAASEM – BAASEM N. A very steep very sinuous road leads up into the upper half of KRONENBURG village. Thence road runs gently over hill and down fairly steeply to BAASEM. The surface of the road is suitable for all horse transport N.of BAASEM for 500 yards road runs down hairpin bends fairly steeply, after which it runs easily to the main road.
   All traffic should enter BAASEM from the East.

9. STADTKYLL – DAHLEM – BLANKENHEIM Road generally similar to (1). A heavy sinuous pull a mile long from WINZENBACH (4 K) northwards surface good, lower half scraped upper half being scraped.
   Steady pull ½ mile into DAHLEM. Sharp rise 800 yards long out of DAHLEM to N.
   Fairly sharp rise 800 yards long N. of level crossing to F. KAISER HAUS. Fall average about 1 in 15 last mile into BLANKENHEIM with 3 or 4 fairly bad pot holes. No metal available handy for repairs.

10. F.KAISERHAUS – SCHMIDTHEIM.Road similar to (1) Fairly steep sinuous hill down about 800 yards into SCHMIDTHEIM generally the main roads are in sound condition and the main mass of the mud has generally been cleared from the centre 10' or 12' of the road. The sides are everywhere very muddy.

15th December 1918.

Lieut.Colonel.
General Staff, 3rd Division.

3rd Division Operation Order No.300.

1. The Division will march on December 15th in accordance with the following March Table.
Reference Sheet Paper Map I.M. 1/100,000.

MARCH TABLE.

Unit.	Starting Point.	Hour of start.	Route.	Destination.	Instructions.
"A" Group.	Point where road bends to N.E. 1000 yards. North of B. in BLANKENHEIM.	10.30.	Cross Roads 1000 yards N.N.W. of 1st H in MULHEIM.	FROHNGAU - BUIR, TONDORF - ROTH, MULHEIM. [ESCHWEILER - SCHONAU - REUSCHEID - HOLZMULHEIM.] Sheet 14. 1/100,000
"B" Group.	Road Junction 1000 yards N.W. of S in STADTKYLL.	11.00.	DAHLEM.	BLANKENHEIM. BLANKENHEIMERDORF SCHMIDTHEIM.
Div.HQ. Transport & Sig.Section.	SETZ	08.30.	ANDLER - MANDERFELD. Junction of Roads 900 yards N.N.W. of A in ALBNUTHEN.	FACTORY ½ mile S.E. of junction of roads 900 yards N.N.W. of A in ALBNUTHEN. BAASEM.
"C" Group.	Junction of roads 900 yards N.N.W. of A in ALBNUTHEN.	11.30.	HALLSCHLAG.	KRONENBURG. KRONENBURGERHUTTE. HALLSCHLAG.
"D" Group.	Road Junction 400 yards W.of S in SCHONBERG.	11.45.	ANDLER.	LOSHEIM - KREWINKEL HASENVENN. MANDERFELD. ANDLER - SCHONBERG.
35 Bde.RGA. 152 A.T.Coy. R.E.	Road junction immediately S.of the D. in HALDINGER.	09.45.	Road Junction 800 yards N.W.of 1st G in GRUFFLIN-GEN. - ST.VITH. ATZERATH.	SETZ. ATZERATH. LOSHEIM. MACKENBACH. HEUEM.

2. Divisional H.Q. will remain at FACTORY ½ mile S.E. of junction of roads 900 yards N.N.W. of A in ALBNUTHEN.

3. ACKNOWLEDGE.

Distribution :-
- G.O.C.
- 8th Inf.Bde.
- 9th Inf.Bde.
- 76th Inf.Bde.
- 35th Bde.RGA.
- 1st Division
- A.D.M.S.
- File.

- "Q"
- Div.Train.
- VI Corps G.
- Camp.Commdt.
- Guards Div.
- VI Corps H.A.
- D.A.D.O.S.
- War Diary.

- G.S.A.
- A.P.M.
- VI Corps "Q".
- 3rd.Div.Sigs.
- 6th Division
- C.R.E.
- 3rd Div.M.T.Coy.

[signature]
for Lieut.Colonel.
General Staff, 3rd Division.

14/12/18.
Issued at 06.30 hours.

G.7683.

O.C. 80th Bde. R.A.

Will you please convey to all ranks under your command my congratulations on their marching and general appearance when crossing the frontier this morning. I fully appreciate their difficulties, and the hard work required to maintain their high standard. The horses had been well cared for and looked very well. The Heavy Artillery has played a great part in enabling us to enter Germany as victors, and all ranks of your command may well be proud.

                                  Sd.C.J.Deverall. Maj.Genl.
14/12/18.   Commanding, 3rd Division.

O.C. 132nd. A.T. Coy. R.E.

Will you please convey to all Ranks under your command my congratulations on their fine marching and appearance when crossing the frontier this morning. All ranks may well be proud of the occasion.

                                  Sd.C.J.Deverall. Maj.Genl.
14/12/18.   Commanding, 3rd Division.

C.R.A. 3rd Division.

Will you please accept yourself and convey to all ranks under your command my congratulations on their fine marching and smart and soldierlike appearance when crossing the frontier. The weather conditions were most unfavourable but I fully appreciate the care and hard work required to bring about the results attained. All ranks may well be proud, and I am certainly proud of them.

                                  Sd.C.J.Deverall. Maj.General.
14/12/18.   Commanding, 3rd Division.

O.C., 3rd Divisional Train.

Will you please accept yourself and convey to all ranks under your command my congratulations on their efficient appearance when crossing the Frontier. The condition of horses and all transport generally was a testimony to the care and hard work taken throughout the march in spite of unpropitious weather conditions. I appreciate the results and feel that all ranks may well be proud.

                                  Sd.C.J.Deverall. Maj.Genl.
14/12/18.   Commanding, 3rd Division.

S E C R E T.

3rd Div.G.S.2002/9.

```
* 8th Inf.Bde.        A.D.M.S.
* 9th Inf.Bde.      * 3rd Div."Q".
* 76th Inf.Bde.       3rd Div.Sigs.
* C.R.A.              A.P.M.
* C.R.E.              3rd Div.M.T.Coy.
  20th K.R.R.C.       3rd Div.Train.
  Camp Commdt.        Mob.Vet.Section.
  D.A.D.O.S.          D.A.G.C.
  35th Bde.R.G.A.
```
----

1. The amended areas allotted to Corps, also the provisional boundaries of the areas allotted to Divisions of the VI Corps in German Territory are shown on attached Map. These areas may have to be amended when it has been possible to make a thorough reconnaissance of the VI Corps area.

   The Map issued with GS/2002/8 dated 2/12/18 is cancelled.

2. The II and Canadian Corps are responsible for the defence of the River RHINE within their respective boundaries.

3. The 1st Cavalry Division is shortly to be withdrawn, and will probably be marching back to its billeting area within the next two or three days.

4. The march of the VI Corps into its area will be carried out as follows :-

   (a) The road allotted to each column is shown on the attached map.

   (b) The Guards Division will continue its march straight into its final area.

   (c) The 2nd Division will continue its march into its area.

   (d) The 3rd Division will continue its march to the area about EUSKIRCHEN, where it will close up. As soon as the tail of the Guards Division has cleared ZULPICH, the 3rd Division will be ordered to move into its final area.

   (e) The dividing lines between Divisions for billeting purposes during the march are shown on the attached map.

/5

(2)

5. The subdivision of Divisional billeting area to Brigades etc. will be guided by the fact that the VI Corps is in support to the II Corps and may be ordered to move forward rapidly at short notice.

As far therefore as billeting accommodation will permit the 3rd Division will be concentrated in the northern portion of the 3rd Division area – Infantry Brigades being billeted along the roads leading to the RHINE.

6. The 35 Bde RbA will be accommodated in 3rd Division area.

H H Traill

Lieut.Colonel.
General Staff, 3rd Division.

14th December 1918.

X Map attached

3rd Division Operation Order No.301.

1. The Division will march on December 16th in accordance with the following March Table. Reference Sheet I.M. and I.L.1/100,000 (Germany).

MARCH TABLE

Unit.	Starting Point.	Hour of Start.	Route.	Destination.	Instructions.
"A" Group.	Road Junction 300 yards W.of 1st E in EIGERSCHEID.	10.00	MUNSTEREIFEL. IVERSHEIM.	EUSKIRCHEN - ROITZHEIM. BILLIG - STOTZHEIM. RHEDER - WEINGARTEN.	Certain accommodation which will be marked is to be reserved for Div.HQ.in EUSKIRCHEN.
"B" Group.	Point where road bends to N.E.1000 yards North of E in BLANKENHEIM.	10.45.	Road Junction 1000 yards WNW of 1st M in MULHEIM.	EICHERSCHEID - SCHON AN BOUDERATH - HOLZMULHEIM FROHNGAU - BUIR - TONDORF.	
"C" Group.	Road Junction 1000 yards N.W.of S in STADTKYLL.	09.45.	DAHLEM.	MULHEIM - BLANKENHEIM - BLANKENHEIMERDORF.	"C" Group will reserve accommodation on night Dec.16/17th in BLANKENHEIM for 8 officers 300 O.R. 30 officers Chargers and 100 horses of Div.HQ. and Div.HQ.Sig.Section which will stage there.
				SCHMIDTHEIM.	Accommodation for 1 Bn. in SCHMIDTHEIM is allotted to "C"Group,remainder of the village to "D"Group. Exact boundaries between "C" & "D"Groups in this village will be notified by 3rd Div."Q".
"D" Group.	Junction of Roads 900 yards NNW of A in ALBNUTHEN.	10.30	HALLSCHLAG.	SCHMIDTHEIM	
				DAHLEM. BAASEM. HALLSCHLAG. SCHEID.	
35th Bde.RGA Road Junction 400 132.AT.Co.RE.yards W.of $ in SCHONBERG.		10.15	MANDERFELD		
Div.HQ. Transport & Sig.Sec.	Junction of roads 900 yards NNW of A in ALBNUTHEN.	08.30	DAHLEM.	BLANKENHEIM. (Starting Area)	

2. Divisional H.Q. will close at present location at 09.00 and open at EUSKIRCHEN on arrival.

3. ACKNOWLEDGE.

Distribution :—
G.O.C.
8th Inf.Bde.
9th Inf.Bde.
73th Inf.Bde.
C.R.E.
D.A.D.V.S.

"Q".
A.P.M.
Camp Commdt.
Guards Div.
A.D.M.S.
File.

G.R.A.
VI Corps G.
3rd Div.Sigs.
6th Div.
D.A.D.O.S.
War Diary.

Div.Train.
VI Corps Q.
35th Bde.RGA.
VI Corps HA.
3rd Div.MT.Coy.
1st Division.

15/12/18.
Issued at 06.30.

/. Lindsey Meyn.
Lieut.Colonel.
General Staff, 3rd Division.

3rd Division Operation Order No.302.

1. The Division will march on December 17th in accordance with the following March Table.

Reference Sheet: I.&.I.I.1/100,000.(Germany).

MARCH TABLE.

Unit.	Starting Point.	Hour of Start.	Route.	Destination.	Instructions.
"A" Group.	Tail of column to be in EUSKIRCHEN by 11.45.		Any	EUSKIRCHEN.	
"B" Group.	Road Junction 300 yards W. of E in EICHERSCHEID.	10.00.	MUNSTEREIFEL.	ROITZHEIM. BILLIG - STOTZHEIM. WEIKGARTEN. KIRSPENICH. IVERSHEIM.	
"C" Group.	Road Junction 1000 yards W.N.W. of M in MULHEIM.	10.15	TONDORF.	MUNSTEREIFEL. EICHERSCHEID. SCHONAN. BOUDERATH. HOLZMULHEIM.	
"D" Group.	Road Junction 1400 yards S. of the 1st H in SCHMIDTHEIM.	09.45.	BLANKENHEIM.	FROHNGAU. ENGELGAU. BUIR - TONDORF. MULHEIM. BLANKENHEIM.	
35 Bde.RGA. 152 AT.Coy. R.E.	Road Junction 1400 yards W. of B in KRONENBURG.	09.30	DAHLEM.	BLANKENHEIMERDORF.	
D.H.Q. Transport & Sig. section.	BLANKENHEIM.	08.00.	TONDORF. MUNSTEREIFEL.	EUSKIRCHEN.	

2. Divisional Headquarters will remain at EUSKIRCHEN.
3. ACKNOWLEDGE.

Distribution:- G.O.C. "Q". Q.R.A. Div.Train.
8th Inf.Bde. A.P.M. VI Corps "G".
9th Inf.Bde. VI Corps "Q". Camp Commdt.
76th Inf.Bde. 3rd Div.Sigs.35th Bde.RGA.
Guards Div. 6th Division,1st Division.
VI Corps H.A. C.R.E. A.D.M.S.
D.A.D.O.S. 3rd Div.M.T.Coy. D.A.D.V.S.
File. War Diary.

16/12/18. Issued at 06.30 hours.

p. Lieut.Colonel,
General Staff,3rd Division.

3rd Division Operation Order No. 503.

1. The Division will march on December 18th in accordance with the following March Table.

Reference Sheet I.M. & I.L. 1/100,000 Germany.

MARCH TABLE.

Unit.	Starting Point.	Hour of start.	Route.	Destination.	Instructions
"A" Group.	*Not to leave EUSKIRCHEN before 1000. Bn.+ Inder to R.E. whose unit will be met later.*		LOMMERSUM. NEIDERBERG.	ERP. EHREM. FRIESHEIM. BORR - WEILER.	
"B" Group.					Will be notified after result of reconnaissance is known.
"C" Group.	Road Junction 700 yards W.N.W. of first E in IVERSHEIM.	10.30.	IVERSHEIM. WACHENDORF. ANTWEILER.	LESSENICH. SATZVEY. OBR GARTZEM. FIRMENICH - ENZEN.	
"D" Group.	Road Junction 600 yards N. of 1st E in ENGELGAU.	10.00.	WEVER. MECHERNICH.	ROGGENDORF. MECHERNICH. KOMMERN. SCHAVEN.	
35th Bde. RGA. 132 A.T.Coy. R.E.	Road Junction 500 yards W. of B in BLANKENHEIM.	10.15	TONDORF. ENGELGAU.	EISERFER - WEYER. ZINGSHEIM.	

2. Divisional H.Q. will remain at EUSKIRCHEN.
3. ACKNOWLEDGE.

Distribution :—

G.O.C.	"Q".	G.R.A.	
8th Inf. Bde.	A.P.M.	VI Corps "G".	
9th Inf. Bde.	VI Corps "Q".	Camp Commdt.	
76th Inf. Bde.	3rd Div. Sigs.	35th Bde. RGA.	
Guards Div.	6th Division.	1st Division.	
VI Corps H.A.	G.R.E.	A.D.M.S.	
D.A.D.O.S.	3rd Div. M.T. Coy.	D.A.D.V.S.	
File.	War Diary.	3rd SW Tmn	

17/12/18.
Issued at 06.30.

[signature] Major

[signature] Lieut. Colonel.
General Staff, 3rd Division.

3rd Division Operation Order No.304.

1. 3rd Division Operation Order No.303 is cancelled.
2. The Division will march on December 13th in accordance with the following March Table.
Reference Sheet 1cM. & 1.M. 1/100,000.Germany.

MARCH TABLE

Unit.	Starting Point.	Hour of Start.	Route.	Destination.	Instructions.
"A"Group. Less Pioneer Bn.& Fld.Co. R.E.	Not to leave EUSKIRCHEN before 09.30 hours, to be clear of it by 10.30.		LOMMERSUM. NIEDERBERG.	EPP. LHILL. FRIESHEIM. BORR - WEILER.	
20th K.R.R. (Pioneers) 529th Fld. Coy.R.E.	Cross Roads in EUENHEIM.	09.00.	DURSCHEVEN.	Pioneer Bn. - FUSSENICH. GEICH. 529th Fld.Co.RE.- FROITZHEIM.	To move under orders of O.C.20th KRRC (Pioneers).
"B"Group.	Not to enter EUSKIRCHEN before 10.30 to be clear of IVERSHEIM by 10.00.		Any	EUSKIRCHEN.	
"C"Group.	Road Junction 200 yds WNW West I of IVERSHEIM.	10.00	WACHENDORF. LESSENICH.	LESSENICH. SATZVEY. OBER GARTZEM - FIRMENICH - ENZEN.	
"D"Group.	Road Junction 500 yards N.of 1st : E in ENGELGAU. 10.00.		WEYER. MECHERNICH.	ROGGENDORF. MECHERNICH. KOMMERN. SCHAVEN.	
35th Bde. RGA. 132 AT.Coy. RE.	Road Junction 500 yards W.of B in BLANKENHEIM.	10.15	TONDORF. ENGELGAU.	EISERFEY - WEYER. ZINGSHEIM.	

3. Divisional Headquarters will remain at EUSKIRCHEN.
4. ACKNOWLEDGE.

Distribution :-
G.O.C.
8th Inf.Bde.
9th Inf.Bde.
76th Inf.Bde.
Guards Div.
VI Corps H.A.
D.A.D.O.S.
Files.
"Q".
A.P.M.
VI Corps Q.
3rd Div.Sigs.
6th Division.
G.R.E.
3rd Div.MT.Coy.
War Diary.
C.R.A.
VI Corps G.
Camp Commdt.
35th Bde.RGA.
1st Division.
A.D.M.S.
D.A.D.V.S.
3rd Div.Train.

12/12/18.
Issued at 10.30.

20th KRRC.
529 Fld.Coy.RE } Through 76 & by Bde.

/A.Lt.Col.
/A.Lt.Col.
General Staff,3rd Division

8th Inf. Bde.
9th Inf. Bde.
~~C.R.E.~~
~~R.A.~~
1st Division.
~~S.~~

G 7670

The road from railway crossing N.E. of ZULPICH to DURBENICH - SIEVERNICH - HAZENEICH is fit for horse transport. The road running along the railway W. of DURBENICH to level crossing thence to MIDDERNICH - GLADBACH and the main road is also fit for horse transport.

Neither of these roads are fit for lorries.

There are one or two field carts standing in the road which should be moved.

The road from the level crossing N.E. of DURBENICH through GEISTINGEN to main road has not been reconnoitred.

Lieut. Colonel,
General Staff, 3rd Division.

17th December 1918.

3rd Division Operation Order No.295.

1. The Division will march on December 19th in accordance with the following March Table.

Reference Sheet - M. & I.L. 1/100,000. Germany.

M A R C H   T A B L E.

Unit.	Starting Point.	Hour of Start.	Route.	Destination. Final Area.	Instructions.
"A" Group. Less Tail to be clear of LECHENICH Monser Bn. & by 11.30. 229 Fld.Co. R.E.			LECHENICH		
20th K.R.R.C. (Pioneers) 529th Fld. Co. R.E.	Road Junction 200 yards S.W. of F in FROITZHEIM.	10.00.	STOCKHEIM.	20th K.R.R.C. (Pioneers) DUREN. 529th Fld.Co.R.E. Destination will be notified.	To move under the orders of O.C. 20th KRRC. (Pioneers).
"B" Group.	Cross Roads in EURNHEIM.	10.00.	ULPENICH.	"B" Group. 1bss MG.Bn. and Field Company ZULPICH. M.G. Battalion. FUSSENICH. GEICH. 56th Fld.Coy.R.E. FROITZHEIM.	
"C" Group.	Road Junction 900 yards N. of 1st N in ENZEN.	09.30.	ULPENICH. ZULPICH. LESSENICH.	CLADBACH. MUDDERSHEIM. DISTERNICH. SIEVERICH.	
"D" Group.	Cross Roads 600 yards N.E. of N in SCHWERFEN.	10.00.	Any route South of and excluding ZULPICH.	GIMNICK. PISSENHEIM. BURG - EMEKEN. WOLLERSHEIM.	
35 Bde.RGA.Road Junction 200 yards 132 AT.Co. W. of the 1st E in R.E. EISERFER.		09.30.	LECHERNICH.	SINZENICH. SCHWERFEN.	

2. Divisional H.Q. will close at EUSKIRCHEN at 09.00 and open at DUREN on arrival.
3. ACKNOWLEDGE.

Distribution :-
G.O.C.,
8th Inf. Bde.
9th Inf. Bde.
76th Inf. Bde.
Guards Div.
VI Corps H.A.
D.A.D.O.S.
3rd Div. Train.

"Q"
A.P.M.
VI Corps Q.
3rd Div. Sigs.
6th Div.
C.R.E.
3rd Div. MT.Coy.
20th K.R.R.C.

C.R.A.
VI Corps G.
Camp Commdt.
35th Bde. RGA.
1st Div.
A.D.M.S.
D.A.D.V.S.
529th Fld.Co. R.E.

File.
War Diary.

18/12/18.
Issued at 08.50.

(signed) M.V. ...
Lieut.Colonel.
General Staff, 3rd Division.

Reference 3rd Division Operation Order No.305.

Divisional H.Q., Transport and Signal Section will move on December 19th as follows :-

Unit.	Starting Point.	Hour of Start.	Route.	Destination.
Div.HQ. Transport & Sig.Section.	Cross Roads, EUENHEIM.	08.15.	ULPENICH. ZULPICH. FROITZHEIM.	DUREN.

Headquarter lorries will leave USKIRCHEN at 10.00 hours, proceed via LOMMERSOM - FRIESHEIM - ERP - GLADBACH - KELZ - DUREN.

19th December 1918.

Lieut.Colonel,
General Staff, 3rd Division.

Copies to :-
"Q".
D.A.D.O.S.
A.P.M.
3rd Div. Sigs.
C.R.E.
VI Corps G.
A.D.M.S.
D.A.D.V.S.
File. War Diary.
Camp Commandant.

3rd Division Operation Order. No.306.

1. The Division will march on December 20th in accordance with the following March Table.

Reference Sheet F.N. & I.L. 1/100,000. Germany.

MARCH TABLE.

Unit.	Starting Point.	Hour of Start.	Route.	Area	Instructions.
"B" Group. Less M.G.Bn. & 56th Fld. Coy.R.E.	Level Crossing ¾ mile N.E. of ZULPICH.	09.00	BESSENICH. DISTERNICH.	Final Area.	
56th Fld.Co. M.G.Bn.	} FROITZHEIM.	09.00	SOLLER. STUCKHEIM.	Will be notified. DUREN.	} To move under orders of O.C. M.G.Bn.
"C" Group. Less 438th Fld.Co.RE.	Road Junction ½ mile W. of G in GLADBACH.	09.30	Any	Final Area.	
438th Fld. Co.RE.	do.	To be clear of starting point by 10.30.	KELZ. FRAUWULLESHEIM.	To be notified.	To move under orders of GOC 8th Inf.Bde.
"D" Group.	To move into Final Area under orders of C.R.A., no restrictions as to routes but NOT to enter ZULPICH before 09.40 or FROITZHEIM before 09.30, if using the ZULPICH - FROITZHEIM - SOLLER Road.				

2. Divisional H.Q. will remain at DUREN.
3. ACKNOWLEDGE.

Distribution :-
G.O.C.   C.R.A.
8th Inf.Bde.   "Q".
9th Inf.Bde.   A.P.M.   VI Corps G.
76th Inf.Bde.   VI Corps Q.   Camp Commdt.
Guards Div.   3rd Div.Sigs.   35th Bde.RGA.
VI Corps HA.   6th Div.   1st Div.
D.A.D.O.S.   C.R.E.   A.D.M.S.
3rd Div.Train.   3rd Div.MT.Coy.D.A.D.V.S.
                               File.   War Diary.

18/12/18.
Issued at 14.00.

Lieut.Colonel.
General Staff, 3rdxDiv.

G.2869/2.

8th Inf.Bde.   G.1.a.
9th Inf.Bde.   1st Division.
76th Inf.Bde.   59th Bde.R.G.A.

ROAD RECONNAISSANCE.

Reference 1/100,000 I.M. & 1.M. German Map.

1. MANNHEIM - TONDORF - HOLZHEIM is road suitable for double lorry traffic. About 12' to 15' of metalling clear in middle 10' but very muddy at sides. The surface is inclined to be soft and gritty but is still holding.
   A hill about a mile long leads up N.out of MANNHEIM only the first 300 yards being at all steep.
   The street in the Eastern end of TONDORF is narrow and rough having been repaired with heavy metal. E.of TONDORF there is a dip down and up but the gradients are not very steep.
   There is a steep very sinuous hill down into HOLZHEIM near the top the left side of the road is badly broken away opposite where a lorry had broken down.

2. Entrance to MULHEIM is suitable for all horse transport, the road slopes fairly steeply down from the main road to the village.

3. TONDORF - ENGELN similar to (1) fairly level throughout.

4. MULHEIM - FREKHAU - ENGELN. About 10 feet of metalling very good condition and no mud. There are two dips between FREKHAU and the main road (1) with hills about 300 yards long each side but not serious for any horse transport.

5. Entrance to MULHEIM suitable for all horse transport slopes fairly steeply down to village.

6. HOLZHEIM - BHONAU. About 12' metalling rough but hard and fairly level suitable for all horse transport.

7. HOLZHEIM - PT.473 - KIRCHSEIFEN. Similar in nature to (1) a steep hill about a mile long out of HOLZHEIM up to PT.473 and a steady fall about 3 kilometres long into KIRCHSEIFEN.

8. ENGELN - MORSBACH - PT.473 Good road fairly level suitable for all horse transport and one way lorry traffic.

9. Entrances to MORSBACH from MORSBACH to PT.473 Both are good hard narrow roads suitable for all horse transport.Both slope down into MORSBACH and the Eastern road is steepest but is not a serious hill for horse transport coming up. There is no through connection direct from MORSBACH to KIRCHSEIFEN.

10. BHONAU - KIRCHSEIFEN is a good level two way lorry route.
    Note. Transport should move by HOLZHEIM - BHONAU - KIRCHSEIFEN and ENGELN - MORSBACH - PT.473 - KIRCHSEIFEN to avoid the hill out of HOLZHEIM.

                                          Lieut.Colonel.
15th December 1918.   General Staff, 3rd Division.

TO ALL RANKS OF THE "IRON" THIRD DIVISION.

I wish you all a Happy Christmas - a Bright and Prosperous New Year and many such in the years to come.

You are spending this Christmas in Germany to ensure a just and lasting peace following upon the efforts of the past four years.

In the victory that has been gained you have played a great and glorious part, and your Division has justly earned the title of an "IRON" Division.

Since April 9th 1917, the day of the commencement of the Battle of ARRAS, you have fought continuously in the front line except for very brief periods necessary to move you from one scene of operations to another.

During 1918, as stated by the Third Army Commander, not only have you been continuously in action since the beginning of the advance and borne the brunt of the culminating operations, but you came to these operations direct from a long period of defensive operations in which you were continuously engaged without any period of rest.

These defensive operations comprised the defence of ARRAS, and the defence of HINGES, a key to the French Coal Mine Districts.

Your share in these operations will be remembered with pride and will be recorded in the History of our country as an example of ceaseless endurance and calm courage against which the mightiest thrusts of the enemy were of no avail.

As was to be expected the Division has suffered heavy casualties in the fierce fighting in which it has taken part and many of our comrades lie gloriously in their last earthly resting places; the memory of their unselfish sacrifice will ever remain with us.

In 1918 alone you have been awarded more than 2,000 decorations for your gallantry and devotion to duty.

Such is the record gained by your ceaseless enterprise, your indomitable courage, your powers of endurance and your loyal support to your leaders.

To all ranks, to all Units and Formations, to all Commanders and Staffs, I express my pride and my thanks.

I trust that you may live long to enjoy the fruits of your labours, and that it may be your privilege to transmit to your children and to your childrens' children, as Christmas Days and New Years roll on, the story of the deeds of yourselves and your comrades in the British Army and in the glorious old Third Division in particular - deeds which have won for you and for them the right to live in Peace and in Honour in your own homes in the British Isles, or in other parts of the Empire under His Majesty The King.

C. J. Deverell
Major General.
Commanding, 3rd Division.

23rd December 1918.

3rd Div.G.7738.

8th Inf.Bde.
9th Inf.Bde.
----

1.   The following moves will take place on the 27th inst.

    8th Inf.Bde.H.Q.   to BINSFELD.
    8th T.M.Battery   to ROMMELSHEIM.
    No.3 Coy.3rd Div.Train   to ESCHWEILER.

2.   The village of FRAUWULLESHEIM is not available for 8th Inf.Bde. as it is required for the 142nd Field Ambulance, attached 9th Inf.Bde.

3.   The villages in para.1 will be vacated by 12 noon on the 27th by any units of 9th Inf.Bde. billeted there.

4.   KERPEN and BLATZHEIM have been allotted to the 9th Inf.Bde. and units can be moved into these villages under arrangements to be made by 9th Inf.Bde.

                             Sd.W.H.Traill.Lt.Col.
                          General Staff, 3rd Division.

26th December 1919.

Copy to 3rd Div."Q" for information.

"A" Form.

Army Form C. 2121.
(In pads of 100.)

MESSAGES AND SIGNALS.

No. of Message ....

Prefix .... Code .... m.	Words.	Charge.	This message is on a/c of:	Recd. at ...... m.
Office of Origin and Service Instructions.	Sent At .... m. To .... By		.... Service. (Signature of "Franking Officer.")	Date .... From .... By ....

TO 8 Inf Bde
9 Inf Bde

Sender's Number.	Day of Month.	In reply to Number.	AAA
* G.O. 257	26		

Para	1	[illegible] 3 of	Div
Ops	G.775	are	cancelled
Moves	will	be	carried
out	as	ordered	in
AQ 207	[illegible]	[illegible]	of
9	Bde	at	present
allotted	to	[illegible]	aaa
FRAUWALLESHEIM		leave	the
clear	of	these	villages
by	1200	hours	on
27th	inst	aaa	
Addressed	8	and	9th Bdes

From [illegible]
Place
Time 1000

The above may be forwarded as now corrected. (Z) [illegible signature]

Censor. Signature of Addressor or person authorised to telegraph in his name.

* This line, except AAA, should be erased if not required.

Wt. W 8253/P511. 500,000 Pads. 1/18. B. & S. Ltd. (E2389.)

3rd DIVISION.

Disposition and Movement Report No.1.
31st December 1918
~~12th January, 1919.~~

UNIT.	Location of H.Q. at 1900 hours.	Probable changes within 24 hours.
3rd Divisional H.Q.	DUREN No.70 Oberstrasse	
8th Infantry Brigade H.Q.	BINSFELD.	
2nd The Royal Scots.	BUIR.	
1st Royal Scots Fus.	MERZENICH.	
7th K.S.L.I.	GOLZHEIM.	
8th T.M.Battery.	BINSFELD.	
8th Field Ambulance.	GIRBELSRATH.	
No.3 Coy Train, R.A.S.C.	FRAUWALLESHEIM.	
9th Infantry Brigade H.Q.	NORVENICH SCHLOSS.	
1st Northld. Fus.	OBR. BOLHEIM.	
4th Royal Fusiliers.	BLATZHEIM & BERGERHAUSEN.	
13th King's L'pool Regt.	KERPEN.	
9th T.M.Battery.	SOFIENHOHE.	
142nd Field Ambulance.	KELZ.	
No.4 Coy Train, R.A.S.C.	OLLESHEIM.	
76th Infantry Brigade H.Q.	GYMNICH BURG.	
8th K.O.R.L.Regt.	TURNICH SCHLOSS.	
2nd Suffolk Regt.	GYMNICH (Southern entrance)	
1st Gordon Hldrs.	KIERDORF (Villa Louise).	
76th T.M.Battery.	GYMNICH BURG.	
7th Field Ambulance.	DIRMERZHEIM Billet No.42.	
No.2 Coy Train, R.A.S.C.	KONRADSHEIM.	
C.R.A.	NIDEGGEN.	
23rd Brigade R.F.A.	NIEDERAU - DUREN Road.	
40th " "	KREUZAU.	
42nd " "	UNT. MAUBACH.	
3rd Div. Ammn. Column.	LENDERSDORF.	
C.R.E.	DUREN, No.127 Oberstrasse.	
56th Field Company, R.E.	DUREN, 2 Friedriche Platz.	
458th " " "	DUREN, 13 Eschstrasse.	
529th " " "	DUREN, 22 Ost Strasse.	
3rd Battalion M.G. Corps.	~~The Barracks, DUREN.~~ The BARRACKS DUREN	
20th K.R.R.C.(Pioneers)	~~SCHLICH - MERODE - DERICHS - WEILER.~~	
A.D.M.S.	The Schools, DUREN.	
XI Mobile Veterinary Section.	LENDERSDORF.	
35th Brigade R.G.A.	BERG.	
111th Heavy Battery.	PISSENHEIM.	
152nd A.T.Coy, R.E.	PISSENHEIM.	
VI Corps H.Q.	DUREN, 2 Eisenbahn Strasse.	
Guards Division.	LINDENTHAL.	
2nd Division.	DUREN, 3 Holz Strasse.	

3RD DIVISION OPERATION ORDER NO. 298.

1. The Division will march on December 13th in accordance with the following March Table.

Reference Sheet 1/100,000.

MARCH TABLE.

Unit.	Starting Point.	Hour of start.	Route.	Destination.	Instructions.
"A" Group.	To be clear of present area by 12.00.		Any.	BAASEM — BERK — KRONENBURG — FRAUENKRON — HALLSCHLAG — SCHEID — LOSHEIM — ALBUTHEN.	
"B" Group.	Railway Crossing 400 yards south of S in ST.VITH (Paper map 1/100,000)	10.00	ATZERATH.	KREWINKEL — HASENVENN — MANDERFELD — ANDLER — WECKERATH — SCHONBERG — HACKENBACH — SETZ.	
"C" Group.	Not to enter new area before 08.50. To be clear of present area by 10.30.		Any.	NEIDINGEN — NEUNDORF — KROMBACH — WEISTEN — BRAUNLAUF — THOMMEN — GRUFFLINGEN.	
"D" Group.	Head of column not to leave present area before 09.30 to be clear of present area except ROGERY by 11.30.			ALDRINGEN — BEHO — ALDRINGEN — ESPELER — DEYFELD — ROGERY.	
35th Bde. R.G.A.	Cross Roads, J.K.28.21.	10.30		BOUVIGNY.	
132 A.T.Coy. R.E.			Cross Roads SALMCHATEAU	COURTIL.	

2. Divisional Headquarters will remain at SALMCHATEAU.
3. ACKNOWLEDGE.

Distribution :—
G.O.C., "Q" G.R.A.
8th Inf.Bde. Div.Train. A.P.M.
9th Inf.Bde. VI Corps "Q" VI Corps "Q".
76th Inf.Bde. Camp Commdt. 3rd Div.Sigs.
35th Bde.RGA. Guards Div. 6th Division.
1st Division. VI Corps H.A.C.R.E.
A.D.M.S. D.A.D.O.S. 3rd Div.M.T.Coy.
D.A.D.V.S. File. War Diary.

12/12/18.
Issued at 07.00

for. *[signature]* Major
for. Lieut.Colonel.
General Staff, 3rd Division.

3rd Division,
G.S.2002/8.

8th Inf. Bde.	A.D.M.S.
9th Inf. Bde.	3rd Div. "Q".
76th Inf. Bde.	3rd Div. Signals.
C.R.A.	A.P.M.
C.R.E.	3rd M.T.Coy.
20th K.R.R.C.	3rd Div'l Train.
Camp Comndt.	XI Mobile Vet. Secn.
D.A.D.O.S.	D.M.G.O.
35th Bde R.G.A.	

Reference para.1 of G.S.2002/2 dated 16th November.

1. During the march through Germany, roads need not be picketed at night, but guards must be mounted over ammunition, also on groups of billets, gun parks, horse lines, and at all Headquarters.
    Inlying picquets must be detailed in every unit, and be ready to turn out at very short notice.

12th December, 1918.

/Lieut.Colonel,
General Staff, 3rd Division.

G.7646.

G.O.C.8th Inf.Bde.

    Will you please accept yourself and convey to all ranks of your fine Brigade by congratulations on their good marching and smart soldierlike appearance when crossing the frontier this morning. I am well aware of, and appreciate highly, the care and hard work required to bring about the results attained. All ranks may well be proud.

12th Dec.1918.
                                    Sd.C.J.Deverell.Major General.
                                    Commanding, 3rd Division.

G.7647.

O.C.3rd M.G.Bn.

    Please accept your self and convey to all ranks of your fine Battalion my congratulations on their fine marching and smart soldierlike appearance when crossing the frontier this morning. I am well aware of, and appreciate, the care and hard work which has been required to produce the results attained.
    All ranks may well be proud.

12th Dec.1918.
                                    Sd.C.J.Deverell.Major General.
                                  Commanding, 3rd Division.

G.7643.

3rd Division Operation Order No.299.

1. The Division will march on December 14th in accordance with the following March Table. Reference Sheet 1/100,000.

MARCH TABLE.

Unit.	Starting Point.	Hour of Start.	Route.	Destination.	Instructions.
"A" Group.	Road Junction 1000 yards N.W. of S. in STADTKYLL. (Paper Map 1/100,000).	11.00	DAHLEM.	BLANKENHEIM. BLANKENHEIMERDORF. SCHMIDTHEIM.	
"B" Group.			Any	BAASEM. KRONENBURG. HALLSCHLAG. SCHEID. LOSHEIM.	Not to enter new area before 09.00. To be clear of present area by 12.00.
Div.H.Q. Transport & Sig.Section.	SALMCHATEAU.	09.00.	CIERREUX. ROGERY–BEHO. Road Junction 800 yards N.W. of AG in GRUFFLINGEN. ST.VITH.	NEUEM (Staging Area). 1st	
"C" Group.	Railway Crossing 400 yards South of S. in ST.VITH. (Paper Map 1/100,000).	10.00.	ATZERATH.	KREWINKEL. HASENVENN. MANDERFELD. ANDLER–WECKERATH. SCHONBERG.	
"D" Group.			Any	ATZERATH. NEIDINGEN. NEUNDORF – KROMBACH. BRAUNLAUF. THOMMEN – GRUFFLINGEN.	Not to enter new area before 08.30. To be clear of present area by 10.45.
35 Bde. RGA 152 A. Coy. RE.	Road Junction 1 mile East of Y in BOUVIGNY.	09.30.	BEHO	MALDINGEN. ALDRINGEN.	

2. Divisional H.Q. will close at SALMCHATEAU at 09.00 and open at Factory ½ mile S.E. of Cross Roads at point 572 in square 4.I.Sheet I.M.Germany 1/100,000 and 1½ miles S.E.of LOSHEIM on arrival.

3. Acknowledge.

Distribution:—
G.O.C.
8th Inf.Bde.
9th Inf.Bde.
76th Inf.Bde.
Guards Div.
VI Corps H.A.
D.A.D.O.S.

"Q". C.R.A.
A.P.M.
VI Corps "Q".
3rd Div.Sigs.
6th Division.
C.R.E.
3rd Div.M.T.Coy.

Div.Train.
VI Corps "G".
Camp Commdt.
35th Bde.RGA.
1st Division.
A.D.M.S. —D.A.D.V.S.
File. War Diary.

Issued at 06.30.
13/12/18.

A. ffrench Heger.
Lieut.Colonel.
General Staff, 3rd Division.

3rd Division.
G.7650.

A.D.M.S.
Will you please convey to all ranks of the 3 Field Ambulances of this Division my congratulations on their fine marching and smart soldierlike appearance when crossing the Frontier. I appreciate the care and hard work required to bring about the results attained. All ranks may well be proud.

13th Dec. 1918.

(Sgd.) C.J.DEVERELL, Major-General,
Commanding, 3rd Division.

C.R.E.
Will you please convey to all ranks of the three Field Companies of this Division my congratulations on their fine marching and smart and soldierlike appearance when crossing the Frontier. I appreciate the care and hard work of all ranks required to bring about the results attained. All ranks may well be proud.

13/12/18.

(Sgd.) C.J.DEVERELL, Major-General,
Commanding, 3rd Division.

"A" Form
MESSAGES AND SIGNALS.

Army Form C. 2121
(In pads of 100.)

Prefix......Code.........m.	Words	Charge.	This message is on a/c of:	Recd. at......m.
Office of Origin and Service Instructions	Sent			Date............
....	At ....m.		......................Service.	From ....
....	To			By ....
	By		(Signature of "Franking Officer")	

TO { ...

Sender's Number.	Day of Month.	In reply to Number.	AAA
JC 201	13/12		

Reference 3rd Rout OO 299
via Staging area for
an all Transport and
Signal Section was to
SETZ and not NEUEM
as stated

From ....
Place ....
Time 1645

G.7634/2.

8th Inf.Bde.
9th Inf.Bde.
76th Inf.Bde.
C.R.A.
35th Bde.RGA.

ROAD RECONNAISSANCE.

1. **SCHONBERG - ANDLER - MANDERFELD.** This road is similar to that between ST.VITH and SHONBERG. There is about 12' to 15' of metalling but the sides are very muddy. Lorries can pass anywhere going slow.
   For 3 kilometres N.from ANDLER there is a heavy winding pull up the first kilometre having a very soft surface though the soling seems very soft underneath. Civilians are cleaning this hill and replacing the surface as far as possible.

2. **MANDERFELD - PT.572 - HALLSCHLAG** similar to (1). About 1000 yards steady pull up S.E. of HULLSCHEID.

3. **MANDERFELD - KREWINKEL to LOSHEIM - PRUM** Road reported by staff officers suitable for all horse transport to KREWINKEL. Beyond KREWINKEL only partly examined and found passable for all horse transport, but so heavy that only transport of troops using KREWINKEL Village should use it, and cookers etc. of troops using the ammunition factory.

4. **PT.572 (4.I) to Munition Factory near WEIDENHOCHST** Road similar to (1) in sound condition but muddy. A railway runs along side the road.

5. **Pt.572 - ALBNUTHEN** good road for all horse transport to entrance of village, then very soft and muddy.

6. **HALLSCHLAG - KRONENBURG - STADTKYLL** - Similar to (1) sound muddy but most of centre scraped. Several rises and falls but none serious.

7. From road (6) above to BERK narrow road. Hard, suitable for all horse transport. Branch to FRAUENKRON stated by Burgomeister to be equally good.

8. Road past 2nd N. in KRONENBURG - BAASEM - BAASEM M. A very steep very sinuous road leads up into the upper half of KRONENBURG village. Thence road runs gently over hill and down fairly steeply to BAASEM. The surface of the road is suitable for all horse transport E.of BAASEM for 300 yards road runs down hairpin bends fairly steeply, after which it runs easily to the main road.
   All traffic should enter BAASEM from the East.

9. **STADTKYLL - DAHLEM - BLANKENHEIM** Road generally similar to (1).
   A heavy sinuous pull a mile long from WENZENBACH (4 K) northwards Surface good, lower half scraped upper half being scraped.
   Steady pull ½ mile into DAHLEM. Sharp rise 600 yards long out of DAHLEM to N.
   Fairly sharp rise 600 yards long N. of level crossing to F. KAISER HAUS. Fall average about 1 in 15 last mile average about into BLANKENHEIM with 3 or 4 fairly bad pot holes. No metal available handy for repairs.

10. **F.KAISERHAUS - SCHMIDTHEIM.** Road similar to (1) Fairly steep sinuous hill down about 500 yards into SCHMIDTHEIM generally the main roads are in sound condition and the main mass of the mud has generally been cleared from the centre 10' or 12' of the road. The sides are everywhere very muddy.

13th December 1918.

Lieut.Colonel.
General Staff, 3rd Division.

1. The Division will march on December 15th in accordance with the following March Table.
Reference Sheet Paper Map I.M. 1/100,000.

MARCH TABLE.

Unit.	Starting Point.	Hour of start.	Route.	Destination.	Instructions
"A" Group.	Point where road bends E. to N.E. 1000 yards North of B in BLANKENHEIM.	10.30.	Cross Roads 1000 yards W.N.W. of 1st M in MULHEIM.	EICHERSCHEID - SCHOWN - BOUDERATH - HOLZMULHEIM - FROHNGAU - BUIR. TONDORF - ROER. MULHEIM.	Meat I.M. 1/100,000
"B" Group.	Road Junction 1000 yards N.W. of S in STADTKYLL.	11.00.	DAHLEM.	BLANKENHEIM. BLANKENHEIMERDORF. SCHMIDTHEIM.	
Div. Hq. Transport & Sig. Section.	SETZ	08.30.	ANDLER - MANDERFELD. Junction of Roads 900 yards N.N.W. of A in ALSNUTHEN.	FACTORY ½ mile S.E. of junction of roads 900 yards N.N.W. of A in ALSNUTHEN.	
"C" Group.	Junction of roads 900 yards N.N.W. of A in ALSNUTHEN.	11.30.	HALLSCHLAG.	BAASEM. KRONENBURG. KRONENBURGERHUTTE. HALLSCHLAG.	
"D" Group.	Road Junction 400 yards W. of S in SCHONBERG.	11.45.	ANDLER.	LOSHEIM - KREWINKEL. HASENVENN. MANDERFELD. ANDLER - SCHONBERG.	
35 Bde. RGA. 152 A.T.Coy. R.E.	Road junction immediately G of the D in HALDINGEN.	09.45.	Road Junction 800 yards N.W.of 1st G in GRUEFLIN - GEN. - ST.VITH - ATZERATH.	SETZ. ATZERATH. MACKERBACH. HEUEM.	

2. Divisional H.Q. will remain at FACTORY ½ mile S.E. of junction of Roads 900 yards N.N.W. of A in ALSNUTHEN.

3. ACKNOWLEDGE.

Distribution :-
G.O.C.   "Q"   G.R.A.
6th Inf. Bde.   Div. Train.   A.P.M.
9th Inf. Bde.   VI Corps G.   VI Corps "Q".
76th Inf. Bde.   Camp Commdt.   3rd Div. Sigs.
35th Bde. RGA.   Guards Div.   6th Division.
1st Division.   VI Corps H.A.   C.R.E.
A.D.M.S.   D.A.D.O.S.   3rd Div. M.T.Coy.
File.   War Diary.   General Staff, 3rd Division.

for [signature] M[...]
Lieut. Colonel.

14/12/18.
Issued at 06.30 hours.

G.7653.

O.C. 35th Bde. RGA.

Will you please convey to all ranks under your command my congratulations on their marching and general appearance when crossing the frontier this morning. I fully appreciate their difficulties, and the hard work required to maintain their high standard. The horses had been well cared for and looked very well. The Heavy Artillery has played a great part in enabling us to enter Germany as victors, and all ranks of your command may well be proud.

Sd.C.J.Deverell. Maj.Genl.
Commanding, 3rd Division.

14/12/18.

O.C. 132nd. A.T. Coy. R.E.

Will you please convey to all Ranks under your command my congratulations on their fine marching and appearance when crossing the frontier this morning. All ranks may well be proud of the occasion.

Sd.C.J.Deverell. Maj.Genl.
Commanding, 3rd Division.

14/12/18.

C.R.A. 3rd Division.

Will you please accept yourself and convey to all ranks under your command my congratulations on their fine marching and smart and soldierlike appearance when crossing the Frontier. The weather conditions were most unfavourable but I fully appreciate the care and hard work required to bring about the results attained. All ranks may well be proud, and I am certainly proud of them.

Sd.C.J.Deverell. Maj.General.
Commanding, 3rd Division.

14/12/18.

O.C., 3rd Divisional Train.

Will you please accept yourself and convey to all ranks under your command my congratulations on their efficient appearance when crossing the Frontier. The condition of horses and all transport generally was a testimony to the care and hard work taken throughout the march in spite of unpropitious weather conditions. I appreciate the results and feel that all ranks may well be proud.

Sd.C.J.Deverell. Maj.Genl.
Commanding, 3rd Division.

14/12/18.

SECRET.

3rd Div.G.S.2002/9.

* 8th Inf.Bde.   A.D.M.S.
* 9th Inf.Bde.   * 3rd Div."Q"
* 76th Inf.Bde.   3rd Div.Sigs.
* C.R.A.   A.P.M.
* C.R.E.   3rd Div.M.T.Coy.
  20th K.R.R.C.   3rd Div.Train.
  Camp Commdt.   Mob.Vet.Section.
  D.A.D.O.S.   D.R.G.O.
  35th Bde.R.G.A.

---

1.   The amended areas allotted to Corps, also the provisional boundaries of the areas allotted to Divisions of the VI Corps in German Territory are shown on attached Map. These areas may have to be amended when it has been possible to make a thorough reconnaissance of the VI Corps area.
       The Map issued with GS/2002/6 dated 2/12/18 is cancelled.

2.   The II and Canadian Corps are responsible for the defence of the River RHINE within their respective boundaries.

3.   The 1st Cavalry Division is shortly to be withdrawn, and will probably be marching back to its billeting area within the next two or three days.

4.   The march of the VI Corps into its area will be carried out as follows :-

   (a)   The road allotted to each column is shown on the attached map.

   (b)   The Guards Division will continue its march straight into its final area.

   (c)   The 2nd Division will continue its march into its area.

   (d)   The 3rd Division will continue its march to the area about EUSKIRCHEN, where it will close up. As soon as the tail of the Guards Division has cleared ZULPICH, the 3rd Division will be ordered to move into its final area.

   (e)   The dividing lines between Divisions for billeting purposes during the march are shown on the attached map.

(2)

5. The subdivision of Divisional billeting area to Brigades etc. will be guided by the fact that the VI Corps is in support to the II Corps and may be ordered to move forward rapidly at short notice.

As far therefore as billeting accommodation will permit the 3rd Division will be concentrated in the northern portion of the 3rd Division area - Infantry Brigades being billeted along the roads leading to the RHINE.

6. the 3.5 Bde RHA will be accommodated in 3rd Division area.

W.M Traill

Lieut.Colonel.
General Staff, 3rd Division.

14th December 1918.

X Map attached

1. The Division will march on December 15th in accordance with the following March Table.
Reference Sheet I.M. and I.L.1/100,000 (Germany).

MARCH TABLE

Unit	Starting Point.	Hour of Start.	Route.	Destination.	Instructions.
"A" Group.	Road Junction 300 yards W. of 1st E in EICHERSCHEID.	10.00	MUNSTEREIFEL. IVERSHEIM.	EUSKIRCHEN – ROITZHEIM. BILLIG – STOTZHEIM. RHEDER – WEINGARTEN.	Certain accommodation which will be marked is to be reserved for Div.HQ. in EUSKIRCHEN.
"B" Group.	Point where road bends to N.E.1000 yards North of L in BLANKENHEIM.	10.45	Road Junction 1000 yards WNW of 1st M in MULHEIM.	EICHERSCHEID – SCHON AN BOUDERATH – HOLZMULHEIM FROHNGAU – BUIR – TONDORF.	
"C" Group.	Road Junction 1000 yards N.W. of S in STADTKYLL.	09.45	DAHLEM.	MULHEIM – BLANKENHEIM – BLANKENHEIMERDORF	"C" Group will reserve accommodation on night Dec.16/17th in BLANKENHEIM for 8 officers 300 O.R. 30 officers Chargers and 100 horses of Div.HQ. and Div.HQ.Sig.Section which will stage there.
				SCHMIDTHEIM.	Accommodation for 1 Bn. in SCHMIDTHEIM is allotted to "C" Group, remainder of the village to "D" Group. Exact boundaries between "C" & "D" Groups in this village will be notified by 3rd Div. "Q".
"D" Group.	Junction of Roads 900 yards NNW of A in ALENUTHEN.	10.30	HALLSCHLAG.	SCHMIDTHEIM.	
				DAHLEM. BAASEM. HALLSCHLAG SCHEID.	
35th Bde.RGA Road Junction 400 132.AT.Co.RE.yards W.of § in SCHONBERG.		10.15	MANDERFELD	BLANKENHEIM. (Staging Area.)	
Div.HQ. Transport & 900 yards NNW of Sig.Sec. A in ALENUTHEN.		08.30	DAELEM.		

2. Divisional H.Q. will close at present location at 09.00 and open at EUSKIRCHEN on arrival.
3. ACKNOWLEDGE.
Distribution :-

G.O.C.	"Q".	G.R.A. Div.Train.
8th Inf.Bde.	A.P.M.	VI Corps G. VI Corps Q.
9th Inf.Bde.	Camp Commdt.	3rd Div.Sigs. 35th Bde.RGA.
76th Inf.Bde.	Guards Div.	6th Div. VI Corps HA.
C.R.E.	A.D.M.S.	D.A.D.O.S. 3rd Div.MT.Coy.
D.A.D.V.S.	File.	War Diary. 1st Division.

15/12/18.
Issued at
06.30.

f. Lindsey Moore
Lieut.Colonel.
General Staff, 3rd Division.

3rd Division Operation Order No.302.

1. The Division will march on December 17th in accordance with the following March Table.

Reference Sheets:- M.& I.L.1/100,000.(Germany).

MARCH TABLE.

Unit.	Starting Point.	Hour of Start.	Route.	Destination.	Instructions.
"A" Group.	Tail of column to be in EUSKIRCHEN by 11.45.		Any	EUSKIRCHEN.	
"B" Group.	Road Junction 300 yards W. of E in EICHERSCHEID.	10.00.	MUNSTEREIFEL.	ROITZHEIM. BILLIG - STOTZHEIM. WEINGARTEN. KIRSPENICH. IVERSHEIM. MUNSTEREIFEL.	
"C" Group.	Road Junction 1000 yards W.N.W. of 1st M in MULHEIM.	10.15	TONDORF.	EICHERSCHEID. SCHONAU. BOUDERATH. HOLZMULHEIM. FROHNGAU. ENGELGAU. BUIR - TONDORF. MULHEIM. BLANKENHEIM.	
"D" Group.	Road Junction 1400 yards S. of the 1st H in SCHMIDTHEIM.	09.45.	BLANKENHEIM.	BLANKENHEIMERDORF.	
35 Bde.RGA. 152 AT.Coy. R.E.	Road Junction 1400 yards W. of B in KRONENBURG.	09.30	DAHLEM.		
Div.H.Q. Transport & Sig. Section.	BLANKENHEIM.	08.00.	TONDORF. MUNSTEREIFEL.	EUSKIRCHEN.	

2. Divisional Headquarters will remain at EUSKIRCHEN.
3. ACKNOWLEDGE.

Distribution :- G.O.C.
 8th Inf.Bde.
 9th Inf.Bde.
 76th Inf.Bde.
 Guards Div.
 VI Corps H.A.
 D.A.D.O.S.
 File.
 "Q". G.R.A. Div.Train.
 A.P.M. VI Corps "G".
 VI Corps "Q". Camp Commdt.
 3rd Div.Sigs.35th Bde.RGA.
 6th Division.1st Division.
 C.R.E. A.D.M.S.
 3rd Div.M.T.Coy. D.A.D.V.S.
 War Diary.

16/12/18. Lieut.Colonel,
Issued at 06.30 hours. General Staff,3rd Division.

3rd Division Operation Order No.303.

1. The Division will march on December 18th in accordance with the following March Table.

Reference Sheet I.M. & I.L. 1/100,000 Germany.   M A R C H   T A B L E.

Unit.	Starting Point.	Hour of start.	Route.	Destination.	Instructions
"A" Group.	*Not to enter EUSKIRCHEN*	before 1000	LOMMERSUM. NIEDERBERG.	ERP. EHREM. FRIESHEIM. BORR - WEILER.	*But field Coy R.E. wishes for which will to meet I.M.*
"B" Group.				Will be notified after result of reconnaissance is known.	
"C" Group.	Road Junction 700 yards W.N.W. of first L in IVERSHEIM.	10.30.	IVERSHEIM. WACHENDORF. ANTWEILER.	LESSENICH. SATZVEY. OBR GARTZEM. FIRMANICH - ENZEN.	
"D" Group.	Road Junction 600 yards N. of 1st E in ENGELGAU.	10.00	WEYER. MECHERNICH.	ROGGENDORF. MECHERNICH. KOMMERN. SCHAVEN.	
35th Bde. RGA. 132 A.T.Coy. R.E.	Road Junction 500 yards W. of B in BLANKENHEIM.	10.15	TONDORF. ENGELGAU.	EISERFER - WEYER. ZINGSHEIM.	

2. Divisional H.Q. will remain at EUSKIRCHEN.
3. ACKNOWLEDGE.

Distribution :-
G.O.C.   "Q".   G.R.A.
8th Inf. Bde.   A.P.M.   VI Corps "G".
9th Inf. Bde.   VI Corps "Q".   Camp Commdt.
76th Inf. Bde.   3rd Div. Sigs. 35th Bde. RGA.
Guards Div.   6th Division.   1st Division.
VI Corps H.A.   G.R.E.   A.D.M.S.
D.A.D.O.S.   3rd Div.MT.Coy. D.A.D.V.S.
File.   War Diary.   3rd Div Train

17/12/18.
Issued at 06.30.

for Huntley.
Major.

A. Lieut.Colonel,
General Staff, 3rd Division.

3rd Division Operation Order No.304.

1. 3rd Division Operation Order No.305 is cancelled.
2. The Division will march on December 19th in accordance with the following March Table.
Reference Sheet I.M. & L.L. 1/100,000.Germany.

MARCH TABLE

Unit.	Starting Point.	Hour of start.	Route.	Destination.	Instructions.
"A"Group. Less Pioneer Bn., Fld.Co., R.E.	Not to leave EUSKIRCHEN before 09.30 hours, to be clear of it by 10.30.		LOMMERSUM. NIEDERBERG.	ERP. LHAR. FRIESHEIM. BORR - WEILER.	
20th KRRC (Pioneers) 529 Fld. Coy.R.E.	Cross Roads in EUENHEIM.	09.00.	DURSCHEVEN.	Pioneer Bn. - FUSSENICH. GEICH. 529th Fld.Co.RE.- FROITZHEIM.	To move under orders of O.C.20th KRRC (Pioneers).
"B"Group.	Not to enter EUSKIRCHEN before 10.30 to be clear of IVERSHEIM by 10.00.		Any	EUSKIRCHEN.	
"C"Group.	Road Junction 700 yds WNW of IVERSHEIM	10.00	WACHENDORF. LESSENICH.	LESSENICH. SATZVEY. OBER GARTZEM. FIRMASICH - ENZEN.	
"D"Group.	Road Junction 600 yards N. of 1st E in ENGELGAU.	10.00.	WEYER. MECHERNICH.	ROGENDORF. LECHERNICH. KOLLEN. SCHAVEN.	
35th Bde. RGA. 152 AT.Coy. RE.	Road Junction 500 yards W. of B in BLANKENHEIM.	10.15	TONDORF. ENGELGAU.	EISERFER - WEYER. ZINGSHEIM.	

3. Divisional Headquarters will remain at EUSKIRCHEN.
4. ACKNOWLEDGE.

Distribution:-

G.O.C.
8th Inf.Bde.
9th Inf.Bde.
76th Inf.Bde.
Guards Div.
VI Corps H.A.
D.A.D.O.S.
File.
20"KRRC
529 Fld.Coy.RE

"Q".
A.P.M.
VI Corps Q.
VI Corps Sigs. Camp Commdt.
3rd Div.Sigs. 55th Bde.RGA.
6th Division.1st Division.
C.R.E. A.D.M.S.
3rd Div.MT.Co. D.A.D.V.S.
War Diary. 3rd Div.Train.

C.R.A.
VI Corps G.

17/12/18.
Issued at 10.50.

Lt.Col.
General Staff, 3rd Division

8th Inf. Bde.
9th Inf. Bde.
~~A.A.~~
C.R.E.
~~50th Div. R.A.~~
1st Division.
"Q".

The road from Railway Crossing N.E. of ZURPICH to BERGHEIM - MEVENHICH - DISTENHICH is fit for horse transport. The road running along the railway W. of DISTENHICH to level crossing thence to MODENHEIM - GLADBACH and the main road is also fit for horse transport.
Neither of these roads are fit for lorries.
There are one or two field carts standing in the road which should be moved.
The road from the level crossing N.W. of DISTENHICH through MERSENICH to main road has not been reconnoitred.

Lieut. Colonel.
General Staff, 2nd Division.

17th December 1918.

3rd Division Operation Order No.295.

1. The Division will march on December 10th in accordance with the following March Table.

Reference Sheet :- M. & I.L. 1/100,000. Germany.

MARCH TABLE.

Unit.	Starting Point.	Hour of Start.	Route.	Destination. Final Area.	Instructions.
"A"Group.Less Tail to be clear of LOMMERSUM Pioneer Bn.& by 11.30. 529 Fld.Co. R.E.			LOMMERSUM.		
20th K.R.R.C. (Pioneers) 529th Fld. Co.RE.	Road Junction 200 yards S.W. of E in FROITZHEIM	10.00.	STOCKHEIM.	20th K.R.R.C.(Pioneers) DUREN. 529th Fld.Co.R.E. Destination will be notified.	To move under the orders of O.C. 20th KRRC. (Pioneers).
"B"Group.	Cross roads in EUENHEIM.	10.00.	ULPENICH.	"B"Group,less MG Bn. and Field Company, ZULPICH. M.G.Battalion. FUSSENICH. GEICH. 56th Fld.Coy. R.E. FROITZHEIM.	
"C"Group.	Road Junction 900 yards N.of lst N in ENZEN.	09.30.	ULPENICH. ZULPICH. LESSENICH.	GLADBACH. MUDDERSHEIM. DISTERNICH. SIEVERNICH.	
"D"Group.	Gross Roads 800 yards N.E. of N in SCHWEFEN.	10.00	Any route South of and excluding ZULPICH	GINNICK. PISSENHEIM BERG - EMBKEN. WOLLERSHEIM.	
55 Bde.R.G.A.,Road Junction 200 yards 152 AT.Co. W. of the 1st E in BESSENHEIM. R.E.		09.30.	MECHERNICH.	SINZENICH. SCHWERFEN.	

2. Divisional H.Q. will close at BUSKIRCHEN at 09.00 and open at DUREN on arrival.
3. ACKNOWLEDGE.

Distribution :-
G.O.C.,   "Q"
8th Inf. Bde.   A.P.M.   C.R.A.
9th Inf. Bde.   VI Corps Q.   VI Corps G.
76th Inf. Bde.   3rd Div. Sigs.   Camp Commdt.
Guards Div.   6th Div.   35th Bde.RGA.
VI Corps H.A.   C.R.E.   1st Div.
D.A.D.O.S.   3rd Div.-M.T.Coy-D.A.D.V.S. A.D.M.S.
3rd Div.Train.   20th K.R.R.C.   529th Fld.Co.R.E.
                                            File.
                                            War Diary.

16/12/18.
Issued at 08.50.

(signed) W.H.Fraser.L/C
Lieut.Colonel.
General Staff,3rd Division.

Reference 3rd Division Operation Order No.305.

Divisional H.Q., Transport and Signal Section will move on December 19th as follows :-

Unit.	Starting Point.	Hour of Start.	Route.	Destination.
Div.HQ. Transport & Sig.Section.	Cross Roads, EUENHEIM.	08.15.	ULPENICH. ZULPICH. FROITZHEIM.	DUREN.

Headquarter lorries will leave USKIRCHEN at 10.00 hours, proceed via LOMMERSOM - FRIESHEIM - ERP - GLADBACH - KELZ - DUREN.

[signature]
Lieut.Colonel,
General Staff, 3rd Division.

19th December 1918.

Copies to :-
"Q".
D.A.D.O.S.
A.P.M.
3rd Div.Sigs.
C.R.E.
VI Corps G.
A.D.M.S.
D.A.D.V.S.
File. War Diary.
Camp Commandant.

3rd Division Operation Order. No.306.

1. The Division will march on December 20th in accordance with the following March Table.

Reference Sheet :- I.L. 1/100,000. Germany.

MARCH TABLE

Units.	Starting Point.	Hour of Start.	Route.	Area.	Instructions.
"B" Group. Less M.G.Bn. & 56th Fld. Coy. R.E.	Level Crossing ¾ mile N.E. of ZULPICH.	09.00	ESSENICH. DISERNICH.	Final Area.	
56th Fld.Co. M.G.Bn.	FROITZHEIM	09.00	SOLLER. STUCKHEIM.	Will be notified. DUREN.	To move under orders of O.C. M.G.Bn.
"C" Group. Less 438th Fld.Co.RE.	Road Junction ½ mile W. of G in GLADBACH.	09.30	Any	Final Area.	
438th Fld. Co.RE.	do.	To be clear of starting point by 10.30.	KELZ. FRAUWULLESHEIM.	To be notified. DUREN	To move under orders of GOC 8th Inf.Bde.
"D" Group.	To move into Final Area under orders of C.R.A. no restrictions as to routes but NOT to enter ZULPICH before 09.40 or FROITZHEIM before 09.20, if using the ZULPICH — FROITZHEIM — SOLLER Road.				

2. Divisional H.Q. will remain at DUREN.
3. ACKNOWLEDGE.

Distribution :—

G.O.C.	"Q".
8th Inf.Bde.	A.P.M.
9th Inf.Bde.	VI Corps Q.
76th Inf.Bde.	Camp Commdt.
Guards Div.	3rd Div. Sigs. 35th Bde.RGA.
VI Corps HQ.	6th Div. 1st Div.
D.A.D.O.S.	C.R.E. A.D.M.S.
3rd Div.Train.	3rd Div.MT.Coy.D.A.D.V.S.
	File. War Diary.

18/12/18.
Issued at 14.00.

M.Farrell
Lieut.Colonel.
General Staff, 3rd Div.

MG Bn } Thro' 9 F Bde
56 F.Co.R.E.

G.2049/2.

8th Inf. Bde.   G.S.A.
9th Inf. Bde.   1st Division.
76th Inf. Bde.   38th Bde.R.G.A.

ROAD RECONNAISSANCE.

Reference 1/100,000 I.D. & I.L. German Map.

1. BLANKENHEIM - TONDORF - HOLZMULHEIM Road suitable for double lorry traffic. About 12' to 18' of metalling clear in middle 10' but very muddy at sides. The surface is inclined to be soft and gritty but is still holding.
   A hill about a mile long leads up N. out of BLANKENHEIM only the first 800 yards being at all steep.
   The street in the Southern end of TONDORF is narrow and rough having been repaired with heavy metal. N. of TONDORF there is a dip down and up but the gradients are not very steep.
   There is a steep very sinuous hill down into HOLZMULHEIM near the top the left side of the road is badly broken away opposite where a lorry had broken down.

2. Entrance to MULHEIM is suitable for all horse transport, the road slopes fairly steeply down from the main road to the village.

3. TONDORF - ENGWAU similar to (1) fairly level throughout.

4. MULHEIM - ENGWAU - INGELAU. About 10 feet of metalling very good condition and no mud. There are two dips between ENGWAU and the main road (1) with hills about 300 yards long each side but not serious for any horse transport.

5. Entrance to MULHEIM suitable for all horse transport slopes fairly steeply down to village.

6. HOLZMULHEIM - SCHONAU. About 12' metalling rough but hard and fairly level suitable for all horse transport.

7. HOLZMULHEIM - PT.478 - EICHERSCHEID. Similar in nature to (1) a steep hill about a mile long out of HOLZMULHEIM up to PT.478 and a steady fall about 2 kilometres long into EICHERSCHEID.

8. INGELAU - BOUDRAU - PT.478 Good road fairly level suitable for all horse transport and one way lorry traffic.

9. Entrances to BOUDRAU from BOUDRAU to PT.478 Both are good hard narrow roads suitable for all horse transport. Both slope down into BOUDRAU and the Eastern road is steepest but is not a serious hill for horse transport coming up. There is no through connection direct from BOUDRAU to EICHERSCHEID.

10. SCHONAU - EICHERSCHEID is a good level two way lorry route.
    Note. Transport should move by HOLZMULHEIM - SCHONAU - EICHERSCHEID and INGELAU - BOUDRAU - PT.478 - EICHERSCHEID to avoid the hill out of HOLZMULHEIM.

18th December 1918.

Lieut.Colonel.
General Staff, 3rd Division.

3rd Div.G.7738.

8th Inf.Bde.
9th Inf.Bde.
----

1.   The following moves will take place on the 27th inst.

    8th Inf.Bde.H.Q.   to BINSFELD.
    8th T.M.Battery   to ROMMELSHEIM.
    No.3 Coy.3rd Div.Train   to ESCHWEILER.

2.   The village of FRAUWULLESHEIM is not available for 8th Inf.Bde. as it is required for the 142nd Field Ambulance, attached 9th Inf.Bde.

3.   The villages in para.1 will be vacated by 12 noon on the 27th by any units of 9th Inf.Bde. billeted there.

4.   KERPEN and BLATZHEIM have been allotted to the 9th Inf.Bde. and units can be moved into these villages under arrangements to be made by 9th Inf.Bde.

                        Sd.W.H.Traill.Lt.Col.
                General Staff, 3rd Division.

26th December 1919.

Copy to 3rd Div."Q" For information.

"A" Form.
MESSAGES AND SIGNALS.

Army Form C. 2121.
(In pads of 100.)

TO: 8th Inf Bde
    9th Inf Bde

Sender's Number: Ga 285
Day of Month: 26

AAA

Paragraphs 1, 2 and 3 of 3rd Div. G.7738 are cancelled Moves will be carried out as ordered in AC 207 aaa Units of 9th Bde at present billetted in BINSFELD and FRAUWULLESHEIM will be clear of these villages by 1200 hours on 27th inst aaa Addressed 8 and 9th Bdes.

From: 3rd Div
Time: 1800

3rd DIVISION.

Disposition and Movement Report No. 4.
~~12th January, 1919.~~ 31st December 1918

UNIT.	Location of H.Q. at 1900 hours.	Probable changes within 24 hours.
3rd Divisional H.Q.	DUREN No. 70 Oberstrasse	
8th Infantry Brigade H.Q.	BINSFELD.	
2nd The Royal Scots.	BUIR.	
1st Royal Scots Fus.	MERZENICH.	
7th K.S.L.I.	GOLZHEIM.	
8th T.M. Battery.	BINSFELD.	
8th Field Ambulance.	GIRBELSRATH.	
No. 3 Coy Train, R.A.S.C.	FRAUWALLESHEIM.	
9th Infantry Brigade H.Q.	NORVENICH SCHLOSS.	
1st Northld. Fus.	OBR. BOLHEIM.	
4th Royal Fusiliers.	BLATZHEIM & BERGERHAUSEN.	
13th King's L'pool Regt.	KERPEN.	
9th T.M. Battery.	SOFIENHOHE.	
142nd Field Ambulance.	KELZ.	
No. 4 Coy Train, R.A.S.C.	OLLESHEIM.	
76th Infantry Brigade H.Q.	GYMNICH BURG.	
8th K.O.R.L. Regt.	TURNICH SCHLOSS.	
2nd Suffolk Regt.	GYMNICH (Southern entrance)	
1st Gordon Hldrs.	KIERDORF (Villa Louise).	
76th T.M. Battery.	GYMNICH BURG.	
7th Field Ambulance.	DIRMERZHEIM Billet No. 42.	
No. 2 Coy Train, R.A.S.C.	KONRADSHEIM.	
C.R.A.	NIDEGGEN.	
23rd Brigade R.F.A.	NIEDERAU - DUREN Road.	
40th " "	KREUZAU.	
42nd " "	UNT. MAUBACH.	
3rd Div. Amm. Column.	LENDERSDORF.	
C.R.E.	DUREN, No. 127 Oberstrasse.	
56th Field Company, R.E.	DUREN, 2 Friedriche Platz.	
458th " " "	DUREN, 13 Eschstrasse.	
529th " " "	DUREN, 22 Ost Strasse.	
3rd Battalion M.G. Corps.	The Barracks, DUREN.	
20th K.R.R.C. (Pioneers)	~~SCHLICH - HERODE - DERICHS - WEILER.~~ THE BARRACKS DUREN	
A.D.M.S.	The Schools, DUREN.	
XI Mobile Veterinary Section.	LENDERSDORF.	
35th Brigade R.G.A.	~~BERG.~~ BERG	
111th Heavy Battery.	PISSENHEIM.	
132nd A.T. Coy, R.E.	PISSENHEIM.	
VI Corps H.Q.	DUREN, 2 Eisenbahn Strasse.	
Guards Division.	LIEDENTHAL.	
2nd Division.	DUREN, 3 Holz Strasse.	

NORTHERN DIVISION
(LATE 3RD DIVISION)

GENERAL STAFF
JAN-JUN 1919

NORTHERN DIVISION
(LATE 3RD DIVISION)

Army Form C. 2118.

WAR DIARY
or
INTELLIGENCE SUMMARY.

(Erase heading not required.)

Instructions regarding War Diaries and Intelligence Summaries are contained in F. S. Regs., Part II. and the Staff Manual respectively. Title pages will be prepared in manuscript.

Place	Date	Hour	Summary of Events and Information	Remarks and references to Appendices
1st Jan. DUREN			Weather. Fine. G.O.C. Proceeded on leave – Brig.Genl.J.S.OLLIVANT, Commanding 3rd D.A. assumed command of Division during G.O.C's absence.	
"	2nd Jan.		Weather. Fine.	
"	3rd Jan.		Weather. Fine.	
"	4th Jan.		Weather. Fine, windy.	
"	5th Jan.		Weather. Fine.	
"	6th Jan.		Weather. Fine.	
"	7th Jan.		Weather. Fine. Cold.	
"	8th Jan.		Weather. Fair.	
"	9th Jan.		Weather. Fair.	

Army Form C. 2118.

WAR DIARY
or
INTELLIGENCE SUMMARY.
(Erase heading not required.)

Instructions regarding War Diaries and Intelligence Summaries are contained in F. S. Regs., Part II. and the Staff Manual respectively. Title pages will be prepared in manuscript.

Place	Date	Hour	Summary of Events and Information	Remarks and references to Appendices
DURAN	10th Jan.		Weather. Fair.	
"	11th Jan.		Weather. Fair.	
"	12th Jan.		Weather. Snow during morning, fine later.	
"	13th Jan.		Weather. Cold and damp.	
"	14th Jan.		Weather. Fair.	
"	15th Jan.		Weather. Fine.	
"	16th Jan.		Weather. Fair.	
"	17th Jan.		Weather. Mainly wet.	
"	18th Jan.		Weather. Fine.	

Army Form C. 2118.

WAR DIARY
or
INTELLIGENCE SUMMARY.
(Erase heading not required.)

Instructions regarding War Diaries and Intelligence Summaries are contained in F. S. Regs., Part II. and the Staff Manual respectively. Title pages will be prepared in manuscript.

Place	Date	Hour	Summary of Events and Information	Remarks and references to Appendices
CUREN	19th Jan.		Weather. Fine. Brig.Genl.J.S.OLLIVANT, proceeded on leave - Brig.Genl. B.D.FISHER, Commanding, 8th Inf.Bde. assumed command of Division.	
"	20th Jan.		Weather. Fine and frosty.	
"	21st Jan.		Weather. Fine and frosty.	
"	22nd Jan.		Weather. do.	
"	23rd Jan.		Weather. A little snow during morning, frost later.	
"	24th Jan.		Weather. Fine and frosty. G.O.C.returned from leave and took over command of Division from General Fisher.	
"	25th Jan.		Weather. Fine and frosty.	
"	26th Jan.		Weather. Frosty during morning, snow during afternoon.	
"	27th Jan.		Weather. Frosty, a little snow.	
"	28th Jan.		Weather. "	

Army Form C. 2118.

WAR DIARY
or
INTELLIGENCE SUMMARY.
(Erase heading not required.)

Instructions regarding War Diaries and Intelligence Summaries are contained in F. S. Regs., Part II. and the Staff Manual respectively. Title pages will be prepared in manuscript.

Place	Date	Hour	Summary of Events and Information	Remarks and references to Appendices
JUBA.	29th Jan.		Weather. Frosty during morning - slightly warmer during afternoon.	
"	30th Jan.		Weather. Frosty. G.O.C.'s inspection of Field Companies R.E.	
"	31st Jan.		Weather. Frosty. G.O.C.'s inspection of 20th K.R.R.C. (Pioneers).	

for Furse
for Lieut-Colonel
General Staff 2nd Division.

No 55

CONFIDENTIAL

GENERAL STAFF

3rd DIVISION

WAR DIARY

1st – 28 FEBRUARY

VOLUME 4

Army Form C. 2118.

WAR DIARY
INTELLIGENCE SUMMARY
(Erase heading not required.)

Instructions regarding War Diaries and Intelligence Summaries are contained in F. S. Regs., Part II. and the Staff Manual respectively. Title pages will be prepared in manuscript.

Place	Date	Hour	Summary of Events and Information	Remarks and references to Appendices
DUREN.	1st Feb.		Cold. Slight thaw during afternoon. Nothing of interest.	
"	2nd Feb.		Cold. Nothing of interest.	
"	3rd Feb.		Frosty. Nothing of interest.	
"	4th Feb.		Frosty. Inspection by G.O.C. of 1st Gordon Highlanders and 8th K.O.R.L.	
"	5th Feb.		Cold. Slight thaw during afternoon. Inspection by G.O.C. of 2nd Suffolk Regt., 76th T.M.Battery, 7th Field Ambulance and No.2 Company, Train.	
"	6th Feb.		Cold. Little snow. Later hard frost. Inspection by G.O.C. of 2nd Royal Scots and No.3 Company, Div.Train.	
"	7th Feb.		Keen frost. Inspection by G.O.C. of 7th K.S.L.I. and 8th Field Ambulance.	
"	8th Feb.		Keen frost. Inspection by G.O.C. of 1st Royal Scots Fus. and 8th T.M.Battery.	
"	9th Feb.		Fine. Nothing of interest.	
"	10th Feb.		Fine. Inspection by G.O.C. of 13th King's Liverpool Regiment.	
"	11th Feb.		Fair. Inspection by G.O.C. of 4th Royal Fusiliers and 9th T.M.Battery.	

Army Form C. 2118.

WAR DIARY
or
INTELLIGENCE SUMMARY.
(Erase heading not required.)

Instructions regarding War Diaries and Intelligence Summaries are contained in F. S. Regs., Part II. and the Staff Manual respectively. Title pages will be prepared in manuscript.

Place	Date	Hour	Summary of Events and Information	Remarks and references to Appendices
DUREN.	12th Feb.		Fine. Nothing of Interest.	
"	13th Feb.		Fine. Inspection by G.O.C. of No.4 Company Train, 1st North'd Fus. and 142nd Field Ambulance.	
"	14th Feb.		Fine. Nothing of interest.	
"	15th Feb.		Fair. Nothing of interest.	
"	16th Feb.		Dull. Nothing of interest.	
"	17th Feb.		Wet. Nothing to report.	
"	18th Feb.		Fine. Nothing of interest.	
"	19th Feb.		Dull. 3rd Division Operation Order No.307 issued to all concerned. (Vide O.O.307 attached).	
"	20th Feb.		Wet. King's L.R., 1st Gordon Highlanders and 7th K.S.L.I. ordered to be prepared to move at short notice. 13th	
"	21st Feb.		Fine. Nothing of interest.	

Army Form C. 2118.

WAR DIARY
or
INTELLIGENCE SUMMARY.
(Erase heading not required.)

Instructions regarding War Diaries and Intelligence Summaries are contained in F. S. Regs., Part II. and the Staff Manual respectively. Title pages will be prepared in manuscript.

Place	Date	Hour	Summary of Events and Information	Remarks and references to Appendices
DUREN.	22nd Feb.		Wet. Forecast of moves and reliefs forwarded to all concerned. (Vide copy attached). Transfer of 20th K.R.R.C. to 2nd Division forwarded to 20th KRRC etc. (Vide copy attached). 3rd Division G.8074/5 forwarded to all concerned. (Vide copy attached).	
"	23rd Feb.		Fine. Nothing of interest.	
"	24th Feb.		3rd Division G.8074/10 issued to all concerned. (Vide copy attached). 3rd Division G.B.249 - amendment to G.8074/10 issued to all concerned (Vide copy attached). Presentation of Colours to 13th King's L.R. by Army Commander. Divisional Commanders "Good-bye" to 20th K.R.R.C. on leaving the Division.	
"	25th Feb.		Wet. 3rd Division G. 8074/12 forwarded to all concerned. (Vide copy attached). Arrival of 1/9th D.L.I. (Pioneers) to join the Division in relief of 20th K.R.R.C. (Pioneers).	
"	26th Feb.		Fine. Forecast of moves and reliefs forwarded to all concerned. (Vide copy attached). 3rd Division G.A.270 forwarded to all concerned. (Vide copy attached). Arrival of 1/6th West Yorks. Regt. in relief of 13th King's Liverpool Regiment. 13th King's Liverpool Regt. on transfer to 32nd Division, leave the Division.	
"	27th Feb.		Fine. Divisional Commanders "Good-bye" to 1st Gordon Highlanders on leaving the Division. Arrival of 20th D.L.I. from 41st Division to join 3rd Division in relief of 8th K.O.R.L.	
"	28th Feb.		Fine. Presentation of Colours by Army Commander to 8th K.O.R.L. Presentation of Colours by Army Commander to 7th K.S.L.I. Arrival of 1/4th York. and Lancs. from 49th Division to join 3rd Division in relief of 1st Gordon Highlanders.	

SECRET.

3rd Division Operation Order No.307.   Copy No. 20

19th February 1919.

Reference the accompanying Map.*

1. The 3rd Division (less Artillery) is to relieve the Guards Division (less Artillery) in the COLOGNE area.

2. The following reliefs will be carried out under arrangements to be made between Brigadiers concerned.

   (a) 9th Inf. Brigade Group will relieve the 1st Guards Brigade Group.

   (b) 76th Inf. Brigade Group will relieve the 2nd Guards Brigade Group.

   (c) Relief of M.T. Co & No.1 Co. Div'l Train Guards Division by 3rd M.T. Co & No.1 Co. 3rd Div. Train will be arranged by "Q" 3rd Division with "Q" Guards Division.

   (d) Orders as regards the move of the 8th Inf. Brigade Group to replace the 3rd Guards Brigade Group, and move of M.G. and Pioneer Battalions will be issued later.

3. Moves in connection with the reliefs mentioned in para.2 (a) and (b) will be carried out in accordance with the attached Table.

4. Billeting parties of units moving in relief will be despatched 24 hours in advance of their Units.

5. The G.O's C. 9th and 76th Inf. Brigades will assume command of their respective Brigade Areas on completion of the reliefs mentioned in para.2 (a) & (b).

6. Guards and Detachments at present found by the 1st Guards Brigade will be taken over by the 9th Inf. Brigade on the 21st inst.

   Guards and Detachments at present found by the 2nd Guards Brigade will be taken over by the 76th Inf. Brigade on the 27th inst.

7. The G.O.C. 3rd Division will assume command of the area now occupied by the Guards Division, on completion of the relief mentioned in para.2 (b) and at an hour to be notified.

   On assuming command the Guards Divisional Artillery will come under the orders of the G.O.C. 3rd Division.

8. Divisional H.Q. will move to COLOGNE and take over the H.Q. at present occupied by the Guards Division on the 1st March.

9. Accompanying map shews the areas and position of H.Qrs.

   Statement is attached shewing location of the H.Qrs. of units of the Guards Division.

10. ACKNOWLEDGE.

Lieut. Colonel,
General Staff, 3rd Division.

Issued at 20 hours.
* Issued to 3 Bdes, C.R.A., C.R.E., "Q", M.G.Bn only.

Distribution/

Distribution :-

Copy No.1. G.O.C.
2. 8th Inf. Brigade. *
3. 9th Inf. Brigade. *
4. 76th Inf. Brigade. *
5. C.R.A. *
6. C.R.E. *
7. A.D.M.S.
8. "Q" 3rd Division. *
9. 3rd M.G. Battn. *
10. 20th K.R.R.C. (Pioneers).
11. D.A.D.O.S.
12. D.A.D.V.S.
13. A.P.M.
14. 3rd Div. Train.
15. 3rd Div. Signals.
16. 3rd M.T.Coy.
17. Guards Division.
18. VI Corps "G".
19. VI Corps "Q".
20. War Diary.
21. War Diary.
22. File.

TABLE OF RELIEFS.

Date.	Relieving Unit.	To.	Unit to be relieved.	Instructions.
1919. February	**9th Inf. Bde. Group.**			
20th.	1 Battn. 9th Inf. Bde.	EHRENFELD Area.	1 Battn. 1st Guards Brigade.	To move under orders of G.O.C. 9th Inf. Bde. KERPEN can be used as a staging area.
22nd.	do.	do.	do.	
25th.	do.	do.	do.	
25th.	Field Company, R.E., Field Ambulance and Co. Div'l Train.	do.	Field Company, R.E., Field Ambulance and Co. Div. Train 1st Guards Brigade.	Field Company R.E., to HUNGERSDORP and BRAUNSFELD area.
February.	**76th Inf. Bde. Group.**			
26th.	1 Battn. 76th Inf. Bde.	RIEEL Area.	1 Battn. 2nd Guards Brigade.	To move under orders of G.O.C. 76th Inf. Brigade.
27th.	do.	do.	do.	
March. 1st.	do.	do.	do.	
1st.	Field Company, R.E. Field Ambulance and Co. Div'l Train.	do.	Field Company, R.E., Field Ambulance and Co. Div. Train 2nd Guards Brigade.	Field Company R.E. to HUNGERSDORP and BRAUNSFELD. area.

GUARDS DIVISION LOCATIONS.

G.O.C.   20 Fürst Puckler Strasse.

Offices.
  "G" and "Q"   264 Durener Strasse.
    D.Signals.   do.
    Education Officer.   do.
    Camp Commandant.   do.

C.R.E.   18 Robert Blum Strasse.
D. Train.   8 Virchow Strasse.
A.D.M.S.   5 Virchow Strasse.
D.A.D.V.S.   do.
D.A.P.M.   do.
Traffic Control Officer.   do.
Intelligence Officer.   do.
Sanitary Officer.   do.
S.C.F. (C of E)   12 Virchow Strasse.
S.O. (P.B.Dept)   19   do.
Soldiers' Club Office.   12 Geibel Strasse.
    so.   Store.   111 Durener Strasse.
D.Baths Officer.   389 Venloer Strasse.
Q.M.Stores.   148 Durener Strasse.
Transport Lines.   165a   do.   (back of).
Band.   22 Scheffel Strasse.
Div.M.T.Coy.   School Pius Strasse, EHRENFELD.
D.A.D.O.S.   Junction of Venloer Str. & Leo Strasse.
O.C. Reception Camp.   12 Geibel Strasse.
G&S. Employment Coy.   Gymnasium, Gyrhof Strasse (facing S. end of
                                Classen Kappelmann Strasse).

Messes.
  G.O.C.   20 Fürst Puckler Strasse
  "A.1"   2 Virchow Strasse.
  "B"   20 Robert Blum Strasse.
  "C"   23 Virchow Strasse.

Brigade H.Q.   13 Kanal Strasse, EHRENFELD.
  Bn. H.Q.   58 Siemens Strasse, EHRENFELD.
  Bn. H.Q.   138 Ehrenfeld Gürtel, EHRENFELD.
  Bn. H.Q.   50 yds W. of BICKENDORF Church.
  Bn. H.Q.   52 Kruth Strasse, EHRENFELD.
  Trench Mortar Battery.   34 Otto Strasse, EHRENFELD.
  Field Ambulance.   98 Vogelsanger Strasse, EHRENFELD.

Brigade H.Q.   57 Hohenstaufen Ring, COLOGNE.
  Bn. H.Q.   88 Stammheimer Strasse) Battalions in
  Bn. H.Q.   67 Niederlander Strasse) Inf. Bks. No.1.
  Bn. H.Q.   109 Stammheimer Str) Pioneer Barracks
  Bn. H.Q.   15/17 Worringer Str)(adjoining above).
  Trench Mortar Battery.   2 Bodinus Strasse, RIEHL.
  Field Ambulance.   10 Bodinus Str RIEHL Pioneer Barracks
                                                        No.10

/Brigade H.Q.

(2).

Brigade H.Q.	107 Bachemer Str.(corner of Bachemer Strasse & Lindenburger Allee)
Bn H.Q.	Corner house Luxemburger Strasse and Sulz Gürtel.
Bn.H.Q.	13 Krieler Strasse.
Bn H.Q.	13 Emma Strasse.
Trench Mortar Bty.	86 Lindenburger Allee
Field Ambulance	EFFEREN.
Bn H.Q.	12 Steilzmann Strasse
Field Coy, R.E.	342 Aachener Strasse.
do.	21 Christian Gau Strasse.
do.	J. CLERMONTS Office, Aachener Strasse.
Pioneer Battn.	3 Geibel Strasse.
M.G.Battn.	H.Q. - School in Lindenborn Strasse.
	Billets - Schiller Gymnasium, and Lindenborn Strasse.
	Transport - Helios Strasse.
Mobile Vetinary Setion.	DECKSTEIN.
Div. Arty. H.Q.	NIPPES - Niehler Strasse.
Brigade R.F.A.	Just N. of second E. in WEIDEN.
do.	Just S. of K, in KONIGSDORF.
do.	300 yds S. of L. in POULHEIM.
D.A.C.	BRAUWEILER.

S E C R E T.
G.S074/7.   22/2/19.

FORECAST OF MOVES AND RELIEFS.

Date.	Unit.	To.	Relieved Unit.	Remarks.
Febr. 20th.	13th King's L'pools	EHRENFELD area.	2nd Gren. Guards.	
22nd.	1st Northld Fus.	do.	2nd Goldstreams Gds.	
24th.	142nd Fld Amblce.	AERPEN.		
24th.	9th Inf. Bde. H.Q.	KERPEN.		
24th.	56th Field Coy. R.E.	KERPEN.		
25th.	4th Royal Fusiliers.	EHRENFELD area.	1st Irish Guards.	
25th.	9th Inf.Bde. H.Q.	EHRENFELD area.	1st. Guards Bde H.Q.	
25th.	142nd Field Amblce.	do.	4th Field Ambulance	
25th.	56th Field Coy.	MUNGERSDORP & BRAUNSFELD area.	Field Coy, Gds Div.	
25th.	No. 4 Gd Train.	EHRENFELD area.	No. 3 Gd Guards Train.	
Febr. 25th.	1/9th D.L.I. (Pioneers)	LINDENTHAL area.	3rd Coldstream Gds. (Pioneers)	Take over billets of 4th Coldstream Gds (late Pioneer Battn.)
26th.	20th K.R.R.C. (Pioneers).			Stand Fast. Transfered to 2nd Div.from midnight 26/27th February.
26th.	1/8th W. Yorks.	EHRENFELD area	13th King's L'pools.	

9th Inf. Bde. Group.

Date	Unit	Location	Unit	Notes
Febr. 25th	13th King's L'pools.	BEUEL (BONN)		To 32nd Div. by train.
26th	2nd Suffolk Regt.	RIEHL area.	1st Scots Guards.	
27th	20th D.L.I.	KERPEN.	8th K.O.R.L Regt.	8th K.O.R.L. stand fast and reduced to cadre. 20th D.L.I. take over horses of 8th K.O.R.L.
28th	1st Gordon Hldrs.	RIEHL area.	3rd Gren. Guards.	
29th	529th Field Co.	KERPEN.		
March 1st	20th D.L.I.	RIEHL area.	1st Coldstream Gds.	
1st	529th F. Co. N.E.	HUNGERSDORF and BRAUNSFELD areas.	Field Co. Gds Div.	
1st	7th Field Amblce.	RIEHL area	9th Field Amblce.	
1st	No.2 Co. Train.	RIEHL area	No.4 Co Gds Div Train.	
1st	Div. H.Q.	COLOGNE.	Div. H.Q. Gds.Div.	
1st	H.Q.Section Div. Signal Co.	COLOGNE.	H.Q.Sec.Guards Div Signal Co.	

764th Inf. Bde. group.

20th K.R.R.C.
"Q".

SECRET.

G.3074/6.

    20th K.R.R.C. (Pioneer Battalion) will be transfered from 3rd to 2nd Division at midnight 26th/27th February and will remain in their present location.

    Reference G.3074/2 dated 21st inst. The only men required to rejoin the Battalion will be those employed within the Division.

(sd) J.N. Lumley Major.,
for Lieut. Colonel.,
General Staff. 3rd Division.

22nd February 1919.

SECRET.

9th Inf. Brigade.
"Q" 3rd Division.

G.0074/5.

1. (a) The 1/9th Durham Light Infantry (Pioneer Battn) will arrive at NIPPES (COLOGNE) by train at about 19-30 hours on the 25th February, and will take over the billets in the LINDENTHAL area vacated by the 4th Coldstream Guards.
   The Battalion will arrive complete with horses and transport.
   On arrival the 1/9th D.L.I. will come under the orders of the G.O.C. 9th Inf. Brigade until the 3rd Division takes over from the Guards Division on the 1st March when the 1/9th D.L.I. will come under the orders of 3rd Div. H.Q.
   (b) The G.O.C. 9th Inf. Brigade will arrange for guides and a band to meet the 1/9th D.L.I. to conduct them to their billets.
   The Divisional Commander will meet the 1/9th D.L.I. on their arrival in COLOGNE.

2. (a) The 1/6th West Yorkshire Regiment will arrive at NIPPES (COLOGNE) by train about 12.00 hours on the 26th February and on arrival will join the 9th Infantry Brigade.
   (b) The G.O.C. 9th Infantry Brigade will arrange for guides and a band to meet the 1/6th West Yorks., to conduct them to their billets.
   (c) The 1/6th West Yorks will be arriving complete with transport but without horses; the G.O.C., 9th Infantry Brigade will therefore arrange to horse their transport from the Station to billets.
   The horses for the 1/6th West Yorks. will be received finally from the 7th Seaforth Highlanders (9th Division).
   (d) The Divisional Commander will meet the 1/6th West Yorks. on their arrival in COLOGNE.

3. (a) The Divisional Commander will see the final practice for the Colour presentation of the 13th King's Liverpool Regiment at 12.00 hours on the 24th February and will say 'good-bye' to them at the conclusion of the parade.
   G.O.C. 9th Infantry Brigade will arrange to have a guide at his Headquarters at KERPEN at 11.15 hours to conduct the Divisional Commander to the place of parade.
   (b) G.O.C. 9th Infantry Brigade will forward to Divisional H.Q. a copy of the Order of parade.

4. (a) The 13th King's Liverpool Regiment will entrain at NIPPES (COLOGNE) about 11 hours on the 26th February for BEUEL on transfer to the 32nd Division. Hour of arrival at BEUEL probably 1500 hours.
   The Battalion will move complete with horses and transport.
   The G.O.C. 9th Infantry Brigade will arrange for a band to play the Battalion off.
   The Divisional Commander will be present on the departure of the Battalion.
   (b) "Q" will notify the exact hour at which the entrainment will take place on receipt of the information from Corps "Q".

5. "Q" will arrange with "Q" 32nd, 49th and 62nd Divisions regarding the transfer of the 13th King's Liverpool Regiment, 1/6th West Yorks. and 1/9th D.L.I. for supplies.
   Train wagons will accompany Units.

(sd) W.H. Traill., Lieut.Colonel.
General Staff, 3rd Division.

22nd February 1919.

SECRET.

G.8074/10.

76th Brigade.
"Q"

Reference Forecast of moves and Reliefs under G.8074/7 of 22nd. February.

1. 20th Durham Light Infantry will detrain at HORREM on 27th February and on arrival will join 76th Infantry Brigade.

76th Inf. Bde. will provide a band to play them to their billets.

20th Durham Light Infantry will arrive with horses according to Cadre "B" and will take over horses to complete establishment from the 8th King's Own Royal Lancaster Regiment.

20th Durham Light Infantry will be billeted in KERPEN.

2. 8th King's Own Royal Lancaster Regiment will not move but will remain in their present area and be reduced to Cadre.

3. Exact hour of detrainment of 20th Durham Light Infantry will be notified by "Q" 3rd Division on receipt of information from "Q" VI Corps.

4. "Q" 3rd Division will arrange with "Q" 41st Division regarding the transfer of the 20th Durham Light Infantry for supplies.

(sd) W.H. Traill Lieut-Col.,
General Staff., 3rd Division.

24th February 1919.

Copy to A.D.M.S.
    Div'l Train.
    20th D.L.I. (through 41st Division.

SECRET. G.8074/12.

76th Inf. Bde.
"Q".

1. Para.1 of G.8074/10 of 24th February is cancelled.

    (a) The 20th Durham Light Infantry (41st Division) will arrive at NIPPES (COLOGNE) on the 27th February in relief of the 8th King's Own Royal Lancaster Regiment which will be reduced to Cadre in its present area.

    The 20th Durham Light Infantry on arrival in COLOGNE will join the 76th Infantry Brigade and will relieve the 3rd Battalion Grenadier Guards.

    (b) The G.O.C., 76th Infantry Brigade will arrange for guides to meet the Battalion at the station and conduct it to billets.

    (c) The 20th Durham Light Infantry will arrive with horses according to Cadre "B" and will take over horses to complete establishment from the 8th King's Own Royal Lancaster Regiment.

    G.O.C., 76th Infantry Brigade will arrange to horse the transport of the 20th Durham Light Infantry from the station to billets.

2. (a) The 1/4th York and Lancaster Regiment (49th Division) will arrive at HORREM probably on the 28th February in relief of the 1st Gordon Highlanders which will be reduced to Cadre in its present area.

    On arrival the 1/4th York and Lancaster Regiment will join the 76th Infantry Brigade and will be billeted in KEMPEN.

    The G.O.C. 76th Infantry Brigade will arrange for guides to meet the Battalion at the station and conduct it to billets.

    (b) The 1/4th York and Lancaster Regiment will arrive with horses according to Cadre "B" and will take over horses to complete establishment from the 1st Gordon Highlanders.

    G.O.C., 76th Infantry Brigade will arrange to horse the transport of the 1/4th York & Lancaster Regiment from the station to billets.

    (c) On the 1st March the 1/4th York and Lancaster Regt. will move to COLOGNE (RIEHL Area) under orders of G.O.C., 76th Infantry Brigade in relief of the 1st Battalion Coldstream Guards.

3. Moves of the 529th Field Company, 7th Field Ambulance and No.2 Company Divisional Train will take place as already ordered in 3rd Division Operation Order 307.

4. Exact hour of detrainment of above Battalions will be notified by "Q".

25th February 1919.

W.A.Traill
Lieut.Colonel,
General Staff, 3rd Division.

Copies to :- Guards Div.
A.D.M.S.
Div'l Train.
20th D.L.I. (thro' 41st Division).
1/4th York & Lancs. (thro' 49th Division).

Forecast of Moves and Reliefs.

Serial No.	Date	Relieving Unit	To	Relieved unit of 3rd Div.	Relieved Unit of Guards Divn.	Remarks
1	Feby. 26th.	2nd Suffolks.	RIEHL Area (COLOGNE)	–	1st Scots Guards.	
2	27th.	20th D.L.I.	RIEHL Area (COLOGNE)	9th K.O.R.L.	3rd Grenadier Guards.	Arrive with horses in accordance with Cadre "B". Take over horses from 9th K.O.R.L. to complete establishment.
3	28th	1/4th Y.&L.	KERPEN (detrain at HORREM).	1st Gordon Hrs.	–	Arrive with horses in accordance with Cadre "B". Take over horses from 1st G.H. to complete establishment.
4	28th.	529 Field Co.	KERPEN.	–	–	
5	March 1st.	1/4th Y.&L.	RIEHL Area (COLOGNE).	–	1st Coldstream Gds.	
6	1st	529 Field Co.	KUNGERSDORP & BRAUNSFELD Area (COLOGNE)	–	–	
7	1st	7th Fd.Amb.	RIEHL Area (COLOGNE)	–	9th Field Amb.	
8	1st	No.2 Coy. Div.Train.	RIEHL Area (COLOGNE)	–	No.1 Coy. Gds.Div. Train.	
9	1st	3rd Div.HQ.& HQ.Sec.Sig.Co.	COLOGNE.	–	Gds.Div.H.Q. & H.Q. Signal Coy.	
10	4th	1/5 W.Yorks.	SULZ Area (COLOGNE)	7th K.S.L.I.	1 Battn. 3rd Guards Brigade.	7th K.S.L.I. Standfast. Reduced to Cadre.
11	5th	1 Bn.8th Inf. Bde.	do.	–	- do -	
12	5th	438 Fld.Co.	KERPEN.	–	–	
13	March 6th.	438 Fld.Coy.	KUNGERSDORP & BRAUNSFELD Area (COLOGNE)	–	–	
14	6th	1 Bn.8th.Inf. Bde.	SULZ Area (COLOGNE)	–	1 Bn.3rd Gds.Bde.	
15	6th	9th Fld.Amb.	do.	–	3rd Fld.Amb.	
16	6th	No.3 Coy. Div.Train.	do.	–	No.2 Co.Gds.Div. Train.	
17	10th	1 Co.3rd M.G.Bn.	KERPEN.	–	–	
18	11th	do.	EHRENFELD Area (COLOGNE)	–	1 Coy.4th Gds.M.G.Bn.	
19	11th	1 Coy.M.G.Bn.	KERPEN	–	–	
20	12th	1 Co.M.G.Bn.	EHRENFELD Area (COLOGNE)	–	1 Co.4th Gds.M.G. Battn.	
21	12th	H.Q.& 2 Coys. M.G.Battn.	KERPEN.	–	–	
22	13th	do.	EHRENFELD Area (COLOGNE)	–	H.Q.& 2 Coys.4th Gds.M.G. Battalion.	

76th Inf. Bde. Group (Serials 1–9)
8th Inf. Bde. Group (Serials 10+)

Orders as regards moves of Serial Nos. 1 to 9 have already been issued.
Orders for moves of Serial Nos. 10 to 22 will be issued later.

Copies to :— 8th Inf.Bde.   A.D.M.S.
9th Inf.Bde.   "Q"
76th Inf.Bde.   M.G.Battn.
C.R.A.   Signals.
C.R.E.   Guards Div.

GENERAL STAFF.
3RD DIVISION.
No. 1/8074/13   25/2/19

"A" Form
MESSAGES AND SIGNALS.

Army Form C. 2121 (In pads of 100.)

TO	1 Bde	aaa	
	CRE	Q	
	Guards Divn		

Sender's Number: GA 270
Day of Month: 26
AAA

Reference	forecast	of	moves
your	Relief	issued	under
58074/13	of	25th	inst
aaa	In	Column	2
against	serial	No	12
1st	5th	March	read
2nd	March	aaa	against
Serial	No 13	1st	6th
March	read	3rd	March
aaa	438th	Field	Coy
will	carry	out	these
moves	on	2nd	and
3rd	March	under	orders
of	CRE	aaa	addsd
CRE	repeated	8	Bde
aaa	8	Guards	Divn

From: Brakin

"A" Form
MESSAGES AND SIGNALS.

Army Form C. ____
(In pads of 100.)
No. of Message............

Prefix........Code........m.	Words	Charge	This message is on a/c of:	Recd. at......m.
Office of Origin and Service Instructions	Sent			Date............
....	At ....m.		............Service.	From............
....	To			
....	By		(Signature of "Franking Officer")	By............

TO { Avonus Train

Sender's Number.	Day of Month.	In reply to Number.	AAA
G5249	24		

Reference this office G80494/10 of date mine first line for 26th read 27th

From Zeebrun
Place
Time
The above may be forwarded as now corrected. (Z)   Wrenly Major
.... Censor. Signature of Addressee or person authorised to telegraph in his name
* This line should be erased if not required.

GENERAL STAFF
NORTHERN DIVISION
MARCH.

WAR DIARY

INTELLIGENCE SUMMARY.

(Erase heading not required.)

Place	Date	Hour	Summary of Events and Information	Remarks and references to Appendices
DUREN	March 1st		Weather fine: Mild. Divisional H.Q. closed at DUREN at 1000 hours and opened at LINDENTHAL (Cologne) same hour.	
LINDENTHAL (COLOGNE)	2/14		Nothing of interest	
"	15		3rd Division renamed "Northern" Division. Col. Inderson assumed command of Northern Division.	
"	16/22		Nothing of interest.	
"	23rd		Having now for more of St. Vde and affiliated field Ambulances coy. from. (Vice S.A.82 attached)	
"	24th		Cancellation of S.A.82 and substitution unit to units concerned. (Vice S.A.93 attached)	
"	25/26		Nothing of interest to report.	
"	27th		Visit of Commander in Chief to Cologne. Units informed (Vice S.89§E attached)	
"	28/31		Nothing of interest.	

P.J. Butler, Major
General Staff, Northern Division

"A" Form
MESSAGES AND SIGNALS.

Army Form C. 2121
(In pads of 100.)

No. of Message..........

Prefix....Code....m	Words	Charge	This message is on a/c of:	Recd. at....m
Office of Origin and Service Instructions	Sent		..................Service.	Date..........
	At........m			From..........
	To..........			
	By..........	(Signature of "Franking Officer")	By..........

TO { 9 Inf Bde / of Inf Bde & northern Div / Cdn vol Lewis / Depot / 76 Canyards / Lewis Team }

| Sender's Number. | Day of Month. | In reply to Number. | AAA |
| SR 82 | 3/3 | | |

Army Order No ... 8th
Inf Bde ... affiliated
and Ambulance cover Train
Company will be prepared
to move to the
area POUCHEIM 9E YEV SOUTHERN
at an early date
and This area is
being vacated by 76th
Army Order RFA (less
BAC) on 26th must
and 9th Inf Bde
will send advance parties
to this area on
26th inst to take
over billets and Government
property from 76th Army

From
Place
Time

The above may be forwarded as now corrected. (Z)
....
Censor. Signature of Addressor or person authorised to telegraph in his name
* This line should be erased if not required.

Order No. 1625. Wt. W3253/ P 511. 27/2. H. & K., Ltd. (E, 2634).

"A" Form
MESSAGES AND SIGNALS.

Army Form C. 2121
(In pads of 100.)

Prefix....Code....m.	Words	Charge	This message is on a/c of:	Recd. at....m.
Office of Origin and Service Instructions	Sent			Date........
....	At ....m.		........Service.	
....	To			From ....
....	By		(Signature of "Franking Officer")	By ....

TO {
....
....
}

Sender's Number.	Day of Month.	In reply to Number.	AAA
Brigade	R F A	has	1/
Inf	Batt	will	the
informed	to	relieve	1st
Brigade	at	present	from
by	of	Inf	Batt
that	the	now	of
the	1/	Inf	Batt
is	relieved	was	Acknowledge
Orders	of	and	by
Inf	Batt	MDS	Batt
train	relieved	all	Watson
down	of	and	16th
coming	Batt	R.F.A	

From J.H. Shawcross
Place
Time 1930
The above may be forwarded as now corrected. (Z)

Censor.   Signature of Addressor or person authorised to telegraph in his name
* This line should be erased if not required.

Order No. 1625. Wt. W3253/ P 511. 27/2. H. & K., Ltd. (E. 2634).

"A" Form
MESSAGES AND SIGNALS.

Army Form C. 2121 (In pads of 100.)

TO	8th & 9th Inf. Bdes.	"Q"	A.D.M.S.	Sigs.
	C.R.A. Northn Div.		Train.	
	76th Army Bde. R.F.A.			

| Sender's Number. | Day of Month. | In reply to Number. | AAA |
| G.A.93 | 24th | - | |

G.A.82 of 23rd inst is cancelled AAA 8th Inf Bde with affiliated Field Ambulance and Train Company will be prepared to move to the area FRECHEN - BACHEM - GLEUEL - HURTH - KENDENICH - FISCHENICH on receipt of orders AAA When the 8th Inf Bde is ordered to move all guards at present found by the 8th Inf Bde will be relieved by the 9th Inf Bde with the exception of the inlying picquet of one company at the NEUMARKT which will continue to be found by the 8th Inf Bde AAA ACKNOWLEDGE AAA Added 8th & 9th Inf. Bdes repeated "Q" C.R.A. Northn Div 76th Army Bde R.F.A. A.D.M.S. Train & Signals

From Northern Div
Place
Time 1615 hours

(Z) W.H.TRAILL, Lt. Col.
G.S.

8th Inf.Bde.
9th Inf.Bde.   1/9th DLI.Pioneers.
76th Inf.Bde.   G.8298.

"Q".
Brig.Genl.H.C.POTTER,CMG.DSO.Comdg.3rd Div.Cadre Group.

1.   The Commander-in-Chief arrives at COLOGNE Station at 09.10 hours tomorrow 28th March and will leave the station at 10.00 hours.

2.   A Guard of Honour consisting of 2 Officers and 50 other ranks with Band will be detailed by G.O.C.,76th Infantry Brigade from the 20th D.L.I. and will be formed up ready to receive the C.-in-C. outside the station at 09.30 hours.
Great Coats will be worn if it is raining.

3.   The C.-in-C. will visit Northern Division Headquarters at 11.00 hours.

    The following will meet the C.-in-C. at the Divisional Commanders residence and will be there by 10.50 hours.

    Brigade Commanders of 8th,9th and 76th Infantry Brigades.
    Brig.Genl.H.C.POTTER,CMG. DSO. Commdg.3rd Div.Cadre Group.
    G.S.O.I.
    A.A.&.Q.M.G.

4.   G.O.C.,76th Infantry Brigade will have the RIEHL Barracks ready for inspection - possibly the C.-in-C. will inspect these barracks between 11.00 and 12.00 hours.

5.   1/9th D.L.I.(Pioneers) will detail a smart guard over the residence of the VI Corps Commander and over VI Corps H.Q.

    This guard will relieve the guard at present found by the 8th Infantry Brigade by 09.30 hours tomorrow morning and will hereafter be found by the 1/9th D.L.I.

    Guard of 1/9th D.L.I. will report to Camp Commandant,VI Corps H.Q. at 09.00 hours tomorrow 28th instant.

6.   All Guards and sentries will be warned to be on the look out for the C.-in-C's Car flying the Union Jack and to turn out and pay the proper compliments.

7.   Acknowledge by wire.

                                                    Lieut.Colonel.
                                  General Staff, Northern Division.

27th March 1919.

Northern Div. "Q"

WAR DIARY

Army Form C. 2118.

HQ G.S. NM 57

INTELLIGENCE SUMMARY.
(Erase heading not required.)

Instructions regarding War Diaries and Intelligence Summaries are contained in F.S. Regs., Part II. and the Staff Manual respectively. Title pages will be prepared in manuscript.

Place	Date	Hour	Summary of Events and Information	Remarks and references to Appendices
LINDENTHAL (Cologne)	April 7th		Captain C. CHIPPER North'n. Div. took up appointment of GSO 3 Northern Division. Lieut. G.W. GORDON HALL, K.O.Y.L.I., took up appointment of GSO 1 Northern Div.	
	10th		Training hours laid down by Divisional Commander as 0900 - 1300, 1400 - 1600 daily except for ½ holidays on Wed. and Sat. and Holiday on Sunday. Minimum of 8 hours Educational training after Church Parade. Minimum one route march each week with weekly transport.	
	17th		GSO 3.. departed on leave to England.	
	23rd		Platoon training started on April 21st. The range at RIEHL and LACKEM were put in order by R.E. during the month and preliminary practice for recruits and backward men were carried out. The number of guards was considerably increased -particularly the whole of a rattalion out of each brigade being taken up in Garrison guard duties. No trouble was experienced with the civil population. Weather fine on the whole.	

C. Chipper Cpt.
[signature] Gen Staff North'n Div

Army Form C. 2118.

WAR DIARY
or
INTELLIGENCE SUMMARY
(Erase heading not required.)

Instructions regarding War Diaries and Intelligence Summaries are contained in F.S. Regs., Part II. and the Staff Manual respectively. Title pages will be prepared in manuscript.

MAY 1919.

Place	Date	Hour	Summary of Events and Information	Remarks and references to Appendices
Cologne.	1st.		Socialist demonstrations (by permission). A good deal of rain fell and most of the demonstrators had recourse to their umbrellas. Everything passed off quietly.	
	6th.		Practice for Review by H.R.H. the Duke of Connaught, on EXERZIER PLATZ, MERHEIM. Very fine day.	
	8th.		Review of Northern Division by H.R.H. (as above). Fine day, but breeze made massed band very difficult to hear at times. H.R.H. complimented the Division on its appearance and smartness.	
	9th.		G.S.O.3 (Capt. C. Chipper, M.C.) returned from leave.	
	12th.		Brigades began Annual Musketry Course (1918 Model)	
	14th.		G.S.O.2 (Major P.R. Butler) proceeded on leave to U.K.	
	16th.		Marshal FOCH arrived by river at landing-stage just S. of HOHENZOLLERN BR. and was received with a guard of Honour of 9th D.L.I. (Pioneers). Large numbers of troops lined the river bank. Some Bolshevist propaganda was discovered by 1st Northern Inf. Bde. near their billets.	
	17th.		Competitors for French Horse Show at WIESBADEN left.	
	20th.		Senior Staff Officers were recalled from leave, which was stopped on account of doubt as to Germans signing.	
	21st.		Ordinary maps of Divisional area issued to complete establishments.	
	22nd.	0930	G.S.O.3, with Staff Captains of the 3 Inf. Bdes., reconnoitred WERMELSKIRCHEN and KURTEN.	
		1200	A Conference held at Corps H.Q. ditto at Div. H.Q.	
	23rd.		Instructions for the advance were prepared, and issued early on 23rd. Maps of country beyond the Bridgeheads received and distributed. G.S.O.2 returned by air. Left Folkestone 10.20 hours; arrived MERHEIM Aerodrme 13.10 hours. It became known that the Germans had been given a week in which to reply.	not attached, owing to matter being in abeyance.

Army Form C. 2118.

WAR DIARY
or
INTELLIGENCE SUMMARY.
(Erase heading not required.)

MAY 1919.

Instructions regarding War Diaries and Intelligence Summaries are contained in F. S. Regs., Part II. and the Staff Manual respectively. Title pages will be prepared in manuscript.

Place	Date	Hour	Summary of Events and Information	Remarks and references to Appendices
COLOGNE.	24th		London Division took over guards on SUD, NEUE, and HOHENZOLLERN Bridges from 1st Northern Divn. 1st Northern Inf. Brigade took over guards on EIFEL TOR Goods Station, and ALTEMBURG Brewery from London Division.	
	26th		2nd Northern Inf. Brigade took over guard on Ordnance Clothing Depot, from London Division.	
	26th 27th }		Corps Commander inspected units of the Division in billets and barracks.	
	27th	0130 hrs.	A large fire broke out in the Ordnance Depot NIPPES, causing serious damage. Possibly the work of incendiaries.	
			G.S.O.3 visited Light Division with reference to scheme for relief of Northern Division guards in the event of an advance. Unauthorised demonstrations took place in COLOGNE in afternoon, directed against rumoured Amended Defence Scheme issued. (formation of RHINELAND Republic.) Time table of reliefs by Light Division issued. Conference of Brigade Majors in "G" Office with reference to March Table for the Advance. Training hours during the summer to be from 0900 hours to 1300 hours. Office hours to be 0900 to 1300 hours and 1400 to 1600 hours. Weather very fine throughout the month.	

11th June, 1919.

C. A. Butler,
Lieut. Colonel,
General Staff, Northern Division.

CONFIDENTIAL.

War Diary
of
General Staff, Northern Division
(British Army of the Rhine.)

———

JUNE 1919.

Original

Army Form C. 2118.

WAR DIARY
or
INTELLIGENCE SUMMARY
(Erase heading not required.)

JUNE. 1919.

Instructions regarding War Diaries and Intelligence Summaries are contained in F. S. Regs., Part II. and the Staff Manual respectively. Title pages will be prepared in manuscript.

Place	Date	Hour	Summary of Events and Information	Remarks and references to Appendices
LINDENTHAL, COLOGNE.	1st.		Weather hot and dry.	P.R.B.
	2nd.		Div. Intelligence Officer visited the industrial areas of HERMULHEIM and KNAPSACK and found all quiet. (Frequent threats of strikes are heard from these places, but no actual disorder has broken out).	P.R.B.
	8th.		Weather very hot, with thunder and showers in evening. G.S.O.2 and Div. Intelligence Officer went by train to COBLENZ, and thence by American Rhine Steamer to CAUB, and back.	P.R.B.
	12th.		Weather continued hot. Dust-storm in afternoon. Div. Commander went on Rhine, as guest of American Army, from COBLENZ to near BINGEN, and back.	P.R.B.
	16th.		Div. Intelligence Officer visited FRECHEN industrial area. All quiet.	P.R.B.
	17th.	06.15	Notification received from Corps that "J" day; would be on 20th June. Today accordingly became J-3 day, and guards found by 2nd Northern Inf. Bde., were relieved by 2nd Light Bde.	See Appendix "A" for complete file of Div. Orders & Instructions
	18th.		J-2 day. Following move took place:- 2nd Nthn Bde. Group from COLOGNE to DUNNWALD area (by march route). Major K.B. FERGUSON (Div. Educ. Officer) reported to H.Q. 1st Belgian Div. ALPEN as Div. Liaison Officer. Orders received in evening that "J" day was to be postponed three days. Thus J-1 day (19 June) was to be followed by J-1 (a) and J-1 (b) days. "J" day to be on 22nd June, but no advance to take place on that day unless definite orders to that effect were received from Corps.	P.R.B.
	19th.		Relief of guards by Light Division completed. "J"-1 day'. Following moves took place:- 1st Nthn Bde. Group from COLOGNE to KURTEN area. (By lorry) 2nd " " " DUNNWALD area to HILGEN area. (By march route) 3rd " " " COLOGNE to WERMELSKIRCHEN area. (By lorry) M.G. Batt. " " TORRINGERT area. (By march route) D.A.W. from KONIGSDORF area to BRUCK area.	P.R.B.

Army Form C. 2118.

WAR DIARY
or
INTELLIGENCE-SUMMARY.
(Erase heading not required.)

Instructions regarding War Diaries and Intelligence Summaries are contained in F. S. Regs., Part II. and the Staff Manual respectively. Title pages will be prepared in manuscript.

Place	Date	Hour	Summary of Events and Information	Remarks and references to Appendices
LINDENTHAL, COLOGNE.	19th	(contd)	In the evening orders were issued for D.A. to continue march on 20th to HOHKEPPEL area, instead of to DURSCHEID area. This change was necessitated by lack of water in DURSCHIED area. Moves took place in beautiful weather over good roads. CORPUS CHRISTI Processions were in progress in most of the villages through which the troops advanced passed, the streets being gaily decorated for the festival. The entire population appeared to be taking part in the processions, and nothing could have been more incongruous than the columns of motor-lorries guns, etc., and the columns of little children and devout people in their "Sunday best" which always seemed to meet at the narrowest points along the roads.	P.R.B.
	20th.		Following moves took place:- M.G. Battalion Group from TORRINGERT area to DABRINGHAUSEN area (By march route) D.A. from BRUCK area to HOHKEPPEL area (D.A., H.Q. remained at LINDENTHAL until move of Div. H.Q.) Weather continued extremely fine, and all ranks appreciated the change from town surroundings to the open country, which was looking its best. The district into which the Division has now moved to was one of great beauty, consisting of well-wooded hills and valleys, with plenty of heavy meadowing, good streams (in places) and comfortable villages. The hay had mostly been cut and was in process of carting. Men and animals stood the marches very well. These, although not long (10 to 12 miles) were undertaken on hilly roads in hot weather. Horses in excellent conditions, if a bit soft. Much speculation with regard to Peace, the consensus of opinion being that the terms would be signed. Our concentration towards the Perimeter undoubtedly impressed the inhabitants, both of COLOGNE and of the district across the Rhine.	
	21st.		Weather showed signs of breaking and some rain fell. Tents and blankets were sent up to the troops in bivouacs. "J" day is now understood to be postponed until 25th inst. When it is definitely announced the days immediately preceding it will be called respectively I. H. G. etc, days.	P.R.B.

Army Form C. 2118.

WAR DIARY
or
INTELLIGENCE-SUMMARY.
(Erase heading not required.)

Instructions regarding War Diaries and Intelligence Summaries are contained in F. S. Regs., Part II. and the Staff Manual respectively. Title pages will be prepared in manuscript.

Place	Date	Hour	Summary of Events and Information	Remarks and references to Appendices
LINDENTHAL COLOGNE.	22nd.		Lieut. LAMBERT, Liaison Officer from 1st Belgian Division, reported for duty. Instructions were sent to our Liaison Officer with 1st Belgian Div. (at ALPEN) to visit H.Q. of XXXIII French Corps at NEUSZ.	P.R.B.
	23rd.		C.-in-C., visited Bde. H.Qs at the front. In the evening, instructions were received that the advance might take place at 03.15 hours on 24th inst. Soon afterwards Corps informed us that the German Government had signified its intention of signing. Brigades etc, were informed accordingly. Orders for a withdrawal to old locations in COLOGNE and vicinity were drafted, but troops to remain in present positions until further notice.	P.R.B.
	24th.		Weather colder, with some rain.	P.R.B.
	25th.		Orders for the withdrawal were issued, to take effect when notified. Weather has turned cold and wet, though with bright intervals.	Appendix "B"
	26th & 27th		Weather wet and cold.	"
	28th		Message received during evening that peace treaty had been signed and that Monday 30th would be "A" day for the withdrawal. This was wired out to Brigades and Units.	"
	29th		Guard-relieving Battalions came back as ordered.	"
	30th		Moves took place as ordered: no hitch, Weather fair & cool. Major General C.J.DEVERELL, left for ENGLAND. Major General A.A.KENNEDY, C.M.G., assumed command of Northern Division. Lt.Col.P.R.BUTLER, D.S.O., G.S.O.2, went on leave to ENGLAND.	"

C. Curtis Capt
for Lieut. Colonel.,
General Staff, Northern Division.

30th June 1919.

See Appx C & D for location

Appendix A

SECRET

Northern Division No. G.8874/17.

1. Reference Northern Division G.8874 of 23rd May.

June 17th was J - 3 day, and the movements laid down for J - 2 day and J - 1 day will be carried out on June 18th and 19th respectively, and the necessary steps will be taken by all concerned in order to undertake the operations laid down for J day on June 20th. No action however, on June 20th is to be taken, nor is the present perimeter to be crossed, until further definite orders to that effect are issued by G.H.Q.

2. Consequent on above :-

    (a) The 2nd Northern Inf. Brigade Group will not move on the 20th June, but will halt at the places reached on J - 1 day.

    (b) The following movements laid down for J day will be carried out on the 20th June, namely,

Nthn Div. Arty Group	to	~~BIESFELD~~ HOHKEPPEL
1st Inf. Bde Transport Group	to	KURTEN.
M.G.C. Group.	to	DABRINGHSN.

3. Positions of the Groups of the Division on June 20th will therefore be as follows :-

1st Nthn Inf. Bde. Group.	KURTEN.
3rd Nthn Inf. Bde. Group.	WERMELSKIRCHEN.
Nthn Div. Arty Group.	~~BIESFELD~~ HOHKEPPEL
1st Nthn Inf. Bde. Transport Group.	KURTEN.
M.G.C. Group.	DABRINGHSN.
2nd Nthn Inf. Bde. Group.	HILGEN and BURSCHEID.

4. When the date for "J" day is notified, the advance will be continued on the general lines given in the revised March Tables issued with G.8874/6 of 27th May, but fresh tables will be issued for each day.

5. ACKNOWLEDGE.

G.W. Gordon Hall

Lieut. Colonel,
General Staff, Northern Division.

18th June, 1919.

Copies to all recipients of G.8874 of 23rd May.

S E C R E T.   Northern Division G.8874/11.

Reference Northern Division G.8874/8 of 28th inst., the following is to be added thereto.

"J plus 1 day. In column of remarks delete reference to SCHWELM."

30th May 1919.

P. R. Butler
Major for
Lieut. Colonel.,
General Staff, Northern Division.

S E C R E T.

Northern Division. G.8874/9.

Reference March Tables issued with G.8874/6 dated 27th May.

J - 2 day.   Delete "7th Field Ambulance less 1 Section".

J - 1 day.   In "Unit" column, after "To 2 Coy Train", add "7th Field Ambulance less 1 Section" (7th Field Ambulance less 1 Section will be under the orders of O.C., 3rd Battn. M.G.C.).

29th May 1919.

Major for
Lieut-Colonel
General Staff, Northern Division.

Copies to all recipients of G.8874/6.

SECRET.

Northern Division G.8874/8.

Reference March Tables issued with G.8874/6 dated 27th May.

J - 2 day.   The 2nd Northern Infantry Brigade Group will cross the
                RHINE by the MULHEIM Bridge, clearing the bridge
                by 10.20 hours.

J - 1 day.   (a) "G" Battery, R.H.A. will clear MULHEIM Bridge
                     by 08.40 hours.

                (b) 1st Northern Infantry Brigade Group will clear
                     SUSPENSION BRIDGE by 11.00 hours.

                (c) 3rd Northern Infantry Brigade Group, head will
                     pass HOHENZOLLERN Bridge at 13.00 hours.

                (d) Northern Div. Artillery Group, head will pass
                     SUSPENSION Bridge at 12.00 hours.

                (e) Transport, 1st Northern Infantry Brigade Group
                     will clear SUSPENSION Bridge by 11.00 hours
                     and MULHEIM Bridge by 09.20 hours.

J Day.   Advanced Divisional H.Q. will leave LINDENTHAL
                at 12.00 hours.

J plus 2 day.   In column of remarks for HAGEN read SCHWELM.

J plus 3 day.   2nd Northern Infantry Brigade in column of remarks
                insert "to be clear of HAGEN by 11.00 hours".

G.W.Gordon Hall

Lieut. Colonel.
General Staff, Northern Division.

28th May, 1919.

Copies to all recipients of G.8874/6.

S E C R E T.   Northern Division G.8874/6.

1st Northern Inf. Bde.	93rd Bde. R.G.A.
2nd Northern Inf. Bde.	London Division.
3rd Northern Inf. Bde.	Southern Division.
C.R.A.	12th Squadron, R.A.F.
C.R.E.	D.A.P.M.
"Q"	D.A.D.O.S.
A.D.M.S.	D.A.D.V.S.
Signals.	Northern Div. M.T. Coy.
3rd Bn. M.G.C.	Train.
1/9th D.L.I.	Cavalry Division.
VI Corps "G".	VI Corps Cyclists Battn.
VI Corps "Q"	File.

Herewith March Tables to replace those issued with G.8874 of 23rd May, which should be destroyed.

Appendix "A", Signal Arrangements should be amended to show the letters of Brigade Calls for use with ground signals as follows:-

1st Northern Inf. Bde.	JB
2nd Northern Inf. Bde.	QW
3rd Northern Inf. Bde.	WD

ACKNOWLEDGE.

G.L.Gordon Hall
Lieut. Colonel.
General Staff, Northern Division.

27th May, 1919.

SECRET.

Northern Division. G. 8874.

Ref. 1/200,000.
Sheets HANNOVER.
       MUNSTER.
       COLOGNE.
       CASSELL.

INSTRUCTIONS FOR THE ADVANCE.

NO. 1.

1.   Under certain eventualities it may be necessary for the Allied Armies to seize as rapidly as possible the RUHR Basin, and to secure the Railway communications, which are essential for a further advance North-Eastwards.

2.   In seizing the railways our object is to ensure that the German rolling stock on the lines is not evacuated in front of us and that the German personnel complete remain at their posts, and work the railway for us. The main railway communication runs COLOGNE - OHLIGS - ELBERFELD - HAGEN - UNNA - Important subsidiary lines are ALTENA - PLETTENBERG - KIRCHMUNDEN - KROMBACH - SIEGEN and SCHWERTE - ARNSBERG - MESCHEDE.

3.   The VI Corps is to advance on a two Division front, with the London Division on the right on a one Brigade front: and the Northern Division on the left on a two Brigade front on the first day, and on one Brigade front on the second day.

       The Southern Division of the II Corps will be on the left of the Northern Division.

4.   The earliest date on which the advance will be ordered (called "J" day hereinafter) will be the 26th May.

5.   The Northern Division will advance as detailed in March table attached.

6.   Composition of leading Brigades:-

       1st Northern Brigade Group.

       1st Northern Infantry Brigade.
       One Squadron Hussars.
       One Squadron Machine Guns (less one Section)
       231st Field Company R.E.
       One Section, 142nd Field Ambulance.
       Detachment of Cyclists (60 strong approx)
       One Machine Gun Company.
       One 18 pounder in lorry manned by personnel detailed by
              Northern Division Artillery.

       3rd Northern Infantry Brigade Group.

       3rd Northern Infantry Brigade.
       one Squadron Dragoons.
       "G" Battery R.H.A.
       One Section Machine Gun Squadron.
       438th Field Coy. R.E.
       One Section 7th Field Ambulance.
       One Detachment of Cyclists (60 strong)
       One Machine Gun Company.
       One 18 pounder in lorry manned by personnel detailed by
              Northern Division Artillery.
       No. 226 Siege Battery, R.G.A. 6" Hows. lorry drawn.

(2)

7. The advance on "J" day will be covered by mounted troops supported by the Cyclists attached to each Infantry Brigade Group.

The mounted troops will be able to advance about 15 miles on this day, but the advance will be continued by the remainder of the Brigade Group in lorries and busses as rapidly as possible to the localities given in the March Tables.

8. On "J" plus one day these Brigade Groups will again push on rapidly to the posts detailed in the March Table. The mounted troops following in rear on this and succeeding days until they overtake the troops carried in busses and lorries.

9. (a) On "J" day the London Division will occupy ATTENDORN and the Southern Division ELBERFELD.

(b) On "J" plus one day the London Division will continue the advance to ARNSBERG.

(c) On "J" plus two day the Southern Division will advance to HAGEN; to SCHWERTE on "J" plus 3 day ; and to DELLWIG on "J" plus 4 day.

10. The 3rd Northern Infantry Brigade will leave troops in HAGEN and SCHWERTE and DELLWIG until relieved by Southern Division when they will rejoin their units under Brigade arrangements.

11. Instructions will be issued later as to the attitude to be adopted in regard to the German civil population.

12. The 12th Squadron R.A.F., will provide aeroplanes to reconnoitre the country immediately on our front, and to bring back information of the progress of the advance. Their machines are provided with W/T to communicate with the Headquarters of each of the leading Brigades, and with Divisional H.Q.

Further details in Appendix "A" attached. (not attached)

13. Brigade H.Q. will be established as far as possible along main signal routes, the position of which will be notified later.

Care must be taken to see that the line is disconnected in front of the advanced telegraph office in use, to prevent messages being read by the enemy.

14. Battalions will move forward complete in personnel &c as per War Establishments, Part VII. Batteries will move on a 4-gun basis. All surplus personnel and stores will be concentrated by Divisions on a Brigade basis. Places will be selected for their concentration and their location reported to these H.Q.

15. Advanced Divisional H.Q. will be established by 1800 hours at WERMELSKIRCHEN on "J" day and by 12.00 hours at ISERLOHN on "J" plus one day.

16. ACKNOWLEDGE.

G.W. Gordon Hall
Lieut. Colonel.,
General Staff, Northern Division.

23rd May 1919.

Distribution of G.8874.

No. 1.   G.O.C.
    2.   1st Northern Inf.Bde.
    3.   2nd Northern Inf.Bde.
    4.   3rd Northern Inf.Bde.
    5.   C.R.A.
    6.   C.R.E.
    7.   "Q"
    8.   A.D.M.S.
    9.   Signals.
    10. 3rd Bn.M.G.C.
    11. 1/9th D.L.I.(Pioneers).
    12. Corps "G".
    13. Corps "Q".
    14. 93rd Bde.R.G.A.
    15. London Division.
    16. Southern Division.
    17. 12th Squadron, R.A.F.
    18. A.P.M.
    19. D.A.D.O.S.
    20. D.A.D.V.S.
    21. Northern Div.M.T.Company.
    22. Train.
    23. Cavalry Division.
    24. VI Corps Cyclist Battn.
    25. War Diary.
    26. War Diary.
    27. File.

MARCH TABLE.

Date	Unit.	Destination.	Route.	Remarks.
J-2	2nd Northern Inf. Bde. 7th Field Ambulance less 1 section. 142nd Field Ambulance less 1 Section. No.4 Coy Train.	DUNNWALD	HOHENZOLLERN BRIDGE.	

NOTE.

1. Attention is drawn to "Notes on March Discipline" issued by G.H.Q. 22/5/19.

2. All movements of troops will be completed daily by 1300 hours to enable lorry traffic to be carried on unimpeded.

MARCH TABLE.

Date.	Unit.	Destination.	Route.	Remarks.
J-1.	"G" Battery, R.H.A.	WERMELSKIRCHEN.	MULHEIM BRIDGE.	To clear bridge by 1000 hours.
	Dragoon Squadron and 1 Section, M.G.Squadron.	WERMELSKIRCHEN.	ODENTHAL.	
	Hussar Squadron and M.G. Squadron less 1 Section.	KURTEN.	BENSBERG.	By Motor Bus.
	1st Northern Inf. Bde Group.	KURTEN.	BERG GLADBACH.	By Motor Bus.
	3rd Northern Inf. Bde Group.	WERMELSKIRCHEN.	SCHLEBUSCH.	To clear bridge over RHINE by 1000 hours.
	Northern Div. Artillery. 9th D.L.I.(P) less 1 Coy. 529th Field Coy, R.E. No.1 Coy Train.	BRUCK.	SUSPENSION BRIDGE	Including 150th Hvy Battery R.G.A. (60-pdrs). 9th D.L.I.(less 1 coy) will act as escort to Artillery during advance.
	Transport 1st Northern Inf. Brigade Group. No.3 Coy Train. One Coy 9th D.L.I.(P).	BERG GLADBACH.	SUSPENSION BRIDGE. MULHEIM BRIDGE.	Coy 9th D.L.I. act as escort to 1st Inf.Bde.Group transport during advance. To clear bridges by 10.00 hrs.
	3rd Bn M.G.C. less 2 Coys. Transport 3rd Northern Inf Bde Group. No.2 Coy Train.	TORRINGERT.	MULHEIM BRIDGE.	M.G.C. act as escort to 3rd Inf.Bde.Group transport during the advance. To clear bridge by 10.00 hours. Not to arrive TORRINGERT before 09.00 hours.
	2nd Northern Inf. Bde Group.	HILGEN and BURSCHEID.	SCHLEBUSCH.	To be clear of SCHLEBUSCH by 0900 hours.

NOTE.
1. Attention is drawn to "Notes on March Discipline" issued by G.H.Q. 22/5/19.
2. All movements of troops will be completed daily by 1500 hours to enable lorry traffic to be carried on unimpeded.

MARCH TABLE.

Date	Unit.	Destination.	Route	Remarks.
J day	1st Northern Inf. Bde Group.	ALTENA and LUDENSCHEID.	WIPPERFURTH.	Positions of mounted troops with advanced Brigades on this and following night will be detailed by their respective Brigade Group Commanders.
	3rd Northern Inf. Bde Group.	SCHWERTE and HAGEN.	SCHWELM and LENNEP.	
	Northern Division Artillery Group.	BIESFELD.	BENSBERG.	
	1st Inf. Bde Transport Group.	KURTEN.	BIESFELD.	
	M.G.C.Group.	DABRINGHSN	ODENTHAL	
	2nd Inf. Bde. Group	BORN and LENNEP		To be clear of HILGEN by 09.00 hours
	Advanced Divisional Headquarters.	WERMELSKIRCHEN.		By M.T.
	1 Company infty to be detailed by 2nd Nthn Inf Bde.			To act as escort to Adv. Div. H.Q.
	Divisional H.Q.	SCHLEBUSCH.		

NOTE. 1. Attention is drawn to "Notes on March Discipline" issued by G.H.Q. 22/5/19.
2. All movements of troops will be completed daily by 1300 hours to enable lorry traffic to be carried on unimpeded.

MARCH TABLE.

Date.	Unit.	Destination.	Route.	Remarks.
J plus 1 day.	3rd Northern Inf. Bde. Group.	SOEST and IERL.	ISERLOHN.	Mounted troops of both advanced Bdes, come under orders of 3rd Northern Inf. Bde. this day.
	1st Northern Inf.Bde. Group.	MENDEN FRONDENBERG and SCHWERTE.	WESTIG and LETMATHE.	A post of cyclists to be detached to cross roads ½ mile E of DELECKE to connect with London Divn, and 2 platoons Infantry to LUDENSCHEID as guard to Corps H.Q.
	Northern Division Artillery Group.	WIPPERFURTH.	-	Follow 1st Inf.Bde. Transport Group.
	1st Inf.Bde.Transport Group.	WIPPERFURTH.	-	Under orders of C.R.A.
	M.G.C. Group.	HUCKESWAGEN.	-	
	2nd Inf.Bde.Group.	SCHWELM.	LENNEP.	To be clear of SCHWELM by 11.00 hrs.
	Advanced Divisional H.Q.	ISERLOHN.	HAGEN.	
	Divisional H.Q.	WERMELSKIRCHEN.	-	

Note :- 1. Attention is drawn to "Notes on March Discipline" issued by G.H.Q. 22.5.19.

2. All movement of troops will be completed daily by 13.00 hours to enable lorry traffic to be carried on unimpeded.

MARCH TABLE.

Date.	Unit.	Destination.	Route.	Remarks.
J plus 2 day.	Northern Divisional Artillery Group. 1st Inf.Bde.Transport Group.	South east of KIERSPE.	RONSAHL.	Under Orders of C.R.A.
	M.G.C. Group.	OCKINGHSN and HALVER.	-	
	2nd Inf.Bde.Group.	HAGEN.	-	To be clear of HAGEN by 11.00 hours.
	Divisional Headquarters.	HALVER.	RADEVORMWALD.	
J plus 3 day.	M.G.C. Group.	ALTENA.	LUDENSCHEID.	
	Divisional H.Q.	ALTENA.	-	Under orders of M.C.; M.G. Group.
	Northern Division Artillery Group. 1st Inf.Bde.Transport Group.	LUDENSCHEID.	-	Under orders of C.R.A.
	2nd Northern Inf.Bde.	ISERLOHN.	LETMATHE.	

Note:— 1. Attention is drawn to "Notes on March Discipline" issued by G.H.Q. 22.5.19.

2. All movements of troops will be completed daily by 13.00 hours to enable lorry traffic to be carried on unimpeded.

M A R C H   T A B L E.

Date	Unit	Destination	Route	Remarks
J plus 4 day.	M.G.C. Group.	MENDEN.	FLONSBERG.	
	Divisional H.Q.	ISERLOHN.		
	Northern Div'l Artillery Group. } 1st Inf.Bde.Transport Group. }	LETMATHE.		Under orders of O.R.A.

NOTE:- 1. Attention is drawn to "Notes on March Discipline" issued by G.H.Q. 22.5.19.

2. All movements of troops will be completed daily by 13.00 hours to enable lorry traffic to be carried on unimpeded.

SECRET.

APPENDIX "A".

(To accompany Northern Division G.8874 dated 23rd May.)

SIGNAL ARRANGEMENTS.

The means of communication available, in case an advance into GERMANY takes place, are as follows :-

    (a) Telegraph and Telephone.
    (b) Visual.
    (c) Wireless.
    (d) Contact Aeroplanes.
    (e) Mounted orderlies and despatch riders.

(a) TELEGRAPH AND TELEPHONE.

During the first two days of the advance, owing to the distances covered, i.e. approximately thirty miles each day by the Leading Brigades, telegraph and telephone communication may not be possible, but every effort will be made to obtain telegraph communication.

(b) VISUAL.

Every possible opportunity of using visual communication within the Battalions, and between Battalions and Brigades must be taken; as during a rapid advance the use of cable is a waste of material and labour.

Visual between Division and Brigades will not be possible until distances are reduced.

(c) WIRELESS.

Divisional Headquarters and each Brigade will be in possession of a trench set C.W. Mk.III. A spare set will be kept at Divisional Headquarters in case of any irreparable breakdown occurring in any of the working sets.

The attention of all officers is drawn to "Army of the Rhine" letter O.B.26/1 dated 30.4.19 forwarded under Northern Division G.8511/3 dated 2.5.19 as to endorsing all messages "I.B.W.Clear" or "I.B.W.Cipher".

The 12th Squadron, R.A.F., who are co-operating with this Division are sending, on the 23rd inst. to Divisional Headquarters and to 1st and 3rd Northern Infantry Brigades one W/T set with the necessary personnel to man it, for use with contact aeroplanes only. These stations will move with and be under the administration of the Signal Units concerned.

(d) CONTACT AEROPLANES.

Daily during the advance. Divisional Headquarters and the 3rd Northern Infantry Brigade will, on arriving at their Headquarters immediately select a spot for their aeroplane dropping station, and ground signals will be laid out as directed in S.S.191 "Inter-Communication in the Field" Appendix iii.

The 1st Northern Infantry Brigade on "J" day only will also select their aeroplane dropping station and lay out their ground signal.

Letters of Brigade call for use with ground signals will be as follows :-

    1st Northern Inf.Bde.   AN
    2nd Northern Inf.Bde.   BN
    3rd Northern Inf.Bde.   CN

(2)

Divisional Headquarters and each Brigade Headquarters should carry two sets of ground signals and calls to enable "stepping up" to be carried out when required.

(e) MOUNTED ORDERLIES AND DESPATCH RIDERS.

These must be made use of to the fullest extent, as during a rapid advance when long distances are being covered daily this means of communication is the only really possible one.

All units should pay special attention to informing all ranks before dismissing the parade on arriving in billets as to the whereabouts of unit and formation Headquarters, with a view to all troops being able to assist Despatch Riders and Mounted Orderlies.

The attention of all formations and units is drawn to S.S. 191 Chapter iii "Communication during open warfare".

Copies to all recipients of Northern Division G.8874 dated 23rd May.

SECRET

Northern Division. G.8971/12.

APPENDIX A.1 to Northern Div. G. 8874 of 23rd May 1919.

1. <u>D.R's</u> The work of Motor Cyclists will undoubtedly be arduous. Special runs should accordingly be avoided as far as possible. In view of the possibility of indiscriminate sniping of individuals in the area behind the leading Brigade, important messages carried by D.R. should be duplicated, the copy being sent by the next D.R. or by some other means.

2. <u>PIGEONS.</u> Pigeons are available from lofts at UNTER ESCHBACH and the BONNER WALL COLOGNE. These lofts will be in touch with Corps and Divisional Hqrs in their locations as on "J" day by telephone. The 3rd and 1st Northern Brigades should take pigeons for their own use and for distribution to advanced troops.
Although in the absence of wire communication forward the transmission (after arrival at the loft) of a pigeon message addressed by a leading battalion to its Brigade may be a lengthly process, a copy of the message handed in to Corps or Divisional General Staff may prove of considerable value.
Demands for pigeons should be sent to O.C. Signals. Requirements for "J" day and "J" plus 1 day should be notified as soon as possible.

3. The following extract from British Army of the Rhine "Instructions to the Troops" will be adhered to.

   (A) The Signal Service of formations will take over such lines as are required for Military use.

   (B) Local Commanders will take steps to occupy and guard important postal and telegraph lines.

   (C) Until the Security Section G.S. (I) has arranged for supervision and control, all civilian Signal traffic through occupied officers must be stopped by means other than the destruction of lines and instruments. German personnel, and especially Postmasters will be forced to remain at their offices, ready to work communication, but German personnel are not to be permitted to touch any Signal Apparatus in occupied offices, except in the presence of a representative of the Signal Service.

   (D) The above order forbidding the destruction of material will still apply in the case of a temporary withdrawal from an occupied office, but in this case instruments should be removed, the lines being left untouched.

   (E) If the enemy offers organised resistance to our advance and fighting ensues or becomes imminent, a new situation will have arisen, and local commanders will then use their discretion as to severing communication in order to prevent tactical information being conveyed from our lines to the enemy.

4. As soon as possible, 6th Corps Signals will extend existing wire communication from KURTEN to LUDENSCHEID, ISERLOHN, SOEST and ARNSBERG along the German telephone route.

   (A) KURTEN
       WIPPERFURTH
       HALVER
       OCKINGHAUSEN
       LUDENSCHEID
       LETHMATHE
       ISERLOHN.

The above route will subsequently be extended probably as follows:-

/2.

  (B) ISERLOHN
    LANDHAU
    MENDEN
    WICKERIE
    WERL
    SOEST

and (C) ISERLOHN
    MENDEN
    MELHEIM
    ARNSBERG

5. Apart from the above, headquarters of leading formations should endeavour to establish communication with the rear, and laterally, on the German system which in many cases may not be damaged. The following information as regards this system is issued as a guide to establishing communication in this way. There is a route from WERMELSKIRCHEN along the railway through LENNEP to SCHWELM. In the SCHWELM-HAGEN-SCHWERTE area there is a maze of telephone routes, mainly along the railways. Lateral routes which may be of use
SCHWELM - BRECKERFELD - HALVER
HAGEN - BRECKERFELD - HALVER
HAGEN - LUDENSCHEID
SCHWERTE - ISERLOHN

  The above is not intended to be a complete list of all telephone routes in the area of the advance, but merely as a guide to possible requirements.

6. If alterations have to be made on the German system they should be done by Signal Service personnel.

7. Supply of cable, to replace any expended during the advance, cannot be guaranteed. In this connection the following points will be observed as far as tactical situation permits.
(A) Signal Offices of Headquarters will be established at German post Telephone Office.
(B) Staff Officers will be located close to Signal Office in houses where subscribers telephones exist. The above should have D.R's etc., difficulty in finding Headquarters, and save labour in establishing communication on the German Telephone system.
(C) Communication within the Outpost system should be as far as possible by visual or runner.
(D) If a cable has to be laid, it must be picked up in good time before the advance is resumed unless taken over by an incoming unit.

            G.O.Gordon Hall
            Lieut-Colonel.,
30th May 1919.   General Staff. Northern Division.

Copies to all recipients of G.8874 of 23/5/19.

S.ECRET.   Northern Division. G. 8874/15.

APPENDIX "B".

(To accompany Northern Div. G.8874 dated 23rd May "Instructions for Advance.")

1. Establishment of Control over German Railways.

    (a) As laid down in para 1., one of the principal objectives of the first stage of the advance is to secure the complete control over the German Railway systems that are considered essential for a further advance.

    (b) The essential measures to be taken by advancing troops to carry this out are as follows:-

    To occupy stations and important junctions; to prevent any destruction of material or the escape of personnel; to put up the notices of which copies will be provided; to occupy the head railway offices of the various German systems; to compel German personnel to remain at their posts, more especially the head managers and sub-managers of the systems; to stop all movements of trains until control of the general management has been taken over by the Sous-Commission of the C.I.C.F.C. (see paras. F & G. below.)

    Any damage done to German lines to be purely temporary (e.g. by breaking a rail in one or two places), and only to be done in case of withdrawal in order to prevent the circulation of German trains whilst awaiting the resumption of the advance.

    (c) In order to assist Commanders of formations in carrying out the above instructions, and to ensure the maintenance of close touch between them and the railway organisation, Railway Liaison Officers are being appointed for the principal railway centres, as follows:-

Location.	Address.	Liaison For.
ELBERFELD.	Advanced Traffic ELBERFELD EISENBAHN DIREKTION.	II Corps and VI Corps.
ARNSBERG.	Railway Liaison Officer ARNSBERG Railway Station.	Right and left Divisions of VI Corps.

    (d) The above Liaison Officers, together with the necessary Railhead Staffs, and Railway Police, will accompany the advanced troops. The necessary arrangements for the attachment of this personnel to the Corps concerned are being made by D.Q.M.G., who is also providing any additional motor transport required for their use.

    (e) The Railway Liaison Officers will act as the technical railway advisers of the formations to which they are attached, and as such, their advice regarding the movement of trains, etc., should be followed, so far as the tactical situation admits.

    (f) As soon as the Railway Sous-Commission has been established at ELBERFELD, all railway movements will be controlled by that body, and no stopping or altering of trains will be made without reference to it through the Liaison Traffic Office there.

(g) Once the Sous-Commission has taken over, Commanders will ensure that:-

(i) No Railway working is interfered with, and no railway officials are molested or interfered with in their work. In the first instance, these railway officials will have no passes, but the Sous-Commission at ELBERFELD will provide them as soon as practicable

(ii) No railway telephones or telegraphs are interfered with; they are vital to the continued working of the railway.

(iii) No railway buildings or premises are commandeered or occupied without reference to the Railway Liaison Officer concerned.

2. <u>OUTPOST POLICY.</u>

Policy for outpost troops on the perimeter from "J" - 3 to "J" - 1 day inclusive will be as follows:-

There will be no change in present procedure, and existing instructions as regards circulation will be carried out.

It may be anticipated that there will be a greater number of individual attempts to evade circulation regulations. Outpost troops will be warned accordingly.

3. <u>AEROPLANE POLICY.</u>

Reference para. 12 the policy as regards action by aeroplanes during the advance will be as follows:-

In the first instance, and until the enemy definitely discloses an intention to resist our advance, aeroplanes will not take any offensive action with machine guns against enemy personnel on the ground, but will confine themselves to reconnaissance and forwarding reports.

If aeroplanes are fired at from the ground from places which are definitely known to be unoccupied by our troops, they will take the necessary action to ensure their own safety by returning the fire.

There will in no case be any bombing from aeroplanes without previous orders from G.H.Q.

4. ACKNOWLEDGE.

G.O.Gordon Hall

2nd June 1919.

Lieut. Colonel.,
General Staff, Northern Division.

Copies to all recipients of Northern Division G.8874 dated 23rd May.

SECRET.

Northern Divn.   Copy No. 32
No. G.8874/16.

Instructions for the Advance.

Appendix "C".

1. Points to be guarded.   Copies of G.H.Q. Ia.95/1 "List of Localities of importance in connection with communications, etc." were forwarded on May 27th. The object of forwarding this list was to give commanders an idea of the most vulnerable places on our communications. In the event of an attempted rising on the part of the enemy they will then be in a position to arrange for the defence of such places as are in their area.

Adequate guards will, however, be provided as early as possible for the protection of the following :-

HAGEN	-	Main Telegraph Office (BAHNHOF Strasse) Railway Offices and Workshops.
HALVER	-	Main Telegraph Office.
SCHWELM	-	Main Telegraph Office (SCHULSTRASSE).
SOEST	-	Railway Junction.
SCHWERTE	-	Railway Junction.

2. Guards to be warned.   In the event of a cessation of the Armistice it is possible that attempts may be made to interfere with communications or to destroy depots of British stores.

All guards will therefore be warned to be specially on the alert from "J" - 3 day inclusive.

3. Intelligence.   INTELLIGENCE ARRANGEMENTS.

(a) P.O.W. Cages.   Divisional P.O.W. Cage will be situated close to Advanced Divisional Headquarters. The Corps Cage will be established at LUDENSCHEID at 12.00 hours on "J" plus 1 day.

(b) Disposal of P.O.W.   Prisoners will be passed back under escort with as little delay as possible to the Divisional Cage, where they will be examined by the Divisional Intelligence Officer. Owing to the possibility of long distances having to be traversed it may be found advisable to pass prisoners back by M.T. if available. Field Ambulances will report at once to Division H.Q. when any wounded prisoners are admitted.

(c) Disposal of documents.   Prisoners will not be searched until arrival at Divisional Cage. If however there is any sign of prisoners attempting to destroy or throw away letters, documents, etc., on the way, they will be searched on the spot, and all letters documents, maps, etc. will be made into bundles labeled with each prisoner's name and delivered to the Intelligence Officer at the Cage.

(d) Intelligence Police.   An N.C.O. of the Intelligence Police will be attached to each of 1st and 3rd Infantry Brigades. A copy of their instructions is forwarded herewith to 1st and 3rd Inf. Bdes. for information as to the duties of these N.C.Os. They will not be used for any other duties than those laid down.

(2).

4. SIGNAL TO DENOTE HOSTILE OPPOSITION.

Signal to denote hostile opposition.

During the advance Red Very Lights (1") will be used by the infantry as a signal to indicate that their advance is being resisted by the enemy.

The R.A.F. will arrange that any such signals that they see are reported with the least possible delay to the formation concerned.

Reports.

5. REPORTS

(a) The following reports will be forwarded by leading Brigades daily from "J" day inclusive.

(i) <u>Morning Situation Report.</u>

By wire or D.R. so as to reach Advanced Divisional H.Q. by 06.00 hours.

(ii) <u>Evening Situation Report.</u>

By wire or D.R. so as to reach Advanced Divisional H.Q. by 16.00 hours. This report will include captures of prisoners and war material, and will be accompanied by a summary of intelligence for the period 12.00 hours to 12.00 hours.

(b) The following return will be forwarded by Infantry Brigades daily from "J" - 3 day inclusive :-

<u>Forecast of Locations</u> of Headquarters as they will be at 08.00 hours on two days ahead, to reach Advanced Division H.Q. by 18.00 hours.

6. ACKNOWLEDGE.

G.W. Gordon Hall

14th June, 1919.

Lieut. Colonel,
General Staff, Northern Division.

Copies to all recipients of G.8874 of 23rd May, 1919.

SECRET.

Northern Division G.8874/18.

INSTRUCTIONS FOR THE ADVANCE.

Appendix "D".

1. **CIVIL ADMINISTRATION OF AREAS.**

   Until 18.00 hours on "J" day, the G.O.C., VI Corps will continue to carry out the Civil administration of the present VI Corps area. If required, Units of the Light Division now in the VI Corps area will be at the disposal of the G.O.C., VI Corps to assist in maintaining order.

   The G.O.C., II Corps is retaining the Civil administration of the area now occupied by the Northern Division and units of the Northern Division are placed at the disposal of the G.O.C., II Corps if required, in the event of civil disturbances.

   Troops in areas other than their own will continue to be administered by their own Corps.

2. **METHOD OF DEALING WITH RUSSIAN PRISONERS IN THE EVENT OF RESUMPTION OF HOSTILITIES.**

   (i) The following instructions have been received from Marshal FOCH as to the reception of Russian Prisoners of War in the event of the resumption of military operations.

   (a) A considerable number of Russian Prisoners of War are actually located in the German territory which the Allied Armies may reach in the event of military operations being resumed.

   (b) It is expected that the Germans will attempt as they did after the signature of the Armistice, to rid themselves of such prisoners by releasing them, or sending them into the Allied lines.

   (c) The sudden influx of these prisoners would be likely to cause considerable inconvenience to our Armies. Their transportation outside the zone of operations and the provision of the necessary guards would necessitate the employment elsewhere of transport and personnel which could be more usefully employed.

   (d) The Allies will therefore only take over and assume responsibility for those Russian Prisoners of War who remain under discipline in their camps. All others will be turned back into the German lines.

   (ii) It is realized that there will be difficulty in carrying out the orders contained in the last part of paragraph (d) of the above instructions; representations pointing out these difficulties are being made. In the meantime, every effort should be made to give effect to these instructions if any Russian Prisoners of War are met with.

3. **MARKING OF CONTACT AEROPLANES.**

   Contact patrols of the 12th Squadron R.A.F., will be marked with coloured streamers on both wing tips.

4. **ACKNOWLEDGE.**

G.W.Gordon Hall

Lieut. Colonel.,
General Staff, Northern Division.

21st June 1919.

Copies to all recipients of G. 8874 of 23rd May 1919.

Northern Division G.С874/19.

SECRET.

INSTRUCTIONS FOR THE ADVANCE.

Appendix "E".

For all inter-communication between aeroplanes and troops on the ground (artillery and infantry) the following system of identifying points will be used with the 1/100,000 and 1/200,000 maps. Both of these maps are squared, though on the 1/100,000 maps the squares are not perfect where the sheets join.

    (a) A point will be identified on the map as follows:-

    First.   The sheet Number, e.g. 59 in case of 1/200,000 or 3K in case of 1/100,000.

    Second.   Break Signal 'X'.

    Third.   The square, identified by the number and letter shown on left margin and top margin of the sheet, the number being placed first i.e. 2H.

    Fourth.   The co-ordinates of the point in the square (or rectangle in some cases on 1/100,000 map), each side being considered as divided into ten spaces in the usual old British system.

For example:-

    (i) OSTHEIM on the 1/100,000 map would be described as 2LX 2 D 40.30.
    (ii) Cross roads 3 miles S.E. of LUDENSCHEID on the 1/200,000 map would be 59 X 3 H 40.35.

    (b) In the case of zone calls a square of 5,000 metres on the 100,000 and 1,300 metres on the 200,000 maps will be considered as a zone and the zone call will be repeated 3 times, e.g. the zone call of the zone containing OSTHEIM would be 2 LX 2 D repeated 3 times followed by the definite description of the point as explained in the first paragraph.

    (c) Co-ordinate cards for use with both the 1/100,000 and 1/200,000 will be issued as soon as possible, meanwhile cards can be easily constructed for use where great accuracy is required.

ACKNOWLEDGE.

G.W. Gordon Hall

Lieut. Colonel.,
General Staff, Northern Division.

23rd June 1919.

Copies to all recipients of G8874 of 23rd May.

SECRET.

Northern Division.
G.8874/21.

1st Nthn Inf. Bde.
9th D.L.I.
"Q" Nthn Div.
C.R.A.
D.A.P.M.
VI Corps.
Southern Division.

Reference Northern Division G.8874/20 of 25th June.

1. On "A" day the 1st Nthn Inf. Bde. Lorry Group will start at 13.00 hours and not at 12.00 hours, as stated.

2. Should notice of the signing of peace be received in time for movements to be carried out on "A" - 1 day, the 9th D.L.I.(Pioneers) will return to RIEHL by march route instead of in lorries, as follows :-

    (a) A - 1 day.   March to LINDE.   No restrictions.

    (b) "A" day.   March to BERG GLADBACH. Passing junction of LINDE-BIESFELD and KURTEN-BIESFELD roads between 08.00 and 09.15 hours.

    (c) "B" day.   To clear BERG GLADBACH by 09.00 hours and not to cross MULHEIM Bridge before 10.30 hours.

3. ACKNOWLEDGE.

G.W.Gordon Hall

Lieut. Colonel,
General Staff, Northern Division.

28th June, 1919.

SECRET.

Northern Division G.8874/20.

1st Northern Inf.Bde.	93rd Bde.R.G.A.	*Nthn Div Signals*
2nd Northern Inf.Bde.	London Division.	*II Corps.*
3rd Northern Inf.Bde.	Southern Division.	
C.R.A.	12th Squadron, R.A.F.	
C.R.E.	D.A.P.M.	
"Q".	Northern Div.M.T.Coy.	
A.D.M.S.	D.A.D.O.S.	
3rd Bn.M.G.C.	D.A.D.V.S.	
VI Corps "G".	Train.	
VI Corps "Q".	Cavalry Division.	
1/9th D.L.I.	VI Corps Cyclists Battn.	
Light Divn.	Camp Commdt.	

1. In the event of Peace being signed without any further advance taking place, orders may be expected for all troops to resume their dispositions as they existed prior to J-3 day.

2. The Northern Division will carry out the move in accordance with the attached March Table.

3. If tents are wet they will be left standing under guards to be arranged by brigade and other commanders, until they are dry, when further orders will be issued as to their removal.

4. Care will be taken to leave all camps and billets clean and in good order.

5. Units will take over from the Light Division all guards previously found by them, in accordance with attached tables.

6. Acknowledge.

G.W.Gordon Hall
Lieut.Colonel.
General Staff, Northern Division.

25th June, 1919.

MARCH TABLE.

Date.	Unit.	Destination.	Route.	Remarks.
A-1 day.	51st North'd Fus.	Original locations in COLOGNE.	BERG GLADBACH & NEW BRIDGE. / SCHLEBUSCH & HOHENZOLLERN BR.	By lorry. Orders may be issued later for this move to be carried out on "A" day.
	1/5th W. Yorks. 52nd D.L.I.			
A day.	51st North'd Fus. 1/5th W. Yorks. 52nd D.L.I.			Take over guards handed over to Light Division in their respective Bde Areas. 1/5th W. Yorks in addition will take up and later over guard of 2 N.C.Os 12 men on anti left attached German Motor vehicles in NEUMARKT.
	1st Nth.Inf.Bde.H.Q. & L.T.M.B. 52nd North'd Fus. 1 section 142nd Fd. Amb. Cyclist Detachment. 18-pdr & Detachment. 231st Fd. Coy R.E. (personnel) 1 Coy 3rd M.G.Bn. (personnel.)	Original locations in COLOGNE.	BERG GLADBACH & NEW BRIDGE.	By lorry. Starting at 12.00 hours.
	2nd Nth Inf Bde H.Q. & L.T.M.B. 1/4th Y.& L.Regt. 142 Fd.Amb personnel (less 1 section)	—do—	SCHLEBUSCH & HOHENZOLLERN BRIDGE.	By lorry starting at 12.00 hours. Detached Coy 1/4 Y & L.Regt will return from RIEHL Barracks to original quarters.
	51st D.L.I. 1 section 7th Fd.Amb. Cyclist detachment. 18-pdr & detachment 1Coy 3rd M.G.Bn (personnel. 226 Siege Bty. R.G.A.	—do—	SCHLEBUSCH & HOHENZOLLERN BRIDGE.	By lorry starting at 12.00 hours. 51st D.L.I. will occupy 9th D.L.I. block RIEHL Barracks over night A/B days.

MARCH TABLE.

Date	Unit	Destination	Route	Remarks
A Day.	3rd Bn.N.G.Personnel (less 2 Companies). 7th Fld.Amb.personnel (less 1 Section).	Original locations in COLOGNE.	ODENTHAL and HOHENZOLLERN BR.	By lorry. Start 12.15 hours.
	529 Fld.Coy.R.E. personnel.	do.	BENSBERG and NEW BRIDGE.	By lorry. Start 12.30 hours.
	1st Nthn.Inf.Bde. Transport Group. No.3 Coy.Train. Transport 231st Fld.Coy R.E.	BERG GLADBACH.		By March Route, start 09.00 hours.
	2nd Nthn.Inf.Bde Transport Group. 142 Fld.Amb.transport. No.4 Coy.Train.	DUNNWALD.		do.
	3rd Nthn.Inf.Bde Transport Group. Fld.Amb.transport. No.2 Coy.Train. Transport 458 Fld.Coy. R.E. Transport 3rd M.G.Bn.	TORRINGERT.	ODENTHAL.	do.
	Nthn.Div.Arty. Transport of 9th DLI. Transport 529 Fld.Coy. R.E. 150 Hvy.Battery,RGA.	BRUCK	UNTER ELSBACH and BENSBERG.	do.
	G.Battery,R.H.A.	Arty.Barracks, MERHEIM.	MULHEIM BRIDGE.	To clear WERMELSKIRCHEN by 07.30 hours.
	Dragoon Squadron. Hussar Squadron. M.G.Squadron.	COLOGNE Area.		

MARCH TABLE.

Date	Unit	Destination	Route	Remarks.
B Day.	53rd North'd Fus.	Original locations in COLOGNE.	BERG GLADBACH and NEW BRIDGE.	By lorry. To cross NEW BRIDGE between 10.30 and 11.00 hours.
	1/5th West Yorks.	do.	SCHLEBUSCH and HOHENZOLLERN Br.	By lorry. Not to enter MULHEIM before 08.00 hours.
	3rd Nthn.Inf.Bde.) H.Q. and L.T.M.B.) 20th D.L.I.) 159 Fld.Coy.R.E.) personnel.)	do.	SCHLEBUSCH & HOHENZOLLERN BRIDGE.	By lorry. Not to enter MULHEIM before 08.30 hours.
	1/9th DLI (Pioneers).	do.	BENSBERG & NEW BR.	By lorry. Not to cross RHINE before 11.00 hours.
	1st Nthn.Inf.Bde.) Transport Group.) No.3 Coy.Train.) Transport 251 Fld.) Coy.R.E.)	do.	NEW BRIDGE.	By March Route. To cross NEW BRIDGE between 10.00 and 10.30 hours.
	2nd Nthn.Inf.Bde.) Transport Group.) No.4 Coy.Train.) Transport 142 Fld.) Amb.)	do.	MULHEIM BRIDGE.	By March Route. To clear DUNNWALD by 06.10 hours.
	3rd Nthn.Inf.Bde.) Transport Group.) 7 Fld.Amb.Transport.) No.2 Coy.Train.) Transport 438 Fld.) Coy.R.E.) " 3rd M.G.Bn.)	do.	MULHEIM BRIDGE.	By March Route. Not to enter DUNNWALD before 06.10 hrs.

MARCH TABLE

Date	Unit	Destination.	Route.	Remarks.
B Day.	Nth.N.div.Arty. Transport 9th D.L.I. Transport 529 Fld.Coy.RE. 150 Hvy.Bty.R.G.A.	} Original Locations in COLOGNE.	NEW BRIDGE.	By March Route. To clear NEW BRIDGE by 10.00 hours.
	Dragoon Squadron. Hussar Squadron. M.G. Squadron.	} Cavalry Division Area.	HOHENZOLLERN BR.	By March Route. To clear BRIDGE by 10.30 hours.
	3rd M.G. Bn.			Relieve M.G. Detachments at MULHEIM BR., Docks and EIFEL TOR Goods Station.

GUARDS TO BE TAKEN OVER FROM LIGHT DIVISION.

1st Northern Inf. Bde.

No.	Details of Guard.	Offrs.	NCOs.	Men.
N. 1.	Docks.	3.	12.	73.
2.	Train Guard (Docks, EIFEL TOR etc)	-	3.	24.
3.	SCHNUR GASSE (Detention Barracks)	-	2.	8.
5.	Powder Magazine, RADERTHAL.	4.	10.	70.
6.	FORT VII (1 platoon min)	2.	3.	22.
36.	E.F.C. Depot. BAYEN STRASSE.	-	1.	6.
35.	44, C.C.S. UBIER RING.	-	2.	10.
38.	EIFEL TOR. Goods Station.	1.	6.	51.
40.	-do- Power Station.	-	2.	6.
41.	Army Troops M.T. ALTENBURG BREWERY.	-	2.	8.
37.	Militar Lazarett, KARTHAUSER WALL, (Ordnance Depot)	-	1.	6.

Railway Patrols between SUD Bridge and EIFEL TOR Goods Station.

2nd Northern Inf. Bde.

No.	Details of Guard.	Offrs.	NCOs.	Men.
N.11.	NIPPES Artillery Depot (1 Coy min)	4.	20.	120.
12.	SUBBELRATHER STRASSE (Ammn)	-	1.	3.
13.	Police Preasidium.	-	1.	3.
	German Motor lorries, NEUMARKT.	-	2.	12.
16.	M.T. Depot, EHRENFELD.	-	2.	12.
29.	Army Ammn Dump, LONGERICH.	2.	2.	18.
	-do- -do- (Fire picquet)	-	2.	14.
39.	Ordnance Clothing Depot, BAYEN Strasse.	-	2.	6.

3rd Northern Inf. Bde.

No.	Details of Guard.	Offrs.	Strength. NCOs.	Men.
N.17.	MULHEIM BRIDGE.	1.	4.	20.
18.	Military Governor's House.	-	2.	8.
19.	Wireless Station.	-	2.	8.
20.	Refilling Point.	-	1.	3.
23.	Monopol Group (1 Coy min)	3.	10.	65.
26.	ARSENAL.	-	2.	12.
27.	Mil. Police Barracks.	-	2.	8.
28.	Town Guard Room.	-	2.	12.
42.	Mil. Governor's Office. Monopol Hotel:- Guard.	-	2.	8.
	Orderlies.	-	1.	8.

3rd Battn. M.G.C.

No.	Details of Guard.	Offrs.	NCOs.	Men.
N.14.	Commander in Chief's Residence.	-	2.	8.

NORTHERN DIVISION.

Location List.   28th May 1919.

Unit.	Place.
Northern Division H.Q.:-	
G.O.C.	20 Furst Pucklor Strasse, LINDENTHAL, COLOGNE.
"G" Office, "Q" Office) Camp Cmmdt, Educ.Office) Signals.	264 Durener Strasse, LINDENTHAL, COLOGNE.
A.D.M.S., D.A.P.M.) D.A.D.V.S., Post Office)	5 Virchow Strasse, " "
D.A.D.O.S.	12, Goibel Strasse, " "
" Stores.	111, Durener Strasse, " "
Train.	90, Bachemor Strasse, " "
Railhead Post Office.	88, Aachener Strasse, COLOGNE.
1st Northern Inf.Bde. H.Q.	107 Bachemer Strass e, LINDINTHAL, COLOGNE.
51st Northld Fus.	REDWITZ Strasse School, " "
52nd " "	BERRENRATHER School, SULZ, "
53rd " "	Artillery Barracks, MARIENBURG, "
8th T.M. Battery.	Fire Station, Gleueler Strasse, LINDENTHAL.
8th Field Amb'ce (Cadre)	EFFEREN.
No.3 Coy Train R.A.S.C.	Weisshaus, Luxomburg Strasse, SULZ.
2nd Northern Inf.Bde. H.Q.	13, Kanal Strasse, SULZ, COLOGNE.
1/5th West Yorks Regt.	New School, Subbolrather Strasse, BICKENDORF.
1/6th " " "	Schillor Gymnasium, PIUS STrasse, EHRLNFELD.
1/4th York & Lancs "	Hartwigstrasse School, NIPPES, COLOGNE.
9th T.M. Battery.	OVERBECK S trasse School, EHRENFELD, COLOGNE.
142nd Field Ambulance.	98, Vogelsanger Strasse, " "
No.4 Coy. Train R.A.S.C.	Helios Strasse, Chemische Fabrik Kal, EHRENFELD.
3rd Northern Inf.Bde. H.Q.	57 Hohenstaufen Ring, COLOGNE.
20th Durham Light Inf.	RIEHL Barracks, "C" Block.
51st " " "	" " "C" "
52nd " " "	" " "C" "
76th T.M. Battery.	" " "D" "
7th Field Ambulance	" " "E" "
No.2 Coy Train R.A.S.C.	" " "D" "
Northern Div. Artillery H.Q.	10. Vincenz-Statz Strasse, LINDENTHAL, COLOGNE.
74th Bde. R.F.A.	just N. of second E in WEIDEN- 1/100,000 sheet 1E
75th Bde. " "	" S. of K in KONIGSDORF. - -do-
76th Bde. Ammn. Column.	GEYEN.
Northn D.A.C.	BRAUWEILER.
No.1 Coy. Train. R.A.S.C.	BOCKLEMU ND.
C.R.E.	11. Robert Blum Strasse, LINDENTHAL, COLOGNE.
56th Field Coy R.E(cadre)	Flora Strasse, RIEHL.
231st " " "	569 Aachener Strasse, BRAUNSFELD.
438th " " "	Entrance to FLORA GARTEN, RIEHL.
529th " " "	21, Christian Gan Strasse, BRAUNSFELD.
1/9th D.L.I.(Pioneers)	RIEHL Barracks. "B" Block.
3rd M.G. Battalion.	RIEHL Barracks. "A" Block.
XI Mobile Vet. Section.	DECKSTEIN.

Northern Div. H.Q.
28th May 1919.

NORTHERN DIVISION.

Location List.   20th June 1919.

Unit.	Place.
Northern Division H.Q.:-	
G.O.C.	20 Furst Puckler Strasse, LINDENTHAL. COLOGNE.
"G" Office, "Q" Office, Camp Cmmdt, Educ.Office, Signals.	264, Durener Strasse, LINDENTHAL. COLOGNE.
A.D.M.S., D.A.D.M.	5, Virchow Strasse, " "
D.A.D.V.S., Post Office	12, Geibel Strasse, " "
D.A.D. O.S.	111, Durener Strasse, " "
" Stores.	90, Bachemer Strasse, " "
Train.	
Railhead Post Office,	88, Aachener Strasse, COLOGNE.
1st Northern Inf. Bde. H.Q.	KURTEN.
51st North'd Fus.	
52nd " "	
53rd " "	
1 Coy. 3rd M.G. Battn	} Bivouacked between KURTEN and BIESFIELD.
231st Field Coy. R.E.	
1 Coy. 9th D.L.I.(Pioneers)	
No.3 Coy. Train R.A.S.C.	
1st T.M. Battery.	
2nd Northern Inf. Bde. H.Q.	HILGEN.
1/5th West Yorks Regt.	
1/6th " " "	
1/4th York & Lancs"	} between HILGEN and BURSHEID.
2nd T.M. Battery.	
142nd Field Ambulance.	
No.4 Coy. Train R.A.S.C.	
3rd Northern Inf. Bde. H.Q.	WERMELSKIRCHEN.
20th Durham Light Infantry.	
51st " " "	
52nd " " "	
3rd T.M. Battery.	WERMELSKIRCHEN.
1 Coy. 3rd M.G. Battn.	
226 Siege Battery R.G.A.	
438th Field Coy. R.E.	
Northern Div. Artillery H.Q.	10, Vincenz Statz Strasse, LINDENTHAL. COLOGNE.
74th Bde. R.F.A.	
75th Bde. "	
Northern D.A.C.	
No.1 Coy. Train R.A.S.C.	} Bivouacked in vicinity of HOHKEPPEL.
9th D.L.I. (less 1 Coy)	
150th Battery R.G.A.	
529th Field Coy. R.E.	
C.R.E.	11, Robert Blum Strasse, LINDENTHAL. COLOGNE.
231st Field Coy. R.E.	KURTEN.
438th " " "	WERMELSKIRCHEN.
529th " " "	HOHKEPPEL.
1/9th D.L.I.(Pioneers)	HOHKEPPEL.
3rd M.G.Battn (Less 2 Coys)	
7th Field Ambulance.	} DABRINHAUSEN.
No. 2 Coy. Train.	
XI Mobile Vet. Section.	DECKSTEIN.
1 sqdn Dragoons.	
"G" Battery R.H.A.	} WERMELSKIRCHEN.
1 section. M.G.sqdn.	
1 sqdn Hussars.	} KURTEN.
1 sqdn. M.G.C.(less 1 section)	

Northern Div. H.Q.
20th June 1919.

www.ingramcontent.com/pod-product-compliance
Lightning Source LLC
Chambersburg PA
CBHW081432300426
44108CB00016BA/2353